W9-ABV-575

SMALL CHANGE

SMALL CHANGE

Women, Learning, Patriotism, 1750–1810

Harriet Guest

THE UNIVERSITY OF CHICAGO PRESS
CHICAGO AND LONDON

Harriet Guest is senior lecturer in the Department of English and Related Literature at the University of York. She is the author of *A Form of Sound Words: The Religious Poetry of Christopher Smart* and the editor of Johann Reinhold Forster's *Observations Made during a Voyage round the World.*

The University of Chicago Press, Chicago 60637
The University of Chicago Press, Ltd., London

Printed in the United States of America

09 08 07 06 05 04 03 02 01 00 1 2 3 4 5

ISBN: 0-226-31051-5 (cloth)
ISBN: 0-226-31052-3 (paper)

Library of Congress Cataloging-in-Publication Data

Guest, Harriet
Small change : women, learning, patriotism, 1750–1810 / Harriet Guest.
p. cm.
Includes bibliographical references and index.
ISBN 0-226-31051-5 (cloth : alk. paper) — ISBN 0-226-31052-3 (pbk. : alk. paper)
1. English literature—Women authors—History and criticism. 2. Women and literature—Great Britain—History—18th century. 3. Women and literature—Great Britain—History—19th century. 4. Women—Education—Great Britain—History—18th century. 5. Women—Education—Great Britain—History—19th century. 6. Patriotism—Great Britain—History—18th century. 7. Patriotism—Great Britain—History—19th century. 8. Great Britain—Intellectual life—18th century. 9. Great Britain—Intellectual life—19th century. 10. Patriotism in literature. 11. Home in literature. I. Title.

PR448.W65 G84 2000
820.9′352042′09033—dc21

00-034333

♾The paper used in this publication meets the minimum requirements of the American National Standard for Information Sciences—Permanence of Paper for Printed Library Materials, ANSI Z39.48-1992.

For Helena

CONTENTS

ILLUSTRATIONS

ACKNOWLEDGMENTS

Since I began work on this book many people have contributed to its ideas and arguments. Rachel Bowlby, Kate Davies, David Glover, Cora Kaplan, Emma Major, Felicity Nussbaum, and Kevin Sharpe have all read and commented helpfully on chapters in different stages of preparation. My ideas have also benefited from discussions with Jacques Berthoud, Veronica Guest, Philippe Harari, Anna Hicks, Robert W. Jones, Valarie Raworth, and Jane Rendall. The readers for the University of Chicago Press also contributed significantly to the final form of this book. I regret that I can no longer thank in person Tony Tanner for his warm encouragement, or Stephen Copley for his good humor and scholarly generosity. The interdisciplinary research environment created by colleagues and students in the Centre for Eighteenth Century Studies at the University of York has been extraordinarily stimulating for my work. I am grateful to the Humanities Research Center in North Carolina, where I began work on this project and enjoyed in particular conversations with David and Susan Southern and Gloria Pinney. A term of research leave funded by the British Academy allowed me to finish the first draft of the book. At the University of Chicago Press, I have been grateful for the support and interest of Alan Thomas, the attention to my text given by Randolph Petilos, and the unintrusive copy editing skills of Evan Young. My greatest debt is to John and Helena Barrell. John Barrell always found time to listen and encourage, despite the demands of his own work, his wayward box hedges, four hundred children, and a crop in the field. This book is for Helena, who cannot remember life without it, and whose opinions and interests have done much to shape it—her understanding of sense and sensibility has been an inspiration and a delight.

INTRODUCTION

> The tender sex . . . assemble their sentiments and their ideas about them, and confine their affections to what interests them most. . . . A man to them, is more than a nation; and the hour in which they live, than a thousand ages after death.
>
> There are certain qualities, which have generally been ranked among the social virtues, but which may more properly be called *the virtues of polished life.* They are the charm, and the bond of company; and are useful at all times, and upon all occasions. They are in the commerce of the world, what current money is in trade: they are sometimes not absolutely necessary, but one can never safely be without them; and they always procure the possessor a favourable reception.
>
> William Russell, *Essay on the Character, Manners, and Genius of Women in different ages*

> From the little pains that have commonly been bestowed on the mental cultivation of our sex, it is not surprising that the powers of Abstraction and generalisation should be so very seldom met with. Happily in the sphere in which it is most frequently our lot to move, these are not so indispensably requisite, as that sound judgement which is vulgarly denominated common sense. The duties of mankind in general, and of our sex in particular, are oftener active than speculative: and an ever wakeful attention to the minutiae of which they are composed, is absolutely essential to their performance: but those who would, for this reason, deny the utility of cultivating the higher powers of the mind, ought, by a parity of reasoning, to consider gold as useless, because small coin is more frequently requisite in transacting the common business of the day.
>
> Elizabeth Hamilton, *Letters on the Elementary Principles of Education*

In the last decade or so, gender relations have played an increasingly important part in studies of the eighteenth century. The emphasis has shifted away from

Figure 1 R. Pollard and J. Wells after Catharine Maria Fanshawe, *Politics,* 1791, aquatint, 15 × 29 ¼ in. BM 8033. © The British Museum.

femininity, from study of the experience or writings of women as a separate category of literary or historical analysis, and toward the complex involvement of women and of gender difference in all areas of eighteenth-century life and thought, from those which demand the "higher powers of the mind" to the "common business of the day." Because eighteenth-century women are seen to be like small change in their virtues, their habits of mind, they enter into every area on which scholars gain a purchase. The analogy employed in my epigraphs links them to the quotidian, the immediate and contingent, to the minutiae of private life. But it also indicates that gender difference is the basis of sociable exchange, that women are the "bond of company" which "one can never safely be without." Femininity may seem of small significance in some of the major transactions of cultural change, but it is always a part of what gives those transactions current value.

In 1791, Ryland of New Bond Street published an aquatint titled *Politics,* engraved by R. Pollard after a sketch by Catharine Maria Fanshawe (fig. 1). It can be used to illustrate some of the ways in which politics and gender have been understood in the eighteenth century. The image shows the grand interior of one of the more "public" rooms of a great house. In the center is a "handsome Adam chimney-piece, on which are a Wedgwood tazza and a pair of ornate candlesticks."[1] In front of the fireplace stands a cluster of men

1. I quote from the description of the aquatint given in F. D. Stephens and M. D. George, *British Museum Catalogue of Political and Personal Satires,* 11 vols. (London: British Museum, 1870–1954),

engaged in animated discussion—apparently debating the politics alluded to in the title. The central figure, warming his backside before the blaze in a proprietorial manner, listens attentively and with the air of a man about to deliver an authoritative opinion. At the margins of the image are two groups of seated women. The elderly woman on the extreme left has fallen asleep, and lolls awkwardly and ungraciously in her chair. The younger woman on the extreme right yawns without restraint or embarrassment. Between the elderly women on the left and the central group of more or less middle-aged men stands a younger fashionably dressed man, who seems to be listening to but not participating in the political discussion.

What the image most obviously portrays is women bored and marginalized by political discussion: a complete failure of common interest between men and women. The image brings to mind the comments of the *Gentleman's Magazine* on Mary Wollstonecraft's *A Vindication of the Rights of Men* (1790), which jeered, "The rights of man asserted by a fair lady! The age of chivalry cannot be over, or the sexes have changed their ground. . . . We should be sorry to raise a horse-laugh against a fair lady; but we were always taught to suppose that the rights of women were the proper theme of the female sex." The *Magazine* asserts, somewhat ironically in light of Wollstonecraft's later career, that women can have no interest in men's political status or debates, and can only be concerned with what they represent as the sexualized pseudopolitics of women: "we were always taught . . . that, while the Romans governed the world, the women governed the Romans."[2] In the aquatint, the men turn their backs on the women, apparently forgetting their presence in the heat of political debate or perhaps intrigue—the men on the left look rather conspiratorial. The women don't all look bored; some of them are talking among themselves, but on the whole their focus of interest is not the central group of men.

It may, however, be possible to read the aquatint differently. If this is a satire on women's inability to follow political discussion, we might ask why a woman chose to sketch it. Or is it a satire on the self-importance of men, and does the politics of the title allude to relations between the sexes—perhaps to the violation of the codes of social politeness by the central group? The women on the right in particular look much more obviously fashionable than most of the men, and the rather foppish young man who is peripheral to the older

---

no. 8033. Catharine Maria Fanshawe's sketches provide the basis for a number of prints, some of which she aquatinted herself. I am grateful to David Alexander for drawing this to my attention.

2. *Gentleman's Magazine,* 1791, quoted in Wendy Gunther-Canada, "The Politics of Sense and Sensibility: Mary Wollstonecraft and Catharine Macaulay Graham on Edmund Burke's *Reflections on the Revolution in France,*" in *Women Writers and the Early Modern British Political Tradition,* ed. Hilda L. Smith (Cambridge: Cambridge University Press, 1998), 145.

men's conversation might be taken to indicate that the women and this young man are the softened and feminized examples of civilized behavior, obtruded upon by the boorish and perhaps barbarous behavior of the men. More plausibly, perhaps, we might pause to wonder why the men are having this conversation in mixed company at all. Couldn't the women have retired alone to the drawing room, while the men stayed to debate round the dinner table, over the port, or couldn't the men have gone to their club or coffee house and left the women at home? Or is the presence of the women necessary to their conversation—are these perhaps men who hold diverse political opinions, or who represent different professions or sections of society, who might not have met together and engaged in debate without women to mark this as sociable behavior, heterogeneous, eclectic? Perhaps the women who appear to be following the men's discussion—there's at least one on each side of the room—are watching their protégés go through their paces; perhaps they're waiting to intervene at the appropriate moment, in the right place, as did aristocratic hostesses such as the Duchess of Devonshire.

I do not mean to suggest that reading this particular aquatint reveals the philosopher's stone—the hearthstone—that will explain eighteenth-century culture and society. I want instead to emphasize that recent advances in scholarship on the history and literary history of women and of gender relations in the eighteenth century have made it possible to ask new questions, to interrogate images like this differently, perhaps with the possibility of gaining more illuminating answers. Because of the work that has gone on in the field of gender in eighteenth-century studies in the last decade or so, we now may look at that child among the women on the right and ask: are these women turning away from the men in order to instruct and enlighten the rising generation? Why is the woman on the left ignoring her playing cards? Has she perhaps been influenced by the thought of bluestocking gatherings in which men and women converse together on all subjects and there is no card-playing? The range of contexts in which we might consider any image of relations between men and women has been opened up. Perhaps it is no longer possible to read this image simply as a sign of the separation of spheres, the division between the masculine world of politics and the feminine world of domestic responsibilities and gossip. The figure of the feminized young man who seems to belong to neither or both of the gendered groups looms larger in our vision than he would have even a decade ago; the marginalization of the women is more problematic than it might have seemed.

Much of the work that has complicated our understanding of gender difference in the eighteenth century—or of how we might review the century through the lens of gender—has been produced by historians. I do not think of my own methods as those of a historian. As a literary critic, I am primarily concerned with texts, and with the discursive relations between them. But despite important methodological differences, I find that I can most readily situate my own project in relation to recent developments in history, and particularly in women's history, not least because the period I am concerned with, from the middle of the eighteenth to the early nineteenth century, is too often carved up in literary criticism between Romanticists and eighteenth-century specialists. Broadly speaking, the most exciting development in women's history has been that "new research breaks down the barriers that still divide women's history and gender history from 'mainstream' history," as Hannah Barker and Elaine Chalus argue in their illuminating analysis of recent trends in this field.[3] Those trends have made it difficult for any student of cultural or "mainstream" history to ignore gender as a powerful category of analysis, and they mean that feminist historians and literary critics are increasingly compelled to consider discourses on femininity in relation to a larger discursive network of which gender difference is one of several foundational categories; they mean that, for example, it is becoming more difficult to think about a domestic sphere without considering it in the context of the perplexed relations between the public, the private, and gender difference in the eighteenth century.

Keith Baker provides a useful short account of some of the key differences between dominant theories of the relation of public and private in the eighteenth century. He discusses the antithesis between the public political realm defined by the discourse of classical republicanism, explored most influentially in the work of J. G. A. Pocock, and the public sphere described in the work of Jürgen Habermas. The first, early modern conception of a realm in which "independent citizens participate in the common exercise of a sovereign, political will" is based in "a recovery of the model of the ancient polis." This discourse articulates an unambiguously masculinist concept of virtue limited to a small political elite which excludes most people all of the time and includes its independent citizens only some of the time. Habermas's public sphere, in contrast, is represented as a "distinctive feature of modern society," which takes form "within the *private* realm of civil society" where people participate in "the critical discussion leading to the formulation of a rational, consensual judgement."[4] If we think of the public as the site for the exercise of the will of independent citizens acting for the common good, then the image shown in the

3. "Introduction," in *Gender in Eighteenth-Century England: Roles, Representations and Responsibilities,* ed. Hannah Barker and Elaine Chalus (Harlow: Longman, 1997), 24.

4. Keith Michael Baker, "Defining the Public Sphere in Eighteenth-Century France: Variations on a Theme by Habermas," in *Habermas and the Public Sphere,* ed. Craig Calhoun (Cambridge, Mass.: MIT Press, 1992), 187–88.

aquatint of *Politics* is private. The central group of men might be independent, they might be classical republican citizens debating privately the course they will uniformly pursue in public; but, apparently engaged in dispute or at least persuasive speech in a private house in the company of women and children, they are not for the moment public citizens and they do not inhabit the domain of political power. Habermas's terms are more difficult to apply to the image. As Baker points out, Habermas's public "can be understood either as a discursive category expressing a normative ideal or as an actually existing social reality." If it is a "normative ideal," it can be understood either as accessible to all "privatized individuals communicating in the world of letters," all human beings who have access to the modes of communication that characterize modernity, or as restricted by education and property rights to white middle-class males.[5] A normative ideal of critical discussion taking place among white, property-owning men might seem more compatible with "an actually existing social reality" than the more utopian vision of an inclusive public involved in the formulation of rational, consensual judgment.

Because Habermas's bourgeois public sphere forms within the private realm of civil society, Dena Goodman, for example, can write that "there was no such thing as a 'public' woman in eighteenth-century France. Most women, like most men, functioned within a private realm that had a public face."[6] Goodman's reading of Habermas implies that *Politics* may portray public faces in a private realm, and asks us to consider what kind of publicity this might be. Baker's essay makes a similar point, but it is more concerned with how we might think about the relation between different notions of the public, between say classical republicanism and Habermas's public-within-a-private. Are the women and the foppish young man included in the arena of *Politics* designated by the title of the aquatint by virtue of their education and common humanity, their potential to participate in critical discussion? Does the image perhaps present a collision between those different notions of publicity? If the men are public citizens enjoying a private conversation, does their rudeness indicate that they have failed to appreciate that the women and the younger man are a part of a newer and more inclusive notion of public debate? Or perhaps they are exemplifying the slippage in Habermas's theory: this is all *Politics,* ideally everyone is included, but actually the property qualification, the position of men as heads of the household and earners of money, means that age and gender exclude most of those present.

5. Baker, "Habermas," 183, 186.

6. Dena Goodman, "Public Sphere and Private Life: Toward a Synthesis of Current Historiographical Approaches to the Old Regime," *History and Theory* 31, no. 3 (1992): 19.

That last possibility perhaps comes closest to the reading of eighteenth-century politics and public life in some of Kathleen Wilson's recent work. She writes: "In the public culture of the period, political articulacy lay in the eye of the beholder, and political consciousness was a many-splendored thing, forged as strikingly through the involvement of individuals in localized contests for power as through participation in national movements that aimed at ousting a minister or reforming the state."[7] This idea of public culture, where political articulateness is a function of reception and consciousness, seems close to what Baker and Goodman make out of their readings of Habermas, though Wilson's work is more directly and explicitly linked to that of Foucault, Pocock, and Stuart Hall.[8] In an essay from 1995, Wilson explores the construction of a notion of a national community of "extra-legal . . . citizenship" in eighteenth-century provincial newspapers. She notes that "the accessible, homogenized national identity cultivated by newspapers was in fact a delimiting one that recapitulated the self-representations of the urban upper and middle classes, and especially their male, white, and English members." She argues that print culture, club life, and other "socially-mixed and potentially transgressive spaces of urban society" cultivated "politically constructed national imaginings" and "efforts to enact a 'national,' rational political public to which the state was to be held accountable"; they cultivate something that resembles Habermas's oppositional public. This urban movement, Wilson argues, "led to stridently gendered and exclusionary notions of political subjectivity that played central roles in consolidating oppositional categories of the domestic and public spheres."[9] In this account, the political imaginary cultivated in urban spaces is potentially accessible to men and women of every class and race. The argument that the potential inclusiveness of the forms of political subjectivity available in these spaces produces a patriotism which is masculinist and exclusionary is reminiscent of accounts of Habermas's public-in-the-private sphere, which indicate that though the normative ideal of the public sphere may be inclusive, in social reality it is restricted to white, property-owning men.

Wilson's argument, however, has a further twist, which may work to reappropriate some of the inclusiveness of the Habermasian ideal to these "sites where extra-legal definitions of citizenship could be enacted or maintained." For Wilson argues that though national and patriotic discourses were overtly and sometimes stridently masculinist, and "depended upon a marginalization

7. Kathleen Wilson, *The Sense of the People: Politics, Culture and Imperialism in England, 1715–1785* (Cambridge: Cambridge University Press, 1998), 15. Originally published 1995.

8. See Wilson, *Sense,* 15.

9. Kathleen Wilson, "Citizenship, Empire, and Modernity in the English Provinces, c. 1720–1790," *Eighteenth-Century Studies* 29, no. 1 (1995): 78, 74, 78.

or subordination of the feminine in their notions of the national character," women were nevertheless perceived as political subjects in some contexts. Wilson writes that "long before the 1790s, the commercialized nature of English politics and culture provided middle class women with wider opportunities to act like political subjects and appropriate the mantel [*sic*] of citizenship for themselves; the injunctions to 'manly rationality' could not be bounded by biological sex and were a source of identity for women as well as men." Women were, Wilson argues, caught in a "double bind" of "being simultaneously urged to promote love of country and yet constrained by their lack of legal and political status and injunctions to domesticity." Her essay suggests that this twist, which ties women back into a political public characterized by their exclusion, may be made possible by the distinction between representations of women and discourses on femininity. She writes, for example, of "convergences and tensions between the symbolic feminine and the empirical positions of women."[10] This distinction is of course fraught with difficulty.[11] But the notion that there may be different discursive registers in play, complicating the historical relations between gender difference, publicity, and politics so that women do not seem necessarily excluded from "extra-legal" or "private" forms of public citizenship, of political articulateness and engagement, is fruitful, and produces in *The Sense of the People* a persuasive account of historical change.

The instability of the public/private divide is lucidly explored in Lawrence Klein's influential essays. Klein argues that "although the distinction between 'public' and 'private' *is* common in the eighteenth century, each term in the opposition has several meanings. Thus, there is no one 'public/private' distinction to which interpretation can confidently secure itself. . . . [R]ecognizing this mobility of meanings increases the complexity of mapping discourse." Having explored a sample of the meanings available, Klein concludes that scholars of the eighteenth century must abandon the "a priori commitment to the publicity of men and the privacy of women." Klein's exposition of the complexity of the public/private opposition is useful, though I think he underestimates the extent to which the eighteenth-century discourses that produce this range of meanings may have different degrees of resonance. Klein's essay is

10. Ibid., 78, 79, 80.

11. See for example Joan Wallach Scott, "Gender: A Useful Category of Historical Analysis," in *Gender and the Politics of History* (New York: Columbia University Press, 1988), 28–50; and Chandra Talpade Mohanty, "Feminist Encounters: Locating the Politics of Experience," in *Destabilizing Theory: Contemporary Feminist Debates,* ed. Michèle Barrett and Anne Phillips (Cambridge: Polity, 1992), 74–92.

structured by his "skepticism about the 'domestic thesis,'" which was inspired by Amanda Vickery's influential article on the "Categories and Chronology of English Women's History."[12] Vickery has since expanded on some of the arguments of her article in her illuminatingly detailed study, *The Gentleman's Daughter: Women's Lives in Georgian England* (1998).

Vickery discusses at some length the availability of public life to polite eighteenth-century women from "commercial professional and gentry families," and finds in it some cause for celebration. She writes enthusiastically that:

> Fuelled by polite ideals, the intellectual horizons of privileged, provincial women rolled majestically outwards in the course of the eighteenth century. . . . The well-turned letter became an unavoidable performance of the long-standing female work of kin, but in addition it enabled unprecedented numbers of women to participate in worldly exchange and debate. It was in their tireless writing no less than in their ravenous reading that genteel women embraced a world far beyond the boundaries of their parish.

The women Vickery studies participate through their literacy in an extensive world of debate. As readers, they "enjoyed unprecedented access to the public world of print." As social beings, they enter and in some cases preside over a considerable range of "public venues." Vickery takes her "reconstruction of the potentialities of public life for polite women"[13] to show that though the women she studies "were obviously severely disabled when it came to institutional power, they did not lack access to the public sphere, *as they understood it.*" She concludes that "it seems likely that eighteenth-century conceptions of publicity were different to those of nineteenth-century feminists and twentieth-century historians."[14]

Vickery's detailed analysis of the lives of a small group of Lancashire families is fascinating, but in its use of the language of public and private it is not without problems. In her discussion of public sites frequented by polite women, Vickery explains that her "selection of venues . . . is guided by the definitions of public life offered by eighteenth-century women themselves."[15]

12. Lawrence E. Klein, "Gender and the Public/Private Distinction in the Eighteenth Century: Some Questions about Evidence and Analytic Procedure," *Eighteenth-Century Studies* 29, no. 1 (1995): 99, 105, 97, and see 107 n. 4. See also Lawrence E. Klein, "Gender, Conversation and the Public Sphere in Early Eighteenth-Century England," in *Textuality and Sexuality: Reading Theories and Practices,* ed. J. Still and M. Worton (Manchester: Manchester University Press, 1993), 100–115.

13. Amanda Vickery, *The Gentleman's Daughter: Women's Lives in Georgian England* (New Haven, Conn.: Yale University Press, 1998), 1, 287, 259, 227.

14. Amanda Vickery, "Golden Age to Separate Spheres? A Review of the Categories and Chronology of English Women's History," *The Historical Journal* 36, no. 2 (1993): 412.

15. Vickery, *Daughter,* 227. See also Vickery's discussion of this issue in her Introduction, 10–11.

As Baker points out, and Vickery acknowledges, the language of public and private has been important to the accounts of the eighteenth century by J. G. A. Pocock and by Habermas, who use the terms differently. It has also, as Vickery emphasizes, been "long deployed in feminist rhetoric and women's history." Carole Pateman, for example, writes that "the dichotomy between the public and the private is central to almost two centuries of feminist writing and political struggle; it is, ultimately, what the feminist movement is about."[16] It carries, then, a considerable and rather convoluted burden of significances. Vickery's work implies a further opposition between the complexity of this baggage, and indeed of the aggregated conceptions of "nineteenth-century feminists and twentieth-century historians," and the simplicity of appealing to what a small group of polite eighteenth-century Lancastrian women understood the public to mean.

In a manner that reminds but also reproves, Vickery writes:

> In no century before the twentieth did women enjoy the public powers which nineteenth-century feminists sought—the full rights of citizenship. Public life for the gentlemen I have studied invariably incorporated some form of office, but there was no formal place for their wives in the machinery of local administration. Customarily, a wealthy woman wielded power as a mother, kinswoman, housekeeper, consumer, hostess and arbiter of polite sociability. If all this adds up to a separation of the public sphere of male power and the private sphere of female influence, then this separation was an ancient phenomenon which certainly predated the misogyny of the 1690s, evangelicism, the French revolution and the factory.[17]

Vickery speaks of the eighteenth century as having "a backdrop of continuity and muted change," and though she claims that "from the late seventeenth century the comfortably off in the provinces benefited from an extraordinary expansion and sophistication of their material and intellectual worlds,"[18] she argues that it is "extremely difficult to sustain . . . the argument that sometime between 1650 and 1850 the public/private distinction was constituted or radically reconstituted in a way that transformed relations between the sexes."[19] Vickery sometimes implies that before the nineteenth century the language of public and private was relatively simple and stable; that it conformed to what

16. Carole Pateman, "Feminist Critiques of the Public/Private Dichotomy," in *The Disorder of Women: Democracy, Feminism and Political Theory* (Cambridge: Polity, 1989), 118.

17. Vickery, "Golden Age," 411.

18. Vickery, *Daughter,* 286.

19. Vickery, "Golden Age," 411–12. Cf. Leonore Davidoff, Megan Doolittle, Janet Fink, and Katherine Holden, *The Family Story: Blood, Contract and Intimacy 1830–1960* (London: Longman, 1999), esp. chapter 2.

Baker describes as "the conventional distinction between the public (as the domain of political power) and the private (as the domain of social reproduction)."[20] Vickery suggests that men inhabited the "domain of political power" and "controlled public institutions,"[21] while women understood and accepted that the public for them had a much narrower meaning, and applied only to social and cultural activity, which they alternated with spells of domesticity. However "extraordinary" was the expansion in what was considered appropriate and available for consumption, both materially and intellectually, it was not so extraordinary, it seems, as not to fit comfortably into more or less static notions of the limited social publicity available to women. Small change.

By contrast, Kathleen Wilson's work on provincial newspapers—research which in some respects overlaps with Vickery's—leads her to conclude that something very similar to Vickery's "extraordinary expansion" produced changes in the relations between political consciousness and public life which "created spaces and sites for a wider range of groups to claim or imagine a status as citizens despite oligarchy and ethnic, class, and gender inequalities."[22] To some extent, of course, differences of this kind may be explained by reference to the different materials Vickery and Wilson study. Barker and Chalus point out that "the historian's choice of sources determines his or her understanding of gender": those who study "prescriptive or satirical literature" find out about how "contemporaries conceptualized and talked about gender," while those who examine "the experiences of real individuals" find out about how "gender was played out in daily life." But the difference is not only about the problematic distinction between empirical experience and representation or conceptualization. It is about the role of discourse, and more specifically of political discourses, in cultural and historical change.

For almost all of the historians and critics I have mentioned, the opposition between a masculine public sphere of political power and a sphere of privacy which is much more difficult to characterize, but which almost always includes or overlaps with the domestic, is understood to be complicated (and here the analogy of spheres becomes a hindrance) by a third site. That third site may take a form derived from Habermas's public-within-the-private; it might take a form suggested by whiggish opposition politics in the 1770s, when the true patriot able to grasp the public good was not usually characterized by involvement in the imminently corrupting exercise of political power, or it might take the form of the capacity to imagine oneself as a citizen possessed of a political

20. Baker, "Habermas," 187.
21. Baker, "Habermas," 187; Vickery, "Golden Age," 413.
22. Wilson, "Citizenship," 78.

subjectivity. What all these forms have in common is that they suggest that the relation between public and private may be permeable, may be fluid. Vickery's account of the publicity available to polite Lancastrian women certainly suggests that what was available to them was expansive and expanding. But it never results in—and perhaps never could result in—even the most tentative or imaginary pressure on the "public/private distinction" in its most conventional form. Vickery writes that her

> rejection of the conceptual vocabulary of "public and private" and "separate spheres" deployed so extensively in women's history rests above all on the fact that it has so little resonance for the prosperous women studied here. . . . [W]omen's own writings suggest that the dominant historiographical debate about elite women's lives has been misfocused, curiously negligent of those women's own concerns; distinctions of limited significance have been over-emphasised, while central preoccupations have been missed altogether.

She cautions that "it is futile to berate Georgian women for 'failing' to perceive their limitations."[23] Obviously I do not want to suggest that women who did not question their own position should be swept under the carpet. But I do think the methodological framework in the context of which we might consider, for example, women's access to printed material needs to be supple enough to allow for the possibility of small changes in readers' consciousness of themselves in relation to public issues: to the idea of the nation, or even to political debate.

Many of Vickery's reservations about "the conceptual vocabulary of 'public and private' and 'separate spheres'" are, of course, salutary. But rejecting the vocabulary can lead to a sort of particularism. Barker and Chalus acknowledge the importance of Vickery's work, though they concede that "the concerns at the heart of older models remain important." They conjure historians to "become more aware and accepting of the sharp contradictions and infinite variations of women's and men's experiences in pre-industrial societies," and they assert that "eighteenth-century English society was earthy, robust and dynamic, yet it remained decidedly diverse."[24] There is a familiar—indeed an overfamiliar—discourse of national character at work in this characterization of an "earthy," implicitly non-urban and non-urbane, Englishness. In Barker and Chalus's account, and to some extent in Vickery's work too, there is an implicit appeal to the notion of a continuous national character which resists change by celebrating diversity and plurality. Perhaps not surprisingly, the

23. Vickery, *Daughter,* 10.
24. Barker and Chalus, *Gender,* 25–26, 24.

crudest version of this tendency toward particularism can be found in Amanda Foreman's useful and entertaining biography of *Georgiana: Duchess of Devonshire* (1998). Foreman claims that for historians such as those who contributed to the Barker and Chalus collection "the argument has turned in favour of idiosyncracy, of integration and pluralism, with a greater dependence on individual case histories rather than theoretical models."[25] It is of course precisely in terms of the value of individual idiosyncrasy and eccentricity that the continued existence of a House of Lords stocked with hereditary peers is argued for, and Amanda Foreman has appeared on BBC's *Newsnight* to make that case. I do not want to suggest that the work of Vickery, of Barker and Chalus, or of those they present, is characterized by quite this kind of conservatism. I want to indicate that while I think their reflections on the models of women's history have been instructive, we should be careful not to throw out infant political possibilities in the discourses of publicity along with the bathwater.

For most of the historians I have mentioned, whether they study eighteenth-century notions of public and private in the terms suggested by Pocock or by Habermas, or perhaps more fruitfully play those terms off against each other, the language of public and private has a political resonance or potential; it implies a consciousness which, however indirectly or obliquely, positions itself in relation to a notion of citizenship, real or imaginary. The social activity of, say, shopping may be very small change in "the commerce of the world," but it is part of the currency of that private world from within which public faces emerge. Small changes in the network of meanings that constitute publicity mean that some women, even as they shop, can imagine themselves as political citizens. When eighteenth-century women engaged in the "tireless writing" of letters, they were perhaps engaged in an activity of very limited public importance, public only in the sense that it created a "bond of company" between them and absent friends; but when they marked parts of their letters as suitable only for the eyes of the addressee, and indicated that other parts could be

25. In *Georgiana: Duchess of Devonshire* (London: HarperCollins, 1998) Amanda Foreman writes that "female participation in any activity outside the domestic sphere was haphazard and unpredictable; character and circumstances were often more important in determining a woman's life than social convention." She cites Barker and Chalus's *Gender,* to which she is a contributor, and states that "the eight contributors argue against the case for separate spheres and therefore, by implication, against the notion that women's history is a separate discipline within the field of history. In the past, historians have argued that men and women lived in increasingly rigid separate spheres, controlled and demarcated by the functions of gender. More recently, the argument has turned in favour of idiosyncracy, of integration and pluralism, with a greater dependence on individual case histories rather than theoretical models" (428 n. 27).

read to assembled company; or when, indeed, they prepared their letters for (most usually posthumous) publication, they made them available to an audience who might hear, or mis-hear, in them not only the "small coin . . . frequently requisite in transacting the common business of the day," but the chink of gold, of public opinions being formed and disputed.[26]

Across the period spanned by this book, a series of small changes takes place in the position of women, or the way women are perceived; and the cumulative effect of these changes is that by the early nineteenth century it had become possible or even necessary for some women to define their gendered identities through the nature and degree of their approximation to the public identities of political citizens. The second half of the eighteenth century, this book argues, was characterized by widespread debate about the nature of domesticity and the public and private roles of women—a debate made all the more pervasive and significant in its implications by the success with which, especially at the turn of the century, it masqueraded as a show of consensus. By the early nineteenth century, the conditions (of consciousness or imagination at least) necessary to nineteenth-century feminist debate were emerging; some women of liberal education could assume that it was their right and duty to have opinions about what happened in the world; they did not see their exclusion from participation in the public life of the nation as natural; indeed, in some senses they did not think of themselves as excluded at all. In the 1790s, for example, the desires and aspirations articulated in the fictions of Mary Wollstonecraft or Mary Hays are marked by the affinity between private pursuits and public ambitions. Both Elizabeth Hamilton and Lucy Aikin, writing a few years later, thought that patriotism was a necessary part of women's education, and argued that middle-class women's exclusion from paid labor allowed them to cultivate a statesmanlike knowledge of the world that was no longer available to professional or landed men.

This book is structured by the belief that this important change in the way middle-class women think of themselves cannot best be explained in terms of a simple linear narrative of cause and effect. Vickery is, of course, right that what we see in this period is not a time, a moment, when the relation between public and private or between men and women is radically reconstituted, but a process of "muted change": shifts, not radical in themselves, which reconfigure relations between those paired terms in ways that are profoundly significant. There is obviously no particular event or moment that brings about this reconfiguration. But less obviously perhaps, this is not a process of change that

26. I discuss letter-writing at greater length in chapter 4.

can best be charted through the progress of a particular argument or discourse. This book is about the small changes that take place across a range of discourses and genres. This is where my project parts company with the various accounts of women's writing, or representations of women in the eighteenth century, that feminist literary critics have produced in the last fifteen years or so, and on whose work of recovery, scholarship and debate this book builds.

Most recent accounts by feminist critics have focused more or less exclusively on novels—on women as writers of novels and romances, or on representation of women in novels.[27] But eighteenth-century novels themselves participate in debates that cut across genres; they assume readers who are also immersed in periodical literature, in poetry, in histories, readers who discuss plays and parliamentary debates, who perform music, and peer into the windows of print shops. Novels echo debates and discourses the implications of which may only be spelled out in, say, polemical essays, or conduct books, or private letters. This book traces issues and arguments between genres, and perhaps partly because of that different focus it argues against the thesis that middle-class women were in the second half of the eighteenth century increasingly confined to domesticity by the demands of propriety. It shows that domesticity is always a contested proposition; it is insufficiently polite or elegant or social, it fails to produce contestants for the international competition in learned women, and it fails to secure to women those forms of personal worth which only participation in the labor market offers. In most of the contexts considered in this book, domesticity gains in value as a result of its continuity with the social or the public, and not only as a result of its asocial exclusion. This project considers domesticity in relation to learning, patriotic politics, and work in order to reveal the extent to which it is only ever one of a set of contradictory demands on women.

A number of critical studies published in the last decade have considered the position of women in relation to notions of earning and labor.[28] Most of these

27. I have in mind here Nancy Armstrong, *Desire and Domestic Fiction: A Political History of the Novel* (New York: Oxford University Press, 1987); Jane Spencer, *The Rise of the Woman Novelist: From Aphra Behn to Jane Austen* (Oxford: Basil Blackwell, 1986); and Janet Todd, *The Sign of Angellica: Women, Writing, and Fiction, 1660–1800* (London: Virago, 1989).

28. I am thinking of, for example, Catherine Gallagher, *Nobody's Story: The Vanishing Acts of Women Writers in the Marketplace, 1670–1820* (Berkeley: University of California Press, 1994); Cheryl Turner, *Living by the Pen: Women Writers in the Eighteenth Century* (London: Routledge, 1992); Liz Bellamy, *Commerce, Morality and the Eighteenth-Century Novel* (Cambridge: Cambridge University Press, 1998); Laura Mandell, *Misogynous Economies: The Business of Literature in Eighteenth-Century Britain* (Lexington: University Press of Kentucky, 1999); and Edward Copeland, *Women Writing about Money: Women's Fiction in England, 1790–1820* (Cambridge: Cambridge University Press, 1995).

studies have explored women's ability to earn money, or their power as consumers. In this project I am primarily concerned with women's access to the languages of moral authority or personal worth that are attached to labor, and particularly to specialized professional careers. Broadly speaking, it might be argued that in the early decades of the period discussed in this book, a part of the value of learning to women is that it gains them moral authority; it is perceived as a substantial property, analogous to landed estate in its ability to confirm the moral worth of its owner. But learning is also a professional qualification, and in later decades that aspect of learning becomes the primary source of the worth it implies. Both conservative and liberal texts on the position of women published in the late eighteenth and early nineteenth centuries appropriate the discourse on the division of labor to feminine employments and occupations, though they do so in the service of widely divergent agendas. A major concern of the second half of this book is an exploration of the ways in which the language of the division of labor might work to afford or deny women access to public life.

Sensibility or sentiment has also been the focus for several important recent critical studies, and it is central to the issue of women's ability to imagine themselves as patriotic or public citizens.[29] It is perhaps most obviously important to that ability because of its role in the sentimental notion of the continuity of affect linking the family and the nation, which assumes particular prominence during the years of conflict between Britain and its American colonies. But it is also important to the emergence of the sense that the nation in its ideal form, as for example the seat of liberal whiggish ideals or of egalitarian principles, is an object of either nostalgic regret or utopian projection. Broadly speaking, my book is concerned with the feminization of patriotism, and the changes which make different forms of patriotic consciousness available to women, and as a literary critic I am primarily concerned with women writers, and their negotiations with patriotism in their writing. But this book is not only about women and patriotism. I continually return to the issues raised by the changing relations among a larger group of terms: nation, sensibility, public and private, and gender difference.

29. G. J. Barker-Benfield, *The Culture of Sensibility: Sex and Society in Eighteenth-Century Britain* (Chicago: University of Chicago Press, 1992); Syndy M. Conger, ed., *Sensibility in Transformation: Creative Resistance to Sentiment from the Augustans to the Romantics* (London: Associated University Presses, 1990); Claudia Johnson, *Equivocal Beings: Politics, Gender, and Sentimentality in the 1790s* (Chicago: University of Chicago Press, 1995); John Mullan, *Sentiment and Sociability: The Language of Feeling in the Eighteenth Century* (Oxford: Clarendon Press, 1988); Janet Todd, *Sensibility: An Introduction* (London: Methuen, 1986); and Jean Hagstrum, *Sex and Sensibility* (Chicago: University of Chicago Press, 1980).

The second half of the eighteenth century is an important starting point for feminist historiography for three different reasons. First, and most familiar, is the history which takes its starting point from the 1790s, when women gain a clearly identifiable feminist political voice. Mary Wollstonecraft, and to some extent Mary Hays, Catharine Macaulay, and Anna Laetitia Barbauld, begin to articulate in the late century claims for women which are, at least from the standpoint of our own time, recognizably claims to political identity. Second, from the middle of the century, catalogues of the lives of eminent women begin to be published, biographical dictionaries which lay the foundations for histories of women. Perhaps as a development from this, the period is characterized by what Susan Staves describes as "nationalistic celebration of the new literary and cultural achievements of the extraordinary English women, the 'British Fair,' celebrated as emblems of British enlightenment."[30] Biographies of women of the past as well as celebrations of living "extraordinary English women" acquire a new significance to emerging—and changing—notions of the national identity. Third, women acquire a new importance in the narratives of the progress of civilization produced, most distinctively, by the theorists of the Scottish enlightenment. Following Addison and Montesquieu, the condition of women is perceived as the index of civilization, and the position of women is, as a result, extensively debated, both in historical studies of British and European culture and in comparative studies of other cultures.

This book discusses each of these issues, and begins to explore the relation between them. Part 1 focuses on the decades of the mid-eighteenth century, and considers the status of women's learning, and of learned women. I look at the relation between the consumption of intellectual and material goods—learning and shopping—and consider in some detail the terms in which learned women are celebrated as the icons of national progress. The status of learned women in these decades gives them, in some sense, a public importance which is tied to the privacy of the activity of learning, and I therefore take this as the starting point for a discussion of the kinds of publicity and privacy available to women which is one of the major themes of this book. In part 2, I study at some length the writings of Elizabeth Carter. Carter was hailed over several decades as the paradigmatic learned woman, and my chapters on her look at the nature of her fame, as it is represented in her letters and those of other women of the "bluestocking circle" and in the wider world of print. I consider the importance of Carter's reputation for domesticity and for piety in licensing

30. Susan Staves, "'The Liberty of a She-Subject of England': Rights Rhetoric and the Female Thucydides," *Cardozo Studies in Law and Literature* 1 (1989): 172.

her fame; her relation to learning as a profession; and, in the context of her significance to notions of the national character, the nature of her patriotism.

In part 3 I extend my discussion of patriotism and gender into the 1770s and 1780s, when representations of the American war as a conflict within the family gave feminine and sentimental patriotism a more public face. As Linda Colley argues, from the 1770s onward "belief in a distinctive feminine sphere could also, paradoxically, legitimise women's intervention in affairs hitherto regarded as the preserve of men."[31] To some extent, it can be helpful to think of this intervention in terms of the ideal of the Roman Matron, and in my chapter on Anna Laetitia Barbauld I discuss some of the many uses of that image in these decades. This model for feminine intervention in the public and political sphere, I suggest, can best be understood in the context of the demands made by the discourse on the division of labor on the notion of domesticity, on the one hand, and by the pervasive politicization of British culture in the 1770s, on the other. I conclude this section with a discussion of Anna Seward's elegiac patriotism, which I suggest signals the new importance of feminized notions of humanity in the wake of Britain's defeat.

In part 4 I turn to the 1790s and, in my conclusion, I consider some of the divergent possibilities of domesticity in the first decade or so of the nineteenth century. My discussion of the 1790s is necessarily brief and partial, for the sheer range and complexity of debate in (and about) the 1790s could only be addressed in a book-length study. However, I explore some of the implications of the antifeminine discourse apparent in Wollstonecraft's *Vindication of the Rights of Woman* (1792) and Hannah More's *Strictures* (1799), and I consider the role of feminine sensibility in the utopian political visions of Wollstonecraft's *Letters Written during a Short Residence in Sweden, Norway, and Denmark* and in Mary Hays's *Memoirs of Emma Courtney,* both published in 1796. In my conclusion, I consider some of the ways in which different accounts of domesticity may represent women as able to fulfill public roles, taking as my starting point Maria Edgeworth's discussion of women's learning in her *Letters for Literary Ladies.* I suggest that whiggish notions of patriotism enable some women—and the examples I am most concerned with are those of Elizabeth Hamilton and Lucy Aikin—to represent domesticity as the site from which an oppositional political discourse can be articulated.

31. Linda Colley, *Britons: Forging the Nation 1707–1837* (New Haven, Conn.: Yale University Press, 1992), 273, and see chapter 6.

PART ONE

Learning and Shopping in the Mid-Eighteenth Century

1

These Neuter Somethings: Gender Difference and Commercial Culture

I

"There are few things by which a man discovers the weakness of his judgement more, than by retailing scraps of common-place sentiment on the trite and thread-bare topic, the degeneracy of the times," remarked Adam Fitz-Adam in the issue of *The World* for February 26, 1756. But for most of the periodical essayists of the mid-century this "trite and thread-bare topic" is the stock in trade, and the narrative of corruption and degeneration is continually alluded to, with ironic acceptance or humorous despair, but above all with a familiarity that indicates the persuasiveness of its account of the times. His tongue pushing more visibly against his cheek, Fitz-Adam goes on to defend modernity, complaining that "really it is a great breach of good-manners, that modern fine gentlemen cannot put a little *rouge* on their faces, but the saucy quill of some impertinent author immediately rubs it off." For, he points out, "Juvenal informs us, that the Roman beaux did the same." Finally, he cites a correspondent who argues that the present age is preeminently uncorrupt because it has achieved that "CONQUEST over the affections and passions" that

Reprinted with permission of the University of California Press from *Refiguring Revolutions: Aesthetics and Politics from the English Revolution to the Romantic Revolution,* ed. Kevin Sharpe and Stephen Zwicker (Berkeley: University of California Press, 1998), 173–94.

philosophers have always advocated, for now Englishmen do not marry for love but, more prudently, for money.[1] The paper, I think, is typical of mid-eighteenth-century social satire, in that it deplores the pervasiveness of what it identifies as degeneracy, but sees its progress as inevitable, and manages to convey almost a perverse pleasure in the absurdities it produces. For periodical papers of the mid-century return repeatedly to the theme of Britain's inevitable imitation of the decline and fall of the Roman Empire, and to the representation of a metropolitan culture as caught up in the historical process where "as the Men became mercenary and effeminate, the Women grew lewd and luxurious,"[2] where errant sexuality and the culture of commercial prosperity are perceived as the intertwined manifestations of national degeneration.

The sense, by mid-century, that the process of degeneration may be as much a matter for wry humor or ironic detachment as for alarm or disgust indicates the extent to which the narrative on corruption has become dissociated from that on commercial progress. For commerce can of course be celebrated with increasing ease in these decades as the source of a culture distinguished by its own characteristic set of virtues and social benefits. Samuel Johnson argues, for example, in *The Adventurer,* that "He, whose mind is engaged by the acquisition or improvement of a fortune, not only escapes the insipidity of indifference, and the tediousness of inactivity, but gains enjoyments wholly unknown to those who live lazily on the toil of others; for life affords no higher pleasure than that of surmounting difficulties, passing from one step of success to another, forming new wishes, and seeing them gratified."[3] In Johnson's account the endless promotion of desire that characterizes commercial culture is wholly removed from and uninfected by the heady mixture of avarice and licentious sexuality which mark desire as the symptom of degeneracy. The processes of this moralization of desire are obviously complex. But in the periodical papers I am concerned with it is effected by the relatively simple maneuver of representing fashionable society in both a synecdochic and an antithetical relation to commercial society. So, a correspondent observes to Adam Fitz-Adam that "the luxury and corruption of any nation is just in proportion to its wealth, and the largeness of its metropolis." He asserts that "one great cause of the

1. *The World. By Adam Fitz-Adam,* no. 165.

2. *Common Sense: Or, The Englishman's Journal. Being A Collection of Letters, Political, Humorous, and Moral,* 23 July 1737. Compare Lady Mary Wortley Montagu, in *The Nonsense of Common-Sense,* no. 9, 14 March 1738: "Bravery and Chastity, the ancient Idols of the two Sexes, are not only left without Worshippers, but trampled on and despis'd. . . . it is a Sort of Merit in People to get the better of natural Shame, when *Money* is in their Way."

3. *The Adventurer,* no. 111, 27 November 1763.

excessive luxury that prevails amongst us" is the "infinite number of people that resort hither, [who] naturally rival each other in their tables, dress, equipage, furniture, and in short, extravagances of all sorts." The move from an inclusive "us," absorbed in luxury, to the metropolis, and then to a "them" who engage their minds in "constant hurry and dissipation," speedily resolves the luxury and corruption that attend commercial prosperity into the problems of "that part of the human species which calls itself the world," or fashionable society.[4] Fashionable society represents, often in the same breath, the same sentence, both the desirous and competitive energies that are seen to characterize commercial progress and the indolence, frivolity, and dissipation to which commercial industry is opposed.

In the first half of this chapter I will explore some of the implications of the ambivalent relation I have outlined between commerce and fashion, first in some more periodical essays, and then in Sarah Fielding's novel, *The Adventures of David Simple.* In particular, I am interested in the way problems about the morality of commercial culture come to be represented as anxieties about sexual difference. In the second half of the chapter I look at the relation between those anxieties and the instability of the distinction between notions of public and private, and the different kinds of morality appropriate to them. What interests me, broadly speaking, is the question of the kind of moral ascendancy women, or perhaps notions of femininity, seem to gain in the mid-century. It is obvious, I think—from, for example, the essays of David Hume, where women are represented as "much better judges of all polite writing than men,"[5] or from the kind of reception that the works of Elizabeth Carter and other learned ladies gained—that during the decades of the mid-century more was demanded of women—affluent or middle-class women were able to do more—by way of a contribution to the notion of the superiority of British culture. By the late 1760s and 1770s, publications by women could be welcomed simply because they were by women, and it became commonplace to claim that Britain was more civilized than other European nations because women were better treated in this culture, and were better educated. This is a considerable cultural shift, which needs to be thought about in a range of different terms and contexts. This chapter will look only at a limited selection of texts

4. *World,* no. 61, 28 February 1754; and [Moore], no. 1, 4 January 1753. On fashion and the metropolis, see James Raven, *Judging New Wealth: Popular Publishing and Responses to Commerce in England, 1750–1800* (Oxford: Clarendon Press, 1992), chapter 8, esp. 162–64.

5. David Hume, "Of Essay Writing," in *Selected Essays,* ed. Stephen Copley and Andrew Edgar (Oxford: Oxford University Press, 1993), 3. The essay was first published in the *Essays: Moral and Political* of 1742.

and issues, but it will introduce some of the contexts in which I want to consider this cultural shift, as well as how it came about.

The kinds of anxieties fashion provokes, in the periodical essayists of the mid-century, stem from its capacity to blur differences seen as necessary to the preservation of the social structure: differences of age—cosmetics make the old appear young, and age the youthful prematurely; differences of nation—as the fashionable adopt the modes, manners, and language of Paris; differences of gender—men are feminized by their absorption in appearance, their desire for trivia, while women are masculinized by the boldness of fashionable manners; and differences of social station, which are no longer clearly indicated by modes of dress, and which give way to differences of wealth or ready cash rather than inherited position.[6] Dress in particular is perceived to have become a system of masquerade, which disguises the differences of social station or class to which it had once been a legible index. But anxieties about dress, of course, which are the subject of numerous periodical essays, function as a means to discuss (or draw a veil over) what are perhaps more profound instabilities in the hierarchy of social difference—instabilities which may be perceived as matter for ambivalent regret. Bonnell Thornton's periodical, *The Connoisseur,* for example, remarks mockingly on the appearance of what it calls "second-hand gentry":

> When I see the wives and daughters of tradesmen and mechanics make such attempts at finery, I cannot help pitying their poor fathers and husbands, and at the same time am apt to consider their dress as a robbery on the shop. Thus, when I observe the tawdry gentility of a tallow-chandler's daughter, I look upon her as hung round with long sixes, short eights, and rush-lights; and when I contemplate the aukward pride of dress in a butcher's wife, I suppose her carrying about her surloins of beef, fillets of veal, and shoulders of mutton.

Like so many essayists of the period, Mr. Town the connoisseur is here deploring the availability of the fashions of the noble and/or wealthy to women of the artisanal or shopkeeping classes, the "red-armed belles that appear in the park every Sunday." But the humor is complicated: it is ridiculous for the

6. For further discussion of these issues see Neil McKendrick, "The Commercialisation of Fashion," in Neil McKendrick, John Brewer, and J. H. Plumb, *The Birth of a Consumer Society: The Commercialization of Eighteenth-Century England* (London: Europa, 1982), esp. 53–56. Complaints about the erosion of the social structure as a result of fashionable consumption and display had of course been common currency for several centuries, but see McKendrick's argument (34–56) that the situation of England in the mid to late eighteenth century was "unique as well as novel" (55). See also Gerald Newman, *The Rise of English Nationalism: A Cultural History, 1740–1830* (London: Wiedenfeld, 1987), chapter 2.

women to dress up, and rob the shop, when Mr. Town can so readily perceive them untransformed by their purchases, or can indeed reverse the reproduction of value, and perceive them to be made absurd by their adornment in the goods they sell. But he accepts the aspiration this implies, acknowledges that the red arms of labor need transforming. He is "vastly diverted" when "Going upon some business to a tradesman's house, I surprised in a very extraordinary deshabille two females, whom I had been frequently used to see strangely dizened out in the Mall. . . . one, who always dresses the family dinner, was genteely employed in winding up the jack, while the other was up to the elbows in soap-suds." It is ludicrous that tradesmen's daughters should wish to be taken for "fine ladies," but their household chores are not wrapped up in any notion of the dignity of labor or proper feminine domesticity—in the eyes of the connoisseur their work is absurdly vulgar, contemptibly demeaning.[7] Politeness demands that women of this class should not be perceived to work, in the same breath as it disparages their "tawdry gentility."

The connoisseur expresses a common complaint of the period when he remarks that "there is scarce one woman to be met with, except among the lowest of the vulgar. The sex consists almost entirely of Ladies."[8] Catherine Talbot lamented, in her essay "On true Politeness," that "regard to the different stations of life is too much neglected by all ranks of people. . . . all sorts of people put themselves on a level."[9] But the desire for exclusive distinction conflicted with the sense, so important to the cultural ascendancy of the manners and aspirations of the middle classes, that politeness is a universal code. In this context, exclusivity is a kind of residual idiosyncrasy inherited from the association of fashion with courtly nobility. Henry Fielding, for example, in *The Covent-Garden Journal,* mocks the attempts of the fashionable "to preserve their circle safe and inviolate . . . against any intrusion of those whom they are pleased to call the vulgar." He suggests that they are obliged to continue to favor the hoop petticoat because it has been "found impossible . . . to slide with it behind a counter." But the point of his satire is to emphasize the permeability of distinctions of station within the middle classes, and between them and a nobility distinguished by no more than the absurdities of fashionable excess. So, for example, he notes that on "observing that several of the

7. *The Connoisseur. By Mr. Town, Critic and Censor-General,* no. 25, 18 July 1754.

8. *Connoisseur,* no. 44, 28 November 1754.

9. *The Works of the late Miss Catherine Talbot. First published by the late Mrs. Elizabeth Carter; and now republished with some few additional papers,* ed. Montagu Pennington, 9th edition (London: Rivington, 1819), 62–63.

enemy had lately exhibited arms on their vehicles, by which means those ornaments became vulgar and common," fashionable people replaced their own coats of arms with cyphers, "cunningly contrived to represent themselves instead of their ancestors"; they replace the signs of aristocratic rank with those of individual difference.[10]

The fashionable and trading classes are, then, ambiguously identified in their aspiration to polite leisure, and the desires of the fashionable are represented in a doubled and ambivalent relation to the energies of commerce. The uneasiness of the perceived relation between the two may be indicated by the frequency with which gambling, which parodies the activities and energies of trade, is represented as central to anxieties about fashionable life. James Fordyce, in his influential *Sermons to Young Women* (of 1765), cites the view that gambling tends "to destroy all distinctions both of rank and sex; to crush all emulation, but that of fraud; to confound the world in a chaos of folly." Gambling is perceived to function like fashion and like trade, and Fordyce agrees that it is an exceptionally laborious calling, for "this trade goes on when all the shops are shut."[11] Adam Fitz-Adam is resigned to the fact that "it is my lot to live in an age when virtue, sense, conversation, all private and public affections are totally swallowed up by the single predominant passion of gaming,"[12] and it is of course appropriate that "Commerce" should be the name of a much-played card game.

In periodical essays, the difference between the habits of expenditure and consumption necessary to commerce and fashion—the difference between good and bad taste—is represented not only as a matter of class difference, but as a matter of the ability of consumers smoothly to assimilate the goods they purchase, preserving their own personalities from becoming dissipated in the variety of objects they desire. Much of the humor of the papers, however, depends precisely on the inability of purchasers to digest what they consume (to borrow the language of Shelley's *Defence*). So, for example, Thornton concludes the discussion of "second-hand gentry" from which I have quoted with the observation that "true oeconomy does not merely consist in not exceeding our income, but in such judicious management of it, as renders our whole appearance equal and consistent." He dwells on the notion that fashionable cosmetics make women appear to be "bedaubed, like an old wall, with plaister

10. Henry Fielding, *Covent Garden Journal*, no. 37, 9 May 1752.

11. James Fordyce, *Sermons to Young Women*, vol. 1 [1765] (London: Cadell, 1809), 193, 185. The first passage may be a paraphrase of *The Rambler*, no. 15, 8 May 1750.

12. [Cambridge], *World*, no. 118, 3 April 1755.

and rough-cast,"[13] or that makeup resembles the paint on portraits offered for sale, but "the picture fails to charm, while my thoughts are engrossed by the wood and canvas."[14] Those who fail to assimilate or digest their purchases to their own consistency expose the mechanics of the reproduction of value; they disclose their own status as things to be bought and sold, units of exchange. Indeed, in an extended fantasy the connoisseur proposes to "open a shop or warehouse . . . under the name of a Mind-and-body-Clothier: two trades which . . . are, in their nature, inseparable." From this establishment he will market personality to the fashionable, packaged in its moral or professional accoutrements.[15]

Fashionable appearance and personality are characterized as an assemblage of bits, "their red, their pompons, their scraps of dirty gauze, flimsy sattins, and black callicoes; not to mention their affected broken English, and mangled French, which jumbled together compose their present language."[16] It is in these terms that the *World* repeatedly and vehemently attacks the fashion for chinoiserie, and censures fashionable dress, remarking, for example, of a young lady seen at Ranelagh: "I could not help condemning that profusion of ornament, which violated and destroyed the unity and τὸ ὅλον [wholeness, completeness] (a technical term borrowed from the toilette) of so accomplished a figure."[17] This fear of severalness, of a dissipation that violates ideal unity, is clearly a language of sexual anxiety, a defensive shoring up of phallic power and taste, which finds expression in the frequent satires on the fashionable erosion of sexual difference. Gendered identity emerges in these papers as something either differentiated or confused, even denied by patterns of consumption. Eliza Haywood's *Female Spectator* comments, in fairly typical terms, in a paper of 1744:

> let it not be said we are the only thoughtless, gawdy flutterers of the human world:—there are *men*-butterflies, as well as *women:—things* that are above the trouble of reflection, and suffer themselves to be blown about by every wind of folly.—Whatever has the name of novelty will carry them through thick and

13. *Connoisseur,* no. 55, 13 February 1755.

14. *Connoisseur,* no. 46, 12 December 1754.

15. *Connoisseur,* no. 77, 17 July 1755. For further discussion of some of these issues see my essay, "Sterne, Elizabeth Draper, and Drapery," *The Shandean* 9 (November 1997): 833.

16. [Moore], *World,* no. 18, 3 May 1753.

17. [J. Warton], *World,* no. 26, 28 June 1753. The sentiment is of course also common in other genres. Talbot comments in more directly moral terms that "the elegant beauty, whose fondest aim is to please and to be admired, has sometimes small regard to that complete harmony of manner and behaviour, which perfects the charm." Essay 15, in *Works,* 152.

> thin;—led by that restless charm, no matter if the chair be overturned, the gilded chariot broke, and the coachman's neck into the bargain, still they press on a mingled motley crowd. . . .[18]

The endless pursuit of novelties, the business of continually "forming new wishes" which Johnson saw as the highest pleasure, is here represented (as is gambling in so many essays of the period) as so absorbing a preoccupation that it erases the gendered and indeed moral or human nature of those engaged in it, who become "*things* . . . blown about by every wind" of fashionable desire.

The periodicals do, of course, acknowledge with some regularity that, in the words of the *World,* "novelty and fashion are the support and source of trade. . . . By increasing the wants, they increase the connections of mankind." This argument emphasizes that the vagaries of desire can "occasion many advantages to the public"—an emphasis that produces a kind of compromise between the ethics of commerce and a more severe civic ideal, but that compromise is achieved by displacing onto the workings of fashion the sense in which commerce is perceived to threaten the fantasy of masculinity central to the civic ideal of public virtue.[19] Fashionable objects of desire are repeatedly represented as both the symptom and the cause of an alarming degeneration of manliness, of a specifically British and heterosexual masculinity. The *Connoisseur,* for example, writes that

> it is too notorious, that our fine gentlemen, in several other instances besides the article of paint, affect the softness and delicacy of the fair sex. The male beauty has his washes, perfumes, and cosmetics. He has his dressing-room . . . a neat little chamber, hung round with Indian paper, and adorned with several little images of pagods and bramins, and vessels of Chelsea china, in which were set various-coloured sprigs of artificial flowers.[20]

The fine gentleman is surrounded by imported luxuries, which may mark his degeneracy,[21] but it is the size of his possessions, his "little chamber" and "little images," perhaps more than their un-Christian diversity, that signals their unmasculine character. In Hogarth's *Marriage à la Mode* (fig. 2) a similar collection of goods is "irrefutable evidence of crude lack of taste, coarse sensuality,

18. Elizabeth Haywood, *The Female Spectator,* book 12.

19. [?Marriott], *World,* no. 117, 27 March 1755. I have in mind the processes Stephen Copley describes as evolving a bourgeois civic humanism, in the Introduction to his anthology, *Literature and the Social Order in Eighteenth-Century England* (London: Croom Helm, 1984).

20. *Connoisseur,* no. 65, 24 April 1755.

21. Henry Home, Lord Kames, for example, writing in the early 1770s, still saw foreign imports as both cause and evidence of effeminizing luxury. See his *Sketches of the History of Man,* 2 vols. (Edinburgh: Creech, 1774), book 1, sketch 8.

Figure 2 S. F. Ravenet after William Hogarth, *Marriage A-la-Mode,* Pl. 4, *The Toilette Scene,* 1745, engraving, $17\frac{1}{2} \times 14$ in. BM 2731. © The British Museum.

and of thriftlessness in buying, for want of a better occupation"; they are a sign of the kind of abandon Henry Fielding implies in his account of the beau, "his body dressed in all the tinsel which serves to trick up a harlot."[22] Mr. Town perceives them primarily as signs of infantilism, but he nevertheless expresses his own homophobic passion in deducing from them that their owner is one of "these equivocal half-men, these neuter somethings between male and female."[23]

22. *Lichtenberg's Commentaries on Hogarth's Engravings,* trans. and introduced by Innes and Gustav Herdan (London: Cresset Press, 1966), 125. *Covent-Garden Journal,* no. 42, 26 May 1752.

23. *Connoisseur,* no. 65, 24 April 1755. For a fuller discussion of the implications of effeminacy, see Felicity Nussbaum, "Effeminacy and Femininity: Domestic Prose Satire and David Simple," *Eighteenth-Century Fiction* 11, no. 4 (July 1999): 421–44, esp. 432–33. See also David Kutcha, "The Making of the Self-Made Man: Class, Clothing, and English Masculinity, 1688–1832," in *The Sex of Things: Gender and Consumption in Historical Perspective,* ed. Victoria de Grazia and Ellen Furlough (Berkeley: University of California Press, 1996), 54–78; and Kristina Straub, *Sexual Suspects: Eighteenth-Century Players and Sexual Ideology* (Princeton, N.J.: Princeton University Press, 1992), chapter 1.

The progress of commerce and the notion of its general utility may be acknowledged in mid-century periodicals to offer a kind of justification of fashionable consumption, but if anything that perception increases the essayists' hostility to particular examples of fashionable taste. Fashionable manners prompt an antagonism that indicates the persistence of anxiety about inhabiting a culture dominated by commerce. In this culture, the periodicals suggest, notions of the public become peripheral, almost accidental to the private interests that are the motor of commercial progress, and within the apparently expanding sphere of the private that is governed by commerce, distinctions—between social stations, between national identities, or between vice and virtue—seem increasingly elusive, seem to melt into air. Gender difference, these papers imply, may provide the means, the basis on which all those other distinctions can be reinstated: if only men can be made less effeminate, and women less lewd or bold, then national degeneration may be checked, and what seems to be mercenary or luxurious, but inseparable from commercial prosperity, may be moralized and made compatible with civilized politeness, or the ideals of public and private virtue. Anxiety about gender difference is of course not exclusively the province of the periodicals. Even Richardson's Sir Charles Grandison, himself no nonpareil of British virility, questions whether "there be characters more odious than those of a masculine woman, and an effeminate man."[24] The relation between fashion and commerce that I have been trying to draw out, however, suggests that commercial culture may require tolerance alongside antagonism toward some forms of blurring of gender difference, that the erosion of gendered identity may crop up so frequently because that identity requires redefinition as well as confirmation.

I want now to focus my discussion on a small group of novels by women—Sarah Fielding's *The Adventures of David Simple* (published in two volumes in 1744, with the additional *Volume the Last* appearing in 1753), and Sarah Scott's *A Description of Millenium Hall* (1762) and *The History of Sir George Ellison* (1766). These novels offer, I think, intriguingly different accounts of gender roles, and of the problems raised by the instability of their definition, and while I do not want to suggest that they typify or represent the diversity of the mid-century, I do think the differences between them can help to indicate something of the cultural changes at issue in this period.

24. Samuel Richardson, *The History of Sir Charles Grandison,* 3 parts, ed. Jocelyn Harris (Oxford: Oxford University Press, 1986), 3.247. For a discussion which reflects thoughtfully on the character of Richardson's hero in terms that have clear implications for his gender, see John Sitter, *Literary Loneliness in Mid-Eighteenth-Century England* (Ithaca, N.Y.: Cornell University Press, 1982), 208–9.

II

Fielding's novel narrates the episodic adventures of its hero as he explores the contiguous worlds of fashion and trade in the microcosm of the "great Metropolis."[25] David Simple is determinedly idiosyncratic in his views, like so many of the narrator-editors of mid-century periodicals, and like them he is largely preoccupied with observing the manifestations of commercial culture in the manners and morals of the middle classes. The key note of this culture for him, as for the *Tatler* and *Spectator* earlier in the century, is struck by his observations on the Exchange, which he visits at the beginning of the book. For Simple, however, the visit to the Exchange does not provide matter for celebration; it is a "melancholy Prospect," a place "where Men of all Ages and all Nations were assembled, with no other View than to barter for Interest," and where the "Countenances of most of the People, showed they were filled with Anxiety" (22). Simple's father kept a "Mercer's Shop on Ludgate-hill" (7), and Simple accepts the primacy of commerce, the importance of visiting the Exchange before anywhere else as he sets out on his quest, but he is also hostile to this world of anxious competition, and excluded from it perhaps by his inherited wealth (though he loses that in *Volume the Last*). His leisure enables him to act as the exemplary embodiment of the private virtues of the Christian gentleman, but the narrator implies that he might be seen as the conscience of commerce, and as a paradigm of the sensibility it ideally produces. When Simple and his friends encounter a beggar, she remarks that their response is "as much actuated by Compassion as ever a Miser was by Avarice, or an ambitious Man by his Pursuit of Grandeur" (313), for their sentimental commerce is transacted in the parallel currency of feeling.

What is problematic about Simple's role in relation to the commercial strife that surrounds him is made most clearly apparent immediately after the woman he loves agrees to marry him, when the narrator's comments are I think so striking that it is worth quoting the passage at length:

> if you are inclined to have an adequate Idea of *David*'s Raptures on that Confession,—think what Pretty Miss feels when her Parents wisely prefer her in their Applause—to all her Brothers and Sisters;—Observe her yet a little older, when she is pinning on her first Manteau and Petticoat;—then follow her to the Ball, and view her Eyes sparkle, and the convulsive Tosses of her Person on the first

25. Sarah Fielding, *The Adventures of David Simple, and Volume the Last*, ed. Peter Sabor (Lexington: University of Kentucky Press, 1998), 21.

> Compliment she receives:—But don't lose sight of her, till you place her in a Room full of Company, where she hears her Rival condemned for *Indiscretion*,—and exults in her *Loss of Reputation*.—No matter whether she rivals her in my Lord—the Captain—or the 'Squire, *&c. &c.*—For as she is equally desirous of engrossing the Admiration of all,—her Enmity is equal towards the Woman who deprives her of *such great Blessings*—which-ever she robs her of.—Imagine—the Joys of an ambitious Man, who has just supplanted his Enemy,—and is got into his Place;—imagine,—what a young Lawyer feels the first Cause he has gained,—or a young Officer the first time he mounts Guard.—But imagine what you will, unless you have experienced what it is to be both a sincere and successful Lover, you have never imagined any thing equal to what *David* felt. (230)

Simple is compared to a spoiled child growing into the fashionable woman who cares only to be the center of admiration; he is like a ruthlessly competitive place-seeker; or a lawyer, that stock figure for greed and self-interest; or an officer, frequently the type of male vanity. Perhaps there is some ambiguity about whether those last two are satirical figures, but on the whole the string of analogies seems free from hesitation or qualification. It is as though the narrative attempts to set up its hero as the exemplar of sincere feeling, the main stockholder of that currency, and must therefore embark on analogies that—almost incidentally, but nevertheless profoundly—destabilize his gendered and moral identity.

I can perhaps best explain why these troubling analogies seem almost inevitable to the narrative by looking briefly at the representation of women elsewhere in the novel. For the moral characters of middle-class women are represented as peculiarly soft and amorphous, only formed into some definite moral shape by the Pygmalion-like desires and projections of men. And the novel suggests two rather different accounts of the significance or the usefulness of this plasticity—accounts which imply that the feminization of the hero might be understood in two contrasting ways. In the first place, the softness of women—or their lack of character, in Pope's famous terms—is important to the argument for the role of fashionable consumption in a providential distribution of wealth. Simple's friends discuss the specific and familiar example of the woman who buys fashionable fripperies, which she has been "brought to think she cannot do without, and is indulging her Vanity with the Thoughts of out-shining some other Lady." They comment that "the Tradesman who receives her Money in Exchange for those things which appear so trifling, to that Vanity perhaps owes his own and his Family's Support." The woman's purchases are not "necessary to preserve Life or Health," but despite appearing "most useless," they "contributed to the general Welfare" (148). Fashion has a positive role in this providential (or perhaps Mandevillian) scheme.[26] The woman's malleable desires are shaped by fashion and custom, which make her no more than a channel for the business of exchange and distribution. Her desires and her desirability—for she purchases in order to shine—make her the central and admired figure for the fantasies that structure commerce, and that produce its benefits to the common weal, for the anecdote on the woman of fashion illustrates the contention that "except all the World was so generous, as to be willing to part with what they think they have a right to, only for the pleasure of helping others; the way to obtain any thing from them is to apply to their Passions" (148).

The consumer's passion, her desire and vanity, are represented here as amoral, but nevertheless capable of supplying the place of philanthropy in the great providential scheme; and her desire is thus, in a sense, like the hero's. David Simple is a private man, and his philanthropy does not extend beyond the "little Society" (237) of his family and friends. His inheritance places him beyond the need to work, and thus in what was coming to seem by the mid-century a position of feminized indolence.[27] As a dispenser of bounty, an idle consumer and successful lover, he is central to those romantic exchanges of desire that structure the private worlds of commerce and fashion, and his position is very close to that of the fashionable woman. When he and his friends finally achieve domestic bliss, at the end of volume 2, the narrator draws this moral from their ideal community: "Let every Man, instead of bursting with Rage—and Envy—at the Advantages of Nature, or Station, another has over him, extend his Views far enough to consider, that if he acts his Part well, he deserves as much *Applause*—and is as useful a Member of Society—as any other Man whatever: for in every Machine, the smallest Parts conduce as much to the keeping it together, and to regulate its Motions, as the greatest" (237). The sentiment here is reminiscent of Lady Mary Wortley Montagu's reflections

26. For a fuller discussion of these terms, see John Barrell and Harriet Guest, "On the Use of Contradiction: Economics and Morality in the Eighteenth-Century Long Poem," in *The New Eighteenth Century: Theory, Politics, English Literature*, ed. Felicity Nussbaum and Laura Brown (London: Methuen, 1987), 121–43. See also Liz Bellamy's discussion of *David Simple* in her *Commerce, Morality and the Eighteenth-Century Novel* (Cambridge: Cambridge University Press, 1998), 131–38; and Linda Bree, *Sarah Fielding* (New York: Twayne Publishers, 1996), chapter 2. Nussbaum sees veiled "revolutionary implications" in the gender relations of the communities represented in Fielding's novel, in her "Effeminacy and Femininity," 436–44 (I quote from 443).

27. See, for example, *Connoisseur*, no. 131, 29 July 1756, which describes the gentleman who is "not obliged to rise to open his shop or work at his trade" as the most "useless idle animal," and compares him to a "celebrated beauty."

on greatness, in *The Nonsense of Common-Sense*, where she argued that "as much greatness of Mind may be shewn in submission as in command, and some Women have suffer'd a Life of Hardships with as much Philosophy as Cato travers'd the Desarts of Affrica, and without the support that the veiw of Glory afforded him. . . . A Lady who has perform'd her Duty as a Daughter, a Wife, and a Mother, appears to my Eyes with as much veneration as I should look on Socrates or Xenophon."[28] For Montagu, of course, the notion that "real Distinction" lies in moral integrity and "consciousness of Virtue" is explicitly offered as consolation to those oppressed by differences of class and gender. In order to appreciate the pleasures of their private station, they need not make the effort of extending their views to encompass an idea of society; they can simply resort to the alternative system of morality which allows them to compare their own integrity with that of the next person. Fielding's use of the familiar image of society as capitalist machine, however, in which individuals are unlikely to be able to extend their views beyond the horizons of their passions, works to obscure social differences as well as to ameliorate them. There is apparently no kingpin here, and no moral ascendancy either, for the image elides those moral differences that have been so important to the characterization of Simple as the hero, and implies a common condition of submission that blurs differences of gender. It is not surprising that after this Fielding turns to comparisons of society with the stage and the prospect view, where "every thing" is "kept in its proper Place," and which can more readily image the kinds of differences of class and of gender she sees as important to the social structure (237).[29] But in their roles as good cogs, Simple and the fashionable girl are equally useful and capable of that "equal and consistent" integrity of appearance or feeling that the *Connoisseur* saw as the mark of good taste and good morals.

I suggested, however, that feminine softness seemed to have two different sets of meanings in this novel, and two different sets of implications for the characterization of the hero. The second of these assumes particular importance in *Volume the Last*, published nearly a decade after the first two volumes of the novel. Montagu commented, rather acidly, that this volume was an improvement on the earlier two because it "conveys a useful moral (tho' she [Fielding] does not seem to have intended it)." She thought that it showed "the

28. Lady Mary Wortley Montagu, *The Nonsense of Common-Sense*, no. 6, 24 January 1738.

29. See John Barrell's discussion of an intriguingly similar passage in Smollett's *Ferdinand Count Fathom* (1753), in his *English Literature in History, 1730–80: An Equal, Wide Survey* (London: Hutchinson, 1983), 185–87.

ill Consequences of not providing against Casual losses, which happen to almost every body."[30] The Simples should have been better insured, but the moral of the tale depends on the fact that they were not. For this imprudence places the hero in a position which resembles what his wife had experienced before her marriage in the second volume of the novel. In a striking episode, Camilla attempts to support herself and her sick brother by begging, but the rich mistake her solicitings for those of prostitution, and when she resorts to the streets she is attacked by other beggars for "begging in their District" (131). She concludes that if impoverished gentlewomen "attempt getting our living by any Trade, People in that Station would think we were endeavouring to take their Bread out of their mouths, and combine together against us. . . . Persons who are so unfortunate as to be in this Situation, are in a World full of People, and yet are as solitary as if they were in the wildest Desart; no body will allow them to be of their Rank, nor admit them into their Community" (132–33). By some rather tenuous route she is, of course, allowed to retain her class status, her gentility, but the emphasis of the episode is on the extent to which she finds herself excluded from any rank or community as a result of her sudden poverty. Her inherited status turns out not to be inherent, but to depend on her lover's recognition of her value. Simple's desire is necessary to reinstate her as someone whose softness and goodness is like "a great Stock in Trade" (121).

In the last volume, Simple has left the metropolis, and become the victim of legal corruption: he has lost all his money, and his poverty is carefully defined to be of the kind where "you pay *Cent. Per Cent.* for every Necessary of Life, by being obliged to buy every thing by retail" (276). He is excluded from the economy of credit, because he has lost that defining attachment to rank or community which credit recognizes. His position now is like that of Camilla, forced upon the town. In this situation, it is difficult to distinguish between the domestic feminization of David and his wife, and what is valuable in them becomes only their capacity for feeling, their capacity to act as the medium of sympathetic exchange. The Simples are exposed to the rigors of adversity, and on the death of their children, Fielding writes of their feelings:

> The true Reason why I dwell not on that Concern, is, that Words cannot reach it—the sympathizing Heart must imagine it—and the Heart that has no Sympathy, is not capable of receiving it. *David* was, on every tender Occasion, motionless with Grief; and *Camilla*, although her Mind was too humble to distort her Countenance, yet did the Tears flow in Streams from her Eyes, and she was

30. *The Complete Letters of Lady Mary Wortley Montagu*, 3 vols., ed. Robert Halsband (Oxford: Clarendon Press, 1967), 3.67.

> at once a Picture of the highest Sorrow and the highest Resignation; for Clamour is rather a Proof of Affectation than of a Mind truly afflicted; and tender Sorrow neither seeks nor wants Language to express itself. (326)

The inexpressive responses of the Simples are contrasted with the behavior of the woman of the world who persecutes them. She displays equally noisy and impassioned grief for the anticipated death of her husband and for the loss of her lapdog, that quintessential fashion accessory, and her capacity for expression inhibits sympathy, inhibits those exchanges of ineffable feeling that structure domestic life in this novel.[31] In this last volume, Simple is much more markedly antagonistic to commercial culture, and more explicitly feminized; and the contrast with the woman of the world suggests that his feminization is no longer the sign of his proximity to fashionable consumers, whose amoral subjection to custom greases the wheels of commercial exchange, but the sign of his affinity with social outcasts who are moral in adversity. In the first two volumes Simple and the fashionable woman had seemed analogous cogs in the social machine, but he had been moralized by his attachment to notions of private community. In the last volume the lack of community, the death of most of his family and friends, makes him an exemplary martyr. His capacity for sentiment makes him central to the commercial culture the novel sets out to moralize, and, I think, to celebrate, but this capacity seems also to make it impossible for him to speak in the languages of that culture. The hero argues, in volume 2, that the anxious competition of the world would become morally acceptable if everyone would "fairly own when they were rowing against each other's Interest" (196), but the conclusion of the novel implies that this sincerity is the prerogative of those who are excluded from the competition, and made speechless and feminine.

III

David Simple represents a culture in which differences of gender are unstable and ambivalent because there seems to be no room, in the insistently private and commercial culture the narrative delimits, for the definition of unambiguously masculine character. This issue is, of course, central to the emergence in the mid-century of the sentimental hero, and its implications structure the narratives of Sarah Scott's two novels of the 1760s, *A Description of Millenium Hall* (cited hereafter as *MH*) and *The History of Sir George Ellison.*

31. See Linda Bree's thoughtful discussion of this passage, in her *Fielding,* 42–43. Janet Todd discusses this passage in comparable terms in *The Sign of Angellica: Women, Writing and Fiction, 1660–1800* (London: Virago, 1989), 168–70.

Scott's novels inhabit, I think, a discursive context rather different from that of *David Simple.* They are also concerned with private and commercial culture, but they indicate a much clearer awareness of the problematic relation between that culture and notions of public virtue and public life—notions that had seemed peripheral or even irrelevant to Fielding's novel. For that reason, perhaps, the instabilities of gender difference are more explicitly at issue in these later texts. In the second novel, Ellison and his companion, Lamont, reflect on their visit to the community of ladies at Millenium Hall, narrated in the earlier novel. Lamont observes that "such a kind of life as they had been witnesses to, was very respectable in women, and was arriving at the highest excellence their sex could reach; but such retirement would be very unfit for man, who, formed with more extensive capacity, deeper penetration, and more exalted courage, was designed to govern the world, to regulate the affairs of kingdoms, and penetrate into the most mysterious arts of human policy."[32] Lamont perceives the opposition between private retirement and public duty to be structured on gender difference. I want, in conclusion, to explore the significance of this structure in Scott's two novels, but first I want to look briefly at the treatment of the relation between gender difference and the public/private axis in a few other texts of the period, for this is, I think, a relation which takes on a particular and troubled importance in these decades.

Lamont's argument resembles one developed in the periodical *Common Sense,* which claimed in 1737 that "women are not form'd for great Cares themselves, but to soothe and soften ours; their Tenderness is the proper Reward for the Toils we under go for their Preservation; and the Ease and Chearfulness of their Conversation, our desirable Retreat from the Labours of Study and Business. They are confined within the narrow Limits of Domestick Offices, and when they stray beyond them, they move excentrically, and consequently without Grace." The periodical, though published nearly thirty years earlier, implies a similar sense that the proper retirement of women confirms their gendered identity; the essayist argues that women who "stray beyond" the "Bounds allotted to their Sex" should "declare themselves in form Hermaphrodites, and be register'd as such in their several Parishes."[33] The paper also

32. [Sarah Scott], *The History of Sir George Ellison,* 2 vols. (London: A. Millar, 1766), 1.108 [40–41]. Page references in the text are to this first edition, but for convenience I have added in square brackets page references to Sarah Scott, *The History of Sir George Ellison,* ed. Betty Rizzo (Lexington: University of Kentucky Press, 1996). For fuller discussion of the representation of slavery in the novel, see Markman Ellis, *The Politics of Sensibility: Race, Gender and Commerce in the Sentimental Novel* (Cambridge: Cambridge University Press), chapter 3; and Moira Ferguson, *Subject to Others: British Women Writers and Colonial Slavery, 1670–1834* (London: Routledge, 1992), chapter 5, esp. 100–111.

33. *Common Sense,* 10 September 1737.

suggests that the confinement of women within "narrow Limits" confirms, and perhaps even produces, a properly protective and masculine identity in those engaged in the "Labours of Study or Business"—labors which might otherwise be seen as potentially feminizing. John Brown's sermon *On the Female Character and Education*, of 1765, echoes the sense that the subordination and domestication of women is necessary to masculine virtue. From his "View of the Female Character," he remarks, with an adroit use of the lexicon of cultivation, that he has "deduced those domestic and Christian Virtues which are naturally ingrafted on it by a Proper Education." But Brown characteristically takes a more apocalyptic line on the dangers of vagrant femininity. He claims that where woman assume "masculine *Boldness* and indelicate *Effrontery*," and "affect a self-sufficiency and haughty Independency; assert an unbounded Freedom of Thought and Action; and even pretend to guide the Principles of Taste, and the Reins of Empire," it is inevitably the consequence that "the Reality of national Virtue vanisheth, and its Shadows occupy its Place; Sincerity is no more."[34]

These arguments depend on a conflation of the differences between what is private, domestic, apolitical, extracommercial, and feminine. That conflation makes it possible to describe the proper activities of men, which range from government to commerce, from military defense to scholarship and guiding the principles of taste, as though they were all forms of masculine public virtue. In an essay from *Sir Charles Grandison* (1753–54) that has been attributed to Elizabeth Carter, she, in the character of Mrs. Shirley, reflects on the strategy of arguing as though masculine "superiority were entirely founded on a natural difference of capacity," which leads men to "Despise us as women, and value themselves merely as men." She points out that

> women have not opportunities of sounding the depths of science, or of acquainting themselves perfectly with polite literature: But this want of opportunity is not entirely confined to them. There are professions among the men no more favourable to these studies, than the common avocations of women. For example; merchants, whose attention is (and perhaps more usefully, as to public utility) chained down to their accounts. Officers, both of land and sea, are seldom much better instructed, tho' they may, perhaps, pass through a few more forms: And as for knowledge of the world, women of a certain rank have an equal title to it with some of them.[35]

34. John Brown, *On the Female Character and Education: A Sermon, preached on Thursday the 16th of May, 1765, at the Anniversary Meeting of the Guardians of the Asylum for Deserted Female Orphans* (London: L. Davis and C. Reymers, 1765), 15, 17, 18.

35. Richardson, *Grandison*, 3.243–44. On the attribution to Carter, see note at 3.508.

The point of Carter's argument is to rehearse the familiar mid-century theme of the need to educate women to be "fit companions for men of sense. A character in which they will always be found more useful than that of a plaything, the amusement of an idle hour."[36] Her way of making the case is more intriguing. For her claim that the education of women is no more limited than that of certain men picks up on the feminization of merchants and the officers of a standing army in the discourse of civic humanism.[37] The final comparison, in Carter's argument, between the "knowledge of the world" acquired by officers and "women of a certain rank," is echoed by Wollstonecraft in her second *Vindication* of 1792, and leads her to ask, "Where is then the sexual difference, when the education has been the same?"[38] Carter's language indicates that what she describes is not, as it were, a space that is neutral in gender, but a set of occupations that are not fully masculine because they imply confined views and superficial knowledge.

Carter's argument suggests the precariousness of the identification of the masculine with the public and the feminine with the private. And the letter also hints at more radical possibilities, for Mrs. Shirley is responding here to an apparently flippant discussion of a topic referred to briefly as "Man's usurpation, and woman's natural independency."[39] The reference is an intriguing indication of the contemporary currency of arguments for women's rights, such as those articulated in the Sophia papers and other mid-century texts more or less directly indebted to Poullain de la Barre's *The Woman as Good as the Man; or, The Equality of Both Sexes* (first published in French in 1673).[40] These texts play on the notion that, on one hand, the gendering of the public/private

36. Ibid., 3.243.

37. See J. G. A. Pocock, *Virtue, Commerce and History: Essays on Political Thought and History, Chiefly in the Eighteenth Century* (Cambridge: Cambridge University Press, 1985), 114.

38. Mary Wollstonecraft, *A Vindication of the Rights of Woman*, ed. Carol H. Poston (New York: Norton, 1975), 23.

39. Richardson, *Grandison*, 3.242.

40. See François Poullain de La Barre, *The Woman as Good as the Man; or, The Equality of Both Sexes*, trans. A. L., ed. Gerald MacLean (Detroit, Mich.: Wayne State University Press, 1988), 26 ff. Other texts in this tradition which are more or less directly indebted to *The Woman as Good as the Man* include: *Woman Triumphant; or, The Excellency of the Female Sex; asserted in Opposition to the Male. By a Lady of Quality* (1721); *Woman not Inferior to Man: or, a short and modest Vindication of the natural right of the Fair-Sex to perfect Equality of Power, Dignity, and Esteem, with the Men. By Sophia, a Person of Quality* (1739); *Beauty's Triumph: or, The Superiority of the Fair Sex invincibly proved* (1751) (*Woman not Inferior* appears as part 1 of this text); *Female Rights Vindicated: or the Equality of the Sexes Morally and Physically proved. By A Lady* (1758); and *Female Restoration, by a moral and physical vindication of female talents; in opposition to all dogmatical assertions relative to the disparity in the sexes. By a Lady* (1780). For an example of the reception of these texts see the review of *Female Restoration* which appeared in *The Monthly Review; or, Literary Journal* for January 1781; and see chapter 5, n. 1, below.

divide removes any justification for excluding women from those employments characterized as private, such as learning, medicine, law and commerce, and that, on the other, in a modern civilization where physical strength is less important, or where the possession of landed estate and the right to bear arms are no longer central to the definition of public and masculine character, there is no longer any reason to exclude women from the more definitively masculine fields of politics, government, and war. In other words, they exploit the unstable definition of public and private spheres in relation to gender difference, to indicate, broadly speaking, that if most powerful or gainful activities and positions can now be thought of as private rather than public, then they can also be thought of as feminizing or feminine, and identified as appropriate to women.

The periodicals of the mid-century can also be understood to articulate and address the cultural nexus of instability formed by the complex of relations between the distinctions of public and private and of gender. It is not something they respond to only with hostility and alarm. So, for example, in a spirit of misogynistic banter, the author of *Common Sense* for February 26, 1737, prescribed that "Ugly Women, who may more properly be called a Third Sex, than a part of the Fair one, should publickly renounce all Thoughts of their Persons, and turn their Minds another Way; they should endeavour to be honest good-humour'd Gentlemen, they may amuse themselves with Field Sports, and a chearful Glass; and if they could get into Parliament, I should, for my own Part, have no Objection to it." Despite the explicit targeting of women here, there is clearly also a dig at the indolence and lack of masculine dignity shown by country gentlemen and parliamentarians—a suggestion, more fully explored in James Thomson's *Liberty*, that corruption has privatized their roles, and made them potentially feminine.

In the *World* for July 3, 1755, the essayist[41] described a dream in which Jupiter allocated people to the "proper calling" suited to their inclinations and abilities. Among the transpositions this involves, he sees scarlet robes, which are probably those of the lords spiritual, "put on by private gentlemen, who, lost in retirement and reserve, were little imagined to be qualified for such important posts"; he sees "princes and potentates" entering "with a good grace into private stations"; and "in a public assembly a junto of patriots, who while they were haranguing on the corruption and iniquity of the times, broke off in the middle, and turned stock-jobbers and pawn-brokers," while "many a man

41. [Mulso], *World*, no. 131.

stept with a genteel air, from behind a counter, into a great estate, or a post of honour." Finally, he turns his gaze to women, and, he writes, "it was with a secret pride that I observed a few of my dear country-women quit their dressing-rooms and card-assemblies, and venture into the public, as candidates for fame and honours." It is important to the nature of this essay that these women do not secure the public roles he imagines for them. He sees a woman who clearly resembles the character usually attributed to Elizabeth Carter about to take office as the warden of an Oxbridge college, "but observing some young students at the gate, who began to titter as she approached, she blushed, turned from them with an air of pity unmixed with contempt, and retiring to her beloved retreat, contented herself with doing all the good that was possible in a private station." In this rather Woolf-like vision, the permeability and progressive erosion of the division between public and private is confirmed, as the dreamer recognizes in private men and women the virtues necessary to public office. The moral sphere of the private has expanded to absorb the public virtues, and the notion of the public has become uncertain, for it is not clear here whether the "public assembly of patriots" refers to a corrupt legislative assembly, which is nevertheless an exclusive public and political gathering, or to a party of coffeehouse politicians, which is public only in the sense of its accessibility. But the paper reinstates the division between public and private even as it marks its blurring. It is here still the most important boundary, the axis in relation to which the virtues of the landed gentry and middle classes are plotted and measured, and in a sense this remains an essentially conservative vision which attempts to reappropriate virtue to public identity, and to indicate that the public sphere is its natural and appropriate habitat. For that to be accomplished, women must remain private and retired, even though their ability to evince what are identified as public virtues is recognized.

IV

These instabilities and uncertainties in the relation between notions of public or private and gender difference are woven into the discursive tissue of Scott's novels of the 1760s. In response to Lamont's comments on the ways of life appropriate to men and women, George Ellison offers a long speech which could be read as an elaboration of Carter's comments in *Grandison.* He points out that Lamont's notions of gender difference might have been appropriate to the "state of equality" that existed before "nature's Agrarian law" had "been abolished by political institutions," but that now "a great estate, or high birth" are necessary to his ideal of masculinity, though they "frequently exalt those who are . . . unfit" (1.110 [41]). He concludes:

> virtue creates the best superiority; therefore I shall not be ashamed of endeavouring to imitate the ladies [of Millenium Hall] . . . and do not fear, lest by so doing, I shall degrade my sex, though I confess to fall short of them may disgrace it; and yet I am very apprehensive that will be the case; for, the truth is, benevolence appears with peculiar lustre in a female form, the domestic cares to which the well educated have been trained, qualifies them better for discerning and executing the offices of humanity. . . . Our sex has long aped the most trifling part of the other in its follies; we are grown dissipated, puerile, vain, and effeminate; a sad abuse of talents, which I readily grant were given us for better purposes; so far I agree with you as to the dignity of man; but . . . the virtues are of no sex; and shall we less esteem any of them, because they are practised by women, when we are not ashamed . . . to adopt their follies! (1.111–12 [42])

I have quoted this passage at some length because I am interested in its shifts, uncertainties, and hesitations; the way Ellison veers between the sense that for men not to outdo feminine virtue is a disgrace to their masculinity, and the sense that virtue may be peculiarly feminine. Throughout the novel Ellison is represented as a resolutely private man, though one who is, of course, more fit for public office than most public men. More firmly than Grandison[42]—and this is clearly a novel which needs to be seen in the context of Richardson's work—he rejects public office because modesty is one of his virtues, and because he perceives it to be inevitably corrupt and corrupting. Most men, he argues, can do more to serve their country in "a private station" (2.28 [132]). It is later confirmed that "the good of the public had no small share even in those actions of Sir George's which are generally looked upon as merely of a private nature" (2.210 [194]). The virtues of a private man, his response to Lamont suggests, are those in which women excel, and which I think John Brown is typical of the period in perceiving as having been "naturally ingrafted . . . by a proper education" on the female character. Ellison puts himself on the spot here, and his hesitations and qualifications indicate his attempts to suggest on the one hand that these are distinctively feminine virtues, and on the other that they transcend gender, and do not make private men effeminate. But the follies or vices that have corrupted masculinity and reduced it to effeminacy are unambiguously those of women. Men can only ape them, and be perversely feminized by them, for they are not natural to them, as they are, he clearly implies, to the "trifling part" of the other sex.

42. See Richardson, *Grandison,* 3.439.

What I think is so interesting about poor Ellison's difficulties is that they indicate the extent to which the cultural hegemony of commercial capitalism produces a context in which virtuous masculinity seems an impossible ideal men can only approximate by emulating feminine virtue. The ladies of Millenium Hall, in the first novel, occupy a position analogous to that of the landed gentleman earlier in the century. Accounts of their interventionist brand of paternalism allude directly to the example of the heroes of Pope's third and fourth Moral Essays, and the account of their role in restoring an old mansion house for the use of "indigent gentlewomen," for example, is an elaborate paraphrase of the passage on Old Cotta and his son in the "Epistle to Bathurst."[43] The description of their estate management is strongly reminiscent of the representations of virtuous public men in retirement in Thomson's *Seasons*. Observing the way they run their estate, Ellison remarks:

> I could not help exclaiming, "In what a heaven do you live, thus surrounded by people who owe all their happiness to your goodness! This is, indeed, imitating our Creator, and in such proportion as your faculties will admit, partaking of his felicity, since you can no where cast your eyes, without beholding numbers who derive every earthly good from your bounty, and are indebted to your care and example for a reasonable hope of eternal happiness. (120)

Like Lyttelton in Thomson's "Spring," the ladies "taste / The Joy of GOD to see a happy World!"[44] The novel suggests, however, that this pseudopublic role is available to the women, and has become problematic for men, because the culture which makes this kind of benevolence possible has changed, as has the idea of the social structure that is implied by the exercise of virtue. This is not Fielding's machine, but it is in terms closer to that than to Thomson's virtuous polity that the women explain their understanding of society as "a state of mutual confidence, reciprocal services, and correspondent affections" (111); they celebrate a more private and commercial view of society as bound together by

43. Sarah Scott, *A Description of Millenium Hall*, ed. Gary Kelly (Peterborough, Ontario: Broadview Press, 1995), 219, and see 219–22. All further references in the text are to this edition.

44. On the significance of the retirement of Thomson's patriots, see Barrell, *Equal, Wide Survey*, 56–78. James Thomson, *The Seasons*, ed. James Sambrook (Oxford: Oxford University Press, 1981), "Spring," ll. 902–3. Susan Lanser argues that the community Scott describes is potentially conservative because it participates in "the work of reproducing patriarchy"; but I suggest that this work involves a feminizing appropriation of patriarchal structures. See her "Singular Politics: The British Nation and the Old Maid," in Judith M. Bennett and Amy M. Froide, *Singlewomen in the European Past, 1250–1800* (Philadelphia: University of Pennsylvania Press, 1999), 303. For an important account of the novel, to which my own discussion is indebted, see Felicity A. Nussbaum, *Torrid Zones: Maternity, Sexuality, and Empire in Eighteenth-Century English Narratives* (Baltimore: Johns Hopkins University Press, 1995), chapter 6, and esp. 149–62.

exchanges of philanthropy and gratitude. Lamont is set up in this novel as a counterpart to the ladies' strange blend of gentlemanly, paternalist virtue and feminine moral strength; he is a feminized "coxcomb" for whom "Fashion . . . has been the guide" (55), but he is also here, as in the second novel, occasionally the mouthpiece of a kind of classical republicanism, and this leads him to comment, when the ladies explain their view of society as a network of mutual dependence, that "You seem . . . to choose to make us all slaves to each other" (113). In their retirement, the ladies combine financial independence with a kind of mutual slavery; they combine what is perceived as Godlike with what is perceived as most abject, and it is in these terms that they effect a kind of feminized moralization of commercial culture.

We could understand the role of the ladies of Millenium Hall in terms of the pre-Smithian formulation that "what oeconomy is in a family, political oeconomy is in a state."[45] In this novel and in *George Ellison* the notion of family extends to embrace almost everyone with whom the protagonists have any contact,[46] so that the family becomes a sort of alternative society of mutual interdependence, and a prototype for the moralization of the expanding private sphere. The "families" in both of these novels interact through what is quite explicitly an affective commerce or economy in which benevolence is exchanged for gratitude, and a part of what is so powerful (as well as perhaps utopian) about this economy is its ability to accord value to unwaged as well as waged labor. The novels seem to endorse a kind of nostalgic feudalism, a society structured on affective ties of obligation and deference, but this is represented as an exchange of sentimental gratifications which is firmly identified as the pleasure of the retirement that industry and self-improvement affords. It is important to the virtue of the familial economies the two novels represent that they should be kept separate from the vices or the amoralism of worldly commerce, and should be purely benevolent paternalist systems. Ellison comments that "as these ladies have no taste but what is directed by good sense, nothing found a place here from being only uncommon, for they think few things are

45. James Steuart, *Inquiry into the Principles of Political Oeconomy* (1767), quoted in Kathryn Sutherland's illuminating essay, "Adam Smith's Master Narrative: Women and the *Wealth of Nations*," in *Adam Smith's Wealth of Nations: New Interdisciplinary Essays*, ed. Stephen Copley and Kathryn Sutherland (Manchester: Manchester University Press, 1995), 107.

46. For his comments on the "endless process of 'familialization'" in *Sir Charles Grandison*, see Tony Tanner's *Adultery in the Novel: Contract and Transgression* (Baltimore: Johns Hopkins University Press, 1979), 178 n. On the importance of "removing the taint of exchange from the domestic sphere," see James Thompson, *Models of Value: Eighteenth-Century Political Economy and the Novel* (Durham, N.C.: Duke University Press, 1996), chapter 5, esp. 180 (from which I quote).

very rare but because they are little desirable; and indeed it is plain they are free from that littleness of mind, which makes people value a thing more for its being possessed by no one but themselves" (*MH,* 64). The ladies distance themselves from the world, which they perceive as resembling a Hobbesian state of nature, where "the same vanities, the same passions, the same ambition, reign in almost every breast; a constant desire to supplant, and a continual fear of being supplanted, keep the minds of those who have any views at all in a state of unremitted tumult and envy. . . . The love, as well as the pleasures of society, is founded in reason, and cannot exist in those minds which are filled with irrational pursuits" (111). The world they reject is that which, in *David Simple,* was represented or embodied in the figure of the fashionable woman: a world of passionate, amoral desires, justified by commerce and sanctified by adversity. The difficulty for the ladies of rejecting this world, of course, is that their own society of reciprocal obligation or mutual slavery exists precisely to help those who are in some way anomalous. They offer asylum for people who, "from some natural deficiency or redundancy" (72), some difference of physical appearance, have been exhibited for profit as an "extraordinary spectacle" (74), and for indigent gentlewomen who, like Camilla in *David Simple,* are excluded from the structures of rank or community; and the narratives of the past histories of the ladies themselves make it clear that they too are unusual, most obviously in their rejection of marriage. People, if not things, repeatedly seem to find "a place here from being . . . uncommon" (64), or as a result of their inability, whether willing or not, to participate in the "same vanities, the same passions, the same ambition" (111) as everyone else. The narrative positions the women as desirable objects of emulation by emphasizing that they are uncommon, the rare manifestation of the ideal retreat from commerce, the ideal leisure and capacity for feeling that commercial culture affords.

The point is perhaps most succinctly expressed in one of the opening chapters of *George Ellison,* where the hero is in Jamaica, industriously occupied in making the fortune on which he will retire. Scott writes that

> business is a shield through which Love's arrows cannot easily penetrate. Amidst all the airs that coquetry could play off upon him, he was frequently computing the profits of his last embarked cargo of sugars and spices; and was in little danger of being captivated by the fairest form, except Commerce, as sometimes personified by the poets, had made her appearance before him; the gums of Arabia, the gems of India, and in short the various riches of different climes, with which they deck her, would have greatly heightened her charms in his eyes; while the egrets, pompons, and bracelets of fashionable nymphs, appeared to him oftener burdensome than ornamental. (1.13 [8–9])

The image of commerce here is most obviously reminiscent of Addison's reflections in *The Spectator* on visiting the Exchange. He writes:

> Nature seems to have taken a particular Care to disseminate her Blessings among the different Regions of the World, with an Eye to this mutual Intercourse and Traffick among Mankind, that the Nations of the several Parts of the Globe might have a kind of Dependance upon one another, and be united together by their common Interest. . . . The single Dress of a Woman of Quality is often the Product of an hundred Climates. The Muff and the Fan come together from the different Ends of the Earth. The Scarf is sent from the Torrid Zone, and the Tippet from beneath the Pole. The Brocade Petticoat rises out of the Mines of Peru, and the Diamond Necklace out of the Bowels of Indostan.[47]

In Addison's famous celebration of trade, of course, the fashionable woman is the emblematic figure of commerce, and there is no possibility of a choice between the two. But Ellison is represented as though he makes the choice of Hercules. His choice is not between pleasure and virtue, though the narrative does seem to strain after that possibility in passing, but between the pleasure of sociability and the pleasure of profit—and even that is hardly a choice. Addison's image of the "Woman of Quality" decked out in the fruits of commerce emphasized the extent to which commercial gain was regarded as a libidinized pursuit,[48] and, when Ellison does choose to marry, only a couple of pages after this choice of the seductions of commerce, the narrator comments that in his eyes "the lady was agreeable, her fortune desirable" (1.16 [9]); the lady unites the barely distinguishable qualities of pecuniary profit and fashionable femininity.

Once Ellison has retired to spend his fortune, he distances himself from the commercial activity that had enabled him to acquire it. He tells his cousin, a landed gentleman who is the less perfect foil for his virtues, that his riches cannot be the source of dignity because "the steps towards riches are seldom virtuous." With a kind of aristocratic disdain, he explains that wealth is "a thing industrious dulness may acquire, or dishonest arts" (1.219 [80]). His herculean choice is now perceived to be between what are represented as the thoroughly eroticized pleasures of philanthropy, and marriage, which he believes "would have degraded me into a mere infatuated husband; and have substituted the ensnaring and intoxicating indulgences of passion, to the calm and solid joys of conscious virtue" (1.172 [63]). His private retirement makes his position

47. *The Spectator*, no. 69, 19 May 1711.

48. For discussion of this issue see Laura Brown, *Ends of Empire: Women and Ideology in Early Eighteenth-Century English Literature* (Ithaca, N.Y.: Cornell University Press, 1993), chapter 4.

much closer to that of Thomson's patriots, or their feminized counterparts at Millenium Hall. But the novel continues to imply that the virtues which make him an exemplary and "useful member of society" (1.172 [63]) are best produced by involvement in commerce, however ambivalently that must be represented, rather than by the inheritance of landed estate. And one of the ambivalent implications of that commercial past is that it both produces the capacity to admire the virtues of women, and feminizes the hero. His cousin, aware that his own indifference toward the good of society, and his embittered disrespect for women, set off the virtues of Ellison, comments that "you are like a statuary who should think the beauties of a Venus would not be sufficiently distinguished, if he did not put a Sybil or a Tesiphone by her side" (1.174 [63]), implying that the hero displays his own beautiful virtues as a figure for desire not so far removed from the figures of commerce or the woman of fashion.

This group of novels, then, indicates that the particular set of virtues associated with commercial culture are peculiarly appropriate to women; they are feminine, and they feminize. That sense combines two different aspects of the discursive terms in which the notion of commerce is most usually represented. On the one hand, commerce is feminizing because it demands or produces confined views and the endless pursuit of self-interested desires—qualities which characterize both Johnson's happy man and the woman of fashion. On the other, women can represent as it were the moralized face of commerce because they are perceived to be excluded from it, and, if they are affluent, confined to the leisure it affords. Financially independent women can be represented as enjoying something like the retirement that could be perceived to be the condition of the disinterested virtue of Thomson's public heroes. The capacity of women, or of notions of femininity, to be represented as at once central and peripheral to the workings of commerce gives them a kind of moral ascendancy. What makes it possible, if problematic, to represent feminine virtues as available to the sentimental hero, in the context I have sketched, may be precisely those anxieties about the erosion of gender difference that appear to make trangression of gendered roles more difficult. Alarm at masculine women and effeminate men is clearly about the desire to return to an imagined golden age of stable differences, but it is also, and perhaps increasingly, a matter of such caricatural representations, such homophobic panic, that it may enlarge the imaginary space in which gender difference is subject to renegotiation, or in which shifts in the definition of gender roles are perceived as tolerable, acceptable, or even neutral. The imaginary space in which instability can be tolerated is most obviously defined by its location at what was beginning to seem the permeable periphery between public and private life, where philanthropy, benevolence, and sympathy seem to link domestic affections with concern for the general good of society. In that space it can seem permissible, or even desirable, for men and women of feeling to be barely distinguishable, united in their ambivalent relation to the commercial culture that produced them.

2

The Female Worthies: Memorializing Learned Women

I

In chapter 1 I discussed some of the implications of commercial culture for the representation of gender difference in the mid-century. In her important article on "Effeminacy and Femininity: Domestic Prose Satire and *David Simple,*" Felicity Nussbaum claims that representations of relations between the sexes in mid-century novels, and in *David Simple* in particular, could "endanger a national identity that depends on strict boundaries between the sexes for its security."[1] Certainly the avid reception of John Brown's jeremiad on the times, for example, suggests that gender difference provided an opportunity or focus for the expression of anxieties about social change. In this chapter I will explore the ways in which representations of learned women in particular are important to the sense of national identity that took shape in the mid-century. I will examine what sorts of qualifications were necessary for entry into the biographical catalogues and lists of eminent women that began to appear in the 1750s, and what those qualities implied about the roles of women and of biography in relation to the emerging definition of the nation.

George Ballard published his handsome volume of *Memoirs of Several Ladies*

1. Felicity Nussbaum, "Effeminacy and Femininity: Domestic Prose Satire and *David Simple,*" *Eighteenth-Century Fiction* 11, no. 4 (July 1999): 443. She refers here to the arguments of John Brown's *Estimate.*

of Great Britain, who have been celebrated for their writing or skill in the learned languages arts and sciences in 1752. It is the earliest of those publications celebrating the achievements of British women as a group distinguished by their gender and nationality which were to become a distinctive feature of the mid to late century. Its successors included John Duncombe's *The Feminiad. A Poem* (1754), Thomas Amory's *Memoirs of Several Ladies of Great Britain* (1755), Mary Montague's *An Original Essay on Woman* (1771), Mary Scott's *The Female Advocate* (1774), and the anonymous *Dialogues Concerning the Ladies* (1785). In broad terms, Ballard's publication might be taken to mark a moment of transition between the more generalized celebrations of the "BRITISH FAIR" of the first half of the century, in for example Thomson's *The Seasons,* and the emergence of a national canon of celebrated women. More specifically, the terms in which the *Memoirs* were conceived provide a way into thinking about the increasing importance of learned women in mid-eighteenth-century Britain as the trophies or emblems of an idea of the nation—an idea fraught with complications both for the way women could understand their relation to it and for the cultural self-conceptions it characterized. My discussion in this chapter will focus on some of the implications of the kind of memorial or biography seen as appropriate to learned women, and will begin to explore the significance of these women to national identity.

Ballard was assisted in the research for his *Memoirs* by the Anglo-Saxon scholar Elizabeth Elstob, who had begun to compile a notebook on this subject before she met him in 1735. Her interest in Ballard's work points to some of its distinguishing characteristics—its antiquarianism, its investment in northern and national historical culture, and its support for the education and scholarship of women. But her comments on its publication also indicate some of the reasons for its initial lack of commercial success. She wrote to Ballard in the mid-1740s:

> I am sorry to have to tell you the choice you have made for the Honour of the Females was the wrongest subject you could pitch upon. For you can come into no company of Ladies and Gentlemen, where you shall not hear an open and vehement exclamation against Learned Women, and by those women who read much themselves, to what purposes they know best. . . . The prospect I have of the next age is a melancholy one to me, who wish Learning might flourish to the end of the World, both in Men and Women, but I shall not live to see it.[2]

2. Ballard MSS. XLIII, 89, quoted in Ada Wallas, *Before the Bluestockings* (London: Allen and Unwin, 1929), "Elizabeth Elstob," 184. My discussion of Elstob and Ballard is indebted to this illuminating essay.

Women who read, the women of whose cause Ballard imagined himself to be the champion, are also those who, in mixed company at least, engage in "open and vehement exclamation against Learned Women." In Elstob's eyes they seem to deny the purpose of their reading, though they might also be understood to be modestly declining the character a reputation for reading might lend them. Ballard's *Memoirs* were reprinted in a new edition in 1775, and their text forms the basis for many of the catalogues of lives that appeared in subsequent decades, but on their first publication they were met largely by silence, disavowed by those whose example had encouraged them.

Ballard explained in his Preface that the "present age" was distinguished for having "produced a greater number of excellent biographers than any preceding times," but that the "ingenious women of this nation" have unaccountably been passed over by these energetic memorialists. He states: "When it is considered how much has been done on this subject by several learned foreigners, we may justly be surprized at this neglect among the writers of this nation; more especially, as it is pretty certain, that England hath produced more women famous for literary accomplishments, than any other nation in Europe."[3] He represents it as natural or inevitable that he should repair this "general neglect,"[4] despite his modest talents. But his brief account of the history of biography implies some hesitation, some qualification of the smoothness of this process. Since the "revival of letters," he believes, memorialists have attempted to set the "great excellencies and attainments" of "illustrious persons" in their "true and proper light." Biographers have been attracted in particular to writers, men who have "distinguished themselves in the republick of letters," whose achievements, he suggests, their own mimic; indeed, Ballard implies that the cultural glory of the present age depends as much (if not more) on the work of biographers and critics as on that of contemporary writers. Those who are distinguished in this republic are usually male, or at least masculinized by the implications of citizenship, and the work of their memorialists focuses on what they have achieved, on what is exemplary in their lives and entertaining about their "peculiarities."[5] In this notion of biography, in contrast to that which he goes on to suggest is appropriate to women, the emphasis is on the history of the individual. The memorable nature of the lives of women is much more directly concerned with the notion that their existence is a matter of

3. George Ballard, *Memoirs of Several Ladies of Great Britain, who have been celebrated for their writings or skill in the learned languages arts and sciences* (Oxford: Jackson, 1752), vi.

4. Ibid., vi.

5. Ibid., v.

national pride, which will be gratified by the number, the quantity of women worth writing about, rather than by their particular achievements.

The difference in the method of memorializing that Ballard's preface points to is most obviously the result of the sense in which biography is perceived, for much of the eighteenth century, as a gendered genre. The emphasis on the individual and his peculiarities, which Ballard notes as a characteristic of masculine biography, could detract from the uniform and ideal masculinity of the public man, and represent him in private and implicitly feminized terms. The problem is clear in, for example, the relation between Pope's first two Moral Essays, "Of the Knowledge and Characters of Men" (1734) and "Of the Characters of Women" (1735). The second essay, according to its rubric, considers women "only as contradistinguished from the other Sex,"[6] whereas the first considers a more generalized notion of mankind, which includes both men and women. The first develops the argument that observation of the ruling passion, the secret spring of behavior, is the most valuable and valid or truthful form of knowledge. Once the peculiar quirks of any individual have been understood, or formulated into a coherent explanatory narrative, their socially perceived or public character will disintegrate, and their private, appetitive personality will be understood as all that is consistent or uniform:

> Search then the Ruling Passion: There alone,
> The Wild are constant, and the Cunning known;
> The Fool consistent, and the False sincere;
> Priests, Princes, Women, no dissemblers here.

Pope argues that private personality, rich in the peculiarities which are the substance of biography, must be understood never to be unambiguously virtuous, selfless, or disinterested, and must take precedence in expository and narrative power, in truthfulness, over public character, so that finally no appearance of public virtue can displace the truth of private appetite. Even Cobham, to whom the epistle is addressed, is subject to his ruling passion when he might appear least passionate, and most disinterested:

> And you! Brave COBHAM, to the latest breath
> Shall feel your ruling passion strong in death:
> Such in those moments as in all the past,
> "Oh, save my Country, Heav'n!" shall be your last.[7]

6. John Butt, ed., *The Poems of Alexander Pope: A One-Volume Edition of the Twickenham Text with Selected Annotations* (London: Routledge, 1968), "Epistle II. To a Lady: Of the Characters of Women," "Argument," 559. See Felicity Nussbaum's illuminating comments in *The Autobiographical Subject: Gender and Ideology in Eighteenth-Century England* (Baltimore: Johns Hopkins University Press, 1989), 149–50.

7. "Epistle I. To Richard Temple, Viscount Cobham," ll. 174–77, 262–65.

In Cobham's case public character and private personality coincide, but it is still the private passion that is the source of truth, and that inevitably deconstructs any notion of disinterested public personality.

The energy of Pope's unpleasant essay on women works perversely to shore up the ideal of masculine character "as contradistinguished from the other Sex" which the first essay had so thoroughly destroyed, for the first essay confirms that to the gaze of the biographer, intent on the peculiarities of personality, neither men nor women have any claim to character, or to any consistent trait that might transcend the vagaries of the ruling passion. It is matter for contempt when the poet remarks, in the second essay, that "A Woman's seen in Private life alone." His assertion that women's "Virtues open fairest in the shade,"[8] where they are hidden, implies that dissimulation and inconsistency are feminine characteristics, and that masculinity is contradistinguished from this. Men display their "bolder Talents in full light," and in contrast to women they again seem capable of supporting public character. In the second epistle, the privacy of their lives, and the primacy of passion in dictating their behavior, are what set women apart, and distinguish their gender; in this context men can again be masculine and constant characters.

The argument of Pope's two moral essays is caught up in a curious double bind: on the one hand, only attention to what is private, contingent, and personal can produce a coherent narrative capable of explaining the individual's role in historical events; on the other, it seems possible to view that private narrative only through a lens which regards the public as the exclusive site of what history can recognize as virtue, as absolute and not adventitious. In this focus, privacy identifies what is feminine and less than virtuous, and masculinity is only able to escape this contaminating embrace when it is juxtaposed with what is unambiguously female. Later in the century, however, personal biography has become not only more plausible than the grand historical narrative of public and heroic action, but more amenable to the description of what can be recognized as virtue. Elizabeth Carter is consistently a strong advocate for the supremacy of the private virtues, but she may not be unusual in her views on this issue. She complains to Elizabeth Montagu that she finds Italian historians "excessively tiresome," and explains:

> The considering man merely as a *political animal,* is not restrained to Machiavel, but seems to be the general principle of every Italian historian I ever read. This is, I suppose, one reason that their characters by appearing only in this single point of view, resembles [*sic*] nothing to be met with in real life. People act, in their general conduct, with regard to the public, conformably to those passions,

8. "Epistle II," ll. 200–202.

> or those principles which influence them as individuals. Unless, therefore, a reader by some acquaintance with them in this capacity is provided with a key to their actions, any character in a mere political display, will appear . . . unnatural and monstrous. . . .[9]

Montagu agreed with Carter that Italian theorists gave primacy to public life at the expense of private virtue. Machiavelli, she writes, "dissolves all private ties & only regards the bond of government." But her comments suggest that for her this is not a choice between the real world of the private individual and the unnatural monstrosities of public politics, but between private rights and public duties, between two different political languages. She writes that Machiavelli "grew a meer State Doctor, consider'd men only as the members of government, & would cauterize, amputate, & bleed them, merely as the health of the body politick required, without any regard to their separate rights or interests."[10]

Montagu's comments on the value of memoirs reflect this perception. She writes to the Duchess of Portland in the mid-1770s:

> The present age is very fond of private anecdotes, and indeed they are interesting, and amusing, and very useful, as notes, to explain the great text of History. They shew the manners and sentiments of the times, and sometimes the causes, sometimes the consequences and effects of great Events. It requires much knowledge, great talents, infinite research to be a good Historian; all these things, on a much smaller scale, will serve to form a writer of Memoirs. The Muse of History is a mighty Dame, and I wd have the Writer of Anecdotes attend on her as a Page, and carry her hat and gloves; if the hat is worn helmet fashion, and the gloves are Iron gauntlets, it lets us into the disposition of the Prince and the Times; if the hat is soft beaver, ornamented with a white feather and the gloves are fringed with silk or silver, we guess the fiddle summoned to the Ball oftener than the Trumpet calld to Battle, so I would ever encourage the dapper Author of Memoirs; . . .[11]

The private memorialist here is the servant of history, administering circumstantial detail and dress, and despite the explicit gendering of the muse of history and her page, the "dapper Author of Memoirs" who supplies biographical anecdotes is feminized by the apparent inequality of their ages and situations,

9. In *Letters from Mrs. Elizabeth Carter to Mrs. Montagu, between the years 1755 and 1800. Chiefly upon literary and moral subjects,* 3 vols., ed. Montagu Pennington (London: Rivington, 1817), 1.276–77, letter lxxvii, Deal, 4 October 1765. Cited hereafter as *Carter to Montagu.*

10. Leonore Helen Ewert, "Elizabeth Montagu to Elizabeth Carter: Literary Gossip and Critical Opinions from the Pen of the Queen of the Blues" (unpublished Ph.D. dissertation, Claremont Graduate School and University Center, 1968), 62, MO 3155, [Sandleford], 1 October [1765].

11. Reginald Blunt, ed., *Mrs. Montagu "Queen of the Blues": Her Letters and Friendships from 1762 to 1800,* 2 vols. (London: Constable, n.d.), 1.340.

and by the relation of his diminutive efforts to those of the authoritative historian—his preoccupation with the "manners and sentiments of the times," the contingent and circumstantial, the feminine details of dress and display. For Montagu, the trivial details which are the stuff of biography and memoir are a pleasing supplement to the truths of history, whereas Carter regards them as the key to the reality of acts which will otherwise appear fantastic.

Biography is perceived to depend on, and appeal to, what moralists represented as a distinctively gendered interest: the interest James Fordyce praised when he spoke of women's "uncommon penetration in what relates to characters, an uncommon dexterity in hitting them off through their several specific distinctions, and even nicer discriminations." But Fordyce's praise here is nicely matched by his condemnation, in the next sermon, of "female curiosity." Here he muses, with evident contempt: "Is it possible, that women could show such amazing eagerness to be acquainted with every minute particular in the life, character, dress, fortune, and circumstances of others, did they possess a fund of domestic entertainment and liberal conversation?" [12] Biography appeals to curiosity as a sensual appetite, as Sarah Fielding implies in comparing the genre to "a sumptuous Feast," the appetite for which feminizes the reader. She writes, comparing biography to the novel: "From the same Taste of being acquainted with the various and surprising Incidents of Mankind, arises our insatiable Curiosity for Novels or Romances: Infatuated with a Sort of Knight errantry, we draw these fictitious Characters into a real Existence." [13] Though the perceived value of biography as a genre is clearly rising in the mid-century, the debate about its propriety—not in terms of its possible invasion of privacy, but in terms of its possible infection of the masculine purity of the public sphere of history—continues to make its status uncertain.

To some extent the dignity and propriety of the genre are perceived to depend on that of its subject. Carter notes:

> However contemptible little circumstances may be considered in themselves, it is by these that we become acquainted with the discriminations of the principal actors in history, more than by their capital exploits. Many a thick headed hero, with the same courage and the same perseverance as Hannibal, might have dragged an equal number of troops over the Alps; but it was by a peculiar stroke of character, when Hannibal converted the fears of his army into mirth and good humour, by the ridiculous answer which he made to Gisco.[14]

12. James Fordyce, *Sermons to Young Women* [1765] (London: Cadell, 1809), vol. 1, s. vii, 218; vol. 2, s. viii, 16.

13. Sarah Fielding, *The Lives of Cleopatra and Octavia* [1757], ed. Christopher D. Johnson (London: Associated University Presses, 1994), 54.

14. *Carter to Montagu,* 3.210, letter ccxlvi, Deal, 18 November 1783.

Biography seems to be valuable either because it reveals what is peculiar about those who are "distinguished . . . from the rest of our Species,"[15] or because it displays manners and customs, but the attention to detail which characterizes it is inevitably "contemptible," debased by its mundanity. Ballard's accounts of eminent women do not, on the whole, benefit from the support of historical significance. What he claims for them, in place of that, is a defining relation to the manners and sentiments of the times, to national identity—a relation that is important to an understanding of the status attributed to learned women in the mid-century.

II

George Ballard was, for most of his life, a tailor, working from Camden, north of London. But his occupation left him time to pursue his antiquarian interests, collecting Roman coins with his sister and researching the lives of women. His friend Joseph Ames, the ironmonger and historian of English printers, wrote of Ballard's work on "Learned English Ladies" that "I may say your Life is spent in the Dress of their Body & Mind."[16] His interest in women may reflect his own marginal position, as well as the antiquarian's sense that British history could best be constructed out of an accumulation of material details. His work is characterized by the pragmatic eclecticism or indiscriminate avidity for detail that was represented as the hallmark of antiquarianism and natural philosophy, and that was frequently satirized as betraying a feminine preoccupation with toys.[17] Ballard's *Memoirs* pay surprisingly little attention to political or religious differences, or even differences of social station among the sixty-four women selected for inclusion. Many of the biographies he included were taken from existing compendia that had been unrestricted by considerations of gender or nationality. Others came from the lives or dedicatory epistles prefixed to published works, some from funeral sermons by well-known orators, and a few from monumental inscriptions, often collected by church historians. Part

15. Fielding, *Cleopatra,* 54.

16. Quoted in George Ballard, *Memoirs of Several Ladies of Great Britain,* ed. Ruth Perry (Detroit, Mich.: Wayne State University Press, 1985), 26.

17. The text I have in mind here is *An Essay in Defence of the Female Sex.* Carter writes: "I perfectly agree with you in the very little esteem I have for a virtuouso task. Besides the useless and undue expence to which it continually offers a temptation, it contracts the understanding, and checks the flights of imagination, while it keeps the attention poring upon minute objects. I agree with you that every work of the great Creator is worthy the utmost attention of man. Yet a scientific scrutiny into natural objects, though it ought to be treated with respect, as productive of the most useful discoveries to society, is not often very beneficial to the mind of the investigator." In *Carter to Montagu,* 3.251, letter cclviii, Deal, 22 September 1785.

of the volume was dedicated to Mary Delany (the eminent social commentator and floral artist), who observed when she saw it that "he does not pretend so much to be an author as a compiler, and gives you very modestly (without assuming any merit to himself) his authorities for what he publishes."[18]

Ballard claimed in his preface that, unlike the biographers of illustrious men, he did "not expect any Character in the learned world" for himself as a result of his work, and his self-effacement as an author mirrors the process in which his *Memoirs* deny more than a quantitative significance to the women whose learned quality they set out to praise. The distinctive feature of his work lay in his editorial policy, his principles of selection: the emphasis on national and gendered character, at the expense of differences between those memorialized. Ballard perceived his project specifically as a matter of competition with other European nations. In order to swell the numbers of learned women that "England hath produced," he introduces those of Ireland and Scotland, and includes women who lived on the Continent, but whom he believed could be claimed as British as a result of their birth, or knowledge of the language. So, for example, he includes Elizabeth Jane Weston, observing that she "seems to have left England when she was very young, and settled at Prague in Bohemia, where (I suppose) she continued the remaining part of her life." He also lists Catherine Tishem, whom he believes to have been a native English speaker though she lived in Antwerp, confessing, disarmingly, that "I am intirely ignorant in relation to the birth, parentage, and the time when this learned gentlewoman died."[19]

He attributes the number of learned women he is able to trace in sixteenth-century Britain to the spread of printing, and to the example of the daughters of Thomas More, and he indicates that the spread of education among women is a sign of cultural progress. He writes: "Parents perhaps, in those times might be of opinion, with a polite and elegant writer, 'That in a country where the women are admitted to a familiar and constant share in every active scene of life, particular care should be taken of their education, to cultivate their reason, and form their hearts, that they may be equal to the part they have to act.'"[20] He is quoting here from George Lyttelton's *Persian Letters* of 1735, and the comment is more obviously appropriate to the mid-eighteenth

18. Quoted in Perry, "Introduction," in Ballard, *Memoirs,* 43.

19. Ballard, *Memoirs,* viii, vi, 243, 144. The appropriation to Ballard's catalogue of women who were not in any obvious sense produced by England might not seem so idiosyncratic in comparison with the habits of eighteenth-century memorialists of men. See John Barrell's comments on Bainbridge Buckridge in his "Sir Joshua Reynolds and the Englishness of English Art," in *Nation and Narration,* ed. Homi K. Bhabha (London: Routledge, 1990), 154–55.

20. Ballard, *Memoirs,* 181.

century than to the sixteenth. Historical, antiquarian study provides him with a means to argue the case for the capacity of women to be educated, and for the necessity, in a modern commercial society, of that education. For history, in his hands, naturalizes and nationalizes commercial culture, representing British society as having been concerned, at least since the Reformation, to educate women in the self-regulation necessary to the discriminating middle-class consumer.[21]

This is a project of national importance, as Ballard's letters indicate, because of the part women should play in modern culture, and because of what the capacity to admire their abilities indicates about men. Lyttelton himself had in fact discouraged Ballard's project, telling him that "he did not know of above one or two [Learn'd Ladys] that deserv'd to be taken notice of. That he knew several of good Parts etc. but then they had Modesty enough to keep their Productions at Home; and that those who had ventur'd 'em abroad seldom met with Success. That the so much talk'd of Madam Dacier was a mere Pedant."[22] Ballard's account of his response to this criticism sweeps aside the comment on the proper modesty of women of parts. He responds first not by defending the merits of Madam Dacier, but by appealing to the judgment of the French: "I am no way concern'd to vindicate the Reputation of Madam Dacier, but nevertheless I cannot forbear saying if she can deserve no better a Character than this, that it is a very severe Reflection upon the French Nation in general, who must be thought from hence not to know how to encourage or reward Merit, having cast away so many extraordinary Favours upon one who so little deserv'd 'em." The French, he adds, are "a Nation fam'd for their Learning & encouragement of Literature." And he goes on to defend his choice of British women in similar terms:

> It was no small satisfaction & Pleasure to me to recollect that most of the Ladys whose Memoirs I am collecting have been applauded & extoll'd by the Pens of some of the greatest & most learned Men that this or any other Nation can boast of. . . . how far soever some Persons may be hurried on by Prejudice & prepossession against Female Learning & what I have in hand, yet I have the satisfaction to think that those great Persons may stand as an impregnable Bulwark between me and Censure.[23]

21. See Mary Poovey, *The Proper Lady and the Woman Writer: Ideology as Style in the Works of Mary Wollstonecraft, Mary Shelley, and Jane Austen* (Chicago: University of Chicago Press, 1984), chapter 1, esp. 20–23.

22. Ballard reports on George Lyttelton's comments in a letter to Charles Lyttelton of December 1745, Ballard MSS 42:29–30, quoted in Perry, "Introduction," 38.

23. Ballard to Charles Lyttelton, quoted in Perry, "Introduction," 38–39.

Prejudice against female learning is for Ballard caught up through a complex process with prejudice against national identity, and against the encouragement of literature as a necessary part of that identity. But this is not to say that what women have produced as a result of their learning is in itself vital to national identity: their work is not given the status of, most pertinently, Shakespeare's plays, which were argued increasingly forcibly in the mid-century to exercise a kind of sympathetic attraction no English subject could resist. It involves, rather, the suggestion that the nation is embodied in its literary critics, and in the institutionalization of learned culture that these men represent. To dismiss the opinion of "the greatest & most learned Men" would be to detract from the nation itself, for Ballard implies that the nation reveals its greatness in encouraging and rewarding displays of women's learning, and in honoring the authority of its critics.

The point for Ballard is not that the achievements of individual women contribute to national greatness. It is rather that the national institution of literary taste and learned criticism should be able to recognize quantities of well-educated women. Again and again, in his collection of memoirs, Ballard cites examples of women about whom he knows very little, but whose education is asserted in monumental inscriptions, epitaphs, funeral sermons, letters, poems, and dedications. Having argued energetically and at length that Lady Pakington (the seventeenth-century Christian moralist and church historian) should be recognized as the author of the *Whole Duty of Man* (now more usually attributed to Richard Allestree), he quotes passages from the text that favor the education of women, and observes: "I am not at all solicitous to know whether those humourous gentlemen think these are the strokes of a female hand, or not, since, if they deny it, they must inevitably acknowledge, that I have the suffrage of one of the best and most learned men of that age, in favour of the principles I have espoused, viz. that women are capable of the highest attainments in literature." Here the opinion of learned men is a more than adequate substitute for the demonstration of learning by a woman. Women should, Ballard implies, be more written upon than writers. What emerges, in passages like this, is that Ballard's work is not intended only to celebrate the learning of women in the past. He points out, in his life of Lady Pakington, that "that vulgar prejudice of the supposed incapacity of the female sex, is what these memoirs in general may possibly remove,"[24] but in the 1750s it is not capacity that is at issue in discussions of women's learning, but the desirability of recognizing learning as a properly feminine accomplishment.

24. Ballard, *Memoirs,* 324, 321.

The passage Ballard quoted from Lyttelton's *Persian Letters* is extracted from a discussion of the need for women's education in modern society, and continues:

> Where great temptations must occur, great virtues are required; and the giddy situations in which they [women] are placed, or love to place themselves, demand a more than ordinary strength of brain. In Persia a woman has no occasion for any thing but beauty, because of the confinement which she lives under, and therefore that only is attended to: but here, methinks, good sense is so very necessary, that it is the business of a lady to improve and adorn her understanding with as much application as the other sex, and, generally speaking, by methods much the same.[25]

This notion of learning as either the preventive or the cure for fashionable dissipation or giddiness runs throughout Ballard's account. He writes, for example, of Mary Astell that "The learning and knowledge which she had gained, together with her great benevolence and generosity of temper, taught her to observe and lament the loss of it in those of her own sex: the want of which, as she justly observed, was the principal cause of their plunging themselves into so many follies and inconveniences." Ballard repeatedly returns to the opposition between women who improve themselves by acquiring learning and women who, he suggests, waste themselves in all the rites of sociability; but his argument is unusual because of the implication, in this account of Astell, that "learning and knowledge" are a natural attribute of middle-class women, who should "lament the loss" their ignorance represents—they should lament the lack of the education that ought to be their property.[26]

John Duncombe's *Feminiad* addresses the relation between fashion and learning more directly, asking:

> But lives there one, whose unassuming mind,
> Tho' grac'd by nature, and by art refin'd,
> Pleas'd with domestic excellence, can spare
> Some hours from studious ease to social care,
> And with her pen that time alone employs
> Which others waste in visits, cards and noise;

25. George Lyttelton, *Letters from a Persian in England to his Friend at Ispahan,* in *The Works of George Lord Lyttelton; formerly printed separately, and now collected together: with some other pieces, never before printed. Published by George Edward Ayscough Esq.* (Dublin: J. Williams, 1775), 156, letter xlvii. Ballard cited letter xlix, apparently by mistake.

26. Ballard, *Memoirs,* 445–46. Ballard seems here to use "loss" to mean the "Lack, default, want" of a property that might normally be expected, rather than the deprivation of something that had been possessed in the past. See *Oxford English Dictionary,* "Loss," sb. 1, 2a, and H 7.

From affectation free, tho' deeply read,
"With wit well natur'd, and with books well bred?"

Duncombe represents this "deeply read" woman as the ideal wife. She combines domestic and social skills with "studious ease," and it is clearly important that her learning should be represented as a matter of leisure, of ease untainted by contact with the marketplace. She exchanges the most adverse signs of fashionable behavior—visiting and gambling—for learning within the home. But she is of course "well bred," an example of refined sociability. Contemplating the "studious band" of learned British women, Duncombe asserted earlier in the poem, was like gazing on portraits of fashionable beauties:

So when, in blended tints, with sweet surprize
Assembled beauties strike our ravish'd eyes,
Such as in Lely's melting colours shine,
Or spring, great Kneller! from a hand like thine,
On all with pleasing awe at once we gaze,
And, lost in wonder, know not which to praise,
But, singly view'd, each nymph delights us more,
Disclosing graces unperceiv'd before.

Duncombe represents women's learning as a desirable supplement to fashionable grace, an activity that alternates fluently with "social care." It does not isolate women, and his muse makes the effort to view "each charmer singly" only in response to the overwhelming sublimity of gazing on them as a grouped effect, a phenomenon of "our polish'd land."[27]

Duncombe goes on to warn against "letter'd nymphs" who "knowledge may abuse":

. . . husbands oft experience to their cost
The prudent housewife in the scholar lost:
But those incur deserv'd contempt, who prize
Their own high talents, and their sex despise,
With haughty mien each social bliss defeat,
And sully all their learning with conceit: . . .

The notion that these women reject or despise their own sexual identity is based on their neglect of social graces as well as housewifery. They seem unsexed because their identity is too close to that of male professional scholars, whose academic seclusion David Hume, for example, had satirized as "totally

27. John Duncombe, *The Feminiad. A Poem* (London: M. Cooper, 1754), ll. 92–99, 83, 56, 68–75, 65, 55.

barbarous." Incipient professionalization desocializes them just as thoroughly as confinement in the seraglio, which Duncombe, like Lyttelton, represents as the orientalized inverse of progressive commercial civilization, excluding women from the social commerce they should refine.[28]

In Ballard's account learning is represented as though it were necessary to female virtue, which is of course how *reputation* was perceived in earlier texts on women's social conduct, and most influentially in the *Ladies Calling*—another of the works he attributes to Lady Pakington. In some cases, indeed, the reputation for learning is almost interchangeable with the reputation for virtue. Ballard includes Catherine Bovey in his *Memoirs,* for example, because although he has no reason to believe that she was "either a linguist or a writer . . . her extraordinary merit, her exemplary life, and the noble use she made of an ample fortune, demand for her an honourable place among the female worthies." He concludes that "if she were not a writer," his knowledge of her reputation "may at least make us wish that she had been so."[29] The reference to "female worthies" is suggestive, for it implies that Ballard's *Memoirs* identify the virtue of learning, or good sense, with the more traditional and aristocratic women's accomplishments of hospitality and charity, or spending an "ample fortune" well. Certainly Ballard perceives the virtue of education as eliding the distinction between aristocratic women and the daughters of tradesmen, as well as between different political affiliations and religious beliefs (except, unsurprisingly, in the case of Queen Mary); so, for example, Margaret Cavendish, the Duchess of Newcastle, is remembered for the fact that she published, and not for the controversial nature of her publications; Anne Finch, Countess of Winchilsea's years of political banishment receive no mention, and the dispute between adherents of Lockean empiricism and of the idealism associated with John Norris and Malebranche, which dominates women's writing of the early century, is here a field for merit to shine in, rather than a ground for any substantive disagreement.

In her valuable introduction to the 1985 edition of Ballard's *Memoirs,* on which I have drawn extensively in this chapter, Ruth Perry argues that his omission or elision of any reference to controversy makes the book bland, and it certainly makes the fact of learning or publication the dominant feature in the lives of many of the women he writes about.[30] With the possible exception of those memorialized for their activities in or responses to the Reformation,

28. Ibid., ll. 83, 84–89; and on the seraglio, see ll. 43–48. David Hume, "Of Essay Writing," in *Selected Essays,* ed. Stephen Copley and Andrew Edgar (Oxford: Oxford University Press, 1993), 2.

29. Ballard, *Memoirs,* 438.

30. See Perry, "Introduction," 28.

the lives tend to represent the women as set apart from historical circumstance by their devotion to the accumulation of what Ballard identified as a "good stock of useful knowledge," which might enable them to fulfill the "considerable share" they have "to Act in the business of Life."[31] The extent to which accumulating this stock excludes them from historical circumstance and becomes the defining peculiarity of the genus is illustrated perhaps rather perversely by the brief memoir of Elizabeth Legge, born in 1580. Ballard notes that she knew five languages, and adds: "What use she made of this learning, or whether she wrote or translated anything I know not. But, as I have the honour of being informed by the Right Honourable Countess of Dartmouth, she was blind many years before her death; which was thought to have been occasion'd by much reading and writing by candle light." The text comes close to admitting that Legge is included to oblige her distant relation, the Countess of Dartmouth, or more directly because of the fascination of the fact that she lived to the age of 105, her brother to the age of 109, and her sister to the age of 112. She emerges as a collector's item, a curiosity, fortuitously marked out for Ballard's particular cabinet by her languages. The involvement of her family in the Stuart cause becomes in Ballard's account an insignificant embellishment to the details of its "very remarkable" longevity and, in her case, learning.[32]

The main features of Ballard's treatment of the relation between femininity and learning are strongly marked in his account of Grace Gethin, and the publication in 1699, shortly after her death at the age of twenty-one, of her *Misery's Virtues Whet-stone. Reliquiae Gethinianae, Or, some Remains of the Most Ingenious and Excellent Lady, the Lady Grace Gethin, Lately Deceased, being a collection of Choice Discourses, Pleasant Apothegms, and Witty Sentences.* Ballard reproduces extensive passages from this text, and cites with evident approval William Congreve's judgment that

> . . . so compleat the finish'd piece appears,
> That learning seems combin'd with length of years;
> And both improv'd by purest wit, to reach
> At all that study, or that time can teach.

It is unlikely that neither Ballard nor Congreve noticed that the text was essentially a commonplace book, made up of extracts from Bacon, Seneca, and others. Their praise of it as completely unified, consummately finished, and their perception of it as an index to the similarly integrated and matured

31. From the manuscript draft of the life of Margaret Roper, Ballard MSS 74:42, quoted in Perry, "Introduction," 36.

32. Ballard, *Memoirs,* 361.

wisdom of its producer, clearly imply conceptions of origination, and of completeness, that are both historically distanced and distinctively gendered. The text assembles and articulates a succession of diverse and apparently incoherent subject positions. The text and its author seem to be attributed a perfect completeness that is strongly reminiscent of the ideal femininity projected by so many of the periodicals addressed to ladies in the second half of the century—the completeness of a compendium of elegant extracts. Gethin is memorable because she expressed herself, and made herself visible, with all the directness and immediacy that are attributed to women's writing in the period, in a text that appropriates and feminizes the body of literary and learned culture. Gethin represents learning fashioned into a feminine form which Ballard believes "all such as were worthy" would have found "extremely agreeable": "they could not have failed to receive both benefit and delight, from those virtues, which in her writings she has recommended with such forcible arguments, and adorned with such beautiful images."[33] Gethin is much written on—her parents arranged for an anniversary sermon on her death to be preached in Westminster Abbey on Ash Wednesday in perpetuity. She is the type, the paradigm, of Ballard's project, for in her gentlemen of learning can celebrate literary history through the medium of a character which is all but transparent, and serves to do no more than confirm the feminized and national nature of that history.

III

The idea of learned women as female worthies is developed in some of the catalogues of learned women that succeeded Ballard's, and most notably in *Biographium Faemineum. The Female Worthies: Or, memoirs of the most illustrious ladies of all ages and nations* (1766). This collection reproduces much of Ballard's book, and announces the relation between the more traditional virtues of aristocratic women and learning in its extended title, where the book claims to memorialize women "who have been eminently distinguished for their magnanimity, learning, genius, virtue, piety, and other excellent endowments, conspicuous in all the various stations and relations of life, public and private." The collection tries to have it both ways, in that it claims to be a universal catalogue, and yet appeals to a specifically national interest, pointing out on the title page that it contains: "(exclusive of Foreigners) the lives of above Fourscore British Ladies, who have shone with a peculiar lustre, and given the

33. Ibid., 366, 364.

noblest proofs of the most exalted genius, and superior worth." The vagueness of "peculiar lustre," implying aristocratic status or independent achievement,[34] is hospitable both to women distinguished by excellent endowments and women who are conspicuous because of a more scandalous notoriety. The preface attempts rather awkwardly to account for the inclusion of women who "very indifferently comport with the title of our book, THE FEMALE WORTHIES, which seemingly implies, that none but such are honoured with a place in it." It argues that some notoriously unvirtuous women must be included because of their historical importance, but the explanation finally peters out, giving way to the lame comment that there is nothing in the book "from which our fair readers can imbibe the least tincture of immorality."[35] The preface is obliged to concede that quality has been sacrificed to quantity, that the notion of "FEMALE WORTHIES" is defined by the need to produce two volumes for the market, to mass the ranks of women who, in Duncombe's poem, "unite / To dazzle and perplex our wand'ring sight."[36] United by their appearance in the book, the quantity of women seems to dazzle and perplex consideration of the qualities, the attributes that qualify them for inclusion.

In the postscript to his curious volume of *Memoirs of Several Ladies of Great Britain* (1755), Thomas Amory describes the landscape of Green Island (which appears to be a fantastic Utopia) in direct and detailed comparison with Cobham's gardens at Stow, and he emphasizes the superiority of the Elysian Fields at Green Island, where there are

> statues of many ladies, and particularly in one group in the middle of those fine fields, twelve images, large as the life, representing Mrs. *Harcourt* and the eleven constituents she chose on the first founding of her society. . . . there is no inscription to any of these images, setting forth their virtues, as at *Stow:* but the name only of every one, on the low pedestal each rests upon; as, *Socrates, Homer, Abernethy, Mrs. Harcourt,* etc.

Amory is not interested in specifying the virtues that have gained the figures a place in the collection of "worthys," or indeed in giving the names of the women. He suggests that their characters are virtually represented because they are statues, which "seem as it were to breath," and not busts, but he also implies that individuating their virtues could only detract from the effect of the

34. See my "A Double Lustre: Femininity and Sociable Commerce, 1730–60," in *Eighteenth-Century Studies* 23, no. 4 (summer 1990): Special Issue, "The Politics of Difference."

35. *Biographium Faemineum. The Female Worthies; or, Memoirs of the most illustrious ladies of all ages and nations,* 2 vols. (London: S. Crowder, 1766), Preface to vol. 1, viii, x.

36. *Feminiad,* ll. 63–64.

group, united in their piety and their rejection of "the *diabolical invention,* that *for ever execrable ensign,* the *impious and unnatural hoop-petticoat.* This *dreadful machine* is never to appear among those wise and amiable women."[37] The significance of the women turns on the fact that they are represented, and on the lifelike detail which indicates the statuary's skill, which Amory's account celebrates to the exclusion of any peculiarity which might distinguish the women themselves.

The structure of Amory's *Memoirs* is curious: are they an early example of the sentimental fragment, or a late flowering of Swiftian digressive and apparently inconsequential satire (Amory claims to have known Swift well, and to have been "put into his seat at St. Patrick's prayers" in mistake for him), or are they just crazy? Amory claims to intend to produce eight volumes of lives of obscure women united by their rejection of the Athanasian creed. These volumes will form "a *Supplement* to a work which the author began many years ago" on the "antient and present State of Great Britain," the manuscript of which, he says, has unfortunately gone up in flames. He begins on the life of Mrs. Marissa Benlow, but after four hundred-odd pages he concedes to the correspondent to whom the book is addressed:

> When I sat down to write to you, I had no thought of making two letters of Mrs. Benlow's history; but various subjects have grown so fast under my pen, in order to give you what I principally intended, several useful informations, and thereby, so small a part of that lady's story hath been related, that I am obliged to refer you to another epistle for the principal events, and most extraordinary transactions in her life. You shall have it when I have breathed a little, and the notes and illustrations referred to in the first letter.

The promised account of Benlow's life is squeezed out, endlessly deferred, because Amory works on the principle that nothing is irrelevant, nothing can be excluded: "Among the rules layd down in my note-book, there was this concluding memorandum: Even love and laughter, a country-dance, and a drinking-bout, are to be articles, if they are uncommon, and accord with good manners." And he argues that memoirs of women are the appropriate occasion for his endless digressions, because any account of the events of their lives is of peripheral importance, and indeed almost irrelevant to his project. He explains:

37. Thomas Amory, *Memoirs of Several Ladies of Great Britain. Interspersed with Literary Reflexions, and accounts of Antiquities and Curious Things. In Several Letters* (London: J. Noon, 1755), Postscript, 412–13, 415.

> Such are the things and entertainment the reader will find in the following heap of minutes and notes, which are called *Memoirs of several ladies of Great Britain,* because the illustrious women therein mentioned are the choicest things in the collection, and every other account, with all the literary reflexions, spring from their storys, and are recited occasionally, as they relate to particulars in their historys. This is the reason of the title. Exclusive of this, the work might have been named *Pandecta,* as it contains a great variety of matter, and that the narrations relative to the ladies are the least Part of the performance.[38]

Women are the occasion for, and in a sense license his extraordinary peripatetic ramblings through the ancient and present state of Great Britain, through theological controversy, through the curiosities of antiquarianism and natural philosophy, and through reflections on the manners and sentiments of the times, because in his account women have no character, no history, no individual peculiarities. They are the ideal subjects for biography because they do not distract from or interrupt the accumulation of curious detail for which they are the excuse.

Ballard's *Memoirs* do not suffer from the eccentricity of Amory's volume, or the rag-bag inclusiveness of *Biographium Faemineum,* but like those volumes they do treat learned women primarily as a means to an end. Ballard suggests that his *Memoirs* will function as a sign of the civility of the national institutions of taste and critical judgment, precisely because the lives of the women listed lack either historical significance or, on the whole, the kind of biographical anecdote and detail that might individuate the women or embellish historical events. Mary Delany wrote of Ballard's dedication to her:

> I don't know how to help myself, but I am vexed at the books being dedicated to me. If I am not too late, I wish it could still be avoided; if it cannot, I don't like "Mrs D., wife of Dr. D." . . . Why could he not say (if he must say anything), To Mrs Delany, (a native of this country,) married to Dr. Delany, Dean of Down, &c. . . . Don't call me cross, but I think I feel a little so on this occasion, though not ungrateful; for I am much obliged and well pleased that a person of so much real worth as Mr. Ballard should have a good opinion of me, but I rather wish for shade and shelter than to be exposed to day's garish eye.[39]

Delany claims that she does not want the dedication, and that it pleases her, and she suggests that it will be more acceptable to her if it is addressed to her

38. Ibid., xxix, xx, 404, 406, xxv. For a thoughtful analysis of the narrative structures of Amory's work see Katie Trumpener, *Bardic Nationalism: The Romantic Novel and the British Empire* (Princeton, N.J.: Princeton University Press, 1997), 105–7.

39. *The Autobiography and Correspondence of Mary Granville, Mrs. Delany,* 3 vols., ed. Lady Llanover (London, 1861), 3.171; quoted in Perry, "Introduction," 41.

as "a native of this country" than as a wife; if she is willing to have a publicly visible character, it is as a British (or perhaps as an Irish) woman that she will accept it. A mutual friend of Ballard and Delany, Sarah Chapone, endorsed Delany's self-assessment, explaining to Ballard that it would be "looked upon as superfluous and indecorous to attempt to distinguish her [Delany] by saying whose wife she is."[40] Delany's response implies a curious mixture of self-effacement and defense of her own independence: if she is important, this is not something she will accept as the effect of her domestic role as the wife of a prominent cleric. Perhaps this is because she is more proud of having been born Mary Granville than of having become Mary Delany, but here she expresses this as a claim to nationality—a claim that was not of course simple for women. She does not claim distinction as an individual. The difficulty of her reply suggests the ambivalence of the relation between an idea of national identity which can be conceived of in terms of the achievements of women, and the acceptance of the public and social authority of educated women. It also indicates the peculiar demands which that ambivalence placed on learned women themselves—demands which I will suggest in part 2 are most apparent in the life and fame of Elizabeth Carter.

Hume's essay "Of National Characters," published in 1742, concluded with the reflection that "the politeness of a nation will commonly much depend" on maintaining "free intercourse between the sexes." For this reason, he argues: "the people, in very temperate climates, are the most likely to attain all sorts of improvement, their blood not being so inflamed as to render them jealous, and yet being warm enough to make them set a due value on the charms and endowments of the fair sex." For Hume, the effects of a temperate climate moderate between inertia and excessive desire—desire which cannot result in general improvement because it is focused on an excessively specific and attainable means of gratification. National character is here critically involved in national sexuality, and in the kind and degree of "free intercourse" available "between the sexes."[41] Duncombe's *Feminiad* alludes to this argument in rejecting "the bold, unblushing mien" of women writers who were associated with sexual scandal (he mentions Delarivier Manley, Susanna Centlivre, and Aphra Behn), and yet claiming that women confined and treated only as objects of sensual desire could not "beguile / The freeborn sons of Britain's

40. Chapone to Ballard, 30 October 1752, Ballard MSS 43:168; quoted in Perry, "Introduction,"
41. I am grateful to Francesca Wilde for information on Delany's life.

41. Hume, "Of National Characters," in *Essays,* 125.

polish'd isle."[42] His explicit aim is at once to praise the women artists and writers he mentions for their modest diffidence, and to coerce and cajole them into making their work more public. Writing the poem, however, provides him with an occasion to praise the talents of Susanna Highmore, his future wife, and the poem's praise of learned ladies might therefore also be seen as a model expression of polite desire.

Hume's and Duncombe's comments on the cultural importance of defining a national sexuality help us to understand perceptions of learned women in the mid-century because they point to the context of newly complicated notions of the domestic, which Johnson's *Dictionary* defines as "Belonging to the house; not relating to things publick," and "Not foreign; intestine." The situation of women in a domestic space which is defined by its lack of publicity was important to, for example, Pope's Moral Essay on the characters of women, where women seemed to conform to Johnson's definition of the domestic as "Private; done at home; not open." Women's lack of publicity seemed to identify them with concealment, and at least to imply duplicity. But the celebrations of eminent women I have been discussing seem to focus more on that sense in which the domestic situation of women identifies them both with what belongs to the familial house and with what is "not foreign," with national character. The domestic space which belongs to the house of women seems to emerge as an ambiguously private and national sphere, structured by affective relations, sentimental ties, sexual desires. In this space the idea of learning as a form of fashionable elegance, and of the learned woman as a moralized figure of display and desire, confirms that national identity is "not wild" (as Johnson also writes of the domestic), not corrupt or a sign of barbaric masculine isolation, but civilized and progressive.[43]

42. ll. 141, 39–40.

43. Samuel Johnson, *A Dictionary of the English Language. In Two Volumes* (London: Strahan, 1755), "Domestical, Domestick," 1, 4, 2, 3. My discussions of Thomas Amory, and of the learned ladies of the Bluestocking Circle, are indebted to conversations with Emma Major, who has always been generous in sharing her extensive knowledge.

3

A Shoping We Will Go

I

This morning is so very fine,
We'll to the meadows walk,
And when we to the town return,
with shop-men we will talk.
And a shoping we will go.
The Ladies Amusement[1]

When Elizabeth Carter's translation of *All the Works of Epictetus, which are now extant* was published in 1758 the *Monthly Review* celebrated the event:

> Many Ladies have been very witty; some few have been very learned; but we have never, till now, seen these accomplishments united with an acute understanding and solid judgement, sufficient to unravel the intricacies of Philosophy. France can now no longer boast her *Dacier,* but must be compelled to own that our women excel theirs in Sense and Genius, as far as they surpass them in Modesty and Beauty.[2]

1. *The Ladies Amusement, To which is added, Hawke's Engagement* (Stirling: C. Randall, c. 1800), stanza 1. It seems likely that the song was first published some decades before 1800, as the song with which it is published celebrates Hawke's engagement at Quiberon Bay, which took place in 1759.

2. *Monthly Review* 18, 1758, quoted in Vivien Jones, ed., *Women in the Eighteenth Century: Constructions of Femininity* (London: Routledge, 1990), 175. For a fuller account of the reception of Carter's *Epictetus,* see Sylvia Harcstark Myers, *The Bluestocking Circle: Women, Friendship, and the Life of the Mind in Eighteenth-Century England* (Oxford: Clarendon Press, 1990), 159–70. My own discussion of some of the women associated with the bluestocking circle is (inevitably) deeply indebted to Myers's scrupulous and thorough research.

For almost two decades of the mid- to late century, praise for Carter's achievements becomes a repeated refrain, a key note in the celebration of British cultural supremacy. Her reputation becomes the sign of the superior capacities of all "our women," and it seems an act of allegiance, a duty necessary to the formation of national identity, to proclaim their excellence "in Sense and Genius," as well as "in Modesty and Beauty." In this chapter I want to explore the relation between those four attributes, and between, on the one hand, the rising status of women's learning in the mid-century, and on the other, the importance of the woman of fashion as a figure for the desires that animate commercial culture.

The growing recognition in the decades of the mid-century that women's learning might be a source of national pride is in some respects a rather surprising development. A paper published in the periodical *Common Sense* in 1737 provides an energetic example of the sort of anxious defense of masculine territory which the idea of learned women quite frequently provoked in the 1730s, and also indicates how closely learning was associated with fashion. The paper claimed, perhaps in allusion to Pope's dictum about women's lack of character, that the model woman, "though she could support any Character, assumes none." Implying that character is no more necessary to feminine than to masculine identity, the essayist suggests that the ideal woman would not choose to put on any character, apparently because to do so would be a departure from a femininity that is universal or natural. Writing of women who attempt to discuss "Politicks and Metaphysicks," he concludes, "how shocking do they become, when the Rage of Ambition, or the Pride of Learning, agitates and swells those breasts, where only Love, Friendship, and tender Care should dwell?" A character for learning or ambition is here incompatible with the feminine capacity for feeling, but it remains unclear whether this character is too elevated for mere women or too low, a debasement of ideal femininity.

The essayist exemplifies this lack of clarity when he writes of a woman who values "Reason and good Sense" that: "If *Eudosia* would content herself with her natural Talents, play at Cards, make Tea and Visits, talk to her Dog often, and to her Company but sometimes, she would not be ridiculous, but bear a very tolerable Part in the polite World."[3] He suggests, with indeterminate irony, that the best therapy for Eudosia's "ridiculous" insistence on discussing "solid Trifles" is the kind of behavior so often condemned as the feminized and undesirable form of politeness: a formal sociability emptied of the bonding power of affective exchange, an excessive sentimental attachment to the

3. *Common Sense*, Saturday, 10 September 1737. On the early eighteenth-century fear of learned women, see Clifford Siskin, *The Work of Writing: Literature and Social Change in Britain, 1700–1830* (Baltimore: Johns Hopkins University Press, 1998), chapter 2.

supplemental accessories of fashion (the lap dog), and an attraction to the imminently addictive pleasures of gambling. It is more usual in the 1730s and 1740s to urge, as does Wetenhall Wilkes, that at least a little learning—enough to result in "conversing and corresponding correctly"—is both "genteel and necessary" because it distracts women's thoughts from "the idle Entertainments and Diversions that are invented to chouse [dupe or swindle] them out of their Cash and Wit together."[4] A little learning helps virtuous women to abstain from fashionable consumption and achieve true politeness in, for example, *The Woman of Taste* (1733) and *The Young Gentleman and Lady Instructed in . . . principles of politeness, prudence, and virtue* (1747). The indeterminate irony of the *Common Sense* paper, however, indicates that while fashionable behavior devalues femininity, learning involves a desire for value, for substance, that is yet more shockingly incompatible with the capacity for feeling and the lack of character necessary to feminine identity.

The comments of the *Monthly Review* on Carter's *Epictetus* confirm that competition with the French is a spur to the reevaluation of learned women as trophies of British cultural superiority. The reviewer claims that, because of Carter, "France can now no longer boast her *Dacier*." That claim is not, of course, simply about Dacier's merits as a translator of the classics, but about the sense in which she or Carter might be seen as representatives of cultural difference and signs of national identity. Dacier's changing reputation in Britain helps to indicate what was demanded of a distinctively British idea of learned femininity. In 1771, *The Town and Country Magazine* printed a memoir of the French scholar which was admiring but rather less enthusiastic than earlier accounts of the standard she posed for national competition. The article remarks for example that "We find, in general, more wit and taste, with less crowded erudition in her works, than in those of her husband. The only reproach she ever really merited, was her unbounded admiration of all that she wrote." If Dacier can no longer be dismissed as a learned pedant, as Lyttelton's earlier comments to Ballard had suggested, then she can be mocked for her vanity—the failing most persistently attributed to learned or witty women in later decades. In keeping with its reputation as a scandal sheet, the *Magazine* goes on to report at some length the "pleasantries" of Dacier's enemies, including for example the observation that

4. Wetenhall Wilkes, *An Essay on the Pleasures and Advantages of Female Literature* (London: Cooper and Caswell, 1741), 25, 24. On the relation between the exchange of goods and of affection, see Marcia Pointon, *Strategies for Showing: Women, Possession, and Representation in English Visual Culture, 1665–1800* (Oxford: Oxford University Press, 1997), chapter 2, esp. 20–21.

> She was outrageous in defending the interests of antiquity—Whenever she talked of the glorious ages of Alexander and Augustus, she fainted with admiration. . . . this learned lady, holding a distaff by her side, recited . . . the tender farewell between Andromache and Hector, with so much enthusiastic rapture, that she was absolutely bereft of her senses. Her external appearance had a certain bibliographic air, quite incompatible with ease and elegance: for, indeed, what an indecency must she have been guilty of, to fix a pompoon with the same hand that could pen Greek?[5]

These "pleasantries" imply that Madame Dacier's response to the classics is marked by a sexualized form of excessive sensibility reminiscent of the passions of learned or ambitious women which had shocked the essayist of *Common Sense.* But in mocking her "bibliographic air" they also suggest that she is guilty of a kind of prudery in finding the signs of "ease and elegance" indecent. The memoir suggests that a more ideal, and perhaps more British, learned woman would moderate her enthusiasm for her studies, and instead display her capacity for feeling in fashionable elegance, in playing that "very tolerable Part in the polite World" that had been the therapy ironically recommended for Eudosia in *Common Sense.*

Feminine learning is perceived with increasing insistence in the mid- to late century in a parallel relation to fashionable elegance. Fashionable consumption is moralized by its relation to the consumption of learning, as a degree of literary taste becomes necessary to polite elegance, while fashionable ease seems to lend an air of femininity to an otherwise prudish or impassioned pursuit, as the portrait of Dacier implies. The ladies of *Millenium Hall* again nicely display the difficult combination required. George Ellison notes that they have produced a self-sufficient economy on their estate, and observes:

> Such a situation . . . would be dangerous to many people, for if, as some have supposed, and, in regard to a great part of the world, I fear with truth, mutual wants are the great bands of society, a person thus placed, would be in danger of feeling himself so independant a being, as might tempt him to disclaim all commerce with mankind, since he could not be benefitted by them. He would look on himself in the light of a rich man gaming with sharpers, with a great probability of losing, and a certainty of never being a gainer. (*MH,* 110)

Here the analogy between "commerce with mankind" and gambling is an intriguing indication of the pervasiveness of the perception of fashionable

5. *The Town and Country Magazine; or, Universal Repository of Knowledge, Instruction, and Entertainment. For December, 1771,* "Memoirs of *Madam* Dacier." The reported "pleasantries" are attributed to the Abbé Carlaud de la Vilate.

activity as a synecdochic representation of commercial culture. The ladies reject the imputation of self-sufficient independence, but they distinguish between their desire for a solitude where "we have no cards, no assemblies, no plays, no masquerades" (112) and what they regard as the substantial currency of social commerce: "Reason wishes for communication and improvement; benevolence longs for objects on which to exert itself; the social comforts of friendship are so necessary to our happiness, that it would be impossible not to endeavour to enjoy them" (110).

The ladies do, to some extent, deny desire: the tales of their pasts, out in the fashionable world, repeatedly involve their refusal to marry men they desire, perhaps most strikingly in the narrative of Miss Selvyn's mother, who refuses to marry the lover by whom she is pregnant precisely because he knows that she desires him (211–17). And their learned seclusion may be both the cause and the reward of this disavowal. But it is also, as they acknowledge in discussion with Ellison, an alternative manifestation of desirous sensibility. Early in the novel, the ladies with some of their pupils perform extracts from Handel, and Ellison comments that

> the songs were sung in a manner so touching and pathetic, as could be equalled by none, whose hearts were not as much affected by the words, as their senses were by the music. The sight . . . made me almost think myself already amongst the heavenly choir, and it was a great mortification to me to be brought back to this sensual world, by so gross an attraction as a call to supper. . . . (63)

The "sublime harmony" (63) of Handel is here a sign of religious sensibility and high culture, rather than of the luxurious extravagance it had represented earlier in the century. In *The Woman of Taste,* for example, sighing over Handel was seen as a specious substitute for genuine piety. The poet complained of "A vicious town and court not half so soon, / Made vertuous by a sermon as a tune," and linked appreciation of the "melting notes" of Handel's oratorios with the financial irresponsibility of the fashionable: "Singing the bait, devotion the pretence, / By music drawn, that modern foe to sense! / . . . / As much each winter sunk, to please your ear, / As wou'd your landlord pay, and sempstress clear."[6] The activities of the ladies do not however indicate any

6. *The Woman of Taste. Occasioned by a late Poem, entitled, the Man of Taste. By a Friend of the Author's* (London: Battley, 1733), epistle 1, 9, 8. The shift in attitudes to Handel might have to do with the fact that the bulk of his sacred oratorios appeared after the publication of the *Woman of Taste,* but should also be considered in the context of the increasing acceptance of the place of emotional display in the Anglican church. Handel was patronized by the Earl and Countess of Huntingdon, and she is said to have visited his deathbed in 1759. Lady Huntingdon's Connexion had not yet been excluded

simple rejection of fashionable culture, as they are themselves keen to emphasize. Ellison's analogy of the rich gambler is appropriate to them, although they reject the immoral social commerce of gambling. They do not, like Ellison, "fear" that "mutual wants are the great bands of society"; they regard those mutual wants as desirable ties of affection. They participate in a learned and elegant community where feeling and financial probity go hand in hand, like the twinned activities of paying bills and listening to Handel.

Learning both promotes the disavowal of desire, with its implications of luxurious consumption and conspicuous display, by teaching women not to be cheated of "their Cash and Wit together," and confirms a capacity for appropriate feeling, for the desirous and affective sensibility produced or demanded by fashionable commerce. In the decades of the mid-century the recognition some learned women receive makes it possible to think of the fashionable world as gaining substance, ballast, by their presence, while ladies of fashion remain immune to infection by their more negative and unfeminine attributes, such as their peculiar or foreign passion and prudery. But we can perhaps best understand their increasing status by the rather roundabout means of considering some of the characteristics of femininity that in these decades are perceived to contribute to the counterimage of polite femininity, and which I think indicate the extent to which ideas of learning are bound up in the languages of affect, financial probity, and elegance.

II

We'll look at ribbons, laces, gloves
And none of them will buy,
But tell the haberdasher lads,
we'll call another day.
And [a shoping we will go.]

Next to the mercers we will haste,
we'll teaze their silks awhile,
And say we're vex'd for troubling them,
then leave them with a smile.
And [a shoping we will go.]

from the Church of England, into which it continued to import an appreciation of the power of music and of passionate oratory until its secession in 1783. See [A. C. H. Seymour], *The Life and Times of Selina Countess of Huntingdon. By a member of the houses of Shirley and Hastings,* 2 vols. (London: Painter, 1839–1840), 1.229; and Edwin Welch, *Spiritual Pilgrim: A Reassessment of the Life of the Countess of Huntingdon* (Cardiff: University of Wales Press, 1995), 199–202. See also Christopher Hogwood, *Handel* (London: Thames and Hudson, 1988), chapter 5, "London: The Oratorios (1737–59)."

Hard ware and pretty glitt'ring things,
now we shall them refuse;
We'll say they're for a country friend,
and therefore cannot chuse.
And [a shoping we will go.]
Ladies Amusement, stanzas 2–4

In the second half of the century, the figure of the woman of fashion as a focus for anxieties about the morality of commercial culture acquires a further and apparently rather perverse attribute. Excessive fashionable consumption by women, and particularly by women of the trading classes, does of course continue to be ridiculed, satirized, and stigmatized as the abomination of polite society; but with increasing insistence, I think, a kind of counterimage of equally undesirable feminine behavior emerges in the figure of the woman who does not consume enough. When Harriet Byron tries to persuade Charlotte Grandison to "Abate . . . of half your other visits" so that they can spend longer together, Charlotte comments: "Of the ten visits, six of the ladies will be gone to the sales, or to plague tradesmen, and buy nothing: Any-where rather than at home: The devil's at home, is a phrase: And our modern fine ladies live as if they thought so. Two of the other four called upon me, and hardly alighted: I shall do so by them. The other two I shall have paid my compliments to in one quarter of an hour."[7] Charlotte's comments represent fashionable women as figures for a sociability that is devoid of the substance of affective exchange, as had numerous earlier texts. *The Young Gentleman and Lady Instructed,* for example, asserted: "I do not know one thing that contributes so much as this article of visits to the lessening the esteem men of sense have to the fair sex."[8] But here that lack of sentimental worth is demonstrated in going to shops and failing to spend money as much as in the "article of visits." The parallel between visiting and shopping without exchange is reiterated in the first edition of William Alexander's *History of Women, from the earliest antiquity to the present time* (1779). Alexander reflects that "employment is not the mode of the times," and details instead "Amusements and methods of killing time." Under this rubric he notes that "in some of the politer nations, modern visiting is not spending a social hour together; it consists only in her ladyship ordering her coachman to drive to the doors of so many of her

7. Samuel Richardson, *The History of Sir Charles Grandison,* 3 parts, ed. Jocelyn Harris (Oxford: Oxford University Press, 1986), 1.191, letter xxxvii.

8. *The Young Gentleman and Lady Instructed in such principles of politeness, prudence, and virtue, as will lay a sure foundation for gaining respect, esteem, and satisfaction in this life, and eternal happiness in a future state,* 2 vols. (London: Wicksteed, 1747), 2.123.

acquaintances, and her footman, at each of them, to give in a card with her name." Immediately after this he writes:

> SHOPPING, as it is called, is another fashionable female amusement; in order to which, two, three, or sometimes more ladies, accompanied by their gallants, set out to make a tour through the most fashionable shops, and to look at all the most fashionable goods, without any intention of laying out one single sixpence. After a whole forenoon spent in plaguing mercers and milliners, they return home, either thoughtless of their folly, or which, perhaps, is worse, exulting at the thoughts of the trouble and disturbance they have given.[9]

Failing to buy, acknowledging the temptation of the goods in the shops but resisting the urge to purchase them, is the sign not of prudence, but of a hard-hearted lack of sensibility.

Later in the century, in Burney's *Camilla* (1796), the heroine is taken window-shopping by Mrs. Mittin, who adopts the "clever device" of asking for directions in "almost every shop" because of "the opportunity it afforded of taking a near view of the various commodities exposed to sale." The incident clearly indicates the exploitative impoliteness of Mrs. Mittin, but apparently because she looks like a woman of fashion and sensibility, Camilla seems "of a figure and appearance not quite so well adapted for indulging with impunity such unbridled curiosity," and she attracts the curious speculations of the shopkeepers: "Some supposed they were only seeking to attract notice; others thought they were deranged in mind; and others, again, imagined they were shoplifters, and hastened back to their counters, to examine what was missing of their goods." The incident suggests that gratifying curiosity without handing over cash is a form of theft, a sort of irrational gratification or "illicit voyeurism," as Elizabeth Kowaleski-Wallace points out.[10] One of the shopkeepers adds that the women must be "idle travellers, of light character,"

9. William Alexander, *The History of Women, from the earliest antiquity, to the present time, giving some account of almost every interesting particular concerning that sex, among all nations, ancient and modern,* 2 vols. (London: W. Strahan, 1779), 1.98–100. This passage did not appear in later editions, perhaps because it gave offense to the female readership Alexander wished to address.

10. Elizabeth Kowaleski-Wallace, *Consuming Subjects: Women, Shopping, and Business in the Eighteenth Century* (New York: Columbia University Press, 1997), 94. See also Deirdre Lynch, *The Economy of Character: Novels, Market Culture, and the Business of Inner Meaning* (Chicago: University of Chicago Press, 1998), esp 174–94. See Jane Austen's account in *Sense and Sensibility* of the vacuously goodnatured Mrs. Palmer, "whose eye was caught by every thing pretty, expensive, or new; who was wild to buy all, could determine on none, and dawdled away her time in rapture and indecision." Marianne's sensibility is of course expressed in her appetite for endless hours at "booksellers, music-sellers, and print-shops." Jane Austen, *Sense and Sensibility*, ed. James Kinsley, Margaret Anne Doody, and Claire Lamont (Oxford: Oxford University Press, 1990), 142, 79.

as though their activity were a form of sexual promiscuity or commerce played by alien rules.

Camilla's embarrassing experience of her own inadequacy as a consumer is inevitably compounded by the presence of the hero of the novel, who meditates sagely that he could have found the incident merely ridiculous

> had he been less uneasy at seeing with whom Camilla was thus associated; Mrs. Mittin might certainly be a worthy woman, and, if so, must merit every kindness that could be shewn her; but her air and manner so strongly displayed the low bred society to which she had been accustomed, that he foresaw nothing but improper acquaintance, or demeaning adventures, that could ensue from such a connection at a public place.

The effects of associating with Mrs. Mittin in a public place can only be improper or demeaning because her vulgarity inevitably tarnishes Camilla, even though the heroine's "face seemed the very index of purity." [11] For Mrs. Mittin's pleasure might be seen as a satire on the gratifications of politeness, on the purely imaginative and scopic act of appropriation that is attributed to the man of taste or of liberal education in a range of eighteenth-century texts. Addison, for example, had argued that the "Man of Polite Education" could feel "a greater Satisfaction in the Prospect of Fields and Meadows, than another does in the Possession." As Robert W. Jones has pointed out, the satisfaction attributed to this man seems to be based in the "contradiction . . . between the politeness of an imagination which is free from particular, property based desires, and the individuated pleasures which are associated with sensible gratification." The man seems to feel "greater Satisfaction" because his ownership is ideal. Window-shopping women like Mrs. Mittin enjoy a debased version of this polite satisfaction; they are not represented as though they (in Jones's terms) "rise above the pleasures of ownership," but as though they sink below them, gratifying the sensible desires of their "unbridled curiosity" without any further recourse to imagination and its polite freedoms. Mrs. Mittin boasts to Camilla that "they might see all that was smartest, without the expence of buying anything," explaining that "these shops are all so wondrous smart, 'twill be a pleasure to go into them." Her pleasure is a form of shoplifting, as the shopkeepers suspect, because she is replete with all the "sensible gratification" the goods can give her, and she has thus, in some sense, erased their

11. Frances Burney, *Camilla; or, A Picture of Youth*, ed. Edward A. Bloom and Lillian D. Bloom (Oxford: Oxford University Press, 1972), 607–9, 610–11. For a perceptive account of the role of the hero in the novel, see Jane Spencer, *The Rise of the Woman Novelist from Aphra Behn to Jane Austen* (Oxford: Blackwell, 1986), 163–67.

value, their desirability.[12] The reactions of the shopkeepers suggest, however, that Mrs. Mittin's imaginative appropriations would hardly have been troubling were Camilla not also present. Because Camilla looks like a woman of fashion, a woman who should have reserves of sentiment or cash, the behavior of the two women becomes a puzzle, a sign of madness or of actual rather than imaginative theft.

Women who take pleasure in shopping as an end in itself, as a source of entertainment that can be divorced from the business of purchasing anything, are represented as a plague on shopkeepers, most obviously in allusion to the rapacity of locusts, to the sense in which they consume without offering anything in exchange. The anxieties they provoke can perhaps best be understood in the context of the rather vexed and uncertain distinctions between different kinds of commercial activity—between, most obviously, the speculations of city merchants and stock jobbers and the business of shopkeepers and small tradesmen, where the former tends to be represented as commerce and the latter as trade. Commerce is perceived to participate in a discourse of credit which articulates a culture of insubstantial appearances, whereas trade is perceived to depend on cash and to offer credit only with great reluctance. Trade involves notions of industry, thrift, and a more moralized notion of trust which seems to deny the necessity of credit on which the shop nevertheless depends. In *Shops and Shopkeeping in Eighteenth-Century England,* Hoh-cheung and Lorna H. Mui point out that "with a few exceptions . . . shopkeepers did not receive a good press in the eighteenth century," but in the later century, in the context of what are represented as the unfeeling transactions of fashionable women who either do not pay their bills or fail to buy at all, shopkeepers seem to emerge as representatives of commercial probity, or sentimental victims of aristocratic indifference.[13]

The distinction between shops and the Exchange, or between trade and commerce, is central to the cases put forward in *The Tryal of the Lady Allurea Luxury, Before the Lord Chief-Justice Upright, on an Information for a Conspiracy* (1757). Lady Allurea is defended by Mr. Burgamot and Mr. Sergeant Perfume, who emphasize the contributions of luxury to commercial progress in prosperity and polite refinement. In his final address to the jury, Burgamot

12. Addison, *Spectator,* no. 412, quoted in Robert W. Jones, *Gender and the Formation of Taste in Eighteenth-Century Britain: The Analysis of Beauty* (Cambridge: Cambridge University Press, 1998), 44–45. Burney, *Camilla,* 607.

13. Hoh-cheung Mui and Lorna H. Mui, *Shops and Shopkeeping in Eighteenth-Century England* (Montreal: McGill-Queen's University Press, 1989), 6.

rehearses the familiar argument that money is "the Blood, the Life of every State," and that luxury, in the person of

> the amiable benevolent Lady at the Bar . . . makes this Life—this Blood flow into every Vein of the Body Politic, so as to preserve all the Members in a due State of Salubrity—She takes from the Rich only to give to the Poor—without her Care of us—Idleness and Want of Exercise must infallibly soon bring on all the Symptoms of Mortality—The Poor must die of Consumptions—the Rich of Plethoras—and Government be defenceless, for want of proper Revenues for its Support.[14]

The witnesses for the defense are mostly tradesmen and shopkeepers, who are encouraged to point out the number of customers luxury brings them. Luxurious commerce is, according to the defense, healthy and therefore moral because it maintains circulation, both social and monetary.

In contrast to the social and economic metaphor of circulation, which the defense claims is energized by luxury, the case for the prosecution turns on metaphors of stability and retentiveness. It is presented by the Attorney General and Learned Council Arthur Manly Esq., and represents luxury as a threat to public spirit, to what is "Manly," but it attempts to distinguish between this and desirable commerce. Those who speak up for luxury are disparaged as suspect Europeans, Jews, and effeminate, denaturalized Englishmen, whereas, for example, the "Lord-Mayor, and the whole Court of Aldermen" appear for the prosecution, complaining that as a result of luxury, "we have had nothing to eat, fit for an *Englishman* to put in his Stomach. High-seasoned Ragouts and masqueraded Poisons have been substituted in the place of honest roast Beef and Plumb-Pudding, and the noble Bacon Chine and Turkey." It is a sign of luxurious taste, the city dignitaries argue, that "the Citizens neglected their several Occupations—were grown indolent and careless in their respective Callings, and minded Stockjobbing and Sharping more than Trade, in order to support their Pleasures and idle Expences." Trade is represented here as though it involves only the exchange of necessary articles of domestic produce, and functions through networks of mutual obligation analogous to the "Bands of Blood and Affinity, that formerly united Families." But this virtuous trade is represented as threatened by the desire for "Superfluities" which is "a vicious, dissolute Expence in our Manufacturers and Trades-people" themselves, and in their customers.[15] In cross-examining the tradesmen who appear for

14. *The Tryal of the Lady Allurea Luxury, Before the Lord Chief-Justice Upright, on an Information for a Conspiracy* (London: F. Noble, 1757), 67–68.

15. *Tryal,* 19, 17, 75, 79.

the defense, the prosecution continually oscillates between sympathizing with them as the victims of customers who cannot or will not pay their bills, customers whose desires for luxuries are represented as bankrupting trade, and condemning the shopkeepers for trading in foreign goods and stimulating insatiable and antisocial desires in their customers.

The uncertainties of the prosecution case are, I think, fairly typical of the way commerce is perceived in the mid- to late century. It seems usual to condemn customers who fail to pay their bills. Elizabeth Carter, for example, writes of noblemen selling chaplainships that "luxury and extravagance must ever be rapacious and dirty. It is certainly not more scandalous for a nobleman to sell his privileges, than to cheat his tradesman, by running into debt." Later she comments that debt resulting from extravagance "is more mischievous to society than robbing on the highway." Hannah More taps into a familiar vein of sentimental literature when, in *Coelebs in Search of a Wife* (1809), she condemns fashionable ladies on the grounds that "a few ostentatious charities are opposed as a large atonement for a *few amiable weaknesses,* while the unpaid tradesman is exposed to ruin by their vengeance if he refuse to trust them, and to a gaol if he continue to do it."[16] But defense of the tradesman as a figure of private virtue involves condemnation of his customers, and sets his interests apparently at odds with those of commerce, making him the representative of the good old days of cash and trust as opposed to the speculative fantasies of credit and commercial modernity. The tradesman seems to be valued despite or at the expense of his trade, and the satirical figure of the fashionable woman is caught in a parallel double bind. For she is tarred with the vices of excessive desire and fashionable display, even as her failure to purchase is deemed somehow ungenerous, a betrayal of trust and a defrauding of the shopman's labor. In the late century, for example, the song *The Ladies Amusement* which I use as a kind of running epigraph to this chapter lists the wicked ploys of window-shoppers, mockingly suggesting that as these idle would-be shoppers flirt with traders, and "teaze their silks awhile," they coquette with the legitimate expectations and honest desires of the shopkeepers they refuse to gratify. In this song, perhaps more obviously than in the other representations of fashionable window-shoppers I have mentioned, the fairly good-humored mockery of the women is shadowed by the uncertainty of the song's address, the question of

16. Montagu Pennington, ed., *Letters from Mrs. Elizabeth Carter to Mrs. Montagu, between the years 1755 and 1800. Chiefly upon literary and moral subjects,* 3 vols. (London: Rivington, 1817), 1.309, letter lxxxvii, Deal, 12 July 1766, and 323, letter xci, Deal, 12 November 1766. This text is hereafter cited as *Carter to Montagu.* Hannah More, *Coelebs in Search of a Wife,* in *The Miscellaneous Works of Hannah More,* 2 vols. (London: Thomas Tegg, 1840), 2.423.

by and for whom it might be sung. The direction of, for example, Hannah More's attack on fine ladies who are bad debtors is clear: More is concerned about the example they offer to their sex. Satires on women who do not run up debts, but tease shopkeepers with their unfeeling refusal to buy, certainly play on the themes of the fashionable woman's lack of sentiment, and the shopkeeper's probity. But in *The Tryal of Lady Allurea Luxury* and other satires, humor arises from the uneasy naturalization of the dominance of commercial relations in the figure of the woman of fashion who does make the purchases, and shines with the polite elegance convenient or appropriate to her station.

III

Upholsterers shall not escape,
  at this our grand review;
We'll price their carpets, tables, chairs,
  their printed hangings too.
    And [a shoping we will go.]

Some brittle wares, we now must see,
  delf, china, glass and stone;
We'll say they're cracked, we'll say their dear,
  and we'll of them have none.
    And [a shoping we will go.]

Ladies Amusement, stanzas 5–6

The desirable alternative to the woman who regards shopping as entertainment is not, in these decades, the notable housewife, who is often referred to as an object of derision. In late 1755 and early 1756, the *Connoisseur* carried three papers satirizing women who followed advice like that given in *Common Sense,* and contented themselves "with the private Care and Oeconomy of their Families, and the diligent Discharge of domestic Duties." The three women exemplify the gendered domestic virtues of notable economy, good nature, and neatness or cleanliness, each of which is represented as driving the three husbands who complain to the *Connoisseur* to ruin and/or distraction. The first wife insists that her husband take a "little box" in the country, and attempts to make the estate self-sufficient, as conduct books had so often recommended.[17] But the cattle and fowl die, the homemade wine either turns to vinegar or explodes, and they have only what the husband considers the doubtful "pleasure of gathering" vegetables "fresh from the garden, after they had

17. See, for example, James Fordyce, *Sermons to Young Women* [1765] (London: Cadell, 1809), sermon vi, "On female virtue, with domestic and elegant accomplishments."

stood us in more than ten times their value in the raising." In town she goes to market "with all the notable airs and housewifely appearance of an old butter-woman," and secures bargains so extraordinary that she buys in bulk, and "above half her marketings stink and grow musty, before we can use them." When she strays from "domestic oeconomy," she acts more like fashionable women, as she is unable to resist buying "useless commodities" going cheap at sales and auctions. But the bulk of the paper focuses on the issue of perversely expensive economies.[18] This woman could perhaps figure as an example of the inadequacy of training in domestic skills that is so frequently lamented in the period, but in the later satires it becomes clear that these are examples of virtues which have become outmoded because they are insufficiently polite.

The good-natured woman is exemplary. Her husband writes that "no woman can excel my wife in the simplicity of her dress, the humility of her desires, or the contented easiness of her nature." Her fault appears to be that her conception of the family and its duties involves an extended sphere of obligation unsuitable to the contracted urban household. The wife "looks upon herself as in duty obliged" to take care of her servants and their children, so that the house "would put you immediately in mind of the *Foundling Hospital.*" She dispenses charity with an "overflowing humanity" the husband regards as more appropriate to "the *Roman* Catholic Chapel in *Lincoln's-Inn-Fields.*"[19] The neat and clean wife upsets and embarrasses her husband, rather as did the domestic economist, by dressing and behaving in ways no longer regarded as appropriate to the polite leisure of the middle-class woman: he records with horrified amazement that he has "often seen her on her knees scouring the hearth, and spreading dabs of vinegar and fuller's earth on the boards," dressed for this drudgery "so that you would rather take her for a chair-woman." Though they possess fine china, the husband is "never allowed to eat from anything better than a *Delft* plate," because the display cannot be disarranged, and their handsome furniture, "except when we have company, is done up in paper, as if the family to whom it belongs, were gone into the country."

In these three papers the appearance of fashionable leisure has become a requirement of middle-class politeness; they may also suggest why, for the ladies of Charlotte Grandison's acquaintance, the devil seems to be at home. For the domestic sphere of these women is contracted, as cleaning becomes the proper province of charwomen, and marketing of butterwomen; as charity and care for servants become the duties of institutions; and dairying, vegetable-growing,

18. *Connoisseur,* no. 91, Thursday, 23 October 1755.
19. *Connoisseur,* no. 98, Thursday, 11 December 1755.

and brewing produce goods that would be better bought from the shop. The neat woman causes her husband a particularly acute degree of painful embarrassment because she fails to act as though the properties of their social position were her own. She behaves like a servant in her own home, and he has "been in pain" for her when, before company, "through her extreme cleanliness, she has not been contented without breathing into our drinking-glasses, and afterwards wiping them with her pocket handkerchief."[20] These three women, in their different ways, fail to consume, fail to participate in the fantastic exchange of display and desire that shopping generates. They are in a position to benefit from the advice of a paper of 1755 on women's education. The essayist describes an "extraordinary academy" called "Kidder's Pastry-School," where girls going into service and "a few notable young girls of the city" are taught to bake, and comments that

> As housewifely accomplishments are now quite out of date among the polite world, it is no wonder that Mr. Kidder has no share in the education of our young ladies of quality: and I appeal to any woman of fashion, whether she would not as soon put her daughter apprentice to a washer-woman, to learn to clear-starch and get up fine linen, as send her to the pastry-school to be instructed in raised crust and puff paste. The good dames of old, indeed, were not ashamed to make these arts their study: but in this refined age we might sooner expect to see a kitchen-maid thumbing Hoyle's Treatise on Whist, than a fine lady collecting receipts for making puddings, or poring over the Complete Art of Cookery.

What the paper advocates is schools for whist, "so that any lady, who never before took a card in hand, may be enabled in a very short time to play a rubber at the most fashionable routs and assemblies." For all its irony, it is I think clear, when this paper is set alongside those satires on "the ordinary employments of domestic economy," that the essayist is not implying that women could or should return to domestic skills "in this refined age."[21] The papers satirize notable housewives who treat shopping too much as though it were an employment, as though they were themselves butterwomen, charwomen, impolite in their failure to become (or pretend to be) leisured generalists. These women reveal a failure of sensibility in their inability to conceal or delegate their labor, to internalize the implications of their social position; they fail to participate in the exchanges of display and desire that should distinguish their femininity. Even the good-natured woman, whose generosity is represented as a form of excessive humanity, fails in sensibility because there is no exchange

20. *Connoisseur*, no. 103, Thursday, 15 January 1756.
21. *Connoisseur*, no. 60, Thursday, 20 March 1755.

for her gifts, the "humility of her desires" asks no return. In that sense, all of these women are too self-sufficient, too insulated from the prototypical commerce of the card table.

IV

Now after we are thus fatigu'd,
  perfumes will give us ease;
We'll visit all the scented shops,
  but nothing there shall please.
    And [a shoping we will go.]

From shop to shop we'll range about,
  'Till ev'nings darkest shades,
And when we can no longer see,
  we must prepare for beds.
    And [a shoping we will go.]
      Ladies Amusement, stanzas 7–8

In the mid- to late century, then, the imperative that women should consume, and not be too nice about cracks in the merchandise or the usefulness of the commodities on offer, generates its own characteristic set of satirical victims, rejects from the exchange of display and desire. The woman of fashion begins to acquire significance not just as the embodiment of the corruptions of commercial luxury, but as the sign of the polished politeness that is the fruit of commercial prosperity, the figure of civilized sensibility and "most extensive Humanity" that the council for the defense recognizes in Lady Allurea Luxury.[22] The idea of women's learning has a central function here, in mediating, like Lady Allurea, between the unhealthy extremes of consumption and plethora, in converting the glitter of fashionable display into the gold of "Education's moral mint."[23] It is hard to see, in the texts I have discussed, much trace of the parsimonious domesticity literary historians of the novel have often represented as the ultimate ideal or inevitable fate of middling-rank femininity in the eighteenth century.[24] Instead these texts emphasize the desirability of discriminating consumerism and polite sociability. The *Ladies*

22. *Tryal,* 62.

23. Hannah More, *The Bas bleu. Or, Conversation,* in *The Works of Hannah More, in eight volumes, including several pieces never before published* (London: Strahan, 1801), 1.27.

24. I am thinking of, for example, Nancy Armstrong, *Desire and Domestic Fiction: A Political History of the Novel* (New York: Oxford University Press, 1987), and Mary Poovey, *The Proper Lady and the Woman Writer: Ideology as Style in the Works of Mary Wollstonecraft, Mary Shelley, and Jane Austen* (Chicago: University of Chicago Press, 1984), both of which have been extraordinarily influential in the last

Amusement concludes with the lines: "And when we can no longer see, / we must prepare for beds. / And [a shoping we will go]," conjuring the image of women shopping in their dreams, or shopping for a place to sleep. The concluding stanza points toward the capacity of consumerism to engender a newly fantastic sensibility, poised between the associations of feminine desire and display with sexual promiscuity on the one hand, and an increased humanity and superadded civility on the other.

The *Connoisseur*'s attitude toward the education of women reflects the ambivalent perception of it as a sign of progress or corruption. Again in 1755, he praises the publication of *Poems by Eminent Ladies:*

> I never imagined, that our nation could boast so many excellent poetesses, (whose works are an honour to their country) as were here collected together: and it is with the highest satisfaction I can assure my female readers in particular, that I have found a great number of very elegant pieces among the compositions of these ladies, which cannot be surpassed (I had almost said, equalled) by the most celebrated of our male-writers.[25]

This is exactly the kind of celebratory language which is becoming commonplace in the mid-century, but the uneasiness of this praise is made clear by the way the paper develops. The essayist narrates a dream occasioned by the sight of the book, in which he is transported to Parnassus to witness a debate over whether English women poets "should be allowed to hold the same rank, and have the same honours paid them, with the men." The contest is to be decided by the skill the ladies show in riding Pegasus, and the dreamer describes a succession of named women, from the Duchess of Newcastle to Laetitia Pilkington, demonstrating their accomplishments. Some of the women are scandalous figures (Behn, Pilkington), but many are respectable (Philips, Killigrew, Leapor, Barber), and they are all represented as riding the horse with skill, though in styles appropriate to their received reputations. What is interesting about the paper is the complete indeterminacy of the satire, which ends with Pilkington slapping the dreamer's face. It is as though the essay could not quite bring itself to offer a straightforward puff for the publication, even though one of its compilers was Bonnell Thornton, who also produced the *Connoisseur.*

---

decade or so in determining readings of eighteenth-century femininity across genres they never attempted to discuss.

25. *Connoisseur,* no. 79, Thursday, 22 May 1755. The paper refers to George Colman and Bonnell Thornton, eds., *Poems by Eminent Ladies. Particularly, Mrs. Barber, Mrs. Behn, Miss Carter, Lady Chudleigh* (London: R. Baldwin, 1755). The collection was reprinted in 1757 in Dublin, and appeared in new London editions in 1773 and 1785.

For the dream unsettles the praise of the opening paragraph, and there is something backhanded about the way living poets are complimented through the account of Catherine Philips: "Her dress was simple, though of a very elegant make: it had no profuse ornaments, and approached very nearly to the cut and fashion of the present age. Though she never ventured beyond a canter or a hand-gallop, she made Pegasus do his paces with so much ease and exactness, that Waller himself owned he could never bring him under so much command."[26] Though the situation the paper imagines is ludicrous, displays of horsemanship are not condemned as unfeminine. Writing poetry seems indistinguishable from dressage, or from dressing elegantly; it is an appropriate feminine accomplishment. The fact that the exemplary Orinda is dressed in a style which resembles that of the present age clothes modern women poets in her respectability, and implies that their writing, like their dress, is a morally valuable form of display. The essayist accepts women's achievements, and endorses the idea that these are "an honour to their country," but at the same time he displays the unease that is part and parcel of that acceptance.

That sense of praise and unfocused disquiet centers on the relation between fashion and literary learning as appropriate feminine accomplishments, "of a very elegant make." For learning functions on the one hand as a sign of politeness, of elegance, a commodity which indicates sensibility, affect, and lends substance to the otherwise formal exchanges of feminine sociability; and on the other as a retreat from fashion, a sign of abstemiousness that may be either virtuous or unfeminine. Learning is the appropriate form of shopping, the means of buying without extravagance, and not buying without impoliteness. The involvement of educated women in the elegant society so often perceived as the most valuable end product of commercial culture is, of course, the theme of Hume's 1742 essay "Of Essay Writing." Hume claims that "women of sense and education (for to such alone I address myself) are much better judges of all polite writing than men of the same degree of understanding," as a result of the "delicacy of their taste, though unguided by rules." He represents himself as "a kind of resident or ambassador from the dominions of learning to those of conversation," promoting "good correspondence," and even "union" between these two clearly gendered states of the "elegant part of mankind." The analogy with foreign policy is picked up again when Hume goes on to suggest that it is to the advantage of France that the ladies there are "the sovereigns of the *learned* world, as well as of the *conversable,*" and it is developed more immediately in his account of his own function:

26. *Connoisseur,* no. 79.

> I shall give intelligence to the learned of whatever passes in company, and shall endeavour to import into company whatever commodities I find in my native country proper for their use and entertainment. The balance of trade we need not be jealous of, nor will there be any difficulty to preserve it on both sides. The materials of this commerce must chiefly be furnished by conversation and common life: the manufacturing of them alone belongs to learning.[27]

The "balance of trade" here is a sensitive subject, as the essayist shows by the qualification he attaches to his initial statement. At first, he figures himself as perhaps a French spy: he is a resident in the state of conversation, but he passes intelligence back to his own country, and promotes the sale of their commodities. But he qualifies this equation of conversation with the consumption of imported goods: the materials the learned manufacture into commodities are the native, raw produce of conversation, sold back to that state in their worked up and refined form. Though the essay suggests that women should be "the sovereigns of the *learned* world," the commerce it describes between conversation and learning is clearly that which defines relations between colony and imperial center—a commerce in which the essayist takes the role of colonial agent for the empire of learning.

Hume's essay inverts that relation by suggesting that "learned ladies" rule a nation of sociable pleasure, which rescues academic and masculine learning from being "totally barbarous" by consuming the commodities it produces. But the essay's praise for learned women is marked by a disquiet that resembles that of the later paper from the *Connoisseur* on women writers. On the whole the essay celebrates a feminization of literary culture, and represents the civilizing of learning through commerce with sociability as a desirable accomplishment; but Hume portrays himself as less than serious, and as carried away by the analogy that dominates the essay, when he suggests that if the learned were not a "stubborn independent race of mortals" he would urge that women be appointed to rule the "republic of letters," or that all those who lack "sound understandings and delicate affections" be persecuted with "severest vengeance."[28] The essay's praise for women's learning because it is the acceptable form of fashionable consumption, and because their polished delicacy (with its implications of luxury) may rub off on the more manly scholar, is equivocal—undermined perhaps by the implied trajectory of imperial decline.

27. "Of Essay Writing," in David Hume, *Selected Essays*, ed. Stephen Copley and Andrew Edgar (Oxford: Oxford University Press, 1993), 3, 2, 4, 1, 4, 2–3. The essay was not republished by Hume after 1742. My discussion of this essay is indebted to comments Stephen Copley made on it in conversation. See also Jones, Gender, 83–85.

28. Hume, *Essays*, 3, 2, 3.

Hannah More returns to the analogy of imperial commerce between learning and conversation in her poem, *The Bas bleu. Or, Conversation* (written in 1783). Apostrophizing conversation as the "Soft polisher of rugged man," she argues that it is "For thee, best solace of his toil! / The sage consumes his midnight oil." But More understands the exchange between learning and conversation in terms different from those of Hume's essay: here the learned man works "to produce / Materials" for conversation's "future use," and, she continues:

> If none behold, ah! wherefore fair?
> Ah! wherefore wise, if none must hear?
> Our intellectual ore must shine,
> Not slumber, idly, in the mine.
> Let Education's moral mint
> The noblest images imprint;
> Let Taste her curious touchstone hold,
> To try if standard be the gold;
> But 'tis thy commerce, Conversation,
> Must give it use by circulation;
> That noblest commerce of mankind,
> Whose precious merchandize is MIND![29]

Here scholarly intellect produces the material, education and taste manufacture it into specie, and the sociable commerce of conversation gives that current value, circulation. In More's poem polite and feminine society assumes the imperial role, and produces exchange value out of the resources learning could barely know it possessed. The poem is able to assume a more confident, celebratory manner than could Hume's essay, because what women do here is removed from the difficult implications of consumption, and transposed more thoroughly into the affective language of social bonding, of conversation which generates a fantastic value for the currency of trade.

29. *Bas bleu,* 26–27. Elizabeth Montagu wrote about More's poem in a letter to Elizabeth Carter of 19 September 1783: "pray what means bas blue or ye progress of conversation? I shd suppose blue stockings were meant, but what connection has stockings with conversation? I do not think ye french ever wear blue stockings." In Leonore Helen Ewert, "Elizabeth Montagu to Elizabeth Carter: Literary Gossip and Critical Opinions from the Pen of the Queen of the Blues" (unpublished Ph.D. dissertation, Claremont Graduate School and University Center, 1968), 174, and see 174 n. 3 on the date of composition of the poem. Note the allusion, in the first line of the passage I quote from the poem, to Milton's Eve. In *Paradise Lost* Eve asks why the stars shine when they have no apparent audience, and is rebuked by Adam in terms that imply that her question is a sign of feminine vanity and dependence on display. See *Paradise Lost,* Book iv, ll. 657–88.

V

In conclusion, I want to look briefly at Ann Penny's lines "Addressed to the Author of the Essay on the Writings and Genius of Shakespeare," published in her *Poems* of 1771,[30] for the poem elaborates themes central to the celebration of learned women in the mid- to late century. Penny writes:

> No more let France her Critick Dacier boast,
> The Queen of Isles a Montague adorns,
> Whose Genius tow'ring as her Albion's Coast,
> Thy pedant Sons of abject Slav'ry scorns.
>
> Fair blooms the Wreath thy gen'rous Hand has wove,
> With Laurels green thou deck'st thy Shakespeare's Head,
> Immortal Genius doth the Task approve,
> And bids his Poet's Glories round thee spread.
>
> Thy gen'rous Pen was destin'd, sure, to guard
> From Gallick-Ignorance his injur'd Name,
> With polish'd Science to adorn the Bard,
> Bold to admire, yet not afraid to blame.
>
> O! could his Shade, where Peace, where Wisdom reigns,
> Thy nervous Page behold, with Wonder fraught,
> Even there the Bard would bless thy friendly Strains,
> And own his Magick felt, his Genius caught.
>
> There would he wish, if there a Wish can be,
> Whene'er his Montague from Earth retires,
> Her Form in those seraphick Realms to see,
> And tell the Gratitude his Bosom fires.

In the preface to the *Poems,* Penny implies that "the very small Group of Female Writers" are beleaguered, their place in literary culture still insecure and subject to "illiberal Reflection" and contempt. But a sense that they have gained more than a foothold is suggested by the direction of her publication "especially" to the reading public "of her own Sex," and by the fact that the ladies of the bluestocking circle and their associates figure prominently in her list of subscribers.[31] Women are acknowledged, directly and indirectly, as a

30. In her anonymously published *Poems, with a dramatic entertainment* (London: J. Dodsley, 1771), 131–32. Anne Penny was a Welshwoman whose husbands had maritime connections. For further details, see Janet Todd's brief outline of the poet's life in Janet Todd, ed., *A Dictionary of British and American Women Writers, 1660–1800* (London: Methuen, 1987).

31. Subscribers include: the Duchess of Bedford, Elizabeth Carter, Jonas Hanway (to whom the volume had been dedicated, apparently without his knowledge), Samuel Johnson, Lord Lyttelton, the Duke and Duchess of Marlborough, Elizabeth Montagu, Mrs. Ord, Lady Vere, and Lady Vernon.

considerable reading public, and the poem treats Montagu, I think, as a particularly striking example of this new cultural importance, rather than as an exception. Montagu is, as it were, the first lady to hand, because her work has associated her so closely with Shakespeare, whom Addison had established as the cultural icon no English audience (or readership) could fail to warm to. Montagu is represented here as reflecting some of his significance, as his "Glories round thee spread." Her genius is, like Shakespeare's irregularities and imperfections, evidence of British liberty, in contrast to the despotic pedantry to which the French are enslaved, and which Montagu condemns in Voltaire's criticisms of the bard. And this makes Montagu, like Shakespeare, part and parcel of what it is to be British, a phenomenon intimately bound up in the national landscape, the British soil. The genius which is ambiguously that of Montagu and that of the "Queen of Isles" itself is "tow'ring as her Albion's Coast," comparable to or functioning as the white cliffs of Dover.[32] But of course what Montagu has, and what Shakespeare, significantly to his status as national bard, lacked, is "polish'd Science," for she is a sign of those "most refined and enlightened ages" about which the *World* expressed such ambivalent enthusiasm.[33] Montagu's work on Shakespeare makes her the exemplar of the sense in which women writers as a group are, I have argued, valued for their peculiar relation to the national Gothic heritage, to that barbarous but productive past which their more sociable learning colonizes and represents in refined and polished form.

Broadly, we might understand Penny's celebration of Montagu as though she were Vera Lynn, conflated with the south coast and national identity, in the context of the increasing importance of the notion that the condition of women in any culture is the index of the degree of civilization achieved—an argument that acquires most currency during and after the 1770s.[34] But more specifically, Penny's praise for Montagu exemplifies the way learning is celebrated from the mid-century as the appropriate accomplishment of a modern and polite femininity which moralizes commercial culture as the basis for an affective community, a kind of extended sentimental family bound together in relations of exchange and consumption, or mutual dependence. In this chapter I have explored some of the features which contributed to the way upper- and middle-rank women, and in particular learned women, were perceived to

32. For further discussion of some of these issues, see my "The Wanton Muse: Politics and Gender in Gothic Theory after 1760," in *Beyond Romanticism: New Approaches to Texts and Contexts 1780–1832,* ed. Stephen Copley and John Whale (London: Routledge, 1992).

33. *World,* no. 191.

34. On the currency of this notion see Sylvana Tomaselli, "The Enlightenment Debate on Women," *History Workshop Journal* 20 (1985): 101–24.

fulfill this function, features which emphasize the sociability and not the domestication of the proper lady. Learned women are undoubtedly private subjects, but that privacy is not only turned inward, and focused on domestic life. As a result of the sociability that is demanded of them, and the relation to the nation they are required to fulfill, learned women begin to assume a more public aspect.

PART TWO

The Fame of Elizabeth Carter

4

The Learned Lady as Public Spectacle

In the opening pages of *Millenium Hall* the narrator comes across an enclosure in the grounds which offers asylum to unusually short and tall people. These people are here protected by the ladies of the utopian community both from exploitation by showmen, and from the pride they had themselves taken in being exhibited as an "extraordinary spectacle." Ellison is allowed to enter and inspect the enclosure, having promised not to stare at its inhabitants, but he nevertheless comments on them:

> they were all passing backwards and forwards, and thus gave us a full view of them, which would have been a shocking sight, but for the reflexions we could not avoid making on their happy condition, and the very extraordinary humanity of the ladies to whom they owed it; so that instead of feeling the pain one might naturally receive from seeing the human form so disgraced, we were filled with admiration of the human mind, when so nobly exalted by virtue, as it is in the patronesses of these poor creatures, who wore an air of chearfulness, which shewed they thought the churlishness wherewith they had been treated by nature sufficiently compensated.[1]

The whole incident is freighted with understated allusions to the analogy between the position of the women and the "poor wretches" they shelter, and the

1. Sarah Scott, *A Description of Millenium Hall*, ed. Gary Kelly (Peterborough, Ontario: Broadview Press, 1995), 74. Hereafter cited as *MH*.

close relation between the "human form . . . disgraced" and the "human mind . . . exalted" is reinforced here by the ambiguous identity of the subject who "wore an air of chearfulness" despite nature's churlishness, which might be either the "poor creatures" or their "patronesses." The sense in which the ladies of Millenium Hall approximate to public and paternal status depends on the modest care with which they "conceal their virtues in retirement" (*MH,* 53), and the moral redemption of the people saved from "being exhibited as public spectacles" (75) is similarly effected by their retirement in the zoo-like enclosure. The fact that the "poor wretches" (72) are hidden is the visible sign of the women's benevolence, and the activity of not staring at them allows the narrator to contemplate at leisure the extraordinary humanity of the women's exalted minds.[2]

The incident provides a suggestive frame for looking at the kind of fame, the kind of public spectacle, afforded by representations of two of the most celebrated English women of the mid- to late century: Scott's sister Elizabeth Montagu and Elizabeth Carter. Montagu was a very wealthy woman who enjoyed considerable social prominence. For the purposes of my discussion, however, I have chosen to focus more steadily on Elizabeth Carter's unusual status, and to overlook some of the complexities of Montagu's position in order to use her as a foil for the scholar. Like the ladies of Scott's novel, Montagu approximates most nearly to public status through the way she spends her money—her patronage and benevolence. Mary Scott's *The Female Advocate* (1774), for example, praises her patriotic defense of Shakespeare from the detractions of Voltaire, but dwells at greater length on the "nobler Fame" deserved by the virtuous use of riches. Of her exemplary subjection to the "soft controul" of "sweet Philanthropy," Scott writes:

Nature's vast theatre her eye surveys,
Studious to trace Eternal Wisdom's ways;
Marks what dependencies, what different ties,
Throughout the spacious scale of beings rise;
Sees Providence's oft-mysterious plan,
Form'd to promote the general good of man.
With noble warmth thence her expanded mind
Feels for the welfare of all human-kind: . . .[3]

2. Lamont and Ellison first imagine the enclosure to contain a menagerie of "foreign animals," and develop the analogy between chattel slavery and the keeping of wild animals in captivity (71–72). On this passage see Felicity A. Nussbaum, *Torrid Zones: Maternity, Sexuality, and Empire in Eighteenth-Century English Narratives* (Baltimore: Johns Hopkins University Press, 1995), 150–53.

3. Mary Scott, *The Female Advocate; A Poem. Occasioned by reading Mr. Duncombe's Feminead* (London: J. Johnson, 1774), ll. 366, 374, 371, 375–82. The lines on Montagu, Dorothea Mallet Celesia,

Montagu's survey of the providential plan is modulated by her privacy and femininity, by warmth and feeling, but like George Ellison in Sarah Scott's later novel, she is represented as achieving a more comprehensive understanding of the "general good" through the exercise of private virtue than public life, in what is perceived as its present corrupt form, could afford.

One of the ways Montagu demonstrates this almost divine capacity is through an employment policy, on her estate at Sandleford (her favorite country seat), which resembles that of the ladies of Millenium Hall, and of George Ellison. Ellison employs "tribes of skipping children, and hobbling old men and women," and explains that a laborer "would become mine only, when noone else has business for him. . . . I content myself with those whom no other person will accept."[4] The ladies of Millenium Hall offer extra pay or financial support to "Those whose youth render them disregarded, or whose old age breeds neglect" (*MH,* 170), and the servants of the house all suffer from some infirmity or "natural disadvantage" (169). The inhabitants of their almshouses are expected to support one another with reciprocal services, as one of them tells Ellison:

> Now, there is neighbour Susan, and neighbour Rachel; Susan is lame, so she spins cloaths for Rachel; and Rachel cleans Susan's house, and does such things for her as she cannot do for herself. The ladies settled all these matters at first, and told us, that as they, to please God, assisted us, we must in order to please him serve others. . . . (66)[5]

On her visit to Montagu's estate in 1791, Mary Morgan noted that many of the men working in the grounds

> had some great defect, occasioned by age, natural infirmity, or misfortune, being either blind, deaf, dumb, or lame; yet she had so paired them, and fitted their employments to their several faculties, that the remaining senses of one served to supply the deficiency of the other. By this stroke of benevolent ingenuity . . . she has the heart-felt satisfaction of making those useful and happy members of society, whom nobody else would employ. . . . I hope it is not profane to say, she has made the blind to see, the deaf to hear, the dumb to speak, and the lame to walk.[6]

---

and Catherine Talbot (i.e., ll. 357–406) were reprinted in *The Annual Register, or a View of the History, Politics, and Literature, For the Year 1774;* see Montagu's comment below.

4. [Sarah Scott], *The History of Sir George Ellison,* 2 vols. (London: A. Millar, 1766), 1.227, 231 [82, 84]. Hereafter cited as *Ellison.*

5. See also *MH,* 243–44.

6. Mary Morgan, *A Tour to Milford Haven, in the year 1791* (London: J. Stockdale, 1795), 39–40, Letter V, To Miss B—., Burfield, 13 July 1791. On Morgan, see Montagu Pennington, ed., *Letters from Mrs. Elizabeth Carter to Mrs. Montagu, between the years 1755 and 1800. Chiefly upon literary and moral*

For Montagu and for Scott's fictional characters, the providential plan is disclosed in an almost feudally paternalistic moralization of the division of labor, where, as Ellison remarks, "all live in a state of reciprocal services, the great and the poor are linked in compact; each side has its obligations to perform" (*Ellison,* 1.38 [16–17]). The role of the landowner, in setting up and maintaining this reciprocal system, approximates to divine intervention. The microcosm of the estate, which they govern with such exemplary benevolence, corrects or alleviates the inhumanity of commerce in the world beyond its boundaries. The housekeeper at Millenium Hall comments on the charitable vigilance of the ladies: "The fashionable tradesman is sure not to have them in the list of his customers; but should he, through the caprice of the multitude, be left without business, and see his elated hopes blasted, in all probability he will find these ladies his friends" (*MH,* 170). The ladies do not intervene to regulate fashionable caprice, the degeneracy of the marketplace, but they do support the shopkeeper when he becomes the victimized representative of honest trade.

This kind of moralization of the effects of capitalism and the division of labor is perceived to depend on private virtue, and on the sentimental social affection and the knowledge of detail and domestic economy that can imply. Mary Morgan commented on Montagu that "She neither is, nor affects to be, above the common business and occupations of life. She attends to every thing that comes within the sphere of her observation; and it is thus, in my opinion, she proves the extent of her genius." Morgan goes on to confirm that the virtues she praises in Montagu are distinctively gendered. "I could never look upon those people as beings of a superior order, whose thoughts are totally absorbed in one pursuit," she writes; but in contrast to this perhaps characteristically masculine model of absorption, she argues that though Montagu seems "occupied with external things"—absorbed by her public or social roles in fashionable and learned company, and in public exhibitions—though Montagu is "never free from interruptions" of this kind, she always gives priority to private benevolence, and "is always thinking of some great or good work, which tends to the encouragement of genius, or the promotion of plans for the benefit of her species. As I have thus pourtrayed her, you will no longer imagine, that conversing with her has made me averse to the society of female friends, or of my sex in general." Montagu's almost divine characteristics are shown to be thoroughly involved in her feminine grasp of domestic detail, in her sentimental ability to respond with rapturous affection when she hears of

---

subjects, 3 vols. (London: Rivington, 1817), 3.160, letter ccxxxv, Bath, 17 December 1781 (hereafter *Carter to Montagu*). On the treatment of deformity in *MH,* see Nussbaum, *Torrid Zones,* 151–52.

Mary Morgan that "there was nothing in the creation I was so fond of as a chimney-sweeper's boy."[7]

The ability of the very rich—and particularly women—to maintain a benevolent economy within the limited sphere of their estates may be what Carter has in mind when she urges Montagu to value the limitations of her position, writing that "you may comfort yourself . . . that you are born a woman, and not a man; for if you had been a man, you would have been a politician; and who with either sense or honesty, would not shudder at the possibility of being engaged in such political *tricasseries* as the present!"[8] In Montagu's hands, Carter implies, "so much money is so much virtue."[9] Her position as an enormously wealthy private citizen, enjoying marital independence after the death of her relatively untroublesome husband in 1775, allows Elizabeth Montagu to assume something like the status of a national monument, renowned for her benevolence and patronage. "In the centre of her own circle," Richard Cumberland wrote, she "sits like the statue of the Athenian Minerva, incensed with the breath of philosophers, poets, painters, orators, and every votarist of art, science, or fine speaking."[10] Her work on Shakespeare confirms and consolidates this reputation, in its entirely appropriate blend of literary taste and national zeal.

Montagu is, of course, perceived to be freakish, deformed by her fame. Cumberland repeats the quite widespread view that her virtues are the effect of vanity, and claims to have mistaken her for a piece of theatrical scenery, a painted city—a show of public spirit.[11] His account of her as Minerva,

7. Morgan, *Tour to Milford Haven,* 43–44, 45, Letter VI, to Miss B—., Haverford West, 14 September [1791]. Montagu was celebrated posthumously as the "Patron of Sweeps" in "The Sweeps' Lamentation For the Loss of their Friend, Mrs Montagu," which recorded that:

> She'd a heart that could melt
> At the troubles we felt,
> And in soothing 'em thought herself blest;
> So that once in a year
> We partook of her cheer,
> And she kindly provided the best.

The lines allude to Montagu's annual feast for sweeps. See *The Lady's Monthly Museum, or Polite Repository of Amusement and Instruction,* vol. 6, January 1801.

8. *Carter to Montagu,* 3.165–66, letter ccxxvi, Deal, 19 June 1782. Carter's comments refer to events following the fall of the North ministry. See Paul Langford, *Public Life and the Propertied Englishman, 1689–1798* (Oxford: Clarendon Press, 1991), 535–36.

9. *Carter to Montagu,* 2.179, letter cliv, Deal, 28 November 1772.

10. Richard Cumberland, *The Observer,* no. 17.

11. See, for example, James Boswell, *Life of Johnson,* ed. R. W. Chapman, with an introduction by Pat Rogers (Oxford: Oxford University Press, 1980): "A literary lady of large fortune was mentioned, as one who did good to many, but by no means 'by stealth,' and instead of 'blushing to find it fame,'

repeated in numerous celebratory and dedicatory addresses, hints at the sense in which her visibility—her fashionable life, her literary prominence, her role as patron and philanthropist, and the entanglement of her published work with the national identity—may make her gender ambiguous, as Mary Morgan's comments on her surprising femininity also imply. Montagu herself commented that "it is the misfortune of women who are reputed to be learned to have the fools of both sexes, and the witlings of both sexes for their enemies, and they must be upon their guard against ridicule." [12]

The difficulty of Montagu's position is nicely caught in a letter written to the younger Pitt at the age of eleven by his tutor, Edward Wilson, recommending Montagu and Carter as an essay topic. He urged:

> The similarity of those Ladies Characters in some points, and their dissimilarity in others, would be finely pourtrayed by your pen, and might give you an opportunity of determining the just merits and standard of a literary female: The *One* is an highly instructive accomplished Woman possessed of great affluence, who endulges herself in a chaste display of fashionable as well as literary Elegance, makes her Drawing Room the Lyceum of the day, maintains a luxurious hospitality for the Votaries of that Science which she loves, and patronises the learning which She has herself adorned. The *Other* in a state of Mediocrity is humble as if she knew nothing, While She is not only the most learned Woman of any age but one of the most learned Persons of that in which She lives: The pure sublime Genius which never swerves from Virtue, accompanied her in the paths of rigid Discretion, and is contented to slumber while its favorite Votary is employed in the Daily habitual exercise of domestic Duties. This Colloquy should take place between Justice, accompanied by Vanity, enforcing Reward, and merit attended by modesty, who will scarce suffer an acceptance.[13]

The tutor's outline makes clear how much it was the lives and characters of these women, as well as or even rather than their publications, that were important to their reputations, their perceived cultural significance. He emphasizes Montagu's "great affluence," which at once licenses her social prominence, her lyceum of "luxurious hospitality," and makes it problematic, a self-indulgent if "chaste display." The taste for literature which Montagu is taken to represent is a properly private and feminine affair, an indulgence which contrasts with the sternly masculine nature of Carter's classical studies. It can

---

acted evidently from vanity." Johnson comments on this account of Montagu: "I have seen no beings who do as much good from benevolence, as she does, from whatever motive. If there are such under the earth, or in the clouds, I wish they would come up, or come down" (April 1776, 750).

12. Reginald Blunt, ed., *Mrs. Montagu "Queen of the Blues": Her Letters and Friendships from 1762 to 1800,* 2 vols. (London: Constable, n.d.), 2.220.

13. Ibid., 2.99.

readily be coupled with fashionable elegance as a matter of adornment, an accomplishment. Hannah More comments, on first meeting her in 1775, that Montagu is "not only the finest genius, but the finest lady I ever saw: she lives in the highest style of magnificence." More's account, rather like Morgan's later letters, veers uneasily between a lingering fascination with Montagu's magnificence (in terms reminiscent of *Hello!* magazine) and praise for her incandescent genius: "her apartments and table are in the most splendid taste; but what baubles are these when speaking of a Montagu! . . . her spirits are so active, that they must soon wear out the little frail receptacle that holds them."[14] Anna Laetitia Aikin (later Barbauld) comments more cautiously, in 1778, that Montagu, "not content with being the queen of literature and elegant society, sets up for the queen of fashion and splendour." She feared that Montagu would be "full as much the woman of the world as the philosopher."[15] The opposition between literature and fashion here seems incomplete, for both participate in Montagu's splendor and elegance. But though learning adds substance to fashionable exchange, fashion wears learning as an ornament for display, and Barbauld may imply that both are in need of the supplement of piety and benevolence on which Mary Scott's account places such stress.

The tutor's comments exemplify how current, how familiar the reputations of a select group of learned women had become. Montagu wrote to Carter a few years later: "Unless we could be all put into a popular ballad, set to a favourite old english tune, I do not see how we could become more universally celebrated." She goes on to acknowledge that "we might have lived in an age in which we should never have had ye pleasure of seeing our features, or characters, in Pocket books, Magazines, Museums, literary & monthly reviews, Annual registers &c &c &c."[16] The celebration of learned women such as Montagu and Carter is a distinctive feature of the 1760s and 1770s, I argued in part 1, because it is "set to a favourite old english tune" of national superiority and progress, as Lord Lyttelton's comments on Carter's introduction to Epictetus, and Hester Chapone's laudatory poem, confirm; in the light of this, claims

14. William Roberts, *Memoirs of the Life and Correspondence of Mrs. Hannah More,* 4 vols. (London: R. B. Seeley, 1834), 1.53, letter to "one of her sisters," London, 1775.

15. Lucy Aikin, ed., *The Works of Anna Laetitia Barbauld. With a memoir,* 2 vols. (London: Longman, 1825), 2.19, letter to John Aikin, Palgrave, 19 January 1778. Comments on Montagu's worldliness become more frequent after she begins the construction of her grand house in Portman Square.

16. Leonore Helen Ewert, "Elizabeth Montagu to Elizabeth Carter: Literary Gossip and Critical Opinions from the Pen of the Queen of the Blues" (unpublished Ph.D. dissertation, Claremont Graduate School and University Center, 1968), 146, MO 3435, Sandleford, 24 November [1777]. See Sylvia Harcstark Myers, *The Bluestocking Circle: Women, Friendship, and the Life of the Mind in Eighteenth-Century England* (Oxford: Clarendon Press, 1990), chapter 11, "Bluestockings in Print and on Canvas."

Lyttelton, "the English ladies will appear as much superior to the French in wit and in learning, as the men in arms."[17] More troublingly, it is also the sign, the index, of the extent to which that trajectory of national progress in civilization is pregnant with the seeds of decline, and bound up with notions of corruption. The *Critical Review* commented, on Carter's *Poems* of 1762, that "learning is now grown so fashionable amongst the ladies, that it becomes every gentleman to carry his Latin and Greek with him whenever he ventures into female company. . . . The men *retreat,* and the women *advance.* The men prate and dress; the women read and write: it is no wonder, therefore, that they should get the upper hand of us."[18] The *Review* stops short of suggesting cause and effect here; the point is not that because women advance men retreat, but that their movements are seen to be part of the same double-edged process of civilization and decay.

In Anne Penny's poetic *Invocation to the Genius of Great Britain. Inscribed to Her Grace the Dutchess of Devonshire* (1778), aristocratic women are represented as the militant guardians of the nation's virtue, defenders of the gender differences on which virtue and national character depend. The Duchess of Devonshire was of course the leader of fashion in the 1770s, but Penny alludes to her increasing involvement in Whig politics, and specifically to her leadership of a "female auxiliary corps" of "beauteous Amazons" at Coxheath camp, where regiments were massed to meet the threat of invasion.[19] She writes:

> Say will not you, like guardian-angels, stand,
> The warm defenders of your native land;
> Say will not you, like Rome's immortal Fair,
> To Public-virtue sacrifice your share;
> The idol Fashion from his altars throw,
> And spurn the fripp'ry gaudes of Britain's foe?
> Illustrious train! in titled honours high,
> Th'alluring beacons of each humbler eye,

17. Montagu Pennington, *Memoirs of the Life of Mrs. Elizabeth Carter, with a new edition of her Poems, Including some which have never appeared before; to which are added some Miscellaneous Essays in prose, together with her Notes on the Bible, and Answers to Objections concerning the Christian Religion,* 2d ed. (London: F. C. and J. Rivington, 1808), 2.213.

18. *Critical Review* 13 (1762), quoted in Vivien Jones, ed., *Women in the Eighteenth Century: Constructions of Femininity* (London: Routledge, 1990), 175.

19. Amanda Foreman, *Georgiana, Duchess of Devonshire* (London: HarperCollins, 1998), 65. *Morning Post,* Saturday, 18 July 1788, quoted in Foreman, *Georgiana,* 65. For a fuller discussion of women's involvement in the camp at Coxheath, see Robert W. Jones, "Notes on The Camp: Women, Effeminacy and the Military in Late Eighteenth-Century Literature," *Textual Practice* 11, no. 3 (winter 1997): 463–76.

Lead the bright van, begin the noble race!
Such acts of glory will your lineage grace.[20]

"Freedom's sons," Penny argues, can best be saved from "their boasted Ton," their feminized thrall to the "idol Fashion," by the combined stimulations of war and the example of great ladies who "in public as in private virtues shine." The virtues of these women largely take the form of benevolence, which Penny represents as the "envied pow'r, the bleeding heart to heal, / And guard, with Godlike care, the gen'ral weal," as a godlike but tender capacity akin to that attributed to Montagu in Mary Scott's account. But in Penny's *Invocation* this is resolutely public, martial in its opposition to "Those treach'rous trifles that unman our hearts," and softened, feminized, only in its role as what "smoothes the unsocial pomp of state."[21] The example of these women will, Penny claims, restore manly national character to men, and make women better mothers. But the women are able to bring about this reconsolidation of gender difference as a result of the blurring or inversion of gendered roles which is implicit in the appropriation to aristocratic women of the masculine language of whiggish patriotism.

Penny's *Invocation* argues directly that public virtue has become the prerogative and the duty of women, but it is exclusively women of the most exalted social station—the rather improbable alliance of Queen Charlotte, the Duchess of Devonshire, and Lady Granby (about to become, in 1779, the Duchess of Rutland)—she perceives in this close relation to the "genius of Britain." As Amanda Foreman details, in her recent biography, both the Duchess and the Marchioness of Granby were publicly involved in encouraging patriotic responses to the perceived threat of the alliance between the French and the rebellious Americans in 1778;[22] and in the years following the publication of Penny's *Invocation* the Duchess did become closely and sometimes scandalously involved in the public life of high politics. She exposed her "charms for the good of the public,"[23] as Barbauld remarked with some

20. The poem was first published separately in 1778, but was reprinted without revision in [Anne Penny], *Poems* (London: J. Dodsley, 1780), 172–73, from which I quote. "Rome's immortal Fair" is Cornelia, the mother of the Gracchi, who is frequently cited as a model for whiggish women's patriotism. See Wendy Wassyng Roworth, "Anatomy is Destiny: Regarding the Body in the Art of Angelica Kauffman," in *Femininity and Masculinity in Eighteenth-Century Art and Culture,* ed. Gill Perry and Michael Rossington (Manchester: Manchester University Press, 1994), 41–62.

21. Invocation, in *Poems,* 173, 174, 175, 174.

22. Foreman notes that "The Marchioness of Granby bought a half share in a sixteen-gun ship and had it renamed after her." *Georgiana,* 65.

23. Aikin, *Works of Barbauld,* 2.26, letter to John Aikin, Palgrave, May 1784. Barbauld writes: "What do you think of the behaviour of our great ladies on the present election? I thought the

astonishment, in canvassing actively and in what Montagu perceived as "a most masculine manner" in support of Fox's election campaign of 1784.[24] Frances Boscawen wrote to Hester Pitt, resorting to French apparently to veil the indecencies she relates:

> You wou'd be shock'd . . . were You to hear the indignities of the Dss of Devonshire [who] exposes herself every day in her Canvass for Mr Fox. Tout le language des Halles, toutes les propositions les plus Scabreuse does she hear with Ears, what she sees with Eyes cannot be told, I am assur'd. What a Shame! She is in this street they tell me every day tampering with an inflexible Oilman, and this has been her sole employ from 9 in ye Morning till Night. She gets out of her Carriage, Walks into Alleys and many feathers replace tails in her Hat, Many black guards in her Suite.[25]

Fox's election procession, in 1784, carried a banner "Sacred to Female Patriotism," which was perhaps the fruition of Penny's hopes, but the Duchess's public exposure also served to confirm the scandal attached to public women, the horrors of the inversion of gendered roles. The numerous satirical prints of the Duchess out canvassing include many which play directly on the association between women's political involvement and sexual scandal, and which represent the public role of the Duchess as a clear sign, and perhaps even a cause, of national degeneracy—a theme which is explicit in, for example, a print of 1784 that bears the inscription: *A Certain Dutchess kissing Old Swelter-in-Grease the Butcher for his Vote O! Times! O! Manners! The Women wear Breeches and the Men Petticoats* (fig. 3).[26] Earlier prints depicting the Duchess's involvement at Coxheath camp suggested that her participation in military life encouraged effeminacy rather than manliness, and promoted the uncertainty of gender definition that her prominent role was perceived to introduce in public life (fig. 4).

I want to emphasize the disparity between the perceived public status of aristocratic women such as the Duchess and that of Montagu the wealthy

---

newspapers had exaggerated: but Mr.—says he himself saw the two Lady—'s and Miss—'s go into a low alehouse to canvass, where they staid half an hour; and then, when the mob at their heels offered them a thousand indignities, proceeded to another. These he mentioned as unmarried ladies, and therefore less privileged. The Duchess of [Devonshire], Mrs.—, and many others, equally expose their charms for the good of the public" (25–26).

24. Blunt, *Montagu,* 2.169.

25. Vere Birdwood, ed., *So Dearly Loved, So Much Admired: Letters to Hester Pitt, Lady Chatham from her relations and friends 1744–1801* (London: HMSO, 1994), 161, letter from Frances Evelyn-Glanville, Hon. Mrs. Edward Boscawen, Audley Street, 12 April 1784.

26. See John Brewer, *The Common People and Politics 1750–1790s,* The English Satirical Print 1600–1832, no. 87 (Cambridge: Chadwyck-Healey, 1986), BMC 6533, and the Introduction, 36–38. For a much fuller account see Foreman, *Georgiana,* part 2, chapter 9, "The Westminster Election: 1784."

Figure 3 R. Lyford, *A Certain Dutchess kissing Old Swelter-in-Grease the Butcher for his Vote,* 1784, engraving, $10\frac{7}{8} \times 7\frac{3}{4}$ in. (pl.). BM 6533. © The British Museum.

mine-owner. Penny's poetical address to Montagu, which I discussed in the conclusion to chapter 3, does not attribute to her the kind of publicity that seems appropriate to the peeresses of her later *Invocation.* The representation of Montagu as a national monument most nearly resembles Penny's account of the peeresses when her benevolent use of her great wealth is discussed—

Figure 4 James Gillray, *The Recruiting Cuckold. A Song,* 1780, engraving, $5\frac{3}{4} \times 7\frac{3}{4}$ in. BM 5779. © The British Museum.

when she displays, in other words, the attributes appropriate to a more traditional idea of the virtues of female worthies. The distance between accounts of Montagu and the peerage is indicated by the very different nature of the vices their virtues are imagined to conceal. Where peeresses seem liable to the sexually abandoned vices of public women, Montagu is criticized for faults in her private personality: for vanity, the failing to which the display of exemplary

Christian worth is most obviously susceptible, and the vice which most obviously undermines the smooth conjunction of polite and fashionable elegance with learning. A yet greater distance, however, clearly separates the different kinds and degrees of public fame available to these women from the celebration of Elizabeth Carter's scholarship.

The relation between representations of Montagu and Carter may resemble, instead, the relation between the ladies of Millenium Hall and the people they save from the fairground. When Montagu, apparently with some trepidation, had asked Carter for her friendship, Carter replied: "I have no painful excellence, alas, to give you any particular apprehension about me! And I shall owe great part of your affection to the generosity of your own heart. It is certainly one of the best natured . . . arts of a great mind, to give consequence to insignificant things."[27] Friendship with Montagu underlines the social insignificance and modesty of the scholar. Carter represents herself here as though she were the diminutive body that set off the "great mind" of Montagu who, according to Hannah More, "has no body."[28] The ladies of Millenium Hall explain to Ellison that they provide asylum because they are firmly convinced of "how much . . . those poor wretches suffer, whose deformity would lead them to wish to be secluded from human view, in being exposed to the public, whose observations are no better than expressions of scorn, and who are surprized to find that any thing less than themselves can speak, or appear like intelligent beings" (*MH,* 72). Carter occasionally expresses something reminiscent of the modest shame the ladies enjoin on their pensioners; she sees herself as monsterized by publicity, protected only by the abstruse privacy of her researches and by her relationships with women more powerful and more public than herself.

Carter's fame, and her responses to it, take place in the contrasting discursive context indicated by Pitt's tutor. For he rehearses a familiar theme in emphasizing her piety, discretion, and domesticity. Catherine Talbot remarked that Carter had "never raised a pye," but Johnson's well-known comment on her culinary and classical accomplishments catches the flavor of her reputation.[29] Carter noted that a "young man of large fortune" had refused to

27. *Carter to Montagu,* 1.32, letter viii, Bristol, 31 March 1759. Pennington's transcriptions do not always seem reliable. A more probable reading here might be "acts of a great mind."

28. Roberts, *Memoirs of More,* 1.53, letter to "one of her sisters," London, 1775. More writes of Montagu that "Her form (for she has no body) is delicate even to fragility; her countenance the most animated in the world."

29. Johnson "respected her domestic qualifications, and though he considered that a man is in general better pleased when he has a good dinner on his table than when his wife talks Greek, he said, 'My old friend, Mrs. Carter, can make a pudding as well as translate Epictetus, and work a handkerchief as

subscribe to her *Epictetus,* claiming that "he would have done it, if the book had been some treatise of oeconomy for the use of the ladies," and her comment pursues the domestic analogy: "Is not this a most notable youth? And might not one be sure, by applying to him, of getting the best receipt extant for making modern dumpling; for I believe he has much too good a taste to have been perverted at Oxford by the soups and sauces of the ancients."[30] The humor is wry, for the exceptional scholarliness of Carter's work was made homely and familiar by the analogy between cooking and learning, inelegant domesticity and philosophical genius. Her extraordinary learning was perceived somehow to resemble plain English cooking and simple housewifery.

My discussion will be based in large part on Carter's letters of the period between about 1750 and the mid-1770s, the years in which she was actively engaged in writing poetry, essays, and translations for publication, and I will first briefly consider the status of her correspondence. After her death, Carter's nephew and executor, Montagu Pennington, published more than six volumes of her correspondence, made up principally of letters to Talbot, Montagu, and Elizabeth Vesey. His decision to publish them caused him a certain amount of uneasy wriggling around, most obviously because in the *Memoirs* he had written of her life, which drew quite extensively on her correspondence, he had stated unequivocally that Carter "expressed a wish to her executor, that her letters should not be published."[31] He assuaged his conscience with the reflection that she appeared to have prepared some of the letters for publication.[32] Catherine Talbot wrote to Carter arguing that she should at least allow her letters to be circulated, because they would give pleasure and improvement to their

well as compose a poem.'" In Alice C. C. Gaussen, *A Woman of Wit and Wisdom: A Memoir of Elizabeth Carter One of the "Bas Bleu" Society (1717–1806)* (London: Smith, Elder, 1906), 165.

30. Pennington, *Memoirs of Carter,* 1.211. The analogy between writing and cooking is not of course exclusive to Carter, though it is, I suggest, unusually dominant in her case. Hester Thrale Piozzi called the commonplace book she began to compile in 1796 "Minced Meat for Pyes."

31. Ibid., 1.20. Pennington did not edit the letters to the standards of modern scholarship, but unfortunately the manuscripts do not survive. I give the dates he attributed to them, but these should be treated with caution, as they can quite often be shown to be wrong, either because the letters refer to specific historical events, or because surviving manuscripts of her friends' correspondence give different dates. Ewert comments that her study of Montagu's letters has also revealed that "Pennington frequently splices together parts of [Carter's] letters written ten or more years apart, and presents them as a single epistle under a very specific date. On other occasions Mrs. Carter's answer to a query predates the question" (Ewert, "Montagu to Carter," Introduction, lxii). Pennington published six volumes which were avowedly collections of correspondence, and included many letters in the *Memoirs.*

32. See Montagu Pennington, ed., *A Series of Letters between Mrs. Elizabeth Carter and Miss Catherine Talbot, from the year 1741 to 1770. To which are added, Letters from Mrs. Carter to Mrs. Vesey, between the years 1763 and 1787; published from the original manuscripts,* 3d ed., 3 vols. (London: F. C. and J. Rivington, 1819), vol. 1, Preface, iv. Hereafter the first two volumes of this edition will be referred to as *Carter and Talbot,* and the third volume as *Carter to Vesey.*

readers, and add to the credit of their author. Talbot concluded (referring to having shared portions of earlier letters): "To eat a whole fine peach one's self, is a greediness I never had any idea of, and I seriously looked on this as no more than helping my friends to a slice of the best I had."[33] Carter responded that while the argument about the peach was plausible, "that is no reason why one may not very allowably devour a whole turnip, if it was as big as one's head."[34] Writing about her admiration for the letters of Ann Pitt, however, Carter comments that "these are the only instances in which she discovers a close incommunicative disposition; for she will not allow me ever to show them to any mortal."[35] Letters function in this circle much as they do in, for example, *Sir Charles Grandison,* where they are selectively used as part of a social currency, enhancing the worth of those who send and those who receive them. Talbot notes, with revealing irony, that Carter's "Letters make me vastly important. . . . As for Mrs. Montagu's, it . . . heightened my importance beyond imagination."[36] They are, perhaps, not a public feast, but appetizers for limited social circulation. So Hannah More comments on her first introduction to the society of "a certain Mrs. Montagu's, a name not totally obscure," that, among the assembled luminaries, "I do not like one of them better than Mrs. Boscawen; she is at once polite, learned, judicious, and humble . . . her letters are not thought inferior to Mrs. Montagu's."[37] Letters circulated in selected extracts and through gossip are the basis for reputation, and whet polite culture's taste for learned women. They grant wide but oblique access to lives whose modest privacy they also serve to confirm.

Carter's published letters are intimate in the sense that they are distinctly flavored by the nature of her relationships with different correspondents—distinctions that may be indicated by the contrast between Montagu's conviction that "at 13 you was exactly Clarissa Harlowe,"[38] and Talbot's recognition that the "lively sallies" of Anna Howe "that we were highly pleased with, did certainly make us all think of you."[39] Pennington also edited some of Montagu's letters, which Barbauld thought were structured like essays (and would have been superior to Johnson's had they been published as such),[40] and in contrast

33. *Carter and Talbot,* 2.284, Lambeth, 30 October 1763.

34. *Carter and Talbot,* 2.285, Deal, 15 October 1763.

35. *Carter to Montagu,* 2.128, letter cxli, Deal, 14 November 1771.

36. *Carter and Talbot,* 2.267, Lambeth, 11 August 1763.

37. Roberts, *Memoirs of More,* 1.52, 53, to "one of her sisters," London, 1775.

38. Ewert, "Montagu to Carter," 81–82, MO 3188, [Denton], 4 November [1766].

39. *Carter and Talbot,* 1.203, Cuddesden, 28 December 1747.

40. See Aikin, *Works of Barbauld,* 2.109–10, letter to Mrs. J. Taylor, 18 June 1810. Montagu's unpublished letters, in contrast, are much more informal and sentimental. I am grateful to Felicity Nussbaum for sharing with me her more detailed knowledge of Montagu's manuscripts on this point.

to these Carter's letters seem more flexible and fluid. She writes to Talbot: "I have strangely rambled from raree-shows to kings, queens, and a serious discourse upon politics and history. To be sure you must think I mean to talk to you and ask you questions about every thing that is or ever was, and when I have gone through this world, to tell you my own, and then enquire your opinion concerning apparitions."[41] This discursive vagary clearly owes something to the supposed informality of the genre, but the more formal structure of Montagu's published letters may indicate that this fluidity is also an effect of Carter's social position, her class and learning. When she traveled to Europe in 1763 with Montagu's entourage, Carter reflected frequently on the freedoms and inconveniences of her own position as one of the "little folks" among the quality. She observes that she does "not find much to engage my attention" at the "public assemblies" of the spa, and comments that the European nations "have such frequent intercourse with each other, have so much resemblance in their manners, that there is very little to gratify the curiosity of a Speculatist."[42] It is what the tutor called her "Mediocrity," her middle-rank obscurity, that licenses the ranging "curiosity of a Speculatist." But what makes that strange, what makes it so interesting, is that she is not only a speculatist but a philosopher, an observer who exploits the extreme and gendered domestic privacy of her position to assume an inversion of those characteristics, a view of extraordinary scope and authority. The fact that by 1817 the bulk of Carter's published work consists of private letters is appropriate to their importance in her life, and, I suggest, to her reputation as a speculative philosopher.

There are several rather different though closely interrelated narratives or strands of argument that I want to draw out from Carter's work: how she represents her experience of fame and national importance, and how she conceives of her own social prominence in relation to her obscure mediocrity, for instance. I explore the ways in which she and her friends represented her as though she were a professional scholar, and I consider the extent to which her identity as a writer might have been supported or made possible by her piety. In a later chapter, I return briefly to a consideration of her concept of the nation and the profound national feeling she perceived as the fruition of private and social virtue. In discussing each of these issues, I am concerned to unpack the ways in which this retiring woman's extraordinary career eroded and made permeable distinctions between public and private life.

41. *Carter and Talbot,* 1.123, Deal, 30 May 1746.

42. Pennington, *Memoirs of Carter,* 1.280, letter to one of "Mrs. Carter's different relations," Spa, 2 July 1763 (and see 1.259n on the addressee).

5

The Independence of the Learned Lady

I

In 1748, Elizabeth Carter read a satirical pamphlet which argued that in this *annus mirabilis* gendered identities had been reversed.[1] Reflecting on it, she considered "what profession I mean to take up . . . and can find but one I am fit for, which is, trudging over hill and dale, from county to county, in quality of a raree-show man."[2] Carter wrote of "my affection for raree-shows in general," including in that affection apparently both the "bawling historian" who accompanied the show and the pageant of heroic actions from the nation's past that it represented.[3] The notion of her as a raree-show man is appealing, because it suggests the pleasure she took in scenes of national glory, and even in her own celebration as a sign of national progress, and because of the ways in which it is more ambivalently appropriate. Carter's frequently remarked

1. The pamphlet was *Mil Sept Cent Quarante Huit, ou L'Annee Merveilleuse. Seconde Edition. A Paris* [i.e., London] *Imprime L'Annee 1748* (1748). Its publication in London and the quality of the French in which it is composed suggest that it was the work of an English author, see *English Short Title Catalogue* (ESTC). Carter and her friends clearly found it mildly amusing.

2. Montagu Pennington, ed., *A Series of Letters between Mrs. Elizabeth Carter and Miss Catherine Talbot, from the year 1741 to 1770. To which are added, Letters from Mrs. Carter to Mrs. Vesey, between the years 1763 and 1787; published from the original manuscripts,* 3d ed., 3 vols. (London: F. C. and J. Rivington, 1819), 1.240, London, 5 August 1748. The first two volumes of this work are hereafter cited as *Carter and Talbot;* the third is cited as *Carter to Vesey.*

3. *Carter and Talbot,* 1.122, Deal, 30 May 1746.

modesty and personal diffidence, her politeness and the self-effacement involved in her role as a translator, a presenter of works not her own, are at odds with the image of the "bawling historian," but her attitude toward fame is also pragmatic, a matter of social duty and financial need overriding the embarrassment of self-display.

In letters of the late 1760s and early 1770s, Carter reflects on her reputation. She writes to Montagu that "possessors of riches, learning, or greatness" should recognize that these are "external advantages," or "artificial distinctions," and acknowledge that "they cannot always subsist on mere representation." She believes that the vicissitudes of life will frequently "strip" the mind "to the natural feelings of unsophisticated humanity," which is a "forlorn and helpless state," in need of "the consoling tenderness of personal attachments."[4] Writing to Elizabeth Vesey, she contrasts "me, Elizabeth Carter, stript to the naked heart," with her friend's attachment to the idea of her as a scholar, which she represents as proving "your attachment not to *people* but to *things,* for what is all this but mere drapery and ornament!" She argues that if Vesey will esteem her "naked heart," then "I will not quarrel with you for any interior [inferior?] degree of value which you may set on the mere external trappings, with which your imagination will find a pleasure in decorating me."[5] These sentimental views are based in Carter's belief that free will, exercised in the context of the peculiar providence that shapes the lives of individuals, is the basis of "all virtue, all happiness," or social pleasure, and "all personal identity."[6] "I am willing to allow indeed," Carter argues, that genius "is not stuck on the outside of the head like a *pompone;* yet on the other hand . . . it is no object of choice, nor constitutes any part of moral character."[7] Genius, and apparently scholarship—despite the importance to her reputation of the claim that Carter's was the result of industry and not natural quickness—are not elective qualities, and are therefore extrinsic to the personal identity of the Anglican. Hester Piozzi reported Carter's conviction that "my religion is my freehold estate, and

4. Montagu Pennington, ed., *Letters from Mrs. Elizabeth Carter to Mrs. Montagu, between the years 1755 and 1800. Chiefly upon literary and moral subjects,* 3 vols. (London: Rivington, 1817), 2.49–50, letter cxxi, Deal, 12 October 1769. This work hereafter cited as *Carter to Montagu.*

5. *Carter to Vesey,* 3.169, letter lxiii, Deal, 10 October 1771. The suggested emendation is my own.

6. Montagu Pennington, *Memoirs of the Life of Mrs. Elizabeth Carter, with a new edition of her Poems, Including some which have never appeared before; to which are added some Miscellaneous Essays in prose, together with her Notes on the Bible, and Answers to Objections concerning the Christian Religion,* 2d ed. (London: F. C. and J. Rivington, 1808), 2.378, "Letters from Mrs. Carter on the same subject" (i.e., "Answers to objections against the New Testament"), letter ii, To Mrs.—.

7. *Carter to Vesey,* 3.77, letter xxvii, Deal, 13 October 1766.

whoever tries to shake my title to it is an enemy."[8] Carter's identity was as securely founded in this "freehold estate" as that of any civic humanist public man in his hereditary property.

The interest of Carter's remarks about the adventitious nature of learning is that it is for her directly analogous to riches or greatness as the basis for social representation; it is decoration, "drapery and ornament." For until her retirement from publishing, and from social visibility, in the mid-1770s, Carter perceived the duties attached to the possession of learning to be as clearly defined as those attached to the use of riches or rank—as those Montagu was thought to fulfill in so exemplary or ostentatious a manner. Carter's career divides quite neatly into two halves. After the mid-1770s, her nephew notes that she "could hardly be considered in the light of a professed literary character,"[9] and there is a marked change in her letters after that period. Where earlier she wrote of publication as a moral duty for herself and her friends, after the mid-seventies she increasingly advocates a kind of quietism. She writes to Montagu in what becomes a characteristic manner: "The situation which renders one unfit for active duties, yet leaves power and opportunities enough for the exercise of the more quiet and silent virtues; and till one has arrived at proficiency in these. . . . It would be insolent to complain of not being appointed to act in a character which would require higher exertions." These reflections on the "incapacity of being important and useful in society," she concludes, are "necessary to render *me* easy and cheerful, under the sense of my absolute insignificance." In this letter she attributes this change to the state of her health, as a result of which "all the faculties of the understanding are blunted, and every spring of action is relaxed."[10] After the death of Catherine Talbot in 1770—a bereavement Carter felt deeply—she seems to become semi-invalided, but she does continue to pursue a rigorous course of study (and of correspondence), and her decision to stop publishing may also have to do with the fact that by this time there was no longer any strong financial incentive for her to publish.

Carter's attitude to publishing in the decades preceding the mid-1770s is marked by the distinction she presses for, in those letters to Montagu and Vesey, between the duties attached to "external" learning and the feelings of the "internal" self, "stript to the naked heart." On the one hand she expresses modesty and even reluctance about publishing her work, describing it as a

8. Oswald G. Knapp, ed., *The Intimate Letters of Hester Piozzi and Penelope Pennington 1788–1821* (London: John Lane, 1914), 279, letter from Piozzi to Pennington, Bath, 29 October 1819.

9. Pennington, *Memoirs of Carter,* 1.440.

10. *Carter to Montagu,* 2.289, letter clxxvii, Deal, 25 November 1774.

prospect which fills her with "a very painful degree of confusion,"[11] and on the other she evidently takes pleasure in its favorable reception, and in her increasing fame. Carter's naked heart may have fluttered—as Chapone puts it, "when you go to the press, I know you will be in twitters"[12]—but she clearly also regarded publishing her translation as a socially useful act. Carter believed that Epictetus advocated "the morality of the Gospel without its encouragements and supports,"[13] and Talbot endorsed her views, urging that the translation "will be of more use and entertainment than most books I have read." Talbot concluded that it would "do honour to Epictetus, yourself, your country, and womankind."[14] The terms in which Carter's Introduction advantageously compares Epictetus's stoicism to Epicurean philosophy are characteristic of the translation. She writes:

> The Stoical Excess was more useful to the Public, as it often produced great and noble Efforts towards that Perfection, to which it was supposed possible for human Nature to arrive. Yet, at the same time, by flattering Man with false and presumptuous Ideas of his own Power and Excellence, it tempted even the Best to Pride: a Vice not only dreadfully mischievous in human Society, but, perhaps of all others, the most insuperable Bar to real inward Improvement.[15]

The ascending scale of benefits is typical of Carter's writing. Stoicism is valuable because it is useful to the public, but the importance of the idea of the public is displaced, set to one side, when the much more ambiguous notion of "human Society" is brought into play, a notion that is allied with but distinct from the "real inward Improvement" that is the hallmark and goal of her piety. Her translation repeatedly emphasizes how greatly Epictetus was disadvantaged by the lack of Christian, civilized enlightenment, the lack of a sense of the social virtues, but she believes that despite this his life has an exemplary value, which "must contribute a good deal to preserve luxurious States from an absolute universal Dissoluteness."[16] Her reflections on the example set by

11. *Carter and Talbot,* 2.222, Deal, 26 September 1761.

12. *The Posthumous works of Mrs. Chapone. Containing Her Correspondence with Mr. Richardson; A Series of Letters to Mrs. Elizabeth Carter, and Some Fugitive Pieces, never before published. Together with an account of her life and character, drawn up by her own family,* 2 vols. (London: J. Murray, 1807), 1.94, letter xxvi, to Carter, 11 November 1755.

13. Pennington, *Memoirs of Carter,* 1.189, letter to Talbot, Deal, July 1755.

14. Ibid., 1.187, letter to Carter, 1755.

15. "Introduction," in *All the Works of Epictetus, which are now extant; consisting of his Discourses, preserved by Arrian, In Four Books, The Enchiridion, and Fragments. Translated from the original Greek, By Elizabeth Carter. With An Introduction, and Notes, by the Translator* (London: A. Millar, 1758), ii.

16. Ibid., xxvi.

Epictetus are clearly addressed as much to modern as to ancient society. She writes for example that "persons of distinguished Talents and Opportunities seem to have been raised, from time to time, by Providence, to check the Torrent of Corruption, and to preserve the Sense of moral Obligations on the Minds of the Multitude, to whom the various Occupations of Life left little Leisure to form Deductions of their own" [17]—a remark which clearly implies a direct application to the perceived effects of occupational specialization in later eighteenth-century England. The work of Epictetus, and the morality of Carter, which the translation of that work gave her the opportunity to display, might, through their example, contribute to preserve from dissoluteness the luxurious state of modern society.

It is significant that in Talbot's itemization of the reasons for publishing Epictetus, doing honor to womankind should apparently be the conclusive achievement, for gender is an important constituent of Carter's attitude toward publishing and fame. Her nephew observes that she had an "extreme partiality for writers of her own sex," and he notes that when, for example, she discovered that Joanna Baillie's *Plays on the Passions* (1798) were the work of a young and obscure woman, "she felt a triumph, which those who know her partiality to those of her own sex will easily believe." [18] Pennington is, as other critics have pointed out, a fairly unreliable editor and memorialist, and his comments on this issue probably reveal rather more about his cautious, post-revolutionary brand of conservatism than they do about Carter's opinions. He identifies her views on this issue as a "prejudice," which he believed "prevented [her] from cultivating the society of men of letters in general so much as might have been expected." [19] He argues rather obscurely that

> She was much inclined to believe, that women had not their proper station in society, and that their mental powers were not rated sufficiently high. Though she detested the principles displayed in Mrs. Woolstonecraft's [*sic*] wild theory concerning the "Rights of Women," and never wished them to interfere with the privileges and occupations of the other sex, yet she thought that men exercised too arbitrary a power over them, and considered them as too inferior to themselves. Hence she had a decided bias in favour of female writers, and always read their works with a mind prepared to be pleased. . . . [20]

17. Ibid., xxvii.

18. Pennington, *Memoirs of Carter,* 1.443. Chapone writes to Carter, referring to her self-esteem: "you carry your partiality to your own sex farther than I do. Indeed you have the strongest reason to think highly of it, and have the best right of any woman in the world to expect others to do so too." Chapone, *Works,* 1.64, letter xiv, 11 October 1752.

19. Pennington, *Memoirs of Carter,* 1.447.

20. Ibid., 1.447–48.

It may be that by the 1790s Carter did take the ambiguous position Pennington outlines. Certainly her views seem closer to those of Hannah More than of Mary Wollstonecraft. Carter's letters of between about 1750 and 1775, however, speak of a life devoted to the virtues of private life, but to an expansive notion of an arena of privacy that embraces the social. Publication may seem to Carter in these decades to be embarrassing, a matter of overcoming confusion and diffidence, but she clearly also perceives it as a kind of duty, and a source of largely pleasurable reputation and money. Publication is achieved, or gone through with, at the expense of personal modesty, but it clearly is an activity in which she thinks women should be involved. It is difficult to piece together, from Carter's surviving writings, what she thought women's "proper station in society" was. The question is bound up in her faith and her patriotism, and I will discuss it further later in this chapter. But the comments of Carter and her correspondents suggest that it involved rather more interference "with the privileges and occupations of the other sex" than her nephew was prepared to countenance. I have argued that the unstable definition of differences of social station and gender in the mid- to late century meant that what was perceived as proper to one sex or the other was more open to dispute than Pennington, in retrospect, could concede, and this instability could allow or endorse the degree of interference Carter and her friends thought appropriate. The "proper station" that Carter did imagine for women who might be neither aristocratic nor enormously wealthy, and the station her reputation led others to imagine as proper to her, needs to be understood, I think, in the context of her commitment to a notion of private life that is finely stratified, and most obviously differentiated by the relation between quite extreme personal self-effacement and the obligation to publish exemplary work.

Carter inhabits a thoroughly private space, in her own eyes as well as in her reputation. It is, of course, predictable that in contrast to Montagu, or even Vesey, she should represent herself as obscure and insignificant, but in her correspondence with Talbot she also chooses to emphasize that she is merely provincial, almost desocialized. Carter spent at least five months of every year in London, enjoying the delights of polite and elegant society. She did not live in a hole in the ground. But it is important to her self-conception that she should sometimes represent herself as though she did. She writes about a fan that Talbot had given her, that "in the vanity of my heart, I had a great mind the fan should be seen," so she displayed it on the table for her aunt to view: "She seemed quite astonished I should have such a creditable thing belonging to me, for she knows I would sooner fan myself with a cabbage-leaf than lay out any sum of money, in ornaments, that would buy a book."[21] Carter slides herself into public view with oblique gestures of self-display.

Other learned ladies of these decades play with ease and pleasure on the image of the slatternly bookish woman. Montagu describes herself as clean for a lady philosopher,[22] and Chapone writes of meeting Carter's sister that

> I saw her . . . exult over me in her housewifely capacity;—when I folded up the gingerbread nuts so awkwardly, I saw it was nuts to her; but I forgive her, and hope she will repent before she dies of all her uncharitable insults on a poor gentlewoman, that never was guilty of more than four poor odes, and yet is as careless, as awkward, and as untidy as if she had made as many heroic poems as the great and majestatic [*sic*] Blackmore![23]

Chapone's remark involves in its humor an intriguing play between, on the one hand, the notion of the domestic inadequacy of the scholarly woman, defeminized by contrast with the notable housewife, and on the other, the politeness of ornamental learning, as opposed to the rustic vulgarity of domestic concerns. But in Carter learning produces a kind of infirmity, an eccentric strangeness. Hannah More wrote on first meeting her that she "has in her person a great deal of what the gentlemen mean when they say such a one is a 'poetical lady.'"[24] In the curious ratings chart that Hester Thrale drew up of the women of her acquaintance, a chart which clearly indicates her own social anxieties, Carter scored a mere two points for "Person Mien & Manner," or "general Appearance," in contrast to the eighteen points awarded to Montagu, and, it should perhaps be mentioned, the *nil points* accorded to both Chapone and More.[25] Carter herself writes about her social awkwardness as though it

21. *Carter and Talbot,* 1.230–31, London, 13 July 1748.

22. Reginald Blunt, ed., *Mrs. Montagu "Queen of the Blues": Her Letters and Friendships from 1762 to 1800,* 2 vols. (London: Constable, n.d.), 1.100. For further comments on scholarship and personal hygiene, see Sylvia Harcstark Myers, *The Bluestocking Circle: Women, Friendship, and the Life of the Mind in Eighteenth-Century England* (Oxford: Clarendon Press, 1990), 41–42.

23. Chapone, *Works,* 1.55, letter xii, to Carter, Canterbury, Wednesday [1751].

24. William Roberts, *Memoirs of the Life and Correspondence of Mrs. Hannah More,* 4 vols. (London: R. B. Seeley, 1834), 1.53, to "one of her sisters," London, 1775.

25. Katharine C. Balderston, ed., *Thraliana: The Diary of Mrs. Hester Lynch Thrale (Later Mrs. Piozzi) 1776–1809,* 2 vols. (Oxford: Clarendon Press, 1942), 1.330–31, July 1778. Thrale's table is based on the system of classification described in Joseph Spence's *Crito, or a Dialogue on Beauty* (1752), and awards marks out of a possible maximum of twenty. So, for example, Montagu scored twenty points for conversation, but, despite her low score for "general Appearance," the pool is scooped by Hannah More, awarded twenty points each for "Worth of Heart," "Useful Knowledge," and "Ornamental Knowledge." On Spence, see Robert W. Jones, *Gender and the Formation of Taste in Eighteenth-Century Britain: The Analysis of Beauty* (Cambridge: Cambridge University Press, 1998), 85–96; and Michael B.

were an infirmity, noting that even when she feels a duty to speak, "I much question whether the strongest arguments in the world could help me to make a graceful curtsey, or enter a room with a becoming air."[26] But this kind of personal reluctance, personal infirmity, needs to be distinguished from the sense in which Carter cherishes the moral supremacy of private life, nursing the conviction that "there is, indeed, no other refuge from the horrors of history, but in the mild majesty of private life."[27]

I will look at the relation between Carter's sense of personal infirmity and her private social role as a scholar through two anecdotes. In the assembly rooms at Canterbury, Carter met "a very sensible and agreeable woman . . . much more deeply learned than beseems a fine lady," who addressed her "with more civility than I had any title to, and with much more than fine ladies usually show to such awkward-looking folks as me." The fine lady, probably Catherine Sawbridge Macaulay, engaged her in philosophical discussion, and Carter comments that "to be sure I should have been mighty cautious of holding any such conversation in such a place with a professed philosopher or a scholar, but as it was with a fine fashionable well-dressed lady, whose train was longer than any body's train, I had no manner of scruple."[28] The incident pursues themes which persist in Carter's correspondence throughout the decades I am concerned with. In relation to each of her correspondents, Carter positions herself as private and obscure in contrast to their fashionable pleasures, public importance, or social ease. Her physical awkwardness, in these contrasts, figures her obscurity—class position and provincial status—and the ambiva-

---

Prince, "The Eighteenth-Century Beauty Contest," in Marshall Brown, ed., *Eighteenth-Century Literary History: An MLQ Reader* (Durham, N.C.: Duke University Press, 1999), 204–34.

26. *Carter and Talbot,* 1.378, Deal, 23 June 1752.

27. Ibid., 1.359, Deal, 2 November 1751. Carter quotes from Akenside's *Pleasures of Imagination,* where the poet asks:

> . . . is aught so fair
> As virtuous friendship? as the candid blush
> Of him who strives with fortune to be just?
> The graceful tear that streams for other's woes?
> Or the mild majesty of private life,
> Where peace with ever-blooming olive crowns
> The gate; where honour's liberal hands effuse
> Unenvy'd treasures, and the snowy wings
> Of innocence and love protect the scene?
> (Mark Akenside, *The Pleasures of Imagination. A Poem*
> [London: R. Dodsley, 1754], Bk. 1, ll. 503–11)

28. *Carter and Talbot,* 2.121–22, Deal, 27 August 1757. See Bridget Hill, *The Republican Virago: The Life and Times of Catharine Macaulay, Historian* (Oxford: Clarendon Press, 1992), 11.

lence of her attitude toward her gender and sexuality. I only want to touch on this issue, but Carter's refusal to consider marriage is an important constituent of the kind of privacy she inhabits. She wrote: "I was never tempted by any voluntary connexion, to engage myself in the interests, passions, and tumults of the world. If I have suffered from the troubles of others, who have more sense, more understanding, and more virtues, than I might reasonably have expected to find, what might I not have suffered from a husband."[29] It is intriguing that connexion with the world here is immediately about marriage, and the curtailment of freedom she believes that would involve.[30] Classing herself with the "awkward-looking folks" involves a retreat from the visibility of her gender into the obscurity of her class and determinedly single status. But conversing with Macaulay creates the possibility of transgressing the limitations of her gender and class in a different direction. Because Macaulay is so fine, so fashionable, they can talk about philosophy without scruple or caution.

In relation to other "fine ladies," as I have said, Carter clearly found it distressing to be valued for what she perceived to be her extrinsic genius. Hearing that Ann Pitt admired rather than loved her, she commented to Montagu that

> she might *admire* me if I were a vocal statue, or a walking tripod; but no such queer curiosity am I, I walk upon two feet like other folks, and there is not one inch of marble in my whole composition. Surely then, it is very hard that Mrs. Pitt should think of sticking me up in a cabinet, like a mere object of *vertu,* to be *admired,* and perish with cold, when I am so much better entitled to be placed in some obscure snug corner by a warm fire-side. I should be quite undone, if you had considered me in the same view of *admiration,* and placed me among your vases, and your Chinese dolls; but you affirmed that you *loved* me, and I felt beyond all comparison more happy in that declaration, than if the most honorable station had been assigned me, by way of curiosity, that could have been found in the British Museum.[31]

In these circles Carter wants to be on terms of sentimental affection, of a kind of equality moderated only by the obscurity of the corner appropriate to her greater privacy. She thinks of her scholarship as having made her into a spectacle, an exotic curiosity that might be displayed in the Museum as a token of

29. *Carter and Talbot,* 1.334, Deal, 21 May 1751.

30. Carter's position was very unusual. On the social positions more usually available to unmarried women, see Amy M. Froide, "Marital Status as a Category of Difference: Singlewomen and Widows in Early Modern England," in *Singlewomen in the European Past, 1250–1800,* ed. Judith M. Bennett and Amy M. Froide (Philadelphia: University of Pennsylvania Press, 1999), 236–69.

31. *Carter to Montagu,* 1.67–68, letter xv, Deal, 26 October 1759.

Britain's cultural prosperity and imperial expansion. But she found some pleasure and amusement in being perceived by less exclusive social circles as a conjurer, a cunning woman, a witch.[32] In 1764, Montagu took Carter to Winchester Cathedral, and later wrote to Lyttelton about the trip:

> We . . . delighted ourselves with many brittish antiquities, and I believe amazed the Clerk with our learning, as we read all, and criticized most of the inscriptions. As he did not know our names, we were very ostentatious of our knowledge, and flatterd ourselves he would tell the Master of Winchester school that he had shewn the Church to two great female schollards. We gave him several anecdotes of his Saxon Kings with which he may edify the next persons to whom he shews the Cathedral, and I dare say he will not omit to do so, as he seemd to look upon us with great reverence.[33]

There are plenty of incidents in Carter's letters which suggest that she did enjoy making a spectacle of her learning. In this incident, the pleasure of the women is also about anonymity, but an anonymity which casts into high relief the conjunction of gender, class, and learning they can display. Rather like the encounter with Macaulay, this is about the propriety of displaying learning not as a personal attribute, but as a gendered achievement, an attribute appropriate to polite English women.

Carter's attitude to her fame seems both quite simple and very complicated. In a sense, her fame is less problematic than that of Montagu. She writes to her friend, reassuring her that "I am just as sensible of present fame as you can be. Your Virgils and your Horaces may talk what they will of posterity, but I think it is much better to be celebrated by the men, women, and children, among whom one is actually living and looking."[34] At the same time, her character as a learned woman seems to give her a publicity that is at odds with the obscurity of her class position, the singularity of her views on marriage, and the way she represents her social awkwardness as a kind of deformity. Publicity seems to make her a freakish curiosity. If Carter's chosen profession is that of the raree-show man, it seems difficult to determine whether it is her extrinsic learning which makes a display of her reluctant and socially infirm personality, or her awkwardness which licenses and unveils her learning. The analogies of Millenium Hall are perhaps more suggestive, for in the incident I mentioned earlier the ladies and those they shelter seemed to be viewed as a kind of composite though heterogeneous unit, a unit that implies that paternalistic

32. See Pennington, *Memoirs of Carter,* 1.245–48.

33. Blunt, *Montagu,* 1.109.

34. *Carter to Montagu,* 3.47, letter ccvi, Deal, 23 November 1777.

benevolence and learning can be admired as feminine and virtuous if they are furtive, concealed, but the admiring gaze which recognizes them as objects worthy of display must also acknowledge that publicity makes them monstrous.[35] Carter could achieve national importance, and a kind of representative status as the woman who indicated the cultural progress of the nation, because she did not in any of the senses available to great ladies claim public status. Instead she inhabited a private sphere, differentiated and stratified with subtle complexity, which allowed her to be "living and looking," rambling "from raree-shows to . . . politics and history"—a private sphere within which her secure possession of the freehold estate of her religion gave her social and national significance.

II

In 1778, Ann Thicknesse published her *Sketches of the Lives and Writings of the Ladies of France. Addressed to Mrs. Elizabeth Carter.*[36] The dedicatory letter that prefaces the book gives two different reasons for the choice of Carter. In the first place, Thicknesse argues that she would not wish her account of "the literary talents of women of another nation" to suggest that she is "unacquainted with the superior excellence of the first writer in our own." And second, she claims to have had "such a number of Princesses, Countesses, and high Titles, to turn over, that it becomes a kind of relief to my pen . . . in speaking of a woman, who, instead of a high title, possesses an elevated genius, a good heart, and an exalted mind."[37] The example of Carter allows Thicknesse to claim that though France has produced the greater quantity of literary ladies, England at least affords better quality; and this "superior excellence" is associated with Carter's middle-rank obscurity, and with what Thicknesse carefully classifies as "your private virtues, and public character," as distinct from "your personal accomplishments."[38] By the late 1770s, as I have already

35. The itemization of the expenses of Millenium Hall includes the following reference to the asylum: "The maintenance of the monsters an hundred and twenty" (Sarah Scott, *A Description of Millenium Hall,* ed. Gary Kelly [Peterborough, Ontario: Broadview Press, 1995], 247). The term "monster" may refer, as Kelly's note suggests, to "congenital malformation" (247 n. 1), or it may refer more directly to the people's employment as spectacles.

36. Carter comments: "Have you seen Mrs. Thicknesse's book? I have just looked into it, enough to see your name . . . in a very private party, consisting of Mrs. Burbault and your humble servant." *Carter to Montagu,* 2.249, Deal, 28 June 1774 [1778].

37. Ann Thicknesse, *Sketches of the Lives and Writings of the Ladies of France. Addressed to Mrs. Elizabeth Carter,* 2 vols. (London: W. Brown, 1778), Dedication "To Mrs. Elizabeth Carter," 1.iv–v.

38. Thicknesse, *Sketches,* Dedication, 1.iii.

mentioned, Carter had retreated from public view, and when Thicknesse produced an expanded three-volume edition of her *Sketches* in 1780–81 she omitted the dedication to Carter; but the dedication of 1778 suggests that then she could still be celebrated as the representative of private virtues which are somehow peculiar to England. Carter is not, however, usually perceived as a national symbol of the kind that Elizabeth Montagu came to exemplify: she does not figure the ambiguous polish of fashionable and learned elegance, the refinement that commercial prosperity and civilized progress engender. The learning Carter represents has more in common with that of Hume's "totally barbarous" philosophers, "shut up in colleges and cells, and secluded from the world." Her image may be softened by conversation, as Ann Pitt implied in recounting her first meeting with Carter: she wrote that Carter was "good-humoured and unaffected . . . though she happens to be one of the greatest scholars and one of the greatest geniuses in England"[39]—as though scholarly genius were expected to be barbarous, and incapable of good humor. But her reputation is most thoroughly feminized by the prominence of her domestic skills. The *Sketch of the Character* of Carter, published after her death in 1806, for example, takes the "perfect propriety and skill" with which she performed "every domestic employment" to be "proof that knowledge does not necessarily set the female character at variance with its peculiar duties."[40]

I have argued, however, that as politeness and elegance increasingly come to be considered as desirable aspirations for British and in particular metropolitan society in the second half of the eighteenth century, domestic skills become more difficult to praise. Montagu writes to Lyttelton in 1770: "I am so entangled in small cases and petty attentions here, that I believe I shall be fit for nothing but to keep a Haberdashers Shop for the rest of my life. I am perfectly that odious thing call'd a notable Woman."[41] Montagu writes from Denton, where her husband owned a colliery (which she was to inherit after his death), and here she uses the image of the housewife to confirm the feminine propriety of her involvement in that business. But then she remembers that the housewife signifies absorption in petty and material cares, and

39. *Letters to and from Henrietta, Countess of Suffolk, and her second husband, the Hon. George Berkeley; from 1712 to 1767. With Historical, Biographical, and Explanatory Notes,* 2 vols. (London: J. Murray, 1824), 2.245, Mrs Anne Pitt to Lady Suffolk, Clifton, 22 June [1758] (date attributed by the editor).

40. *Sketch of the Character of Mrs Elizabeth Carter, who died in London, on February the 19th, 1806, in the eighty-ninth year of her age* (Kelso: A. Ballantyne, 1806), 14. This appears to be Miss Sharpe's "well-written character" of Carter; see *Memoirs of Carter,* 1.457–58 and n. Myers attributes it to Sharpe in *Bluestocking Circle,* 330. Sharpe's comments can also of course be taken to indicate the revalorization of feminine domestic skills after 1800.

41. Blunt, *Montagu,* 1.240.

is therefore "odious," inappropriate to her social prominence and learning. Carter writes about her own "good housewifery" with self-deprecating irony, explaining to Talbot at some length that she has perfected "a special good sweet cake" only because her earlier disastrous efforts had made the "children all set up their little throats against Greek and Latin."[42] Carter's domestic skills consolidate the sense in which her scholarship marks her out as impolite, unladylike. Learning is a desirable addition to the elegant accomplishments of Montagu, and an admirable if apparently more eccentric supplement to the finery of the young Macaulay; even Carter can exploit its fashionable status in their company. But it is interesting that when she relates that encounter with the "fashionable well-dressed" Macaulay she contrasts her willingness to dispute with her with the wariness that would have been necessary in "holding any such conversation in such a place with a professed philosopher or a scholar"; for in her case I think learning is more nearly professional.

Carter and her correspondents maintain, over many years, a kind of running joke about her semiprofessional status, along the lines suggested by that paper in the *World* for July 3, 1755, which imagined a modest female scholar resembling Carter becoming the warden of an Oxbridge college.[43] Talbot commented in 1760 that "supposing a university of ladies, where could they find a fitter representative" than Carter?[44] Carter herself writes in 1763, humorously disparaging her claim to "preferment": a mere professorship is no "dangerous temptation" to her, "for as I never heard that any professor or professoress had any claim to the ornament of a blue ribbon, mere musty manuscripts, sine blue ribbon, have no attractions for me."[45] In 1773, the question of Carter's professional status is raised by an article in the *Westminster Magazine,* and Montagu writes to inform Carter:

> How do you do Brother Doctor? You seem not to answer readily to ye salutation; in all that is good, you chuse ye thing without ye affiche, but pray consider your

42. *Carter and Talbot,* 1.181–82, Deal, 15 September 1747. Carter may not have accepted the demands of domesticity as easily as her reputation would suggest. She writes: "'Tis a most vexatious thing to be perplexed for want of time, and find one-self always in an uproar of business. Besides all my other important engagements, I have been working my eyes out in making shirts for my brother; I want mightily to reform the world in this particular, and therefore, am resolved when I come into your neighbourhood, and am blessed with a family of boys, they shall all learn to make their own shirts." *Carter and Talbot,* 1.157, Canterbury, 25 January 1747.

43. [Mulso], *The World,* no. 131; see above pp. 40–41.

44. *Carter and Talbot,* 2.192, Lambeth, 17 September 1760. Talbot is responding to the discovery that a proposal for a "national charity" that has been sent to herself and Carter has also been circulated to the universities.

45. *Carter to Montagu,* 1.199, letter liv, Deal, 29 September 1763. Carter refers to the blue ribbon of the order of the garter.

> Partner in trade, ye Learning is all yours, let a little of ye airy title breathe on me, then we shall each have our portion. If you do not understand why I addressd you thus, you must be inform'd, that a Writer in one of ye Magazines, says ye honour of a Doctors degree had been more properly conferred on Mrs Eliz Carter & Mrs Montagu, than on a Parcel of Lords, Knights, & Squires, who are unletterd, to Mrs Macaulay Mrs Aikin & some others he wd bestow a Masters of Arts degree. I ought (perhaps) to have been ashamed to have been *named in a day* with Mrs Carter, but I will confess, I am always delighted with this enormous flattery. . . . you do not know how great [an] honour it is to me. . . .[46]

In response, Carter acknowledges that the company she is placed in flatters her, but adds that "I felt very little elevated by my appointment to the cap and gown," and explains: "I have infinite ambition in my views both for you and myself, which soars beyond all sublunary honors, and looks forward to the 'prize of that high calling,' which leads our hopes to the starry wreaths of immortality. May heaven unite us in this supreme attainment!"[47]

Sylvia Harcstark Myers claims, in her valuable study of *The Bluestocking Circle,* that "Montagu, Carter, and Chapone were all reluctant to seem to be writing for financial gain." She argues that none of these three would have wished to be perceived as "needy and dependent."[48] But for Carter, I think, the implications of a kind of professional identity were more attractive than Myers allows.The lightheartedness of the correspondence between Carter and Montagu licenses the perception of Carter as professionally learned, honored by recognition of her accomplishments, but also involved in the trade of learning, the barbaric seclusion or antisocial specialism of academia. In 1782 Carter and Montagu reflect on marriage. The widowed Montagu writes of the pleasures of independence for women like themselves, who "can think for ourselves, & also act for ourselves," and concludes with the observation, on husbands as masters, "I do not see how they can be necessary to a Woman unless she were to defend her Lands & Tenements by sword or gun."[49] In this and the subsequent letter Montagu suggests that the marital independence she advocates for herself and Carter is directly connected to their status as learned ladies:

46. Leonore Helen Ewert, "Elizabeth Montagu to Elizabeth Carter: Literary Gossip and Critical Opinions from the Pen of the Queen of the Blues" (unpublished Ph.D. dissertation, Claremont Graduate School and University Center, 1968), 122–23, MO 3317, [Sandleford], 6 August 1773. Emendation is Ewert's. For a fuller account of the essay which appeared in the *Westminster Magazine,* July 1773, see Myers, *Bluestocking Circle,* 271–72.

47. *Carter to Montagu,* 2.210, letter clxi, 14 August 1773.

48. Myers, *Bluestocking Circle,* 155.

49. Ewert, "Montagu to Carter," 168, MO 3530, Sandleford, 11 July 1782.

> You my dear Friend have much outdone my vulgar performances: you have purchased an estate on Parnassus which yr Heirs cannot sell or mortgage, & you have built yourself a noble apartment in ye Temple of Fame which is not liable to ye injuries of the elements. While you understand ye Greek language better than all ye Professors in our Universities, & write your own with greater elegance than any of our Litterati or Beaux esprits, you have not any reason to regret your celibacy, nor do I feel any distress or deficiency in my widowed state. . . .

Montagu goes on to assert more positively that she and Carter have a duty to remain single, pointing out that

> It wd be a great joy to some of our Sex if we were to be guilty of matrimony. The demi reps wd say, see what happens to ye Prudes! ye ignorant of both sexes see what befalls les femmes savantes. If we did not mind disgracing ourselves we ought not to bring disgrace on discretion & learning, they will remain when we are no more.[50]

Because Carter and Montagu are single—unmarried or widowed—they enjoy legal independence, and a degree of agency most married women could not exercise. In this context, Montagu represents Carter as though she aspired to gentlemanly independence of fortune, as though her learning were the "freehold estate" in which her identity is based. Carter's devotion to scholarship is perceived to give her the kind of claim to independence that is, in these decades, becoming more typical of the liberal professions.[51]

Carter discussed the theme of independence through learning in the short poem she addressed to her father, and published in her *Poems on Several Occasions* of 1762. Like many of the short pieces included in the collection, the poem to her father has an almost lapidary quality; it displays a degree of technical accomplishment, a smoothness of surface, that creates an air of simplicity. It explores the relation between piety, learning, and paternal authority, suggesting that what the three require or nurture in her is a difficult combination of freedom and obedience. She expresses her gratitude for her father's "Fondness, and paternal Care," explaining that

> Whate'er the tuneful Muse, or pensive Sage
> To Fancy warbled, or to Reason show'd,
> The treasur'd Stores of each enlighten'd Age
> My studious Search to thy Direction ow'd.

50. Ibid., 169, MO 3531, Sandleford, 23 [July] 1782. See also Montagu's comments on Catharine Macaulay's second marriage of 1778, in John Rylands Library, Eng. MS 551, no. 29.

51. See John Barrell, "Visualising the Division of Labour: William Pyne's Microcosm," in *The Birth of Pandora and the Division of Labour* (London: Macmillan, 1992), 89–118, and Froide, "Marital Status."

The movement of the stanza is characteristic of the poem: the poet does not deny her own labor—learning was a "studious Search." But that search was eased by the willingness of the classic texts to warble or show their treasures, and directed by her father—which might of course involve anything from pointing her in the right general direction to detailed instruction and supervision. That theme develops in the following stanzas:

> Ne'er did thy Voice assume a Master's Pow'r,
> Nor force Assent to what thy Precepts taught;
> But bid my independent Spirit soar,
> In all the Freedom of unfetter'd Thought.
>
> Nor e'er by blind Constraint and servile Awe,
> Compell'd to act a cold external Part:
> But fixt my Duties by that sacred Law,
> That rules the secret Movements of the Heart.
>
> Blest Law of Liberty! with gentle Lead
> To regulate our erring Nature giv'n,
> And vindicate, from slavish human Dread,
> The unreserv'd Obedience due to Heav'n.

Carter explains earlier that her father's "Hand my infant Mind to Science form'd," and here the command implied in those notions of his forming and directing power is picked up again in the claim that his voice "bid" her spirit soar, and "fixt my Duties." But those suggestions of paternal government are counterbalanced by the emphasis on her independence and "Freedom of unfetter'd Thought." That doubled movement culminates in the address to the "Law of Liberty," which produces a sort of oxymoronic inversion that reveals that servility is found not in the "unreserv'd Obedience" of piety, but in the "slavish human Dread" which fears its duty.[52]

The poem's emphasis on the combination of law and liberty, individual agency and obedience, characterizes much of Carter's writing, but what is particularly interesting about it in the context of this discussion of Carter's approximation to professional status is the way it suggests that her attitude to her scholarship is all of a piece with her religion and upbringing. These endow her with a moral direction which recognizes liberty and independence as the reward of industry. In the opening lines of the poem, she addresses her father: "THOU by whose Fondness and paternal Care / Distinguish'd Blessings glad my chearful Days." She might refer here to her peculiar happiness in living

52. "To—," ll. 1, 13–16, 17–28, 5, in Elizabeth Carter, *Poems on Several Occasions* (London: John Rivington, 1762), 62–63.

next to her father—that use of "by" is typically adroit—but by the time these poems were published, the distinctive blessings of her life were more obviously the fruits of her scholarship (which indeed gave her the financial means to set up house with her father). In the final lines of the poem, she concludes that if she continues to follow the "sacred Law" of liberty, "Then ev'ry generous Care, thy Youth apply'd, / Shall form the Comfort of declining Age." The lines conflate the "declining Age" of the poet and her father: if she is the daughter he taught her to be, then his old age will reap the rewards of his early care in her solicitude, and in her own old age she will take comfort from what he taught her—she will be morally and financially independent.[53] The moral language of the poem is equally appropriate to the pious virtue and the earning power of the good Protestant, and both make independence a central term of value.

The difference between Carter's and her correspondents' attitudes to professionalism has not only to do with the notion that she is more learned than they are. It may also have to do with her class status and financial position, for Carter had a greater interest in making a trade of her learning than did other women of her circle. Montagu, of course, did not need to take any interest in the financial profits of her work, and was reported to have "given away the profits of the Essay [on Shakespeare] to a widow in distress."[54] Talbot was reluctant to circulate, let alone publish her work, and refused the dedication of Carter's Epictetus because of "the impropriety and absurdity of placing so insignificant a name in so public a point of view." She explained that the publicity would give her "inexpressible pain."[55] Chapone supplies a closer parallel to Carter, since after her husband's death in 1761 she "had some pecuniary embarrassments to encounter," and was obliged to live in lodgings between what appear to have been extended visits to her friends.[56] Despite her straitened circumstances, Chapone claimed that she published because "it appeases in some measure, that uneasy sense of helplessness and insignificancy in society, which has often depressed and afflicted me."[57] But what appeases her is a sense of fulfilling her moral and religious duty as a woman, and not the notion of earning her living, or fulfilling the role that the division of labor might have made available to her if it were not based in the exclusion of women's work. When the bookseller was preparing a second edition of her enormously successful

53. Ibid., ll. 1–2, 29, 31–32.

54. *Carter to Montagu,* 2.191, letter clvii, Deal, 5 June 1773. Montagu denied this report. See Myers, *Bluestocking Circle,* 155.

55. Pennington, *Memoirs of Carter,* 1.206, letter from Talbot to Carter, St. Paul's Deanery, 8 January 1757.

56. Chapone, *Works,* 1.143.

57. Ibid., 1.171, letter lvii, to Carter, 15 June 1777.

Letters on the Improvement of the Mind (1773), Chapone wrote to Carter complaining that

> My friends all fret and scold at me for having sold my copy, and grudge poor Walter his profits. But for my part I do not repent what I have done, as I am persuaded the book would not have prospered so well in my hands as in his. Though I love money reasonably well, yet I fear I have still more vanity than avarice, and I am therefore very happy in the approbation the letters meet with, though my pockets are not the heavier.[58]

Chapone did not see financial gain as a reason for women to publish, preferring to wrestle with her conscience over the precise degree of permissible vanity.

Carter, in contrast, writes to Montagu, with, I suspect, frankness thinly veiled by irony, that "whatever you may think about it, nobody loves money better than I do, both for my friends and myself";[59] for though by the 1770s she could describe her situation as "quite easy,"[60] she never lived in the kind of style to which her friends were accustomed, and always appreciated the financial rewards of publishing. The posthumous *Sketch* of her character observes that she "was extremely attached to her little habitation at Deal. It is probable this attachment was strengthened by its being a purchase made by herself, with the money produced by her translation of Epictetus."[61] She bought the house, which Montagu liked to refer to as her vinegar bottle, with the sum of around £1,000 which she received in subscriptions for the translation, and her father paid her rent for the set of rooms he occupied.[62] After the death of Talbot, in 1770, her papers were left in Carter's hands, and were "printed on her own account, Mrs. Talbot (Catherine Talbot's mother) having nothing to do either with the first expence, or subsequent profits, which eventually were not inconsiderable."[63] She also received annuities from William Pulteney (after the death of Lord Bath in 1767), and from Elizabeth Montagu (after the death of her husband in 1775), and over the years she inherited some money from members of her own family, but the income she received from publishing

58. Ibid., 1.163, letter liii, Farnham Castle, 20 July 1773. Chapone's *Letters* were first printed in 1773 for the bookseller J. Walter, to whom she appears to have sold the book outright.

59. *Carter to Montagu,* 2.104, letter cxxxiv, Deal, 2 July 1771.

60. Ibid., 2.199, letter clviii, Deal, 12 June 1773.

61. [?Sharpe], *Sketch,* 12–13.

62. Carter seems to have been embarrassed as well as pleased by the success of the subscription, and wished to have the copies sent out bound in order to "frustrate the intention" of her friends—Pennington, *Memoirs of Carter,* 1.211. Montagu referred to the house as Carter's vinegar bottle in allusion to the classic fairy story. See Montagu's letter to Carter in 1781, in Blunt, *Montagu,* 2.112.

63. Pennington, *Memoirs of Carter,* 1.413.

was significant, and allowed her to achieve financial independence from her father without accepting what she considered the "voluntary dependence" of marriage.[64]

Carter's understanding of her own role as a kind of professional may be reflected in her decision to produce the translation of Epictetus rather than to build on her reputation as a poet. For translations from the classics have a rather mixed status in these decades. As the reception of her work indicated, the elucidation of difficult classical texts was perceived to involve a degree of learning and judgment that would distinguish male as well as as female scholars. This translation is seen as work of a quite different order from her translation from the French of Crousaz's *Examination of Mr. Pope's Essay on Man* (translation published 1738), or from the Italian of Algarotti's *Sir Isaac Newton's Philosophy Explained* (translation published 1739). Pennington observes that though these early translations helped to establish Carter's reputation, she "never willingly spoke of either . . . and seemed to wish that they should be wholly forgotten."[65] Chapone, however, offered the following comments on Carter's work on Epictetus:

> I hope and believe that you will gain all the honour that a translation can claim. But as that is much less than your genius is capable of acquiring in other ways, I heartily wish this may be the last you will ever be employed in. I do grudge you to such a task! You ought to be an original writer, and let your works be translated by those who can only help the world to words, but not to new ideas or new knowledge. . . . I rejoice that you are likely soon to rid your hands of this laborious work, which has so much engrossed your time, and confined your fancy. I know I speak peevishly about it, for it has always vexed me.[66]

To some extent, I think, Chapone has simply failed to grasp the implications of Carter's translation of a work central to the most exclusively masculinist and Shaftesburian forms of civic humanism, as Chapone may herself acknowledge when she writes of how the publication has "thrown the learned world into the utmost astonishment."[67] Catherine Talbot's remarks on reading a translation of Pliny's letters provide a useful contrast to Chapone's comments. Talbot writes:

> a faithful and elegant translator is a character of the highest virtue in the literary republic. It implies public spirit the most void of ostentation; a kind regard for the illiterate; a love of our native country, shown by enriching its language with

64. *Carter and Talbot,* 1.281, Deal, 28 April 1750. For a more detailed account of Carter's financial circumstances, see Myers, *Bluestocking Circle,* 170–71.

65. Pennington, *Memoirs of Carter,* 1.47.

66. Chapone, *Works,* 1.93–94, letter xxvi, 11 November 1755.

67. Ibid., 1.106, letter xxxii, [1758/59].

> valuable books; a just regard for merit of whatever country, by placing the merit of some valuable foreigners in the truest and fairest light; a care, a judgement, and exactness that original writings do not require, and some degree of humility in scarce aspiring to the name of an author!

Talbot sees skillful translators as "heroes and heroines"[68] of self-effacing virtue. But Chapone may also have a point in emphasizing the laboriousness of translation, the sense that it displays learned judgment and industry rather than the more feminine qualities of fancy or sensibility. The work of translation appropriates to the female scholar both gentlemanly "public spirit" in a form which can be aligned with feminine modesty because it is "void of ostentation," and, in its academic professionalism, a form of the "privileges and occupations of the other sex."[69]

Carter welcomed publishing as a trade or profession appropriate to women much more explicitly than did her correspondents. She is, for example, pleased to hear praise of Mary Collyer's translation of Gessner's *The Death of Abel* in 1761, because "writing for the support of her family is a laudable employment,"[70] and hopes that Charlotte Smith's *Emmeline* (1788) will be "fashionable enough to be of . . . essential benefit to the author" financially.[71] This is not simply a matter of hard-luck stories providing sentimental justification for conduct that would otherwise be shameful; it is a feminine appropriation of literary culture. Despite her disagreement with republican or democratic principles, Carter is still expressing cautious but surprisingly positive pleasure in the publications of Charlotte Smith and Helen Maria Williams in mid-1792,[72] and she defended the "judgement and spirit" of Macaulay's history to Montagu, who thought the historian's politics made her work unreadable.[73] Beyond the largely middle-class domain of the literary republic, Carter expressed concern about the exclusion of women from employment, which she believed had "very serious ill effects on society." She argued that "if the strength which lies dormant at the trifling occupations of the thimble and the loom was exerted to subdue the stubborn soil, our country would not be disgraced by such tracts

68. *Carter and Talbot,* 1.158–59, Cuddesden, 9 February 1747. Pennington's note attributes the translation of Pliny to Melmoth.

69. Pennington, *Memoirs of Carter,* 1.448.

70. *Carter to Montagu,* 1.152, letter xxxviii, Deal, 21 December 1761. Carter also expresses her approval of Collyer's secular novel, *Felicia to Charlotte. Being letters from a young lady in the country, to her friend in town* (1744), in *Carter to Montagu,* 1.151. See Myers, *Bluestocking Circle,* 149–50.

71. *Carter to Montagu,* 3.295, letter cclxviii, Deal, 30 June 1788.

72. See *Carter to Montagu,* 3.333, letter cclxxx, Deal, 22 July 1792.

73. Ibid., 2.310, letter clxxxi, Deal, 3 June 1775.

of uncultivated land, and the poor women might be rescued from want and absolute idleness by finding employment proportioned to their strength."[74]

Montagu's notions of the "proper station" of women made her reluctant to take full advantage of her legal independence as a widow; she told Vesey in 1777 that she wished to pay for her grand new house out of income in deference to "a matter of punctilio," explaining that "writing Eliz. Montagu to bond or Mortgage wd appear to me a masculine action, rather like swearing such an oath as Ventre blue, or odsbodikins; no real harm, but merely an indecorum."[75] Carter in contrast celebrates the financial independence and legal, property-owning agency that is proper to the station of women, at least within the limited sphere of the "literary republic," and perhaps beyond. That does involve an appropriation of the "privileges and occupations of the other sex," even though the persistent analogy with domestic work may veil this appropriation in the implication that these occupations are not fully recognized by the language of the division of labor.

Carter's position, then, is complex. I have tried to show how we might understand her status in relation to Montagu's wealth and social visibility, and in contrast to the more directly public status of aristocratic women. Carter's social standing, as the daughter of a provincial perpetual curate, is important both to the nature of the fame her reputation gains and to the way she represents her own learning. Her obscurity, I claimed, worked to distinguish her scholarship from the polished world of fashionable learning that Montagu dominated, and that brought Montagu both respect and ridicule as on the one hand a shining spectacle for the civilized progress of the nation, and on the other a figure of vanity whose learning is tainted by the doubtful glitter of fashionable display. Carter in contrast is unaffected—the term crops up again and again in accounts of her—and she figures a kind, even a degree, of privacy that is marked on the one hand as pious simplicity, and on the other as inelegant, unfashionable awkwardness. Carter's worth, as a national symbol, is bound up in that persistent analogy between her scholarship and her imputed culinary skills. Domesticity works to place her learning in the frame of something old-fashioned, almost quaint—something that indicates an idea of femininity that has a kind of nostalgic value in its opposition to fashionable gloss, but that is also, and because of that opposition, almost unfeminine, too much like an occupation in its absorption in specialized detail. That frame might license the

74. Ibid., 2.58–59, letter cxxiii, Deal, 1 December 1769.

75. Blunt, *Montagu,* 2.18. Montagu seems to mean that claiming agency as a legal person who can bear responsibility for debt would be indecorous.

sense in which her learning is perceived as almost professional, uncivilized in its isolated absorption. Her learning is exceptional, idiosyncratic, because it bears the double weight of representing both a barbaric and masculine academicism, and a triumph of civilized national progress.

In 1732, an early date in the story of the rise of the learned lady, Catherine Trotter Cockburn asked Queen Caroline to "patronise in her the sex's cause," so that she might "thus the blest occasion prove, / Fair emulation in the sex to move!" If the "female world" used learning to escape the "tyrant sway" of quadrille, she argued,

> Then, as this happy isle already vies
> In arms with foes, in arts with her allies;
> No more excell'd in aught by *Gallia's* coast,
> Our *Albion* too should of her *Daciers* boast.[76]

The persistence of this theme, linking arms with specifically female learning, indicates the extent to which Carter's reputation and character are perceived as necessary to fulfill a profound national aspiration. It is worth thinking about the nature of her career in comparison with that of Elizabeth Elstob (1683–1756), the Anglo-Saxonist and linguist, whose life history is skillfully and sympathetically pieced together in Ada Wallas's *Before the Bluestockings.* Elstob initially lived with her brother, an antiquarian parson, but she was left destitute and "encumbered with debts" after his death in 1715. She ended her life as a nursery governess to the Duchess of Portland, a post she gained through the influence of Mary Delany. Before that she kept a school for "poor children" in Evesham, and wrote to George Ballard of her life that "when my School is done my little ones leave me incapable of either reading, writing or thinking, for their noise is not out of my head till I fall asleep."[77] Ada Wallas's account of Elstob's life does not suggest that the ladies who patronized the scholar regarded her as an equal, or as a companion with whom they could condescend to be on intimate terms. She made neither financial nor social capital of her learning. Carter, in contrast, is like a mascot, a sign of the learned inclinations of others, rather as the short and tall people were the signs of the benevolence of the ladies of Millenium Hall. She comments wryly to Talbot: "The bon ton

76. "A Poem, occasioned by the busts set up in the Queen's Hermitage; designed to be presented with a book in vindication of Mr. Locke, which was to have been inscribed to her Majesty," in *The Works of Mrs. Catharine Cockburn, Theological, Moral, Dramatic, and Poetical. Several of them now first printed. Revised and published, with an account of the life of the author, by Thomas Birch, M.A.F.R.S.,* 2 vols. (London: J. and P. Knapton, 1751), 2.574–75.

77. Ada Wallas, *Before the Bluestockings* (London: Allen and Unwin, 1929), 145, 159–60.

at Paris is *furieusement* to have every thing *a la Grecque.* It must necessarily be the ton in London too, and as no fine gentleman can be happy without a wife a la Grecque, I expect soon to have my choice of the most splendid parties; for though I am not Minerva, I may make my fortune very prettily as her owl."[78] Where Elstob figured the obscurities of antiquarianism, Carter's position at the margins of fashionable society allows her to function as both its ornament and its conscience. She confirms that this is a progressive civilization, capable of celebrating the achievements of learned ladies. But at the same time her oddness underlines the difficulty of reconciling polite femininity with publicly acclaimed scholarship.

78. *Carter and Talbot,* 2.299, Clarges Street, 6 February 1764.

6

The Public Profession of Faith

The nature of Carter's religious faith is central to the question of the kind of combination of publicity and privacy her fame enjoined on her, and to the question of how the particular brand of scholarly femininity she represented acquired such key indexical status. When she died in 1806, she was buried in Grosvenor Chapel, where the inscription on her gravestone recorded that she was "a lady as much distinguished for piety and virtue, as for deep learning, and extensive knowledge." The inscription on the monument erected to her memory at Deal was still more emphatic about the primacy of her character as a Christian: "In deep learning, genius, and extensive knowledge, she was equalled by few; in piety, and the practice of every Christian duty, excelled by none."[1] It was, by this time, more than thirty years since Carter had been active in publishing, and it seems to have become more important to celebrate the extent to which her learning was veiled by her piety than to admire the superiority of her scholarship as a sign of national prowess. Hannah More recommends Carter's example in *Coelebs,* celebrating in her "profound and various learning chastised by true Christian humility. . . . acquirements which would have been distinguished in a university, meekly softened, and beauti-

1. Both inscriptions quoted in Montagu Pennington, *Memoirs of the Life of Mrs. Elizabeth Carter, with a new edition of her Poems, Including some which have never appeared before; to which are added some Miscellaneous Essays in prose, together with her Notes on the Bible, and Answers to Objections concerning the Christian Religion,* 2d ed. (London: F. C. and J. Rivington, 1808), 1.498–99.

Figure 5 Sir Thomas Lawrence, *Elizabeth Carter,* exhibited 1790, pastel, oval, $12\frac{1}{4} \times 10\frac{3}{4}$ in. Reproduced by courtesy of the National Portrait Gallery, London.

fully shaded by the gentle exertion of every domestic virtue, the unaffected exercise of every feminine employment."[2] More's praise implies that learning would have been shameful had it not been "chastised" into a suitably unobtrusive feminine form by pious domesticity. To a reviewer of Montagu's letters (perhaps Walter Scott), writing in 1813, Carter seemed "very learned, very excellent, and very tiresome"; she was "once very celebrated and now almost forgotten" apparently because of the qualities for which she had once been famous.[3] The pastel portrait executed by Thomas Lawrence in 1788–89 (fig. 5) seems to indicate the privacy of her retirement: her face is turned away, her gaze directed modestly downward. That privacy is of course mediated most obviously by the style and signature of the fashionable society portraitist; but

2. Hannah More, *Coelebs,* in *The Miscellaneous Works of Hannah More,* 2 vols. (London: Thomas Tegg, 1840), 2.575. Carter's virtues are paired here with those of Elizabeth Smith, the religious poet.

3. *Quarterly Review,* cited in Reginald Blunt, ed., *Mrs. Montagu "Queen of the Blues": Her Letters and Friendships from 1762 to 1800,* 2 vols. (London: Constable, n.d.), 1.6.

within the terms of the painting itself, only the prominent expanse of her forehead seems to indicate the intellectual vigor that had once distinguished her obscurity.[4] The epitaphs and memorials that appeared after her death may emphasize her piety because this was the dominant characteristic of the last three decades of her life, and because, by the early nineteenth century, it had become the most acceptable aspect of her fame: piety may seem to imply a retired and modest privacy that domesticates her learned reputation. But there is an important sense, in the decades I am most concerned with, that religion is also what makes a kind of publicity available to and even an obligation for women.

Carter's faith was staunchly Anglican. Her early *Remarks on the Athanasian Creed,* published in 1752, establish as their basis that she is "sincerely attached to the Church of *England,*" though she was clearly influenced by "the doctrinal temper of the age, which tended to Deism or Unitarianism."[5] All "unofficial schemes" published by Anglican authors for the revision of the liturgy in the decades following the publication of John Jones's *Free and Candid Disquisitions* in 1749 omit the Athanasian Creed,[6] with its emphasis on the mystery of the Trinity, and Carter's criticisms of the Creed's logic and clarity identify her with these reformers. She argued that biblical accounts of Christ's divinity had "no Sort of Reference to his metaphysical Nature or Essence," but acknowledged rather "the Authority, Dominion and Power with which he was invested by his Father."[7] It seemed to her self-evident that these invested qualities might, in the eyes of believers, exalt Christ "in Majesty *next,* tho' they cannot admit him to be *equal* to his Father." These convictions were based in her insistence that there can be no "necessary Doctrine of Scripture" which cannot be explained "in such Words, or Phrases, or Manners of Expression as are generally well understood,"[8] and place her close to a more distinctively Unitarian position, which argues that the "*trinity in unity*" is, in the dismissive words of Thomas Amory, "spectacle and pleasure";[9] that it is, as *The Progress*

4. By the late 1780s, Lawrence was enjoying the patronage of Carter's London circle, and by 1789, that of the court.

5. [Elizabeth Carter], *Remarks on the Athanasian Creed; on a Sermon, preached at the parish Church of Deal, October 15, 1752; and on a Pamphlet, lately published, with the Title, "Some short and plain Arguments, from the Scripture, evidently proving the Divinity of our Saviour." In a letter to the Rev. Mr. Randolph, Rector of Deal. By a Lady* (London: R. Griffiths, n.d. [1752]), 3. G. J. Cuming, *A History of Anglican Liturgy,* 2d ed. (London: Macmillan, 1982), 135.

6. Cuming, *Liturgy,* 136.

7. [Carter], *Remarks,* 49.

8. Ibid., 48, 47.

9. Thomas Amory, *Memoirs of Several Ladies of Great Britain. Interspersed with Literary Reflexions, and accounts of Antiquities and Curious Things. In Several Letters* (London: J. Noon, 1755), vi.

of the Female Mind (1764) argues, a confused idea which causes the faithful to abandon the attempt to understand and "so [to] fall into idolatry." [10]

My interest in Carter's faith lies not so much in attempting to identify her precise doctrinal position as in trying to understand the centrality of her faith in reconciling her intense privacy with her considerable fame. There is, however, a significant connection between her conviction that "All Men are required to be Believers; But all Men are not required to be Scholars, and Subtle Disputants" [11] and a more distinctively Unitarian distrust of the obfuscations of Anglican doctrine; more specifically, between Carter's views and those of the more recognizably dissenting author of *The Progress of the Female Mind.* The author, identified only as a lady, argues in the earliest of these chronologically arranged essays that because women inhabit a world they can neither control nor understand, they are obliged to turn inward, and to find in religion an idea of direction and progress within which the individual can at least exercise self-control. In the later essay, "Letter to a Christian Divine," she acknowledges that by "common consent" women

> seem given up implicitly to tread the path in which education happens to have introduced them, doomed never to cast a glance beyond it, nor ask whence it derives, or where it leads. Supposed to see no farther than the surface of things, and not to be made for the labours of investigation; the very pretence to it is thought to be a breaking in upon that order of nature which allotts to them a lower sphere of action.[12]

All of this, she claims, "perfectly accords with my own sense of the matter," but she goes on to argue that in the context of the duty of religion this hierarchy must be set aside:

> the differences which seem great among us at present vanish under so extensive a thought; nay, the most grovelling capacity carries an impress of dignity and importance far exceeding that of monarchs and kingdoms, and has as much to do with the universal rule or law of truth as the most soaring genius in the scale of intelligence. I shall therefore take leave to drop such distinctions as reach no farther than this *transitory* scene, because my present enquiries take their meaning

10. *The Progress of The Female Mind, in some interesting enquiries. Containing, I. A Soliloquy, II. A Letter to a Jew, on the Evidences of Revelation. III. A Letter to a Christian Divine on the Gospel System; with some References to a late Free Enquirer. IV. A Remark on the Importance of the Hebrew Language. By a Lady* (London: A. and C. Corbett, 1764), "A Letter to a Christian Divine," 71.

11. [Carter], *Remarks,* 47.

12. *Progress,* "A Letter to a Christian Divine," 31. The editor's introductory address explains that the essays are arranged chronologically in order to illustrate "the progress of the female mind" (2).

> from my being interested in common with the whole race of mankind in a succeeding one which is to endure *for ever.* (32)

Her argument seems to turn on the opposition between gendered and personal identity: she appears to accept that women are perceived to possess "faculties thought equal to little more than domestic science," but to argue that because religion is, as she puts it, "personal," a sphere in which "we are to make *ourselves* moral or religious," the distinctions of the "order of nature," or of "this *transitory* scene," are here set aside (31, 32). So religion might seem to figure (as it may have done in the "Soliloquy" printed earlier in the volume) as nothing more significant than the consolation of the dispossessed, the means of demarcating an internal space in which women could exercise some self-determination. But the argument here is more complicated and perhaps more radical than that account would suggest.

In the opening sentences of the "Letter to a Christian Divine," the author defends her decision to "venture to intrude" on the titular divine's "hours of study or recreation," writing of her letter as "a scribble which will in a peculiar manner provoke you to impatience on account of its being a woman's, unless you allow us a larger scope for mental exertions than we can boast as our privilege by the suffrage of mankind; for it is but too notorious that women are generally regarded as the inferior part of the rational creation" (30–31). The perceived inferiority of women, which the author seems at such ambiguously ironic pains to acknowledge, is based in the notion of their inadequate rationality. But "God has made us rational," and capable of "a bare discernment of moral difference." This discernment is all that is necessary to the choice between "the possibility of *infinite* improvement" in this world as well as the next, and "a character . . . not only defective, but in the highest degree detestable, a burden to itself, a nuisance to society, a rebel to the laws of truth, an opposer to the end of creation, without relish of present, without hope of future existence" (32, 31–32). Her argument clearly implies that were the divine to be impatient with her "scribble" because he did not allow women "a larger scope for mental exertions," he would be denying their rational, moral, and Christian character, aligning himself with the ignorant views of man in general, and consigning women to their fate as detestable nuisances. It implies that the "*equal* concern" of women in the moral and religious "consequences of *rationality*" makes nonsense of the distinctions of "this *transitory* scene" in an immediate sense as well as in the eye of eternity (31, 32). What I find so interesting about this argument is the immediacy of the transition it makes from the personal to the all-inclusive nature of religion—the transition which underpins the claim that women may only think superficially about everything but religion, but if they think profoundly about religion, as their rational and moral nature requires that they should, then they will be unable to think superficially about anything, because nothing is irrelevant to religion.

The Progress of the Female Mind argues that the fundamental rational decision is "to be religious, or not to be religious," and claims that the irreligious person injures both their own happiness and that of society, whereas the religious person is both personally improved, and able to sweep aside or overlook the irrelevant distinctions between people to perceive the common good (32, 31, 32). The author explains that she sees "error, more or less . . . in *every* party and denomination of men," and her view therefore transcends or makes transparent these differences:

> I therefore enlarge my views beyond the boundaries of *party*, and consider every *good* man as aiming at *one* point, travelling in *one* road. It is true, in *various* companies, under colours and sounds as *various:* but these distinctions, though striking to the superficial observer, are *superficial* indeed; a closer view discovers them to have an uniform that is *characteristic*, and will survive every distinction. . . . (75)

In the last essay in the collection, she discusses the need for women to learn Hebrew, in order to understand difficult points in the Bible which are not clarified by "the defects of our translation."[13] Here she argues for the importance of learning for those women "who have leisure to read history, and learn polite languages" on the basis of that model of example and emulation which eighteenth-century culture found so persuasive as an account of class relations.[14] She writes:

> I am sensible these [learned ladies] would be few compared with the numbers, whose sphere in life does not admit of such an education, but was real learning more in fashion among the *rich only* of both sexes, I am apprehensive its influences would extend farther than we are apt to imagine. Opinions as fashions, descend from the higher to the lower ranks of men.
>
> Thus are not the politics of a nation, formed by the court? In religion, by the clergy? The particular sentiments of a family, or circle, perhaps are modelled by a single person in it. Inferiors copy after their superiors, in their mode of *thinking* as well as dress: interest and various attachments operate we know not how far.[15]

13. *Progress*, "Importance of the Hebrew Language," 77.

14. The theoretical model of social emulation, especially as it may be applied to account for the increasing demand for consumer goods, has been criticized by a number of historians, and perhaps most persuasively and influentially by Lorna Weatherill, in her *Consumer Behaviour and Material Culture in Britain, 1660–1760* (London: Routledge, 1988), see esp. 194–96. However, I refer here only to cultural consumption, and to the terms in which eighteenth-century culture, in texts produced by social commentators ranging from Adam Smith to this anonymous lady, conceived of and represented itself.

15. *Progress*, "Hebrew Language," 87.

Learning here gives women the unacknowledged authority of influence, and the analogies she draws with the court and the clergy suggest that she does understand this silent authority to be, as it were, imminently or incipiently public. She goes on to argue that "some few (*and very few they are*) form their own manners; and these as centres of a system direct the motions of all bodies within their influence; so that a small part of mankind do really give the spirit and taste of the world."[16] The use of the Newtonian system as an analogy for cultural hegemony indicates the extent to which this author understands her concern about specific theological questions to be a kind of limitless (though not explicitly political) aggrandizement of the role of middle-class women of liberal education. In the third essay in her *Progress,* the author is still asking the cleric she addresses "if I am herein stretching beyond my proper limits as a *woman?*"[17]—though she has clearly established to her own satisfaction that the "proper limits" religion makes available to her are extensive. By the fourth essay the claim to the basic rational choice to be religious has become a claim to direct "the spirit and taste of the world."

Carter's religion, like that of the author of *The Progress of the Female Mind,* produces a set of values which might seem to make the hierarchies of "this *transitory* scene" redundant, but it does so in rather different terms, which juxtaposition with those letters may help to clarify and which I want now to explore. Carter writes to Montagu in 1772 about her faith:

> It is indeed very possible to live in an exact observance of moral and social duties, so far as respects a popular character, and yet be totally void of real virtue. All external performances derive their true value, with respect to the soul, from the disposition from which they proceed, with regard to the Supreme Being. Wherever his will and his approbation are made the supreme object, all talents, all opportunities, however different in their appearances, become equal possibilities for the acquirement of virtue and of happiness. The most insignificant action, the most unobserved motion of the mind, upon this principle, become great and important, and extend their consequences to eternity; while the most splendid effects, that are produced from merely human or selfish motives, vanish into nothing, and are lost in the chaos of succeeding events.[18]

This is a curious statement, in that it does not appear to be exactly about the private, in the sense that, say, the biographical details of private character might

16. Ibid.

17. *Progress,* "A Letter to a Christian Divine," 77.

18. Montagu Pennington, ed., *Letters from Mrs. Elizabeth Carter to Mrs. Montagu, between the years 1755 and 1800. Chiefly upon literary and moral subjects,* 3 vols. (London: Rivington, 1817), 2.160, letter cl, Deal, 18 August 1772. This work cited hereafter as *Carter to Montagu.*

provide a key to public actions, or even in the sense that Carter is urging when she asks her friends to value the naked heart stripped of the external accomplishments of learning or social position. Private character in the sense that Carter's comments on the value of biography imply is, I think, precisely about "an exact observance of moral and social duties," about the commonplace observation of the age that there can be no public virtue without private morality. And Carter's notion of her naked self is also of a social personality—it is about the domestic intimacy, the warm corner by the fireside, into which she wishes to be enfolded; about the terms on which she wishes to be a member of a circle more metropolitan, more affluent, and more elegant than her domestic situation in Deal could afford her. But this statement is apparently both about intention or motive, about making God's will and approbation "the supreme object," and about the sense in which the disposition of the "most insignificant action, the most unobserved motion of the mind" can be known and evaluated only by God.

Carter's letters to Montagu, advising her on what she should publish, clarify the distinction she makes here between moral or social duty and religious disposition. She writes to Montagu about the success of her essay on Shakespeare:

> I certainly rejoice, upon every account, in the justice which the world does to this fine piece of criticism, and very particularly as an established character will give an additional weight to whatever you produce on a more serious and important subject. There is no doubt great merit in every work that helps to polish the understanding, and give an innocent and improving amusement to the imagination; but it would give me infinite joy, to see such talents as your's [*sic*] more immediately consecrated to the honour and service of Him from whom you received them.[19]

Literary criticism here is a polishing agent, contributing to the progress of polite civilization, whereas the religious work Carter repeatedly urged Montagu to produce is more indirectly social and moral in its aim. Carter suggests that "some improvement" is always effected by the exemplary display of devotion by those "deeply affected by a sense of its importance, and . . . influenced by it in the tenor of their lives"; but the direction of the improvement she is most concerned about is inward: endeavors in religious writing, she suggests, "will certainly be beneficial to yourself, whatever their effect may be, with regard to others; as they will be the discharge of an important duty, and the noblest application of those powers, for which you are so singularly indebted

19. Ibid., 2.20–21, letter cxiv, Tunstal, 26 May 1769.

to heaven."[20] The direction, the purpose, of the sort of publishing Carter urges on her friend is both more private or interior and more public than her essay on Shakespeare could be, for in Carter's view religion is concerned with both what is most personal and what is absolute, permanent, and universal.[21] She writes: "No pleasure can be capable of giving any real delight to the human mind unless it is connected with immortal ideas! I feel this so strongly that I can scarcely enjoy a rose or a sprig of myrtle, till my imagination transplants it to the walks of Paradise, where it will be secure from fading."[22] In the same vein, she argues that knowledge of the Holy Land must be a superstitious distraction from the business of piety, "when it is considered how little connection there is between the starts of a local and temporal devotion, and the constant temper of the spiritual religion of the Gospel."[23] Religion is to her both a duty which improves the most personal self, and a constant temper abstracted from the occasions or accidents of circumstance.

What Carter argues for, in passages such as these, however, is not an idealistic transcendence of the material and contingent world, but a religious sublime that discloses its "real delight." In her letters and poems she frequently writes directly or obliquely of this transfiguration of circumstance as involving a transition from the private and solitary to the transcendent which returns her to quotidian and social life with a renewed sense of its significance in an enlarged figurative sphere. She writes to Montagu, for example, of the pleasure she takes in "sitting on the sea-shore, soothed by the murmurs of the ebbing tide, and the glimmerings of moon-light on the waves," and reflects on whether this situation "would have any effect on . . . an unconnected hermit." She concludes that it would not, because

20. Ibid., 2.166, letter cli, Deal, 21 September 1772.

21. Carter's religion sometimes seems to involve an idealism comparable to that of Mary Astell or John Norris (whose work Astell admired). Samuel Richardson wrote to Carter, about his unauthorized use of her "Ode to Wisdom" in *Clarissa,* explaining that all he had been able to find out about her as an author, apart from her gender, was that she was "conjectured . . . to be a descendant of the famous Mr. Norris, of Bemerton" (Pennington, *Memoirs of Carter,* 1.101–2, 18 December 1747). Talbot writes in a letter dated 30 December 1760, that "I have been reading a treatise on humility written by Mr. Norris . . . which I will keep till you come up, because I think it will strike and please you, as much as it did me." Montagu Pennington, ed., *A Series of Letters between Mrs. Elizabeth Carter and Miss Catherine Talbot, from the year 1741 to 1770. To which are added, Letters from Mrs. Carter to Mrs. Vesey, between the years 1763 and 1787; published from the original manuscripts,* 3d ed., 3 vols. (London: F. C. and J. Rivington, 1819), 2.198, Lambeth. The first two volumes of this work are hereafter cited as *Carter and Talbot;* the third is cited as *Carter to Vesey.*

22. *Carter to Vesey,* 3.226, letter lxxxiii, Clarges-Street, 4 May 1774.

23. *Carter to Montagu,* 2.306, letter clxxxi, Deal, 3 June 1775.

> The pleasures of solitude have almost always a reference to society, and often mean no more than that we retire from the companions whom we do not like, to those whom we do. The views of nature aid us in this ideal commerce, as they then strike us only with universal objects, and general participation, and exclude all the particular and distinguishing circumstances, which separate us from those who so agreeably engage our thoughts.

The movement of this passage is typical of Carter's letters. She begins with a specific situation, which here is pleasurable because it is solitary, but that specificity and solitude lead her to reflect on the universal and the social. Views enjoyed in solitude lose their "local and temporal" characteristics, and "strike us only with universal objects," abstracted quantities of sea or moonlight. In this instance, the darkness works in conjunction with the processes of solitary reflection to obscure distracting detail. The idea of "general participation" in the passage refers to a painterly notion of overall and shared effect. Nothing then reminds the viewer of that sense of place and circumstance—or perhaps even of individual difference—that would otherwise confirm their distance from their preferred companions. This, Carter suggests, is a kind of religious sublime, for she writes that "the sentiments of religion, with which every striking view of nature is always accompanied, inexpressibly heighten the pleasure which we feel from any other subject of our thoughts." But religion returns her to the everyday and social, in this letter to "the inexpressible delight which arises from a consciousness, that our heart is in its best disposition, both with regard to the Supreme Being, and our friends,"[24] but in others more directly to "humbler exercises and employments."[25] This transition from the circumstantial to the theoretical and then, in this instance, to the sociable virtues is, I think, important to an understanding of the implications of Carter's faith.

In a letter of 1762, Carter writes to Montagu of the pleasure she takes in "the true sublime" of a prospect view:

> I rambled till I got to the top of a hill, from whence I surveyed a vast extent of variegated country all round me, and the immense ocean beneath. I enjoyed this magnificent spectacle in all the freedom of absolute solitude. Not a house, or a human creature was within my view, nor a sound to be heard but the voice of the elements, the whistling winds, and rolling tide. I found myself deeply awed, and struck by this situation. The first impression it gave me, was a sense of my own littleness, and I seemed shrinking to nothing in the midst of the stupendous objects by which I was surrounded. But I soon grew more important by the

24. Ibid., 3.35–36, letter cciii, Deal, 25 August 1777.
25. Ibid., 1.168, letter xliii, Deal, 2 July 1762.

> recollection that nothing which my eyes could survey, was of equal dignity with the human mind, at once the theatre and spectator of the wonders of Omnipotence. How vast are the capacities of the soul, and how little and contemptible its aims and pursuits?

Evidently Carter has been reading Burke, but what interests me more is the combination of elevation and abjection, ambition and modesty, that is characteristic of her writing. The view is, as it were, specified by absences: "Not a house, or a human creature . . . nor a sound"; and those seem to confirm the sense that the "freedom of absolute solitude" involves an erasure or annihilation of the self as "I seemed shrinking to nothing." But that shrinking sensation also involves a return to self, and prompts the recollection that the mind is at once "theatre and spectator." Finally the isolation that makes nothing of "little and contemptible . . . aims and pursuits" confirms the vast "capacities of the soul," which may not be expressed in its aims or intentions, but in that almost involuntary religious disposition Carter valued. The passage concludes:

> The view of great and astonishing objects is sometimes very useful, and gives a noble extension to the powers of the mind; but for wise ends, it is not formed to dwell long upon them, without a weariness that brings it back to its duties in the ordinary affairs of the world, and to common business and amusements. And so after all the elevation of the thoughts from a view of the sublime and stupendous objects of nature, one is very glad to return to enjoyments of a gentler kind, the song of linnets, and the bloom of roses.

In descending from her elevation, Carter seems again to assert that the trajectory of these experiences of religious exaltation finds its inevitable conclusion in leaving her "very well contented to descend" and to perceive pious significance in "the ordinary affairs of the world."[26]

Carter enjoys, as it were, Wollstonecraftian transports: "My mind was calm, my spirits elevated, and my heart glowed with all that delightful gratitude which is so naturally felt from an enjoyment so innocent, so unmixed."[27] But the point of these sublime reveries is that they return her to the social world, and console her for its vicissitudes because they indicate the religious disposition of their unobserved insignificance. She writes:

> The hopes of immortality certainly afford a noble subject of contemplation to the elevated faculties, and progressive powers of the soul: but they ought to be received with peculiar gratitude by the social and friendly affections of the heart. The vigour and spirit of merely intellectual pursuits bear up the mind, and in

26. Ibid., 1.167–69, letter xliii, Deal, 2 July 1762.

27. *Carter to Vesey,* 3.334, letter cxxvi, Deal, 5 December 1779.

> some degree transport it beyond the perception of human concerns: but the soft and gentle dispositions of our nature, exposed to every accident of painful sensibility, stand in need of perpetual consolation and support.[28]

Here "intellectual pursuits" are analogous to the experiences of the "unconnected hermit": Carter doubts their value because they "in some degree transport" the mind "beyond the perception of human concerns." The religious value and the pleasure of the "true sublime" depend for her on that "reference to society" which she argued was almost always necessary to the "pleasures of solitude." The "soft and gentle dispositions of our nature" need the comforts of religion, and it is because religion speaks to and is thus dependent on them that it is superior to merely "intellectual pursuits."

This perception of the significance of the religious sublime, as a kind of ideality that returns her to what she saw as the realities of private life, is important to Carter's conception of her own scholarship, and of historical progress. She writes to Montagu, early in their correspondence, that

> If I have any qualifications that entitle me to a share in your esteem and affection, as some I hope I have, I owe them entirely to my being a Christian: some of the least evils perhaps that would have discovered themselves in my composition was I anything else, are, that I should have been a stoic, a metaphysician, a bear, and a wit. Do not be frighted; I am no such beast at present. . . .[29]

The remark is an illuminating indication of the extent to which Carter understands her own views as moving between, on one hand, a kind of stoical insistence on absolute value, in terms of which modern culture seems immersed in "all the corruptions of civilization," and on the other, a Christian endorsement of the value of the private and contingent, the customary and sentimental, which led her to believe that civilization was accompanied by a progressive and "general diffusion of illumination" in religion.[30] Her letter admonishing Montagu about her duty to use her talents for the "honour and service of Him from whom you received them" points to the sense in which though merely "intellectual pursuits" might imply no obligation to publish, religious belief makes it a necessary obligation to involve personal experience in the contingent, to contribute, with whatever degree of modest reluctance, to the "general diffusion of illumination."

Carter repeatedly claims that the strength of her religion lies in its capacity to find value in and appeal to both "the elevated faculties" and "the soft and

28. Ibid., 3.47, letter xvii, Clarges Street, 19 February 1766.

29. *Carter to Montagu,* 1.17–18, letter v, Deal, 13 January 1759.

30. Both quotations from *Carter to Montagu,* 3.354, letter cclxxxviii, Deal, 3 September 1799.

gentle dispositions of our nature." She writes, in *Epictetus,* of the difference between stoicism and Christian faith:

> What ought to be our Dispositions towards Good and Evil, may be learned from Philosophy: but what that certainly-attainable Good, and that Evil which, without our own Faults, we need never incur, are, Christianity alone can teach. That alone can enable us to unite the Wisdom, Courage, Dignity, and Composure of the Stoics, with the Humility that belongs to our frail Nature, and the various Affections that are inseparable from Humanity.[31]

Her emphasis on the importance to her faith of human affections, of private virtues, may help us to understand the significance of her emphasis on Christ's humanity, in her early comments on the Athanasian creed. She writes to Elizabeth Vesey that

> A steady attention to the rule of duty as such, is the surest path to conviction. The natural feelings and interests of a good heart, and the divine assistance, will, sooner or later, subdue any mere constitutional scepticism to such a degree, as will be sufficient to calm the mind into tranquillity, and encourage it by cheerful hope. This is all that is necessary to comfort and to virtue: and high transports of divine enthusiasm, though a great blessing, when founded on real principles of true religion, can, like other distinguished advantages, fall to the lot of very few.[32]

Carter's own experience of "high transports"—whether the sublime reveries the landscape inspires, or the "intellectual pursuits" which transport the mind "beyond the perception of human concerns"—find their validation in private duty, and disclose how what is most insignificant in that may "become great and important" in its contribution to progressive civilization.

In this chapter I have argued that religion makes available to women a sense of social duty that overrides the modesty appropriate to femininity. The religious language of the essayist in *The Progress of the Female Mind,* and of Carter's poetry and prose, creates a peculiar context which sweeps aside the conventions of gendered identity to invoke from educated women a liberal moral authority and comprehensiveness of vision reminiscent of that appropriate to public men. In *The Progress of the Female Mind* this was an effect of the representation of religion first as a sort of marginal, peripheral area where women enjoy an unusual freedom from restraint, and then as the most central, most authoritative and all-embracing sphere. In the final essay the authority of women in this area becomes directly comparable with the emerging cultural authority of the middling ranks as something which achieves hegemonic sta-

31. *Epictetus,* Bk. 1, ch. 4, 18 n. (e).
32. *Carter to Vesey,* 3.131–32, letter xlvi, Sunning Hill, 23 August 1769.

tus through the polite mechanism of example and emulation. Carter's position is more complex. In her writing, a pious reverence for private virtue does produce something like the negation or inversion of the perceived social hierarchy argued for in *The Progress of the Female Mind,* for example in the observation that "heroes or conquerors . . . are characters I look upon with so little reverence, that I think many an honest old woman who cries hot dumplings, a much greater ornament to human nature than a Caesar or an Alexander."[33] But an observation of this sort confirms the distance between the private virtue of the dumpling-seller and the public heroism of Caesar, and does not challenge that, as had the arguments of *The Progress of the Female Mind.* Carter's faith leads her to emphasize that privileges of rank, riches, or learning are external adornments, attributes which imply the visible and social performance of appropriate duties. It is the nature of that performance that is interesting, because the performance of duty does seem to override or sweep aside those other feminine duties associated with modest self-effacement. It requires that Carter or Montagu should publish not to polish or improve civilization, but as a religious observance which is both intimately inward and all-encompassing in its implications.

Carter's meditations on landscape repeatedly involve the sense that her perceiving self leaves behind—perhaps transcends—the absorption in detail and difference that on the one hand gives the place its particular and identifiable character and on the other emphasizes what is local, temporal, variable in the spectator. In the passages I have discussed there is a still moment of calm, of transport. But what her writing repeatedly adds into or insists is already present in that moment is a form of the contingency that seems to have been denied. It is important to Carter that pleasure should be "connected with immortal ideas"—that, as she claimed, "I can scarcely enjoy a rose . . . till my imagination transplants it to the walks of Paradise, where it will be secure from fading." But the passages I have discussed also emphasize that her conception of Paradise always has "reference to society," to contingency and the "accidents of painful sensibility." The relation she imagined between paradise and the temporal enjoined on her the obligation to publish while she imagined publication could contribute to personal or public improvement.

The sense in which Carter's faith demands from her, or makes available to her, a kind of public profession is clearly indicated by her early "Ode to Wisdom," the poem Richardson published without having been able to gain the permission of its author in the second volume of his *Clarissa* (1747). The

33. *Carter and Talbot,* 1.193, Deal, 29 October 1747.

opening stanza of the poem represents the owl as the sign of a philosophic melancholy situated in occluded retirement:

THE solitary Bird of Night
Thro' the pale Shades now wings his Flight,
And quits the Time-shook Tow'r:
Where, shelter'd from the Blaze of Day,
In philosophic Gloom he lay,
Beneath his Ivy Bow'r.

Summoned by this "Fav'rite of *Pallas,*" the poet expresses her gratitude that the goddess has taught her not to cherish the "wild Desires" of "Av'rice, Vanity, and Pride." Instead she requests:

To me thy better Gifts impart,
Each moral Beauty of the Heart
By studious Thought refin'd:
For Wealth, the Smiles of glad Content,
For Pow'r, its amplest, best Extent,
An Empire o'er my Mind.

But the poem does not simply celebrate the virtues of retirement. Carter goes on:

From Envy, Hurry, Noise, and Strife,
The dull Impertinence of Life,
In thy Retreat I rest:
Pursue thee to the peaceful Groves,
Where *Plato*'s sacred Spirit roves
In all thy Graces drest.

He bade *Illyssus'* tuneful Stream
Convey thy philosophic Theme
Of Perfect, Fair, and Good:
Attentive *Athens* caught the Sound,
And all her list'ning Sons around,
In awful Silence stood.

Reclaim'd her wild licentious Youth,
Confest the potent Voice of Truth,
And felt it's just Controul:
The Passions ceas'd their loud Alarms,
And Virtue's soft persuasive Charms
O'er all their Senses stole.

Thy Breath inspires the Poet's Song,
The Patriot's free unbias'd Tongue,

The Hero's gen'rous Strife:
Thine are Retirement's silent Joys,
And all the sweet endearing Ties
Of still, domestic Life.[34]

In the opening stanzas of Gray's (almost exactly contemporary) *Elegy,* for example, the comparable discursive situation of the poet produces a nostalgic vision of past community in contrast to the isolation and atomization of the present. But Carter's stanzas emphasize the relation, the difficult and ambiguous continuity between the "silent Joys" and virtues of retirement and domesticity and the more absolute public virtues appropriate to the poet, patriot, and hero.[35] The poem implies that virtuous retreat from the "dull Impertinence of Life" may result in the reclamation of "wild licentious Youth" to civic virtue, to domestic quiet and public authority.

In Richardson's novel, Clarissa sets the last three stanzas of the ode to music "as not unsuitable to my unhappy situation." She writes to Anna Howe that "after I had re-perused the ode, those three [stanzas] were my lesson," implying, perhaps, an ambiguous attitude to their relation to the earlier sections of the poem.[36] The final stanzas work to provide a strongly pious conclusion to the poem:

No more to fabled Names confin'd,
To Thee! Supreme, all-perfect Mind
My Thoughts direct their Flight:
Wisdom's thy Gift, and all her Force
From Thee deriv'd, unchanging Source
Of intellectual Light!

Oh send her sure her steady Ray
To regulate my doubtful Way,
Thro' Life's perplexing Road:
The Mists of Error to controul,
And thro' it's Gloom direct my Soul
To Happiness and Good.

Beneath her clear discerning Eye
The visionary Shadows fly

34. Carter, "Ode to Wisdom," ll. 1–6, 10, 27, 34, 37–42, 55–78, in *Poems on Several Occasions* (London: John Rivington, 1762), 85–90.

35. For a detailed and illuminating reading of Gray's *Elegy,* see Suvir Kaul, *Thomas Gray and Literary Authority: A Study in Ideology and Poetics* (Stanford, Calif.: Stanford University Press, 1992), chapter 3.

36. Richardson, *Clarissa,* letter 54, 231.

Of Folly's painted Show:
She sees, thro' ev'ry fair Disguise,
That all, but *Virtue's* solid Joys,
Is Vanity and Woe.[37]

The stanzas restate, in the context of their pious address to the deity, some of the dominant themes of the preceding lines, which turn on the opposition of what is solid with what is misty, transitory, and disguised or illusory. But Richardson's heroine may need to take them as her lesson in isolation from the earlier stanzas because this separation strengthens the sense in which they can be taken to describe only a private, even internal sphere of pious devotion appropriate to the way she is represented in the novel.

Clarissa's selective highlighting of extracts from Carter's poem emphasizes the possibility of reading it as a celebration of the moral superiority of the disempowered—at the stage where she copies out the poem, Clarissa is still shutting herself in her rooms in the family home in order to resist being forced into marriage. But the continuity the poem insists on between the private virtues of retirement and those of public life, or between stoic and Christian virtue, suggests a more authoritative role. It echoes the arguments of Carter's *Epictetus,* where her faith is the context that embraces and modernizes the philosopher's moral and political ethics. The poem does take the form of a prayer for retired virtue, but it does not suggest that this offers only personal consolation. The duty involved in the aspiration "The Mists of Error to controul" participates in an extensive and inclusive sphere access to which is afforded, perhaps licensed, by a kind of modest denial. This is a moral language which turns away from any explicitly political inflection, and yet claims authority because of that. But it is at the same time intriguingly close to that of, for example, Wollstonecraft's *Vindication* of 1792, where she writes:

> The stamen of immortality, if I may be allowed the phrase, is the perfectibility of human reason . . . in the present state of things, every difficulty in morals that escapes from human discussion, and equally baffles the investigation of profound thinking, and the lightning glance of genius, is an argument on which I build my belief of the immortality of the soul. Reason is, consequentially, the simple power of improvement; or, more properly speaking, of discerning truth. Every individual is in this respect a world in itself. More or less may be conspicuous in one being or another; but the nature of reason must be the same in all, if it be an emanation of divinity, the tie that connects the creature with the Creator; for, can that soul be stamped with the heavenly image, that is not perfected by the exercise of its own reason? Yet outwardly ornamented with elaborate care, and so

37. Carter, "Ode to Wisdom," ll. 79–96.

> adorned to delight man, "that with honour he may love," the soul of woman is not allowed to have this distinction, and man, ever placed between her and reason, she is always represented as only created to see through a gross medium, and to take things on trust. But dismissing these fanciful theories, and considering woman as a whole, let it be what it will, instead of a part of man, the inquiry is whether she have reason or not. If she have, which, for a moment, I will take for granted, she was not created merely to be the solace of man, and the sexual should not destroy the human character.[38]

In Wollstonecraft's argument, of course, spiritual identity is also resolutely civic; it is unambiguously about the obligation to do more than "adorn the land."[39] In Carter's writing the recognition that religious identity involves or implies civic duty is more oblique. Her writing repeatedly insists on the connections between the pleasures of solitude, the absolute values of religion, and mundane contingency. Those connections explain her commitment to the belief that the publication of the fruits of solitary scholarship is an obligation of her faith. They also help to explain why Carter and her friends should be recognized as important contributors to the complex processes which reconfigure relations between gender difference and the public/private divide in the second half of the eighteenth century.

38. Mary Wollstonecraft, *A Vindication of the Rights of Woman* (1792), ed. Carol H. Poston (New York: Norton, 1975), 52–53.

39. Ibid., 53.

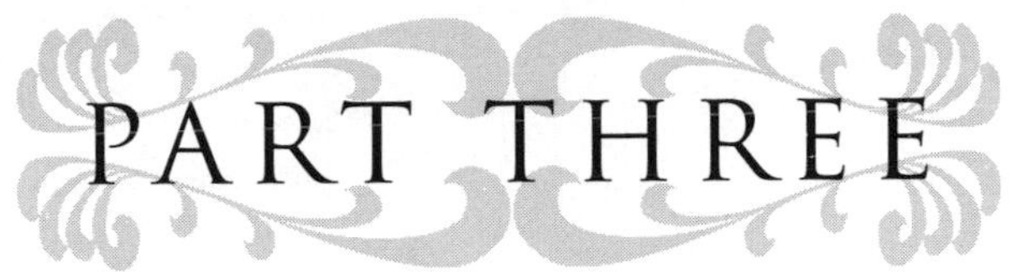

PART THREE

Femininity and National Feeling in the 1770s and 1780s

7

From Learning to Patriotism

In his *History of Women from the Earliest Antiquity to the Present Time* (first published in 1779, and reissued in a revised third edition in 1782),[1] William Alexander noted that in "all ages" there had been women who "either by being endowed with more genius, or by turning it into another channel, have acquired no incompetent share of the learning of the times in which they lived"; and he concluded his short list of examples with the rather weary acknowledgment that "France has had a Dacier, England a Carter, and many others too tedious to mention." He went on to reflect that "These particular instances . . . have no influence on the women in general. A genius of either sex, will infallibly soar above the common level; but the herd of mankind, who feel not the same impulse, nor are actuated by the same fire, will still jog on in the ordinary track."[2] Alexander's rather desultory comments suggest that women's learning is so exceptional that it is a matter of indifference to an author concerned to discuss women's history and condition in general terms. The idea of Carter or Dacier as the representatives of national prowess seems to have lost its edge, its pertinence to the indexical function of the sex as a whole. Alexander's central thesis is that

1. Alexander's *History of Women* was reprinted in what was called a second edition in Dublin in 1779, and appeared in German and French translations, and also in two Philadelphia reprints. For further details of its publishing history, see Jane Rendall's introduction to the reprint of the 1782 edition, 2 vols. (Bristol: Thoemmes Press, 1995), 1.xxiv–xxv. All references to the 1782 edition are to this reprint.

2. Alexander, *History* (1782), 1.87–88.

> the rank . . . and condition, in which we find women in any country, mark out to us with the greatest precision, the exact point in the scale of civil society, to which the people of such country have arrived; and were their history entirely silent on every other subject, and only mentioned the manner in which they treated their women, we would, from thence, be enabled to form a tolerable judgement of the barbarity, or culture of their manners.[3]

But the focus of that argument has shifted, so that here it positively excludes all those learned women whose catalogue is "too tedious"—too long or too troublesome—to reiterate.

James Fordyce had spoken against the idea of "Learned Ladies of any kind" in his *Sermons to Young Women.* He cautioned that "I should be afraid, lest the sex should lose in softness what they gained in force; and lest the pursuit of such elevation should interfere a little with the plain duties and humble virtues of life." But this objection allowed him scope to recommend the example of Carter, whom he believed "had the sense and worth to join every domestic quality that can adorn a woman in her situation" to her learning.[4] A decade later, however, the idea of women's learning has become much more troubling for him. Revisiting the theme of *The Character and Conduct of the Female Sex* in a short discourse published in 1776, he alludes to the role of women as indices of the stadial progress of civilization in asking his audience

> what age or country, distinguished in the annals of fame, has not received a part of that distinction from the numbers of women, whom it produced, conspicuous for their virtues and their talents? Look at this, in which you live: does it not derive a very considerable share of its reputation from the female pens, that eminently adorn it?

In his argument, valuing the society of virtuous women is identified with the capacity to appreciate high culture; it confirms the discriminating taste of the polite man:

> Virtue arrayed by the Graces, attended by the Smiles, and beheld in the person of . . . a woman, will look so supremely engaging, that the low arts, and unhallowed labors, of profligates and harlots to beguile you, must appear in your eye contemptible and hateful. Who, that has been accustomed to a palace, would quit it for a sty? Who, that has contracted a taste for whatever is excellent in poetry, or in painting, would descend to take pleasure in a wretched dauber, or a common versifier? Who, that is smitten with "the beauty of holiness," can look with delight on the loathsomeness of sin?

3. Ibid., 1.151.
4. James Fordyce, *Sermons to Young Women* [1765] (London: Cadell, 1809), sermon v, 1.155–56.

But the emphasis of his argument is solidly on the advantage of appreciating the number and spectacle of women noted for virtues and talents, while he devotes a perverse and prolix energy to the portrait of the woman afflicted with "the Affectation of a Superior Understanding" as a "clamorous, obstinate, contentious being, universally disgustful and odious; fit only to be chased from the haunts of humanity." The woman with pretensions to learning, in his intemperate discourse, is not only irrelevant to the function of women as indices of cultural refinement, but an unsexed being—"Feminality is gone"—that threatens the civilized delicacy of the polite male spectator, who implores heaven to "shelter us from its violence."[5]

Linda Colley concludes her chapter on "Womanpower" in *Britons: Forging the Nation 1707–1837* with the observation that "for both sexes, the last quarter of the eighteenth century and the first quarter of the nineteenth century saw a sharper rate of change at home, massive and demanding wars abroad and the challenge of new forms of patriotism. This was the period in which women first had to come to terms with the demands and meanings of Britishness." Colley argues that a key feature of how women were conjured to meet the challenge of the "new forms of patriotism" was expressed in the repeated invocation of "the supposed behaviour of Frenchwomen as exemplifying what must at all costs be avoided in Britain." More specifically, Colley points out that it was claimed, "usually by men . . . that Frenchwomen had too much of the wrong kind of power."[6] It is frequently argued in these decades that the social and political power and visibility of French women is a sign of excessive civilization, of a degree of polish that involves corruption, and that the British would do well to avoid. Nobody was likely, for example, to mistake the reference to France when one of the participants in the anonymous *Dialogues Concerning the Ladies* (1785) said: "I am afraid, that in some countries, because they would not be thought uncivilised, or unpolished, the men have . . . treated the women with a degree of respect, that has only tended to render them insolent and intractable."[7] William Alexander observes that what he regards as the essentially feminine

5. James Fordyce, *The Character and Conduct of the Female Sex, and Advantages to be derived by Young Men from the Society of Virtuous Women. A Discourse, in three parts, delivered in Monkwell-Street Chapel, January 1, 1776,* 2d ed. (London: Cadell, 1776), Part I, 6; Part III, 96, 78, 83–84.

6. Linda Colley, *Britons: Forging the Nation 1707–1837* (New Haven, Conn.: Yale University Press, 1992), 281, 251.

7. *Dialogues Concerning the Ladies. To which is added, An Essay on the Ancient Amazons* (London: T. Cadell, 1785), dialogue v, 101.

> virtues of modesty and chastity do not flourish most, where they are endeavoured to be forced upon the women by locks, bolts, and gouvernantes, as in Spain; nor where unrestrained liberty and politeness are carried to the greatest length, as in France and Italy; but rather, where refinement is not arrived so far, as to reckon every restraint upon inclination a mark of rustication and ill-breeding.

An important sign of this "unrestrained liberty and politeness" is of course "female influence over literature, as well as over every other thing in France." It is, as Colley's argument suggests, no surprise to find Britain leading the list of countries fortunate in "not having yet arrived at that point in the scale of politeness."[8]

Competition with France had seemed to be a spur to the recognition and celebration of learned British women in the mid-century, however, and the acknowledgment that French women may be more elegant and learned—indeed too learned—in the 1770s does not explain the decline in interest in exceptional women in Britain. For James Fordyce, significantly in the light of his views, the notion that "in France the Women are supreme" creates the problems associated with the corruptions of excessive civilization only for young men. "Can it be thought surprising," he asks, if the company of women "should, in a climate which gives animal spirits light as air, infect the latter with a vanity, a giddiness, and an effeminacy, that characterise their youth to a proverb?" But on the other hand, he claims "it must happen in such a country" that older men

> will be found much the more courteous and amiable, as well as entertaining and accomplished, for their constant intercourse with a sex whom they are taught from the beginning to treat with attention and respect; a sex whose society in general, where-ever it is cultivated with proper regard for decorum and elegance, cannot fail to soften the temper, enliven the genius, and give an agreeable polish to the whole deportment.[9]

Fordyce's comments point to that leitmotif of later eighteenth-century theories of civilization in which the position of women is represented as the key—sometimes the cause, sometimes the effect—of the nice and difficult distinction between corruption and refinement, degeneration and progress. That the women he discusses here are French perhaps allows him to spell out their ambiguous position more fully; but the ambiguity he dwells on removes the possibility that they might offer a cautionary example about the effects of women's

8. Alexander, *History* (1782), 1.440–41, 445–46, 460.
9. Fordyce, *Character and Conduct,* Part I, 27–28.

learning in Britain, and for Fordyce instead they offer a lesson in the need for improved polish in the manners of British men.

The increasingly problematic status of learned women in the 1770s and 1780s can best be understood as involved in a larger cultural shift that is manifested in various ways: in George III's representation of himself as a paternal authority, governing the nation through bonds of affection that extend his private and familial role into his relation to his subjects and his colonies; in the dominance, after so many years of Whig hegemony, of a Tory administration that supported George's right to enforce filial submission on the Americans; in the polarization of political debate in the wake of the Wilkes controversy of the early 1770s, which drew into a sort of heterogeneous cluster disparate groups of the radical and disaffected, and to some extent colored them with Wilkes's reputation for blasphemy and libertinage; and in the rise of a cautiously conservative sense of middle-class propriety and distance from the mob in the wake of the Gordon riots of 1780. For the 1770s and 1780s are characterized by a new emphasis on the values of the private, domestic, and familial as the basis for public morality, and by the apparent politicization of those excluded from the public sphere of parliamentary politics.[10]

The Temple of Fashion (1781), a rambling and rather inept long poem published in Shrewsbury for the author, S. Johnson, intriguingly draws together some of these strands. The poet contrasts "*Modern Patriotism*" with the "lovely Virtue" of the patriotism of the past, claiming that the "time has been" when patriotic inspiration "Could bravely stab the Tyrant in the Friend; / Could, spite of Nature, act the patriot-part, / And steel against his Sons a Father's heart." In the modern age, however,

> How chang'd is She, whose modern JANUS' mien
> In full length at ST. STEPHEN's may be seen;

10. See Eugene Charlton Black, *The Association: British Extraparliamentary Political Organization, 1769–1793* (Cambridge: Harvard University Press, 1963); John Brewer, "The Wilkites and the Law, 1763–74: A Study of Radical Notions of Governance," in *An Ungovernable People: The English and Their Law in the Seventeenth and Eighteenth Centuries,* ed. John Brewer and John Styles (London: Hutchinson, 1980); Jay Fliegelman, *Prodigals and Pilgrims: The American Revolution against Patriarchal Authority, 1750–1800* (Cambridge: Cambridge University Press, 1982); Paul Langford, *Public Life and the Propertied Englishman, 1689–1798* (Oxford: Clarendon Press, 1991), esp. chapter 7, "Just Authority"; Caroline Robbins, *The Eighteenth-Century Commonwealthman: Studies in the Transmission, Development and Circumstances of English Liberal Thought from the Restoration of Charles II until the War with the Thirteen Colonies* (Cambridge: Harvard University Press, 1961); and Kathleen Wilson, "The Good, the Bad, and the Impotent: Imperialism and the Politics of Identity in Georgian England," in *The Consumption of Culture 1600–1800: Image, Object, Text,* ed. Ann Bermingham and John Brewer (London: Routledge, 1995).

Whether a perfum'd Fop purloin a seat,
Or sweaty Oil-man from THAMES' savoury street;
Whether in pay she spaniel it at Court,
Or out of pay the *Bill of Rights* support,
Still is her cause the cause of solid sense:
The Taste of Patriots is a Taste for Pence.[11]

The corruption of the modern age is explicitly laid at the door of radical whiggery—of those who support the Bill of Rights, and whose cause is associated with the increasing power of the city, in the person of the "sweaty Oil-man." In the sort of polarizing move that characterizes these decades, the provincial versifier names and blames together the improbable company of Wilkes, Fox, the Duke of Richmond, and Lord George Gordon.[12] The corruption these men are responsible for, as a result of having encouraged "Anarchy's rude voice,"[13] is located in the House of Commons, which was often known as St. Stephen's, in reference to the chapel where the House sometimes sat. But the lines suggest a further possibility as a result of the emphatic feminization of modern patriotism, and the oddly literal assertion that its personification can be seen "in full length." In 1777, the Reverend Thomas Wilson had erected "a superb white marble statue" of Catharine Macaulay, the radical whig historian, in his parish church at St. Stephen's Walbrooke (fig. 6).[14] Wilson's action caused considerable scandal because Macaulay was both a living and a controversial figure. The statue represented her in classical dress leaning on the five volumes of her history—as the personification of feminine and whiggish patriotism. In the context of Johnson's attack on the Whig politicians with whom Macaulay was closely associated, her statue seems to haunt his poem, to appropriate the image of modern patriotism to itself. For the polarization of political debate in the 1770s works to enfold women, willing or reluctant, in the binary terms of its embrace. In the 1770s and 1780s femininity acquires a public role and definition which, as Linda Colley argues, obliges women "to come to terms with the demands and meanings of Britishness."

The changing status of the learned woman in these decades may be illuminated in retrospect by Richard Polwhele's poem of 1798 on *The Unsex'd Females.* Polwhele's poem takes its cue (and its epigraph) from a passage in Mathias's

11. S. Johnson, *The Temple of Fashion: A Poem. In five parts* (Shrewsbury: Sandford, 1781), Part iv, 27, 35–36.

12. See Black, *The Association,* and Robbins, *Eighteenth-Century Commonwealthman* on the widely divergent views and allegiances of these four men.

13. Johnson, *Temple of Fashion,* Part iv, 35.

14. *Gentleman's Magazine* 47 (1777): 458; quoted in Bridget Hill, *The Republican Virago: The Life and Times of Catharine Macaulay, Historian* (Oxford: Clarendon Press, 1992), 99; and see Hill, 99–102 for a fuller discussion of the incident.

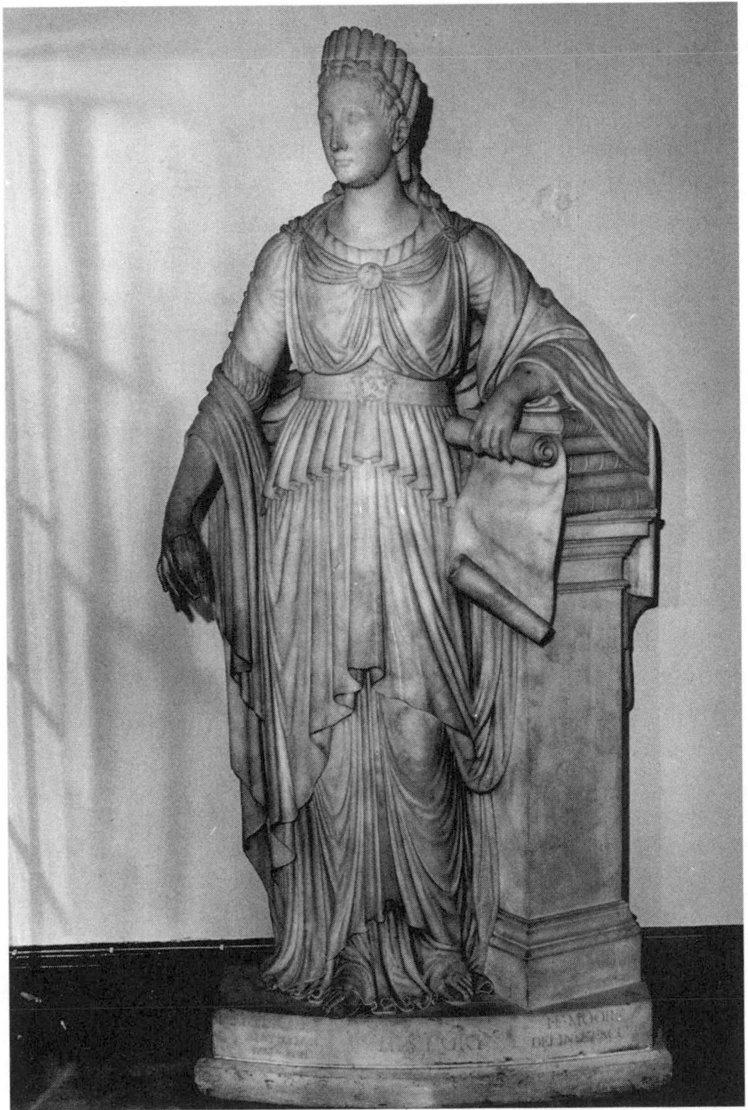

Figure 6 Statue of Catharine Macaulay as *History*, by J. F. Moore (1778). Reproduced by courtesy of the National Portrait Gallery, London, with the permission of Warrington Library.

The Pursuits of Literature. A Satirical Poem. In his Preface to the fourth Dialogue of the poem, Mathias had deplored the availability of revolutionary texts, and in particular of Paine's writings: "Our peasantry now read the *Rights of Man* on mountains, and moors, and by the way side; and shepherds make the analogy between their occupation and that of their governors. Happy indeed, had they been taught to make no other comparison. Our *unsexed* female writers now instruct, or confuse, us and themselves in the labyrinth of politicks, or turn us wild with Gallick frenzy." In the good old days of the indefinite past, he claims, learning had been restricted to "the retreats of academic erudition, and . . . the seats of religion," but now "all learning has an index, and every science it's [*sic*] abridgement"; an incoherent and confusing form of learning has become available to women and the poor. Earlier in the poem he refers explicitly to Charlotte Smith, Elizabeth Inchbald, and Mary Robinson, who, he writes, "are all very ingenious ladies, yet they are too frequently *whining* or *frisking* in novels, till our girls' heads turn wild with impossible adventures, and now and then are tainted with democracy."[15] Polwhele, of course, takes Mathias's remarks as the occasion for a personal and vicious attack on Mary Wollstonecraft. The terms of his attack follow those of Mathias's satire in setting up a contrast between the present state of literature and an idealized past; but where Mathias had opposed an apparently desirable past "age of ignorance" with a present endangered by mass literacy and the diffusion of print culture,[16] Polwhele contrasts those whom he identifies as radical women writers in the present with a past apparently distinguished by learned but not politicized women writers.

Polwhele deplores the politics of Wollstonecraft and the women writers he believes she has influenced—including Barbauld, Robinson, Smith, Helen Maria Williams, and Mary Hays—as examples of modernity. They are "what ne'er our fathers saw," figures in "the new unpictur'd scene, / Where unsex'd woman vaunts the imperious mien."[17] He claims that in the idealized past women's writing had been exclusively concerned with the poetics of consolation and conciliation:

> Ah! once the female Muse, to NATURE true,
> The unvalued store from FANCY, FEELING drew;
> Won, from the grasp of woe, the roseate hours,
> Cheer'd life's dim vale, and strew'd the grave with flowers.

He argues that in "ancient days" women "chas'd from the public scene the fiend of strife" through the display of their maternal virtues. But he asserts that since the advent of Christianity "woman owns a more extensive sway," which

15. Thomas James Mathias, *The Pursuits of Literature. A Satirical Poem in four dialogues,* 8th ed. (London: Becket, 1798), Preface to dialogue 4, 238, and dialogue 1 n. ZZ, 58. Polwhele cites the 7th ed.

16. Mathias, *Pursuits,* Preface to dialogue 4, 238.

17. [Richard Polwhele], *The Unsex'd Females: A Poem, addressed to the author of The Pursuits of Literature* (London: Cadell, 1798), 6, 7.

is exemplified in the work of the women of the Bluestocking circle, as well as in some younger writers:

> . . . vast its influence o'er the social ties,
> By Heav'n inform'd, if female genius rise—
> Its power how vast, in critic wisdom sage,
> If MONTAGUE refine a letter'd age;
> And CARTER, with a milder air, diffuse
> The moral precepts of the Grecian Muse;
> And listening girls perceive a charm unknown
> In grave advice, as utter'd by CHAPONE. . . .

To this list he adds praise of more recent writers, including Anna Seward, Frances Burney, Anne Radcliffe, Hester Piozzi, and of course Hannah More. What he suggests these writers have to offer, in contrast to the libidinized Gallic frenzy and cold philosophical politics of Wollstonecraft and her followers, are the more traditional feminine functions of cultural polish and humanization. Burney, for example, is praised for her ability to "mix with sparkling humour chaste / Delicious feelings and the purest taste." The priority he gives to difference of generation allows the poet to suggest that where the women writers of the 1780s and 1790s engage in faction and the unfeminine violence of political debate, and, at the urging of Wollstonecraft, attempt to "wield the sceptre in yon blaze of day," the earlier generation of women writers had been devoted to the more modest and feminine tasks of strengthening "social ties," and "silken fetters"[18]—they had abjured sexualized sensibility and political faction.

Polwhele's argument is marked with some difficulty; as Mathias had suggested in the comment that Polwhele used for his epigraph, the problem with the work of modern women writers is that it turns "*us* wild with Gallic frenzy" (my emphasis); and Polwhele's poem certainly shows signs of incoherence. In his footnote on Carter, for example, he remarks that he prefers her poetry to the translation of *Epictetus* praised in the text, but adds that her poetry is not as good as Barbauld's. When he mentions that "veteran BARBAULD" has "caught the strain" of women's rights from Wollstonecraft he adds a long and embarrassed footnote which complicates considerably the opposition between new

18. Stephen C. Behrendt argues that "the source of Polwhele's outrage" is "the spirit of personal and social independence that was prompting women to venture outside the tight domestic circle." But this argument ignores the poet's praise for an earlier generation of women writers. See Behrendt, "British Women Poets and the Reverberations of Radicalism in the 1790s," in *Romanticism, Radicalism, and the Press,* ed. Stephen Behrendt (Detroit, Mich.: Wayne State University Press, 1997), 87. [Polwhele], *Unsex'd Females,* 11, 30, 31, 32, 34, 14, 32, 31.

and old women writers on which his argument is based, and which is worth considering briefly. Polwhele writes:

> In this country, a female author was formerly esteemed a Phenomenon in Literature: and she was sure of a favourable reception among the critics, in consideration of her sex. This species of gallantry, however, conveyed no compliment to her understanding. It implied such an inferiority of women in the scale of intellect as was justly humiliating: and critical forbearance was mortifying to female vanity. At the present day, indeed, our literary women are so numerous, that their judges, waving [*sic*] all complimentary civilities, decide upon their merits with the same rigid impartiality as it seems right to exercise towards the men.

The women whose work Polwhele deplores for its Wollstonecraftian taint are, he claims, "a groupe whose productions have been appreciated by the public as works of learning or genius—though not praised with that extravagance of panegyric, which was once a customary tribute to the literary compositions of women." Polwhele hints, and indeed explicitly argues in his comparison of Carter and Barbauld, that the work of these modern women is more valuable than that of the (on the whole older) women whose example he recommends. Writers of Carter's generation had been praised, he observes, because it was remarkable they wrote at all, and as a sign of the courteous gallantry that distinguishes the critics of "this country." But now the "tribunal of criticism . . . no longer imagines the pleading eye of feminine diffidence that speaks a consciousness of comparative imbecility," even though this imagined "crimsoning blush of modesty, will be always more attractive, than the sparkle of confident intelligence."[19] Polwhele claims that in the past national character had resulted in a sort of eroticized admiration for the productions of women, but in the present critics and women writers have lost the national and gendered characters that had made that admiration possible; they are both "*Unsex'd*," and neither can claim to represent the national character or to speak for more than a political faction.

The catalogues of notable British women that continue to appear in the late 1770s and 1780s are marked by an increasing unease about how women can be celebrated, how their achievements in anything other than domestic virtues can be recommended; and it is the nature of that unease, rather than their different ways of dealing with it, that Polwhele's later poem helps to indicate. Thomas Gibbons's *Memoirs of Eminently Pious Women, Who were Ornaments to their Sex, Blessings to their Families, and Edifying Examples to the Church and World,* published in two handsome volumes in 1777, for example, seems on fairly safe ground in recommending the book to parents:

19. [Polwhele], *Unsex'd Females,* 15 and n. On Carter and Barbauld's poetry, see 32–33 n.

> you will in the following Sheets meet with some remarkable Memoirs of pious Women in different ages, spheres, and connexions of life, and . . . I am persuaded, if you have any sincere regards to religion and virtue, and above all if you have felt the effectual impressions of them upon your own minds, that you will be most earnestly desirous that your children may be formed according to the holy Exemplars here held up to view. . . .[20]

Gibbons, who was a dissenting minister, also hopes that the volumes will serve to "confirm and comfort" the piety of the Countess of Huntingdon, to whom they are dedicated.[21] The Countess was, of course, one of the more prominent and spectacular religious leaders of the century. After becoming a widow, she devoted her very considerable fortune to funding the string of chapels that were, after secession from the established church in 1783, to become known as Lady Huntingdon's Connexion; to founding and running a college for ministers and preachers of her Calvinist persuasion at Trefeca, near Talgarth in Brecknockshire; and to promoting missionary activities in North America (especially Georgia, New Brunswick, and Nova Scotia), the South Pacific, and Jamaica.[22]

In 1773, Horace Walpole writes of a "beatific print" he has seen of Lady Huntingdon's portrait, commenting that "with much pompous humility, she looks like an old basket-woman trampling on her coronet at the mouth of a cavern" (fig. 7).[23] The print, produced for Carington Bowles after a painting by J. Russell, is interesting because it indicates the ambivalence central to Huntingdon's religious role. She is, as Walpole notes, not dressed with the magnificence thought appropriate to her social station; instead she wears a sort of shapeless nun-like or anchorite-ish habit. Her (occasionally unreliable) biographer records that because she "devoted her all" to the support of her Connexion, she was "often . . . reduced to a simple change of raiment."[24] She leans

20. Thomas Gibbons, "An Address to Parents on the Education of their Children, and particularly Their Daughters," in *Memoirs of Eminently Pious Women, Who were Ornaments to their Sex, Blessings to their Families, and Edifying Examples to the Church and World* (London: Buckland, 1777), 1.vii.

21. Gibbons, Dedication, in *Memoirs,* 1.vi. On Gibbons's association with the Countess, see Edwin Welch, *Spiritual Pilgrim: A Reassessment of the Life of the Countess of Huntingdon* (Cardiff: University of Wales Press, 1995), 71–72.

22. See Welch, *Spiritual Pilgrim,* 165, 205.

23. Peter Cunningham, ed., *The Letters of Horace Walpole Earl of Orford,* 9 vols. (London: Bohn, 1861), 5.504, letter 1386, to the Earl of Strafford, Strawberry Hill, 24 September 1773.

24. [A. C. H. Seymour], *The Life and Times of Selina Countess of Huntingdon. By a member of the houses of Shirley and Hastings,* 2 vols. (London: Painter, 1839–1840), 2.492. Walpole's reference to the basket-woman suggests, perhaps, that Huntingdon looks like a poor woman who sells goods from a basket, or that she looks as though she should be imprisoned, and eating from the basket, as did the poorest prisoners (see *Oxford English Dictionary,* "Basket," sb. 1.c.). Possibly the reference alludes to her work in freeing small debtors from Newgate—see *Life of Huntingdon,* 2.378.

Figure 7 Carington Bowles after J. Russel, *The Right Honorable Selina Countess Dowager of Huntingdon,* 1773, engraving, $9\frac{7}{8} \times 13$ in.

on what appears to be a hermit's cave, which led Walpole to exclaim, perhaps reflecting rather lewdly on the eroticization of pious fervor, "Poor Whitfield! If he was forced to do the honours of the spelunca! [cave]."[25] And, as Walpole notes, she has her foot on her coronet, as if to indicate her superiority to worldly vanity. But, of course, the coronet is prominent, rather like the football in a sporting photograph, as though it were a trophy, an identifying sign or pedestal, perhaps, as well as the spurned object that Huntingdon seems to have exchanged for the wreath of thorns (or perhaps laurels) that hangs from her fingers.

The Huntingdon Connexion did involve, for its founder, some apparent denial of the privileges of her class: the Duchess of Buckingham found the preachers associated with Huntingdon "most repulsive, and strongly tinctured with impertinence and disrespect towards their superiors. . . . It is monstrous to be told that you have a heart as sinful as the common wretches that crawl on the earth"; she found it extraordinary that Huntingdon could "relish sentiments so much at variance with high rank and good breeding."[26] Edwin Welch, in his authoritative biography of the Countess, notes that the congregations of her chapels were largely made up of "tradesmen and merchants," but her fine chapel at Bath was a fashionable resort, and services conducted at her house in Chelsea were attended by Lords Chesterfield, Bath, and Bolingbroke, Lady Fanny Shirley (the Countess's aunt and Chesterfield's mistress), and Lady Archibald Hamilton (the mistress of the Prince of Wales).[27] The existence of the Connexion depended on the Countess's rank, which (until 1783) made it possible for her to authorize private Anglican chapels so long as they were connected to her various houses, even as the severe demands of its creed made her reject so many of the signs of her status; and her religion itself seems to have involved a curious blend of self-abjection and limitless ambition or self-aggrandizement.[28]

This self-abasement was of course a necessary part of the process of recognition as one of the redeemed elect; it carried its own kind of glory, as Walpole noted in comparing her portrait to that of Charles the Martyr, engaged in the exchange of "*a corruptible* for . . . *an incorruptible crown.*"[29] She used her social position to attract others of rank, wealth, or political power to her beliefs;

25. *Letters of Walpole,* 9.504.

26. Quoted in L. E. Elliott-Binns, D.D., *The Early Evangelicals: A Religious and Social Study* (London: Lutterworth Press, 1953), 139.

27. See Welch, *Spiritual Pilgrim,* 69–70.

28. On this combination see Colin Campbell, *The Romantic Ethic and the Spirit of Modern Consumerism* (Oxford: Blackwell, 1987).

29. *Letters of Walpole,* 9.504.

adorning her chapels with elegance—Walpole was pleased to note of the Bath chapel "that luxury is creeping in upon them before persecution"[30]—and engaging fashionable practitioners to compose music for them.[31] In some respects, indeed, the delights of an incorruptible crown seem rather similar to those of a corruptible one: George Whitefield writes of a meeting of her chaplains at her house that

> Good Lady Huntingdon goes on acting the part of a mother in Israel more and more. For a day or two she has had five clergymen under her roof, which makes her Ladyship look like a *good archbishop,* with his chaplains around him. Her house is a Bethel: to us in the ministry it looks like a college. We have the sacrament every morning, heavenly conversation all day, and preach at night. This is to *live at Court* indeed.[32]

The Countess's rank and piety made her a powerful and controversial figure. Gibbon praises her for having "added to the honours of nobility the sublimer honours of piety and goodness." But in his "Female Piety and Virtue. An Ode," which he "takes leave to annex" to the *Memoirs,* he concludes by recommending the example not of Huntingdon's "illustrious course" of life,[33] but of Queen Charlotte's perhaps less spectacular and less easily specified virtues:

> Be such as *Jane,* or *Parr,* or *Mary* were,
> Or such as *Charlotte, Albion*'s pride, is now;
> Wife, mother, queen, *how good?* rash muse, [for]bear,
> *How good* excells the pow'rs of verse to show.[34]

The Queen is above all the exemplary "Wife, mother," and this unspeakable praise for her serves to confirm that it is the domestic virtues, and not any more saintly or contentious heroism, that merit "*Albion*'s pride," and that Gibbons wishes to impress on his readers.

The anonymous *Dialogues Concerning the Ladies,* published in 1785, is in some respects much closer to the spirit of those celebrations of learned women that had been common in the 1750s and 1760s, and indeed the text borrows substantially and with acknowledgment from Ballard's *Memoirs,* which had been republished in 1775. One of the cast of characters participating in the dialogues does suggest that learned women—the examples here are Cockburn and Macaulay—should be seen as exceptions which "prove nothing respect-

30. *Life of Huntingdon,* 1.477.
31. See *Life of Huntingdon,* 1.229–30.
32. *Life of Huntingdon,* 1.163.
33. Gibbons, Dedication, in *Memoirs,* 1.v.
34. Gibbons, *Memoirs,* 2.528.

ing . . . general propensities," and goes on to argue that "if women ordinarily possessed the same dispositions as men, they would certainly be much less fitted than they are for those duties to which their sex are more particularly called." But the *Dialogues* conclude with a celebration of the notion that "at former periods we have had, in this country, very ingenious literary ladies; but at no preceding period has there ever been in England, at the same time, so many female authors as at present, and possessed of such indisputable merit."[35] The text discusses a range of named living women in some detail, though this does occasionally produce problems or incongruities more marked than those of Ballard's earlier catalogue. The text praises Montagu's *Essay on Shakespeare,* for example, in juxtaposition with the observation that "we have a female historian, whose productions are distinguished by an ardent love of liberty, and by a mode of thinking that is just, masculine, and nervous. The historical works of Mrs. MACAULAY GRAHAM will transmit her name to future ages; and she is also entitled to applause for her political and metaphysical performances."[36] The desire to produce an extensive list of women writers of "indisputable merit" seems to make the endorsement of Macaulay's involvement in political debate, and indeed of her political views, possible or even necessary for what is otherwise a fairly conservative publication, concerned to praise the domestic virtues of those women who "in the shade of privacy and retirement, practise, in the most estimable manner, those duties which render their sex most estimable and most amiable."[37] But there is nevertheless something odd, something uneasy, about the juxtaposition of praise for the "spirit, force, and elegance" of Montagu's work, and the explicit politics of the historian whose work Montagu refused to read. Macaulay's work is "just, masculine, nervous," and directed by "love of liberty"; it is distinguished by a masculinizing whiggish patriotism which demands praise in a register markedly different from that appropriate to Montagu. The praise for Montagu is clearly concerned with the patriotism of her defense of "our immortal SHAKESPEARE" against the "absurd attacks of Voltaire," but "elegance"—rather than justice or masculinity—is central to the form of national identity that involves.

It is a sign of new difficulties in discussing women that this text should be so firmly and aptly cast in the dialogic mode, for it is not a text that produces an argument, or a clear view; it reads much more like a compilation of more or less incompatible views, ways of talking about women, in current circulation.

35. *Dialogues concerning the Ladies,* Dialogue II, 85; Dialogue VII, 152.
36. Ibid., Dialogue VII, 145 and see 144.
37. Ibid., Dialogue V, 106.

There is here no explicit relation, no argumentative continuity, between dialogues which conclude that "the warmth and affection with which they [women] perform the duties of wives and mothers, must give them the justest claim to our regard and esteem," and those which celebrate the notion that "England has certainly produced, and especially in the present age, ladies who have been justly distinguished for their literary accomplishments, their knowledge, their fine taste, the good sense, and the elegance of their compositions."[38] The living women who are celebrated for their achievements include both Carter and Montagu, as well as Barbauld and Anna Seward. The discussion of Barbauld involves praise for her dissenting father's "exemplary piety," and for her own work as a teacher, though the participants note that as a result of her work as an educationalist "one cannot . . . avoid feeling some regret, that this lady has not more leisure to employ those fine talents of which she is possessed, in the composition of literary works of taste and genius."[39] Seward is praised for her poetry, but the dialogists object to her criticisms, in her poem on the death of Major André, of Washington—"no character of the present age is more truly illustrious"—and overlook these only because they believe "the laws of war are not a very natural or ordinary subject of female inquiry."[40]

What interests me about these remarks is that they indicate the extent to which the sort of cataloguing of famous women that the *Dialogues* offer is no longer easily able to ignore the differences between women, the distinctive nature of their politics, or their religious beliefs. The women discussed in the *Dialogues* are not offered as exemplary role models. They are still perceived here to contribute something to the status of the nation when they are taken *en masse,* and to some extent that function of the list does still seem to override the differences between them, to make it possible to include them regardless of their political or religious beliefs. But it does seem that some consideration has to be given to those beliefs; they have to be discussed with a seriousness that was not apparent in the celebrations of the 1750s or 1760s. Biographical dictionaries published in the early 1800s may in retrospect illuminate the difficulties posed by these earlier texts. Neither Mary Hays's *Female Biography; or, Memoirs of Illustrious and Celebrated Women, of all ages and countries* (1803) nor Matilda Betham's *Biographical Dictionary of the Celebrated Women of Every Age and Country* (1804) confines itself to national biography. Betham's lives are distinguished most obviously by their blandness, and their

38. Ibid., Dialogue V, 107; Dialogue VII, 138.
39. Ibid., Dialogue VII, 146, 147.
40. Ibid., Dialogue VII, 150, 149.

ostentatious display of inclusiveness (a claim they do not of course fulfill)—a brief life of Eve is included, though it is hard to imagine whom it might edify. Hays's lives, in contrast, abandon the dictionary form. She repeatedly seems to become so interested in the different lives of individual women that a substantial proportion of the six volumes of her *Female Biography* is taken up with histories of a selected few—most notably Catherine II of Russia, Elizabeth I, and Mary Queen of Scots. Hays retains some of the oddities of Ballard's collection; she includes, for example, the strange tale of the longevity of Elizabeth Legge. But more characteristically these biographies explore the possibilities offered by a moral language of sentimental humanism for representing the complexity of relations between public and private personality. Hays's memoirs are about history and the judgments it involves, rather than about representative or exemplary lives.

The collection which indicates the state of the genre most clearly may be *Eccentric Biography: or, Memoirs of remarkable Female Characters, Ancient and Modern* (1803). This volume claims on its title page to include

> Actresses Gipsies Adventurers Dwarfs Authoresses Swindlers Fortune-tellers Vagrants And other who have distinguished themselves by their Chastity, Dissipation, Intrepidity, Learning, Abstinence, Credulity, &c. &c. Alphabetically arranged. Forming a pleasing mirror or reflection to the Female Mind.

The Advertisement suggests that a moralizing principle of order will be apparent in the work, which "contains a variety not only calculated to entertain, but to improve." It claims that this improvement results from

> *notorious Swindlers,* being contrasted with *Ladies of Honour; Women of astonishing Weakness and Credulity,* with those of *superior talents, or learning;* others of *loose morals,* with some of *the strictest Chastity, designing Gypsies, artful Vagrants,* and *whimsical old Maids;* with *Ladies of wonderful fortune, enterprise, courage.*[41]

The lives themselves, however, illustrate variety, and provide few clues about how these contrasts might be formed, or the category to which any particular individual might most appropriately be consigned. This might imply a comic or satiric comment on the "Female Mind" for which the collection purports to offer "a pleasing mirror or reflection"; but again, this is by no

41. *Eccentric Biography; or, Memoirs of remarkable Female Characters, Ancient and Modern* (London: J. Cundee for T. Hurst, 1803), title page, and Advertisement, iii–iv.

means apparent in the lives themselves. Of Wollstonecraft, for example, the collection records:

> Quick to feel, and indignant to resist the iron hand of despotism, whether civil or intellectual, her exertions to awaken in the minds of her oppressed sex a sense of their degradation, and to restore them to the dignity of reason and virtue, were active and incessant.

The values evident here have almost nothing in common with those that seem appropriate to, say, the life of Elizabeth Montagu in the same volume. The text defines itself most clearly when it notes that "under the epithet *Eccentric* are properly included characters remarkable for some extraordinary deviation from the generality of the sex": when it claims to record the lives of these women only in order to demarcate and confirm the boundaries to which the lives of the "generality of the sex" should conform.[42]

These collections illuminate the difficulties of the genre as a whole, but they also suggest some of the problems peculiar to compiling the lives of women in indicating the lack of a sense of how these lives might be evaluated without resort to the more sophisticated tools of historical analysis. Aristocratic women, and of course monarchs, may have public roles, but these collections cannot distinguish the lives of middle-class women who are exemplary patterns of feminine behavior from those involved in politics, in sexual scandal, or in crime; it is as though they must all be exceptional and eccentric insofar as their names are known beyond the immediate circle of their family and acquaintance. This may be because by the turn of the century domesticity imposes extraordinary constraints on women, though in the last chapter of this book I shall suggest that the narrative of middle-class women's confinement to domesticity is not as simple or uniform as it might seem. At this point I can most fruitfully suggest that if the memoir of every woman seems to have become a tale of eccentric divergence from domestic normality, that may be because gender difference has ceased to have much positive meaning as a category; femininity explains the inclusion of these women in the list, but there is no single discourse appropriate to all of the different lives catalogued, and capable of articulating the terms in which they might be compared and evaluated. Their differences stand out more than their similarities.

It is, of course, evidently the case that the number of women writing and publishing their work increases enormously in the later decades of the eighteenth century, and "female education," if not perhaps "the more intense and

42. *Eccentric Biography,* 141, and Advertisement, iii.

severe studies," does become "an object more considered" as desirable for the marriageable middle-class woman. *The Ladies Magazine; or Entertaining Companion for the Fair Sex* noted in 1790:

> The prevailing taste for improvement in female education, and the happy effects of that education, have enabled us to extend our plan beyond its original intention. The days are passed when Men Writers were afraid lest they should be too learned for the comprehension of female readers, when they were compelled to mould their writings into childish forms, and when the presumption of literary pride led many to believe that learning and genius, taste and study were incompatible with the duties of female life, superior to their understanding, and pernicious to the morals of the sex. The days are passed, when learning in a woman was accounted miraculous, when servile duties were the only duty they were capable of, and the ornament of the person the only pride they could boast.[43]

The Address emphasized that this "happy revolution" extended to contributors as well as readers. It did not advertise the magazine's contents as extending beyond the "pleasing variety of MORALITY, AMUSEMENT and LITERATURE"[44] that might later have consoled a critic such as Polwhele, but it did represent itself as working in the service of the national interest, which required "improvement in female education."

The Frontispiece to the volume shows "The Genius of the MAGAZINE presenting it to Minerva and Britannia, who recommend the Work to the Perusal of the Fair Sex" (fig. 8).[45] The Genius, we seem invited to imagine, has successfully extracted the contents of his volume from the litter of weighty tomes in the foreground, which a woman given to "more intense and severe studies" might otherwise have been tempted to read. But his body conceals them from the figure representing the "Fair Sex," who seems too modest to shift her gaze from the volume he holds, or perhaps from the chastely robed stomach of Britannia beyond that. The winged genius, with his proffered volume, also divides her deferential figure from the helmeted figures of Britannia and Minerva. There is no direct relation in the image between the woman in modern dress who will presumably consume the "Entertaining Companion" and these military figures, who seem to recommend her the volume in rather the manner of employers handing out an improving tract to their servant. But the image does suggest that the woman reader's acquisition of "learning and genius," her improvement in "taste and study," is a kind of patriotic duty—that the wise Minerva is the inseparable companion of Britannia.

43. "Address to the Public," *Ladies Magazine* 21 (January 1790): 3–4.
44. Ibid., 4.
45. "Explanation of the Frontispiece," *Ladies Magazine* 21 (January 1790): 2.

Figure 8 Frontispiece to *The Lady's Magazine; or Entertaining Companion for the Fair Sex*, vol. 21 (1790), engraving, $3\frac{3}{4} \times 5\frac{5}{8}$ in.

In the 1770s and 1780s, the representation of individual women exceptional for their learning or literary ability had become much more problematic in its implications, and less directly important as a sign of national power or civilization. On the one hand, national politics had become increasingly factionalized and polarized. During the Regency Crisis, the Duchesses of Devonshire and Gordon were credited with having "divided [fashionable] society down party lines," their followers adopting uniforms indicating their political allegiances.[46] It was also no longer possible to overlook the conflicting political identities of women who did not move in aristocratic or fashionable circles. On the other hand, these decades are marked by an increasing emphasis on the role of middle-class women as carers and directors of the household economy. Learning is uneasily positioned between the demands of domesticity and politics. It could perhaps be neutral, neither too obviously politicized nor too incompatible with domestic duty, but that neutrality is always imminently partisan or undomesticating, about to force the political differences between women on the public eye. In earlier decades, I have argued, the celebration of learned women had been necessary to the formation of national identity; their eminence had fulfilled a patriotic duty. In these decades patriotism becomes more prominent than learning, or at least it ceases to be possible to display that patriotism simply by adding to the numbers of women who in their quantity establish national prowess. The nature of patriotism, and the form in which it might be appropriate to women, is in these decades a difficult and contentious issue.

46. Amanda Foreman, *Georgiana, Duchess of Devonshire* (London: HarperCollins, 1998), 225, and see Part II, chapter 13, "The Regency Crisis 1788–89."

8

This Sentiment of Home

I

The importance of women to a national literary culture in the 1750s was based on what appears to be a necessary contradiction. In 1757 Carter writes to Talbot describing, with a strange combination of enthusiasm and detachment, troop movements she has observed in Deal, and reporting news of defeat in North America. She comments: "Our present national prospects may be bad . . . [but] at all events, beyond good wishes and prayers, what need have people in private life to think at all about them? If you had no other cause for low spirits, I am persuaded that amidst all the 'briars of this working-day world' you would enjoy the roses." [1] Talbot agrees that "quiet acquiescence" is the role "private persons ought to have in the fate of nations." [2] The women seem to agree that class and gender remove them from any positive identification with or internalization of the national. Elizabeth Montagu became

1. Montagu Pennington, ed., *A Series of Letters between Mrs. Elizabeth Carter and Miss Catherine Talbot, from the year 1741 to 1770. To which are added, Letters from Mrs. Carter to Mrs. Vesey, between the years 1763 and 1787; published from the original manuscripts,* 3d ed., 3 vols. (London: F. C. and J. Rivington, 1819), 2.109–10, Deal, 16 July 1757. The first two volumes of this work are hereafter cited as *Carter and Talbot;* the third is cited as *Carter to Vesey.*

2. Ibid., 2.111, Cuddesden, 29 July 1757. See however Talbot's letter on the surrender of Havana: "Joy to you of the glorious news. . . . What period of our history was ever so glorious as the reign of George the Third? I have smiled and nodded to-day to all the people in the Clapham Road, and notified the good news on the highway to two or three." 2.242–43, Lambeth, 30 September 1762.

much more directly concerned in public and national affairs than Carter or Talbot, but in the 1750s her thoughts on the role appropriate to women other than herself nevertheless seem to confirm Carter's views on the consolations of private life. She writes to her husband in 1753, describing the portrait of an elderly woman that she has seen in a stately home near Doncaster, and adds: "The house is furnished with the good woman's work; I dare say her pleasures were all of the domestic kind, and dairy and poultry her care, her garden her amusement; perhaps to know no more, is woman's highest honour and her praise, and more in our proper character than the cabal and intrigue of state, in which the French ladies place their happiness and glory."[3] The domestic privacy of women is for Montagu here a matter of national as well as gendered character. Women who continue to enjoy the roses preserve their proper character as Englishwomen precisely because they turn away from it.

This characteristic emphasis on the primacy of the private is complicated in the 1770s by the unpopularity of the American war. As Jay Fliegelman has shown, discussion of the American war in the mid- to late 1770s as a conflict between an oppressive, anachronistic patriarchy and its offspring, which claimed representation or independence as a right of maturity, intertwined that political struggle with the languages of novels and other genres which were more obviously concerned with private and familial relations.[4] In this context, in the later decades of the eighteenth century, the language of private relations between parents and children, husbands and wives, with its vocabulary of either monarchs and subjects or contractual partners, acquires a specific political resonance. The terms in which Elizabeth Carter, like so many of her contemporaries, understands the American war give priority to the moral language of private life, but that moral language seems inevitably in this context to become involved in making judgments on political decisions she might earlier have regarded as properly public, and properly beyond the concern of private persons.

She writes to Montagu on July 20, 1777:

> Alas! how can things look with a favorable aspect in America! It has from the beginning, I think, been clear, that all but peace is useless. I am no American, but every reader of history must be convinced, that colonies are always, after a certain time, destructive to the mother country, whenever there is a contest; and that

3. *The Letters of Mrs. Elizabeth Montagu, with some of the letters of her correspondents,* 4 vols., ed. Montagu Pennington (London: T. Cadell, 1813), 3.235, 8 June 1753.

4. Jay Fliegelman, *Prodigals and Pilgrims: The American Revolution against Patriarchal Authority, 1750–1800* (Cambridge: Cambridge University Press, 1982), chapter 4.

> when they wish for independence, the truest policy is at once to give up the point.[5]

She perceives the colonies' development toward mature independence as an inevitable natural progression. Only a month later she adds:

> American affairs seem to be in a very bad train, but that they always were, with regard to the nation. It grieves one's heart to think of the miserable suspense of so many poor individuals, who are informed that places are going to be stormed, and must wait till the next express for intelligence about the fate of their dearest friends. I thank God, I know but few engaged in this dreadful service, but enough to make me anxious for every account.

Her letters of this period again and again express her sympathy for the relations of men fighting in America, and her dismay at English and American loss of life. She returns repeatedly to the sentiments she expresses here in conclusion: "God grant a speedy end to this fatal war, in which there must be so much private loss, and, to speak very moderately, no public advantage."[6] Four months later she writes: "It grieves one's heart to read the list of names, which conveys so much distress and sorrow to the families of the brave men who have fallen in this dreadful quarrel, equally productive of public and private ruin."[7] In these comments—and her letters of this period are of course peppered with allusions to the war—her sympathy with private loss seems to overtake and shape her sense of public policy, as she contrasts the virtuous mother grieving in private for the loss of her sons with the obstinate and unreasonable public mother (or sometimes father) who demands filial obedience from her colonies. Private affliction here seems the basis for a kind of social tie that is violated by a corrupt politics.

Carter's patriotism may also, in a sense, sidestep national politics, to find a focus in private sympathies and prejudices. In a letter of 1749, Talbot wrote: "I believe, in your English zeal, you are, my good Miss Carter, a little of the ancient savage Briton," and Carter agreed that in her dislike of "French fashions and French fooleries" she showed "the spirit of the true original British crab."[8] But her sense of national identity was not constructed only or primarily in opposition to France. Carter thought of herself as a Kentish woman, and wrote to Talbot with an air of flippancy that she would have to "have divested myself

5. Montagu Pennington, ed., *Letters from Mrs. Elizabeth Carter to Mrs. Montagu, between the years 1755 and 1800. Chiefly upon literary and moral subjects,* 3 vols. (London: Rivington, 1817), 3.30–31, letter ccii. This work hereafter cited as *Carter to Montagu.*

6. Ibid., 3.33, letter cciii, Deal, 25 August 1777.

7. Ibid., 3.52, letter ccvii, Deal, 20 December 1777.

8. *Carter and Talbot,* 1.267, London, 25 December 1749, and 269, Deal, 1 January 1750.

of all national prejudices, to make a fair comparison between the pretty ladies of Oxfordshire and those of Kent."[9] As is so often the case with these letters, there is a sense here that humor allows her to drop what is nevertheless a pertinent comment about the extent to which national feeling is based in feelings of regional, local, and sentimental identity.

Carter frequently writes, though almost always with some degree of irony, about her "true patriot prejudice,"[10] which is usually represented as based in her antiquarian investment in the Gothic past. She writes, for example, to Montagu, thanking her for the gift of Richard Hurd's *Letters on Chivalry and Romance* (1762):

> you too well know what a very Goth I am, not to believe that I am very often of the author's opinion, and a rebel against the usurped authority of the classics. Indeed the light and delicate turn of the Greek genius, and the cool correctness of the Roman writers, do not seem capable of those vast and terrific powers, that fill and awe the imagination, in the productions of the Gothic muse.[11]

That investment in the Gothic past which made her "so zealous in the politics of our forefathers"[12] clearly informs the way she writes about landscape, the sense of strong local attachment, in her case to the southeast coast in particular, that is important to a kind of sentimental national identity. In 1763, for example, she writes to Montagu that she is "too good a patriot" not to hope that the comparison between English landscapes and those of the Rhine "may furnish you with many an observation in favour of England." And she produces an illustration reminiscent of Coleridge's "This Lime-Tree Bower" in relating how in "my walk up Dover-hill . . . I saw and thought for you as well as myself." Contemplating the "rude greatness" of Dover Castle, she remarks on "how you would have been charmed by an immediate transition from this savage landscape, into a country smiling in all the ornaments of cultivation."[13] In the local landscape of her native county she seems to find the ground on which she can identify in herself "a little of the ancient savage Briton," and indicate how thinly covered by the surface "ornaments of cultivation" that ancient savagery may be.

9. Ibid., 1.62, Deal, 9 October 1744.

10. Montagu Pennington, *Memoirs of the Life of Mrs. Elizabeth Carter, with a new edition of her Poems, Including some which have never appeared before; to which are added some Miscellaneous Essays in prose, together with her Notes on the Bible, and Answers to Objections concerning the Christian Religion,* 2d ed. (London: F. C. and J. Rivington, 1808), 1.359, letter from Carter to Vesey, Hague, 6 September 1763.

11. *Carter to Montagu,* 2.311–12, letter clxxxii, Deal, 14 June 1775.

12. *Carter and Talbot,* 2.218, letter from Talbot, Lambeth, 26 September 1761.

13. *Carter to Montagu,* 1.194–95, letter liii, Deal, 21 September 1763.

She wrote to Elizabeth Vesey in 1780, in the rather admonitory tone that she often adopted in her later letters to her, sympathizing with her reveries of Gothic times, her pleasure in "losing all modern transactions amidst the adventures of chivalry." But she warns that

> Imagination is a capricious rover, fond of every object that carries it out of the track of daily and familiar occurrences. It loves to traverse the pathless desart and enchanted forest, to roam amidst the wilds of uncultivated nature, and to amuse itself with the extravagent effects of untutored passions. But while we listen to the entertaining relations of the sportive wanderer, let our reason, my dear friend, teach us to be thankful for the blessings of living under the security of civil government, amidst the illuminations of intellectual improvement, and the gentle endearments of regulated society and polished life.[14]

She writes here to a friend whose wandering imagination she feels it increasingly her duty to correct, and perhaps for that reason she stresses her sense of the divide between Gothic fantasy and the realities of civil government.[15] But perhaps she corrects herself as much as her friend, reminding herself of the extent to which her "true patriot prejudice," her strong sense of local attachment, depends on the "immediate transition" between "savage landscape" and the cultivation that is the sign of good government. Throughout the 1770s, Carter, like so many other writers of the period, writes with an increasing sense of disillusionment and disgust about the conduct of public political life, of "the folly of that taxation scheme . . . which brought on the fatal quarrel with the colonies," of the "humiliating sense of shame" induced by the treatment of Ireland, of the sense that "our national provocations against heaven are very great; but there are, I trust, in the walks of private life, so many who proceed on uniformly in a course of duty, that the proportion one may hope is much greater than that which would once have averted the stroke of divine vengeance from a devoted city."[16] This remark, in its reference to Sodom and Gomorrah, may allude as much to public scandals such as the trial of the Duchess of Kingston for bigamy as to parliamentary politics, for the terms of opposition to the American war bring together the excesses of the fashionable world and the guilt of unearned wealth, corrupting political as well as fashionable morality.

Carter's letters, then, suggest that her capacity for national feeling is based in private sympathy, in the affective family unit, in sentimental local ties, and in a sense of the Gothic past which she sets in opposition to the notion of civil government. In some respects, this form of national identification, based in a

14. *Carter to Vesey,* 3.349–50, letter cxxxiv, Deal, 14 August 1780.

15. See Reginald Blunt, "The Sylph," *Edinburgh Review* 242 (1925): 364–79.

16. *Carter to Vesey,* 3.304–5, letter cxiv, Deal, 3 June 1778.

turning away from the public sphere of politics, might seem to accord with traditional notions of the relation—or lack of relation—between femininity and the state. It is useful to take as a starting point here the discussion of women's capacity for patriotism offered in William Russell's *Essay on the Character, Manners, and Genius of Women in Different Ages. Enlarged from the French of M. Thomas* (1773).[17] The *Essay* claims that in order to establish the equality of the sexes "it would be necessary to examine if women, so susceptible of friendship, of love, of pity, of benevolence to individuals, can elevate themselves to that patriotism, or disinterested love of one's country, which embraces all its citizens, and to that philanthropy, or universal love of mankind, which embraces all nations."[18] Unsurprisingly, the text finds that women are incapable of either patriotism or philanthropy as the text defines them. It claims that because women are excluded from honors and offices they cannot "attach themselves to the state." Laws which restrict the terms on which they can possess property "must make them in a great measure indifferent to public welfare." The discussion of patriotism concludes that women do not participate in that "enthusiasm which robs men of themselves, to transform their existence entirely into the body of the state," because they have "less share" in civil institutions, "existing, in short, more in themselves, and in the objects of their sensibility."[19] That characteristic attachment to or identification with "the objects of . . . sensibility" also prevents women from experiencing the "abstract sentiment" of "universal love of mankind": "They must have an image of what they love. . . . They assemble their sentiments and their ideas about them, and confine their affections to what interests them most. Those strides of benevolence to woman are out of nature. A man, to them, is more than a nation; and the hour in which they live, than a thousand ages after death."[20] The directness with which the text attributes the public spirit of men to the tangible

17. William Russell's *Essay on the Character, Manners and Genius of Women in Different Ages. Enlarged from the French of M. Thomas,* 2 vols. (London: G. Robinson, 1773), is based on Antoine-Leonard Thomas's *Essai sur les femmes* (1772), which however appeared to Russell "*to want a good deal more than translation to make it satisfactory to the English reader. . . . He therefore in some measure decompounded it; he split the sentences, broke the paragraphs, and divided the work into parts and sections: he omitted some things, and added others. What relates to the progress of society in Britain is entirely new*" (Preface, 1.v–vi). See Jane Rendall's discussion of the relation between Thomas's work and Alexander's *History* in her Introduction to Alexander, *History of Women* (1782), reprinted in 2 vols. (Bristol: Thoemmes Press, 1995), viii–ix, and on Russell, xi. On Thomas's *Essai,* see also Lieselotte Steinbrugge, *The Moral Sex: Woman's Nature in the French Enlightenment,* trans. Pamela E. Selwyn (Oxford: Oxford University Press, 1995), 90–99.

18. Russell, *Essay,* 2.48.

19. Ibid., 2.49–50.

20. Ibid., 2.52–53.

benefits and rewards they receive is perhaps a little unexpected, but the sketch of women's lack of capacity for patriotism or public spirit is familiar enough as the explicit refrain or implied echo of British eighteenth-century texts on civic virtue.

Women seem to be above patriotism, insofar as that is represented as "almost always a composition of pride and selfishness, generated by the ideas of interest and property," but below it insofar as those ideas are represented as capable of abstracting men from themselves and into an identification with "the body of the state."[21] The situation of women, in their short-focused attachment to their physical surroundings, the images and people they can see and touch, seems to approximate to that attributed to the savage in, for example, John Millar's *The Origin of the Distinction of Ranks* (first published in 1771). He writes:

> As they have . . . little intercourse with those of a different community, their affections are raised to a greater height, in proportion to the narrowness of that circle to which they are confined. As the uniformity of their life supplies them with few occurrences, and as they have no opportunity of acquiring any great variety of knowledge, their thoughts are the more fixed on those particular objects which have once excited their attention; they retain more steadily whatever impressions they have received, and become the more devoted to those entertainments and practices with which they are acquainted.

Millar explains that "hence it is, that a savage is never without difficulty prevailed upon to abandon his family and friends, and relinquish the sight of those objects to which he has been long familiar."[22] What Millar identifies as the savage's "maladie du pays"[23] seems close to that strong sense of local attachment which I suggested characterized Carter's patriotism, and it is, I want now to claim, important to the way patriotism is more widely refigured and reconceived in the 1770s and 1780s.

Patriotism in the sense of what Russell's *Essay* describes as "that enthusiasm, which makes a man prefer the state to his family, and the collective body of his fellow citizens to himself,"[24] rather than of sentimental national or local partisanship, seems incompatible with feminine sensibility. Yet patriotism of that kind is perceived in the later decades of the eighteenth century to be appropriated to distinctively whiggish or even republican positions; and to

21. Ibid., 2.49.

22. John Millar, *The Origin of the Distinction of Ranks,* 4th ed. (Edinburgh: Blackwood, 1806); reprinted with introduction by John Valdimir Price (Bristol: Thoemmes, 1990), 142.

23. Millar, *Origin,* 143.

24. Russell, *Essay,* 2.50–51.

some extent, insofar as that appropriation may make patriotism seem more partisan and less comprehensive in its scope, this may make the identity of the patriot seem more readily compatible with femininity. The heroine of William Hayley's influential poem, *The Triumphs of Temper* (1781), for example, is touched with "patriotic fire" when a scandalous report published about her in the newspaper angers her father, and "Rage from his lips in legal language broke; / Of juries and of damages he spoke. . . ."[25] Serena argues that her sense of "public spirit" means that her innocence would

. . . bear those pangs she knows not to deserve,
Much rather than be made a senseless tool,
To aid the frenzy of tyrannic rule,
Or forge one dangerous bolt for power to aim
At sacred Liberty's superior frame.[26]

She urges her father to "Disdain the vengeance of litigious strife," apparently out of respect for the freedom of the press and distrust of the judicial system, and he, suitably awed and amazed, responds: "Come to thy father's arms!—By Heaven, thou art / His own true offspring, and a Whig in heart."[27]

The canto clearly suggests that though Serena is indeed too virtuously passive to wish to engage in "litigious strife," she is inspired to voice her appeal in this patriotic language because she knows this is the way to her father's heart. She is, naturally, too nice a girl to be interested in the newspaper:

Tho' mild SERENA's peace-devoted mind
The keen debate of politics declin'd,
And heard with cold contempt, or generous hate,
The frauds of party and the lies of state;
Nor car'd much more for fashion's loose intrigues,
Than factious bickerings or foreign leagues;
Yet, while she saunters idle and alone,
Her careless eyes are on the paper thrown.[28]

She takes the paper up for idle amusement, not because she takes an interest in the "keen debate of politics." But she declines that debate, interestingly enough, not just because of her domestic inclinations, her "peace-devoted mind" which might seek to offer private reconciliation for or asylum from public dispute, but because she is superior to the "frauds of party and the lies

25. Hayley, *The Triumphs of Temper; A Poem: In six cantos,* 8th ed. (London: Cadell, 1795), Canto IV, 95, 93.

26. Hayley, *Triumphs,* Canto IV, 96.

27. Ibid., 97.

28. Ibid., 85.

of state," which she is represented as regarding with high-minded contempt and hatred. Serena seems able to speak a language of patriotism which is more disinterested than that of her father because it is purified of party feeling, superior to the newsworthy business of high politics.

The Edinburgh periodical *The Lounger,* which was controlled and largely written by Henry Mackenzie, the sentimental Tory, printed in 1786 a letter purporting to come from "Liberculus" on the shortcomings of Whiggish patriotism. The correspondent explains that while "yet a young man, and full of the classic remembrances of Roman virtue, I connected with the love of Liberty every thing that dignifies and humanizes man."[29] But after a stay at the house of "a warm partisan of Liberty," he finds himself

> very happy to leave this champion for independence, to return to the government of an elderly aunt, who keeps house for me; who, though of old-fashioned Tory principles, is yet very fond of her nephew, very indulgent to her servants, and very hospitable to the neighbours; and who, though she does not trouble herself about the good of her country, feeds the best fowls, and makes the best mince-pies, and brews the best ale in the world.

The limited interests of the aunt are strongly reminiscent of the domestic pleasures of the old woman Montagu had praised in 1753, whereas the patriotic partisan of liberty turns out to exercise "dictatorial sway" over his wife and daughters, not allowing the latter "education like other girls in town, because, he said, in a town they would learn nothing but French dances and French fashions, both which he hated, because the French were slaves." He is represented as an enemy to every kind of innovation, every sign of modernity. His tenants suffer because he "left the very soil at liberty, and neither constrained it by culture, nor fettered it by enclosures." He encourages "proper ideas of freedom and independence" in the neighboring town, where "thriving manufactures" had "been driven out as hostile to its freedom." His patriotic principles are represented as incompatible with politeness, hospitality, and domestic ease, and hostile to agricultural, commercial, or industrial production.

A later number satirizes, in rather different terms, the man whose "great object is the public good."[30] This public-spirited man is more forward-looking than the partisan of liberty whose values were identified with the precommercial past. He is represented as "constantly occupied in contriving schemes for the advancement of agriculture and the improvement of manufactures.

29. *The Lounger,* no. 65, 29 April 1786.
30. *Lounger,* no. 88, 7 October 1786.

He has written a number of little treatises upon those subjects, and his house is constantly filled with those pamphleteers and projectors, who, like him, talk of nothing but the good of their country." But the two satirical portraits share a common moral basis in what John Dwyer identifies as the "view of the domestic arena as the critical ethical environment."[31] The second correspondent asks:

> are there not private virtues, are there not private interests and attachments, that are as important as necessary to constitute a virtuous character, as regard for the public interest? . . . His love for the public is such, that he pays no attention to his family; the public engrosses him to such a degree, that he has no time for private friendship, or for the exercise of private virtues.

This emphasis on the value of the private and familial is shared by the liberal Whig, Vicesimus Knox, in his discussion of the character of the patriot in his essays of 1778. He writes: "The truest patriotism is not always to be found in public life. Selfish motives commonly instigate the noisy votive of ambition and popularity. But what can influence him who secretly serves his country in the retired and unobserved walks of private life? His motives must be pure, and he *is a patriot.*" This insistence that "a bad husband, a bad father, a profligate and an unprincipled man, cannot deserve the name of a patriot"[32] produces a different notion of patriotic feeling, of what it means to be involved in or concerned with "the good of . . . country."

In 1779 *The Mirror,* the parent periodical of *The Lounger,* had portrayed Mr. Umphraville, the moral exemplar of many of its essays, as the model for this different, privately based patriotism. The essayist describes Umphraville's country house, pointing out that "my friend, from the warmth of his heart, and the sensibility of his feelings, has a strong attachment to all the ancient occupiers of his house and grounds, whether they be of the human or the brute, the animate or inanimate creation." The essay gently mocks Umphraville's sentimental affection for the inconveniences of his house. Umphraville will not, for example, remove a "withered stump, which . . . greatly incommoded the entrance to his house . . . because it had the names of himself and some of his school-companions cyphered on its bark." But the essayist concludes that from these attachments

31. John Dwyer, *Virtuous Discourse: Sensibility and Community in Late Eighteenth-Century Scotland* (Edinburgh: John Donald, 1987), 113, and see chapter 4.

32. Vicesimus Knox, *Essays, Moral and Literary,* 3 vols., 17th ed. (London: J. Mawman et al., 1815), Essay no. 9, "An Idea of a Patriot," 1.53, 49.

> the principle of patriotism has its earliest source, and some of those ties are formed, which link the inhabitants of less favoured regions to the heaths and mountains of their native land. In cultivated society, this *sentiment of Home* cherishes the useful virtues of domestic life; it opposes, to the tumultuous pleasures of dissipation and intemperance, the quiet enjoyments of sobriety, economy, and family-affection; qualities which, though not attractive of much applause or admiration, are equally conducive to the advantage of the individual, and the welfare of the community.[33]

This notion that Umphraville's sentimental affections are somehow the source of patriotic feeling may find some indirect support in Samuel Johnson's *Journey to the Western Islands of Scotland* (1775). Boswell notes, of the "very fine passage upon landing at Icolmkill":

> Had our Tour produced nothing else but this sublime passage, the world must have acknowledged that it was not made in vain. Sir Joseph Banks . . . told me, he was so much struck on reading it, that he clasped his hands together, and remained for some time in an attitude of silent admiration.[34]

The sublime passage which left Banks speechless was this:

> We were now treading that illustrious island, which was once the luminary of the Caledonian regions, whence savage clans and roving barbarians derived the benefits of knowledge, and the blessings of religion. To abstract the mind from all local emotion would be impossible if it were endeavoured, and would be foolish if it were possible. Whatever withdraws us from the power of our senses, whatever makes the past, the distant, or the future, predominate over the present, advances us in the dignity of thinking beings. Far from me, and from my friends, be such frigid philosophy, as may conduct us, indifferent and unmoved, over any ground which has been dignified by wisdom, bravery, or virtue. The man is little to be envied, whose patriotism would not gain force upon the plain of Marathon, or whose piety would not grow warmer among the ruins of Iona.[35]

The extreme admiration Banks and Boswell felt for this passage was, I imagine, a response to the rapidity, the sublimity of its transitions, which allow Johnson to claim, first, that the mind cannot and should not be abstracted from local emotion, and then that that local emotion itself abstracts the mind "from

33. *The Mirror*, no. 61, 7 December 1779. Dwyer argues that this passage is a "foreshadowing" of Burke's *Reflections on the Revolution in France*, in *Virtuous Discourse*, 110–11. While he is undoubtedly right to suggest that there is a strong connection between these arguments, I am in this chapter more concerned to explore a cultural shift which does not seem to me easily reducible to the terms of bipartisan political debate.

34. James Boswell, *Life of Johnson*, ed. R. W. Chapman, with an introduction by Pat Rogers (Oxford: Oxford University Press, 1980), 854–55 n. 3, 19 September 1777.

35. Quoted from Boswell, *Life of Johnson*, 854–55 n. 3, 19 September 1777.

the power of the senses." The capacity to be moved by local emotion becomes perhaps yet more attenuated in the reference to the plain of Marathon. This was the site of the Athenians' decisive victory over the much larger army of the invading Persians, in 492 B.C. The victory cost the lives of more than half the defending forces, but it consolidated the Athenians' alliance with Sparta, and the Greeks' sense of themselves as a nation. If Johnson's reference to the patriotic paradigm of Marathon alludes to the parallel between the relations of England to Scotland and Sparta to Athens, then this may have been readily apparent to his first readers. What is I think more difficult, more problematic, is the analogy Johnson draws between the patriotism that gains force upon the plain of Marathon and the piety which warms on Iona. Iona prompts in him an emotion reminiscent of the accounts of landscape in Carter's poems and letters—an emotion which is at once local, a response to the specific physical features of the place, and atemporal, appropriate to humanity as thinking beings free from the "power of our senses." Marathon, in contrast, signifies the ideal of freedom the Athenians fought to defend; an ideal which is imagined to evacuate of meaning the sentimental attachment to place or person, the contingent love of home appropriate to women and savages. But when Johnson writes: "Far from me, and from my friends, be such frigid philosophy, as may conduct us, indifferent and unmoved, over any ground which has been dignified by wisdom, bravery, or virtue," he seems to suggest that the "local emotion" of patriotism or piety experienced at one site or the other involves the same syntax of feeling—that just as he and his friends form a group united by affection, so Marathon and Iona are united in their power to prompt sentimental attachment. The sublime achievement which struck Banks dumb with admiration here seems to be that of making sentimental local emotion the basis of attachment both to home in all its particular contingency and to an ideal that transcends place.

These notions of patriotism, as based in local emotions, sympathetic identifications, and the love of home—in those sorts of attributes which make national identity a matter of customary second nature—may, I have suggested, make national feeling more readily appropriate to femininity, and to the notion of women as "existing . . . more in themselves, and in the objects of their sensibility."[36] In a poem ostensibly written to comfort the widow of Admiral Boscawen, who had died in 1761, Hannah More represents sensibility as a

36. For discussion of the implications of the phrase "second nature," see James K. Chandler, *Wordsworth's Second Nature: A Study of the Poetry and Politics* (Chicago: University of Chicago Press, 1984), esp. chapter 4.

domestic quality and as the basis for women's capacity to serve their country.[37] She suggests that "th'ethereal flame" of sensibility "Makes the touch'd spirit glow with kindred fire, / When sweet Serena's Poet wakes the lyre," and her account of the workings of sensibility may clarify the connection between domestic affection and patriotic feeling in Hayley's *Triumphs of Temper*.[38] More's poetic epistle argues that sensibility is the quality which enables women to promote "kindness, love, and concord" within the family:

> The sober comfort, all the peace which springs,
> From the large aggregate of little things;
> On these small cares of daughter, wife, or friend,
> The almost sacred joys of *Home* depend:
> There, SENSIBILITY, thou best may'st reign,
> HOME is thy true legitimate domain.[39]

Admiral Boscawen had died of a "bilious fever" at Hatchlands Park in Surrey, the stately home he had built with the prize money from his naval triumphs. But the poem suggests that his widow is the appropriate recipient of its praise because she shows her charming capacity for sensibility in sacrificing her family to her country's need. Frances Boscawen, the poem argues, is one of those who have "deepest felt" the pains that complement the pleasures of sensibility:

> You, who for Britain's Hero and your own,
> The deadliest pang which rends the soul have known;
> You, who have found how much the feeling heart
> Shapes its own wound, and points itself the dart; . . .[40]

But Boscawen's grief at her bereavement, More argues, is evidence of "the large soul which takes in human kind," of a capacity for feeling which is profoundly philanthropic, social, and public spirited, and which clearly distinguishes Boscawen from the unfeeling vulgar:

> Whose disconnected hearts ne'er taste the bliss
> Extracted from another's happiness;

37. The poem was published in 1782, and much of it appears to have been written after Garrick's death in 1779, but the final lines refer to the Battle of Lexington (1775) as though it were still continuing. Jerome McGann discusses it in some detail in his *Poetics of Sensibility: A Revolution in Literary Style* (Oxford: Clarendon Press, 1996), chapter 6.

38. More, *Sensibility*, in *The Works of Hannah More, in Eight Volumes: including several pieces never before published* (London: Cadell, 1801), 1.154.

39. More, *Works*, 1.151–52.

40. For an account of Admiral Boscawen's death, see *Dictionary of National Biography* (*DNB*). On his heroism, see for example *An Ode occasioned by the Success of Admiral Boscawen. By a Gentleman of the University of Oxford* (London: R. Baldwin, 1759). More, *Works*, 1.141.

Who ne'er the high heroic duty know,
For public good the private to forego.[41]

It is because she possesses abundant domestic sensibility, and feels deep affection for her family, that Boscawen is also capable of feeling for the "public good." She is represented as able to effect that difficult transition from familial to public feeling as a result of the division James Fordyce made explicit in the claim that "men and women of enlightened understanding, and polite behaviour, are in all countries and ages as like one another, as they are different from the vulgar of whatever rank."[42] But while her rank—her enlightened politeness—trumps her gender, it is her feminine sensibility, her heart, that More claims connects her sense of "heroic duty" with her private affections.

Like almost every other account produced in these decades, the poem emphasizes that sensibility implies the capacity to experience pain as well as pleasure—indeed, as the price of pleasure. The final lines of the poem attempt to analyze the complicated mixture of pleasure and pain this transition between domestic sensibility and national feeling must produce:

Yet why those terrors? Why that anxious care?
Since your last hope the deathful war will dare?
Why dread that energy of soul which leads
To dang'rous glory by heroic deeds?
Why mourn to view his ardent soul aspire?
You fear the son because you knew the sire.
Hereditary valour you deplore,
And dread, yet wish to find one hero more.[43]

The note to these lines explains that "Viscount FALMOUTH, Admiral BOSCAWEN's only remaining son was then in America, and at the battle of Lexington." More's poem certainly seems marked by the difficulty of the transition from the idea of sensibility on which "The almost sacred joys of Home depend" to the sympathy which is imagined to identify itself with the national interest. It is hard to believe that those final lines did much to comfort Frances Boscawen, who, in June 1775, wrote that reading the newspaper reports on events in America "made me sick, and ready to faint."[44] In August 1775, she writes:

41. More, *Works,* 1.143, 142.

42. James Fordyce, *The Character and Conduct of the Female Sex, and Advantages to be derived by Young Men from the Society of Virtuous Women. A Discourse, in three parts, delivered in Monkwell-Street Chapel, January 1, 1776,* 2d ed. (London: Cadell, 1776), Part 1, 31.

43. More, *Works,* 1.155.

44. Brig.–General Cecil Aspinall-Oglander, *Admiral's Widow: Being the life and letters of the Hon. Mrs. Edward Boscawen from 1761–1805* (London: Hogarth Press, 1942), 64, letter to Julia Sayer (Frances Boscawen's cousin), Glan Villa, 28 June 1775.

> I will not enter upon the subject of America; it is too serious! I know not whether there will be peace, but I do firmly believe there ought to be, on any terms whatever—even those that would be call'd dishonourable. My poor boy would not say so, but what honour could result from destroying our own people and our own territory. Will they, when destroyed, yield either taxes or traffic. O no—put out the fire anyway, so you do but put it out soon. It has consumed enough.[45]

Boscawen here seems perhaps surprisingly unconcerned about national honor. But her sentiments here, her conviction that the war is not worth the candle, is strongly reminiscent of Carter's sense of the priority of private morality. Here and in More's poem she shows a patriotism based in private sympathies, a patriotism that has moved away from the view of the *Essay on the Character of Women* to become compatible with and perhaps dependent on feminine sensibility.

In his *Sketches of the History of Man* (1774), Henry Home, Lord Kames, wrote of what he saw as the "capital difference of character" between the sexes: "The master of a family is immediately connected with his country: his wife, his children, his servants, are immediately connected with him, and with their country through him only. Women accordingly have less patriotism than men; and less bitterness against the enemies of their country."[46] In the 1770s and 1780s, I have argued, this distinction is complicated by the changing meanings of patriotism, the changed perception of the relation between the state and the country. In her letters on *The History of England from the Revolution to the Present Time* (1778), a thinly veiled attack on the then government, Catharine Macaulay argued that the inability or unwillingness of the government to keep strict public accounts "has rendered parliaments obnoxious to the great part of the community, who consider them as an expensive, burthensome part of the constitution, and the instruments by which the people are fleeced and beggared with impunity."[47] Macaulay is ostensibly talking about the debate over the restitution of Gibraltar in the late 1720s, but her remarks might just as well apply to the sense of disillusionment with the political process that seems common in the 1770s—a sense that is reflected in the increased moral value of the private and domestic as the source of public virtue and patriotic feeling. The texts I have discussed indicate the extent to which this renegotiation of the re-

45. Ibid., 69, letter to Julia Sayer, Audley Street, 19 August 1775.

46. Henry Home, Lord Kames, *Sketches of the History of Man. In two volumes* (Edinburgh: Creech, 1774), Sketch vi, 1.169. Kames's account of the gendering of patriotism clearly alludes to Milton's account of Adam and Eve's different relations to God in *Paradise Lost.*

47. Macaulay, *The History of England from the Revolution to the Present Time. In a series of letters to a friend* (Bath: Cruttwell, 1778), letter 5, 350.

lation between domestic affection and national sentiment might make possible a remoulding of the feminine characteristics of Britannia to afford women a more direct or immediate connection with their country.

Serena's capacity for patriotic virtue in Hayley's *Triumphs of Temper* is moderated, perhaps feminized, by its basis in domestic virtue and familial affection. The poem concludes with the presentation of a "mystic tablet" supported by the figures of "Connubial Love" and friendship, on which is inscribed the "moral" of the poem:

> "VIRTUE's an ingot of Peruvian gold,
> SENSE the bright ore Potosi's mines unfold;
> But TEMPER's image must their use create,
> And give these precious metals sterling weight."[48]

The "bright ore" of sense alludes to Serena's earlier visit to the allegorical kingdom of sensibility, which, though she was of course warned of its dangers and excesses, was represented as her "congenial sphere."[49] Temper, in these final lines, transforms the heroine's sensibility and virtue into freshly minted currency, in what becomes in the 1770s and 1780s one of the most recognizable images of the value of feminine sociability.

Hannah More had employed the image of a feminine sociable currency in her poem on *The Bas bleu. Or, Conversation,* and Helen Maria Williams took it up in a very similar context in her *Ode on the Peace* (1783).[50] *The Mirror* used the image in 1779, in discussing the qualities necessary to marital happiness: "the lesser virtues must be attended to as well as the greater; the manners as well as the duties of life. They form a sort of *Pocket Coin,* which, though it does not enter into great and important transactions, is absolutely necessary for

48. Hayley, *Triumphs,* Canto VI, 161–62.
49. Ibid., Canto V, 110.
50. See above, p. 89. Helen Maria Williams writes:

> Ah! still diffuse thy mental ray,
> Fair Science! on my ALBION's plain,
> While oft' thy step delights to stray
> Where MONTAGU has rear'd her Fane;
> Where Eloquence shall still entwine
> Rich attic flowers around the shrine,
> View hallow'd Learning ope his treasured store,
> And with her signet stamp the mass of classic ore.

An Ode on the Peace (London: Cadell, 1783), 19. See stanza xxx of the *Ode* in Williams's *Poems* (1786), for the revised version, in which learning is female.

common and ordinary intercourse."[51] Russell's *Essay on the Character of Women,* in concluding the discussion of women's incapacity for national or universal patriotism, had argued, almost as though implying a compensatory virtue, that

> There are certain qualities, which have generally been ranked among the social virtues, but which may more properly be called *the virtues of polished life.* They are the charm, and the bond of company; and are useful at all times, and upon all occasions. They are in the commerce of the world, what current money is in trade: they are sometimes not absolutely necessary, but one can never safely be without them; and they always procure the possessor a favourable reception. Such is that mild complacency, which gives a softness to the character. . . .[52]

This idea of feminine sociability as the small change of the "commerce of the world" indicates, I think, the ambivalence central to the emerging sense of the relation of femininity to the idea of the nation. Feminine qualities are "the bond of company . . . useful at all times," but curiously peripheral to the real business of life, its "great and important transactions."

Frances Boscawen's sensibility is praised by Hannah More because it seems able to assume a kind of patriotic importance, and to appropriate the proportions of "high heroic duty," but what seems most admirable about Boscawen's sensibility is that it is accompanied by or expressed in no public statement, and claims only the public recognition appropriate to epitaphs, elegies, and of course More's poetic epistle itself. The idea of femininity, in More's poem, is I think clearly distinct from that implied in Talbot's notion of the "quiet acquiescence" that "private persons ought to have in the fate of nations," for it seems important that Boscawen's sacrifice and sense of duty should be visible and written about, but her importance to the idea of the grieving national family is deeply bound up in its involvement in the "almost sacred joys of *Home,*" that "true legitimate domain" of sensibility.[53] It is clearly of critical importance that the feminine sensibility characteristic of modern patriotism should have a domestic definition, and a basis in familial privacy. The analogy between sensibility and small change suggests that this is because feminine feeling has a contingent and diminutive status—it is involved in the lesser virtues, the manners of polished life, which acquire value in social exchange. The basis in the affective family, I want now to show, is necessary to guarantee this value, and to distinguish it from those forms of sensibility that might seem to be merely about polish and superficial affect.

51. *Mirror,* no. 33, 18 May 1779.

52. Russell, *Essay,* 2.53–54.

53. *Carter and Talbot,* 2.111, Cuddesden, 29 July 1757; More, *Sensibility,* in Works, 1.142, 151–52.

II

Eliza Draper, the object of Laurence Sterne's sexualized and sentimental fascination, wrote about the value of feminine virtues in a letter she sent from Masulipatam, north of Madras, to her cousin in England in 1774, advising him on his choice of a wife. She wrote that "the Sublimities of Character have less weight with you, than the Bagatelles . . . and in this you are as much sway'd by Wisdom as in any one of your Pursuits." She goes on to give examples: "a Pompadour or a Mrs Cauley might perhaps excite more attention from a Courtier in a Circle than an amiably reserved English Woman with the Virtues of an Octavia, but it seldom, very seldom happens, that the Sage, the Statesman, or the mere man of Business finds his Happiness in the Society of these." The men Draper admires would not, she adds, "choose a Companion of Genius" for a wife. Most intriguing, perhaps, is the suggestion that "the Sublimities of Character" which distinguish the women Draper names are somehow un-English because they contravene the amiable reserve necessary to the feminine national character. What distinguishes that reserved English character, Draper explains, is her "Home Designation," her capacity for the "Cheerful Converse" that makes domesticity the site for nourishing "the Sensations of the Heart rather than the refinements of the Understanding."[54] The homeliness of English women, the letter suggests, is bound up in what it also recognizes as their triviality; their character as bagatelles is what makes them necessary to everyday exchange, what gives them sociable currency. If women become too directly and actively involved in the business and intercourse of society, they seem to acquire a sublime excess of value, which comes to the same thing as having no value or influence at all.

Employing one of the most frequently cited examples of that sublime excess, William Alexander writes of Roman matrons that "they scarcely exhibit any amiable qualities, except some imperfect relics of their ancient patriotism, a virtue, which unless exercised with the greatest moderation, scarcely ever adorns the female character."[55] He is of course talking about the corrupt manners of the period when "the Romans became acquainted with Asia." He argues that "before the Republic was contaminated with the riches, which from every quarter of the plundered globe flowed to Rome, they were the best of wives, of mothers, and of citizens"; but after that influx of wealth, "as

54. Arnold Wright and William Lutley Sclater, *Sterne's Eliza: Some account of her life in India: with her letters written between 1757 and 1774* (London: Heinemann, 1922), 160, letter to William Sclater, Rajahmundry, 20 January 1774.

55. Alexander, *History* (1782), 1.388.

wives . . . the Roman matrons were frequently unchaste. As mothers, not less frequently careless and unnatural. As citizens, endeavouring to overturn all decency and decorum, and sacrificing every thing at the shrine of pleasure and ambition."[56]

The prominence of women in imperial Rome is, of course, closely associated with the collapse of Roman civilization into barbarism. The *Essay on the Character of Women* notes of this "period of corruption" that

> the era of the talents of women at Rome, is to be found under the emperors; when society was more perfected by opulence, by luxury, by the use and abuse of the arts, and by commerce. Their retir[e]ment was then less strict; their genius, more active, was more exerted; their hearts had new wants; the idea of reputation sprung up in their minds; their leisure increased with the division of employments.[57]

In *The Origin of the Distinction of Ranks,* John Millar comments in similar terms on the position of women in modern polite society. He writes:

> in refined and polished nations there is the same free communication between the sexes as in the ages of rudeness and barbarism. In the latter, women enjoy the most unbounded liberty, because it is thought of no consequence what use they shall make of it. In the former, they are entitled to the same freedom, upon account of those agreeable qualities which they possess, and the rank and dignity which they hold as members of society.[58]

The rank and dignity which are the basis of this newfound consequence are explained a few pages earlier, where Millar concludes that in "the modern nations of Europe," women's "consideration and rank . . . came to be chiefly determined by the importance of those departments which they occupied, in carrying on the business and maintaining the intercourse of society."[59] The consequence of women, Millar suggests, depends on their ability to maintain sociable intercourse, to circulate the pocket coin of those pleasures which "become the source of an elegant correspondence, and are likely to have a general influence upon the commerce of society."[60] But that pocket coin is always perilously close to seeming superfluous, unnecessary as it is to any important transaction, and where it is worthless, civilization lapses into barbarism again. Millar adds to his account of the similarity between the barbaric liberty and civilized freedom of women the observation that

56. Ibid., 1.388–89.
57. Russell, *Essay,* 1.58.
58. Millar, *Origin,* 101.
59. Ibid., 97–98.
60. Ibid., 100.

> In a simple age, the free intercourse of the sexes is attended with no bad consequences; but in opulent and luxurious nations, it gives rise to licentious and dissolute manners, inconsistent with good order, and with the general interest of society. The love of pleasure, when carried to excess, is apt to weaken and destroy those passions which it endeavours to gratify, and to pervert those appetites which nature has bestowed upon mankind for the most beneficial purposes. The natural tendency, therefore, of great luxury and dissipation is to diminish the rank and dignity of the women, by preventing all refinement in their connection with the other sex, and rendering them only subservient to the purposes of animal enjoyment.[61]

As women "are introduced more into public life" they lose precisely the rank and dignity which their social role had gained them.

My discussion of feminine sensibility and patriotism has emphasized that familial affection was particularly important during the years of the war with the thirteen colonies because it worked to confirm that Britain, far from being the unfeeling parent the Americans claimed it to be, was motivated by a proper sense of its parental responsibilities. The maternal emotions More celebrates in her poem on *Sensibility,* for example, led Boscawen herself to wish to see the war ended at any cost, but they also made her available as a figure whose emotion moralized the continuation of the war. The form of patriotism More takes her to represent is intimately bound up in the politics of Britain's imperial role. But the implications of feminine sensibility in that imperial context are complex, and they continually escape from the moralized and familial form that poetry such as More's attempted to articulate. For, as the theories of the development of civilization I have mentioned confirm, displays of feminine sensibility are also part of the currency of imperial corruption, signs of the luxury that empire promotes and that causes its decline. In women's prominent patriotic role in the 1770s, the function of women as indices of civilized progress coincides with their alternative discursive significance as indices of decline or agents of corruption. In the next two sections of this chapter I will look at representations of feminine feeling and of fashion as signs of decay in the 1770s and 1780s, and focus in particular on the contradictory meanings attached to Catharine Macaulay's public image.

As patriotism acquires, in the 1770s and 1780s, a discursive character apparently more compatible with femininity, it is the association between femininity and the private virtues appropriate to the domestic and maternal role that underpins the alliance, and affords femininity an acceptable public face. In recognition of the Duchess of Devonshire's support for Fox's successful

61. Ibid., 101–2.

election campaign of 1784, his supporters carried banners reading "SACRED TO FEMALE PATRIOTISM" in the victory parade.[62] But though the polarization of political opinion in the 1770s and 1780s made it more difficult to think of women as excluded from political debate, elevated above or debased below political identity, feminine patriotism only remains securely a virtue when it is based in privacy and thus "exercised with the greatest moderation." In its more politicized forms, and especially in its association with whiggish or republican views, it can acquire some distinctively feminine vices or signs of degeneracy. If Eliza Draper's letter from India refers to Catharine Macaulay—and it is difficult to imagine who else "Mrs Cauley" might be in 1774—then it is intriguing that her reputation as a "republican Virago"[63] and patriot has made her, for Draper, the public woman most nearly approximating in status to the notion of the excessive power of French courtesans—the image of a femininity Draper can only conceive of in the context of a court. For the representation, in the late seventies, of Catharine Macaulay marks an important turning point in the way women prominent for their learning or for their intervention in political debate could be represented.

The decline in Macaulay's reputation was remarkably rapid. In 1776, Sir William Pepys wrote recommending her *History of England* to a correspondent as a salutary antidote to Hume's "Apology for the Stewarts."[64] He explained that

> Macaulay is equally extravagant on the other side. I took up her book with the expectation of finding little more than furious declamation on the side of Republicanism, unsupported by authentic Documents, but though her style is so exceedingly inferior to Hume, is not the cause she has embraced that of human nature and the liberties of Mankind? And in support of it, does she not appeal, to the very frame and genius of our constitution, and to that Eternal Standard of all Political Truth "That Government is founded not for the gratification of an individual, but for the safety and happiness of the Governed."[65]

62. See Amanda Foreman, *Georgiana, Duchess of Devonshire* (London: HarperCollins, 1998), 155, and Linda Colley, *Britons: Forging the Nation 1707–1837* (New Haven, Conn.: Yale University Press, 1992), 248.

63. Edmund Burke, quoted in Bridget Hill, *The Republican Virago: The Life and Times of Catharine Macaulay, Historian* (Oxford: Clarendon Press, 1992), 173, and see chapter 8. My discussion of Macaulay owes much to the work of Kate Davies. See her "Gender and Republicanism in Britain and America: The Meanings of Catharine Macaulay" (unpublished Ph.D. dissertation, University of York, 1999).

64. *A Later Pepys: The Correspondence of Sir William Weller Pepys, Bart., Master in Chancery 1758–1825,* 2 vols., ed. Alice C. C. Gaussen (London: Bodley Head, 1904), 1.207, letter of 1776 to William Franks.

65. *Later Pepys,* 1.210–11, letter of 1776 to William Franks.

Pepys's comments do not acknowledge Macaulay's gender as a significant factor in the reception of her history, which is impassioned, "extravagant," and so forth, but no more so than Hume's. Pepys had expected it to be weakened by intemperance and poor scholarship, but those qualities are here associated with republicanism, and not identified with the "femalities" Polwhele later congratulated himself on discovering.[66] What Pepys finds instead is a history conducted on principles he can admire because they seem to rise above party—a history he praises for qualities which have no explicit gendered connotation.

Carter, as I have mentioned, also admired Macaulay's "very considerable share of both sense and knowledge," and, in a letter of 1775, singled out for particular praise the "judgement and spirit" of her account of James I.[67] Macaulay had written that if James were "ever exempt from our hatred, the exemption must arise from motives of contempt."[68] She later qualified that view, suggesting that she had "taken some liberty in ridiculing" James, for though his "cautious timidity" had prevented him from making war, that caution had at least enabled "the large foundations of the trade of England" to be laid.[69] But the point is that Carter was able, like Pepys, to see judgment rather than partisan zeal in Macaulay's *History,* even in passages Macaulay herself came to regard as too severe. By December 1778, however, Carter is lamenting to Montagu that Macaulay should have "contrived to render herself so consummately ridiculous, by a total want of all common sober sense."[70] By that time three events had taken place, which Carter found increasingly "painful to observe," and which sunk Macaulay's reputation in the press: the celebrations of her forty-sixth birthday in 1776, the erection by Macaulay's friend Wilson of her statue in his parish church in 1777, and her second marriage to William Graham, a young man of twenty-one, in 1778. Those events are all fully and lucidly detailed in Bridget Hill's excellent biography, *The Republican Virago: The Life and Times of Catharine Macaulay, Historian* (1992), to which my discussion is indebted.

Carter was able more or less to stomach the first two events as they came to her attention, though in retrospect they became signs of a lack of common sense. Even in 1778, the birthday celebrations seemed to her to reflect more severely on Wilson, their organizer, than on Macaulay herself. She wrote

66. [Richard Polwhele], *The Unsex'd Females: A Poem, addressed to the author of The Pursuits of Literature* (London: Cadell, 1798), 37 n.

67. *Carter to Montagu,* 2.309–10, letter clxxxi, Deal, 3 June 1775.

68. Catharine Macaulay, *The History of England from the Accession of James I to that of the Brunswick Line,* vol. 1 [1763], 3d ed. (London: Dilly, 1769), 257.

69. *History . . . in a series of letters* (1778), letter 5, 314–15.

70. *Carter to Montagu,* 3.98, letter ccxviii, Deal, 7 December 1778.

that "surely nothing ever equalled that farcical parade of foolery with which she suffered herself to be flattered, and almost worshipped, by that poor old wrong-headed firebrand of party, who now pays so dearly for his nonsense." When she heard about the statue of History, in 1777, it was Wilson she criticized, writing to Montagu:

> Are all the strange representations about Dr. Wilson's statue true? To be sure if he had chosen to raise a statue to Mrs. Macaulay, as high as that which Nebuchadnezzar placed in the plains of Dura, nobody has anything to do with it; but to chuse his inscription from a book written by two nameless writers, and then to call those two writers Lord Lyttelton and Mrs. Peach, is such an instance of absurdity and impertinence as one shall not often meet with.[71]

Carter, the devout Anglican, seems unconcerned by the erection of the image of a living and controversial historian in Wilson's parish church. It is the inscription that troubles her, and it does seem to have involved a complicated and egregious mistake. Wilson quotes from a curious publication titled *The Correspondents. An Original Novel; in a series of letters* (1775), which was thought to be based on letters between Thomas, Lord Lyttelton and Mrs. Apphia Peach, whom he married in 1772 but soon abandoned in order to elope with a barmaid. Wilson compounded the error by attributing his quotation to the "late Lord Lyttelton," the father of Thomas. George, Lord Lyttelton, who had died in 1773, was celebrated because "in public, or in private life" he "abounded in virtues not barely sufficient to create reverence and esteem, but to ensure him the love of all who knew him": in contrast to his "wicked" son, he was renowned for his public and private virtue.[72] To add insult to injury, the terms in which the letters printed in the "novel" of 1775 referred to Catharine Macaulay were less than flattering. The correspondent supposed to be Mrs. Peach mentioned Macaulay in a list that included Carter and Montagu and celebrated the achievements of modern women. The correspondent supposed to be Lord Lyttelton argued in response that "generally speaking, each sex appears to most advantage in the sphere particularly assigned it by Providence," and offered some praise of Macaulay apparently as the exception that proved the rule: "once in every age I would wish such a woman to appear, as a proof that genius is not confined to sex . . . but . . . at the same time . . . you'll pardon me, we want no more than *one* Mrs. *Macaulay*." Wilson seems to have chosen this passage for the inscription because the letter writer did announce that "I would

71. Ibid., 3.40, letter cciv, Deal, 20 September 1777.

72. "A Sketch of the Character of the late George, Lord Lyttelton," in *The Annual Register, or a View of the History, Politics and Literature, For the Year 1776* (London: Dodsley, 1777), 21. On Thomas, Lord Lyttelton, see *Dictionary of National Biography* and *English Short Title Catalogue.*

have her taste the exalted pleasure of universal applause. I would have statues erected to her memory"—presumably after her death.[73] The choice helps to explain Carter's perception of Wilson as the "poor old wrong-headed firebrand" of Wilkesite whiggery: to attempt to defend his statue with a quotation attributed to a man notorious for the vices of blasphemy and obscenity seems perverse enough; but to attribute a letter purporting to be from the vicious son to the father who embodied the combination of public and private virtues so highly prized in the 1770s further undermines Wilson's own reputation.

Carter writes, in 1778, referring more directly to the marriage of Macaulay and Graham, that "I hope the letter which you quote was not really written by herself, but that she contents herself with acting preposterously, and does not add any unnecessary disgrace to her sex, by expressing herself so very indecently." She concluded, perhaps more generously, that "the individual instance of Dr. Wilson and Mrs. Macaulay" might be attributed to the "general folly and corruption of the times."[74] Carter wrote about Macaulay apparently more in sorrow than in anger because she understood her behavior as a reflection both on "her sex" and on "the times." The intrusion of Macaulay's personal life on her public image is bound up for Carter in the acrimony of parliamentary debate over the continuation of the American war: "Did personal rage ever rise so high, or personal abuse ever sink so low, in such an assembly? Dark indeed is the cloud which hangs over our national prospects."[75] Carter is dismayed that personal abuse should infect public debate, and shocked by the possibility that Macaulay's public status as a female patriot should be compromised by a letter to Wilson apparently written by her on her remarriage, and satirized in "three scurrilous, satirical pamphlets."[76] Macaulay's career was enormously damaged by her remarriage. Edmund Rack did not exaggerate its immediate impact when he wrote to Richard Polwhele at the close of 1778:

> Poor Mrs. Macaulay! She is irrecoverably fallen. "*Frailty, thy name is Woman!*" Her passions, even at 52, were too strong for her reason; and she has taken to bed a stout brawny Scotchman of 21. For shame! Her enemies' triumph is now complete. Her friends can say nothing in her favour. O, poor Catharine!—never canst thou emerge from the abyss into which thou art fallen![77]

73. *The Correspondents, An Original Novel; in a series of letters*, 2d ed. (London: Becket, 1776), 114–15.

74. *Carter to Montagu*, 3.98–99, letter ccxviii, Deal, 7 December 1778.

75. Ibid., 3.99, letter ccxviii, Deal, 7 December 1778.

76. Hill, *Republican Virago*, 115.

77. Richard Polwhele, *Traditions and Reflections; Domestic, clerical, and literary; in which are included Letters*, 2 vols. (London: Nichols, 1826), 1.122–23, letter from Rack, Bath, 29 December 1778. Macaulay was of course forty-seven, not fifty-two, but accounts of her marriage frequently exaggerated the difference in age between her and her spouse. See Hill, *Republican Virago*, chapter 5.

But what must have particularly delighted her enemies was the sexual nature of her "crime." Macaulay's reputation as a patriot was, as Pepys suggested, marked by a degree of disinterest that might be seen as defeminizing rather than unfeminine. It is this that Wollstonecraft seems later to pick up on when she praises Macaulay's writing in which "no sex appears."[78] The whiggish or republican nature of Macaulay's work had given her a particular claim to seem disembodied, to participate in that "enthusiasm which robs men of themselves, to transform their existence entirely into the body of the state."[79]

If her politics had in some sense robbed her of a sexualized body, then that transformation had attracted sly detraction: "There was Talk one Evening about Catherine Macaulay; Baretti abused her as usual—She mends however says Reynolds archly—Her last performance was *Loose Thoughts,* and now She is publishing a *Modest Plea.*"[80] Joshua Reynolds's joke about the titles of Macaulay's publications is repeated in the anonymous satire, *A Remarkable Moving Letter, which was Suggested by an Extraordinary Epistle Sent by Her on Her Second Marriage to Her Clerical Admirer* (1779), where she is represented as writing to Wilson that had it not been for his advanced age, "politics had pav'd the road of love," and "All my LOOSE THOUGHTS had toy'd the night away / And thrilling REVOLUTIONS mark'd the day."[81] The point that both Reynolds and the author of the *Remarkable Moving Letter* seem to find so entertaining turns on the analogy between "the body of the state" and the body of the historian. Unlike patriotic men, who "transform their existence," Macaulay has, from the point of view of her satirists, gloriously failed in the act of transubstantiation, and remains a figure of female frailty.

Macaulay's fall can be represented as a lapse always imminent or implicit in women's patriotism. *The Female Patriot: An Epistle from C-t-e M-c-y to The Reverend Dr. W-l-n On her late Marriage. With Critical, Historical, and Philosophical Notes and Illustrations* (1779) offered a rather more skillful, detailed, and handsomely presented satire on Macaulay than the *Remarkable Moving Letter.* Macaulay is portrayed as having made a mock heroic sacrifice of the

78. Mary Wollstonecraft, *A Vindication of the Rights of Woman* (1792), ed. Carol H. Poston (New York: Norton, 1975), 105.

79. Russell, *Essay,* 2.49.

80. Katharine C. Balderston, ed., *Thraliana: The Diary of Mrs. Hester Lynch Thrale (Later Mrs. Piozzi) 1776–1809,* 2 vols. (Oxford: Clarendon Press, 1942), 1.42–43, 28 May 1777. Thrale adds that "Baretti had a comical Aversion to Mrs Macaulay and his Aversions are numerous and strong" (43). Reynolds alludes to Macaulay's *Loose Remarks on Certain Positions to be found in Mr. Hobbes's "Philosophical Rudiments of Government and Society"* (1767), and *A Modest Plea for the Property of Copyright* (1774).

81. *A Remarkable Moving Letter, which was Suggested by an Extraordinary Epistle Sent by Her on Her Second Marriage to Her Clerical Admirer* (London: Foulder, 1779), 6–7.

tomes which had inspired her politics on the altar of her love. The "British Heroine" is then represented as captivated by the "female arts" of poetry and music, bound by the "magick thraldom" of "am'rous fetters." The poet compares these in some detail with the "fatal snare" which imprisons "some poor insect" in the plant identified as "Venus's mousetrap," or "a species of the Mimosa, or Sensitive," and has Macaulay claim that "Stern Patriotism ceas'd my soul to move, / And all the Heroine languish'd into love." Remarriage is represented as a transition between genres, between the heroic and manly patriotism of her history and the eroticized sensibility of the romantic heroine.[82]

The incongruity of that image of Macaulay trapped by her sensibility is underlined when it is set alongside the personification of sensibility portrayed in Hayley's *Triumphs of Temper*. There the figure poised with apparently irresistible allure "just between the woman and the child" hovers over the sensitive plant:

> Her fair left arm around a vase she flings,
> From which the tender plant mimosa springs:
> Towards its leaves, o'er which she fondly bends,
> The youthful fair her vacant hand extends
> With gentle motion, anxious to survey
> How far the feeling fibres own her sway: . . .

One of the engravings after Stothard which illustrate the poem shows the figure of *Sensibility* watching the plant respond to her hand, as "her tender breast with pity seems to pant, / And shrinks at every shrinking of the plant" (fig. 9). In Stothard's image, sensibility is girlish, chastely attired, and appropriate to Hayley's implication that youthful sensibility will in time mature into the "mild maternal form" of benevolence, or love without desire.[83] But Hayley also cherished less chaste fantasies about feminine sensibility. At Hayley's suggestion, a shrub mimosa that he supplied accompanied Emma Lyon (later Emma Hart, and then Lady Hamilton) in George Romney's portrait of her as *Sensibility* (1786, fig. 10); Lyon was of course already notorious as the embodiment of scandalous sexuality, of the kind that was scurrilously attributed to Macaulay.[84]

82. [?Richard Paul Jodrell], *The Female Patriot: An Epistle from C-t-e M-c-y to The Reverend Dr. W-l.n On her late Marriage. With Critical, Historical, and Philosophical Notes and Illustrations* (London: Bew, 1779), ll. 169 n., 146, 151–52, 147, 149, 148 n., 93–94.

83. Hayley, *Triumphs,* Canto V, 111–12, 124. Stothard's illustration, engraved by Neagle, is published by T. Cadell, 1 February 1788.

84. See George Paston, *George Romney* (London: Methuen, 1903), 91–92. See the discussion of this image in Markman Ellis, *The Politics of Sensibility: Race, Gender and Commerce in the Sentimental Novel* (Cambridge: Cambridge University Press), 23–24.

Figure 9 Neagle after Stothard, *Sensibility,* illustration of 1788 in W. Hayley, *The Triumphs of Temper,* 8th ed. (London: Cadell, 1795), engraving, $2\frac{3}{4} \times 4\frac{1}{4}$ in.

Sensibility is central to the conception of desirable femininity in these decades, and to the image of a female patriotism that extends from familial to national affection. But sensibility in conjunction with the stern patriotism of Macaulay the public historian becomes a dangerously sexualized excess, a distortion of the delicate relation between private and public affect. The *Essay on the Character of Women* had suggested that women were not capable of patriotism or a "universal love of mankind" because "a man, to them, is more than a nation," but in the 1770s, I suggested, that sort of capacity for an immediate affection had become increasingly necessary to notions of patriotism—so that,

Figure 10 George Romney of Emma Lyon (later Hamilton) as *Sensibility,* painted c. 1784–86. Oil on canvas. 59 × 47 $\frac{3}{4}$ in. Reproduced by permission of Sotheby's, London.

for example, Johnson's celebration of Iona had involved a difficult mixture of abstract concern for the public good and a more immediate, almost physical response of local emotion. In More's poetical epistle on *Sensibility,* Boscawen had seemed capable of the heroic duty of sacrificing her family for the good of the country because the immediate physical affection she felt for them was imagined somehow to extend to embrace the public good; but in More's account in contrast to Johnson's no process of abstraction seemed involved. Instead, Boscawen's ability to feel for all those who make up the nation was represented as an extension of the sensibility appropriate to her gender, her class, and, more personally, the evidence of her dedication to her family. The sensibility necessary to rehumanize the face of Britain as an imperial power in the context of the American war is however carefully distinguished from the libidinized form of patriotic enthusiasm satirized in representations of Macaulay's marriage. For where a properly patriotic sensibility extends domestic affection into feeling for the nation, Macaulay's politics are taken to represent a public patriotism devoid of sentimental local emotion, and a private life overcharged with physical desire.

The position of femininity in relation to the nation which is represented in the fate of Macaulay, following her second marriage, is aptly portrayed in a song, "The Patriot Fair," published later in the century, but perhaps with an earlier currency. The song begins:

When young and artless as the lamb,
Which plays about its fondling dam,
Brisk, buxom, pert, and silly,
I slighted all the manly swains,
And put my virgin heart in chains,
For smiling, smooth fac'd Willy.

But when experience came with years,
Which rais'd my hopes and quell'd my fears,
My heart was blyth and bonny:
I turn off every beardless youth,
So gave my word, and fix'd my truth
On honest sturdy Johnny.

In subsequent stanzas the patriot fair works her way through a succession of diverse lovers, attracted in turn by their power, fashion, riches, and musical skill, until she concludes:

So now alike the fools and wits,
Fops, fidlers, foreigners and cits,
All struck me by rotation.
Come learn of me ye patriot fair,
Nor make a single man your care,
But sigh for all the nation.

In that final stanza there may be some possibility that the patriot fair has learned from the rotation of fools and wits, "Fops, fidlers, foreigners and cits," to appreciate the joys of a more abstracted, disinterested love for the nation; but the song more obviously indicates that her patriotism consists in an attempt to conduct "amorous parley" with as much of the nation as possible. Either way, her patriotism seems to be founded in a gleefully indiscriminate sexual promiscuity.[85]

85. "The Patriot Fair," in *A Song, on the Grand Illuminations in Glasgow. To which are added The Bush aboon Traquire. The Prevailing Fashions. The Patriot Fair. And, the Rapture* (Stirling: M. Randal, n.d., c. 1800–1810?), ll. 1–12, 25–30, 21.

III

The idea of modern patriotism figured in representations of Catherine Macaulay, in satire or in celebration, is closely associated with the discourse on fashion as the sign of civilized polish or decadence. Elizabeth Montagu, as I have already mentioned, was perceived in the 1770s to have become "the queen of fashion and splendor" as well as "the queen of literature and elegant society,"[86] and had appeared to Cumberland, in the *Observer,* to be as it were wrapping herself in the flag of learned antiquity in the magnificence of her dress. But where comments on Montagu focused on the ambivalent relation between the elegance of her learning and of her manner of living, the fashionable elegance of Macaulay is more usually satirized as the sign of feminine frailty and debasement, as the sign of a sexuality incompatible with the idea of the disembodied patriot. Horace Walpole commented in 1769 on the reception of Paoli, the hero of Corsican independence, that "the Court have artfully adopted him, and at least crushed one egg on which fashion, and her brood-hen, Mrs. Macaulay, would have been very glad to have sat." He suggests that Macaulay's political convictions are no more than fashionable whims.[87] James Boswell reported to Samuel Johnson from Bath, in 1776, that

> It had been mentioned, I know not with what truth, that, a certain female political writer, whose doctrines he [Johnson] disliked, had of late become very fond of dress, sat hours together at her toilet, and even put on rouge:—JOHNSON. "She is better employed at her toilet, than using her pen. It is better she should be reddening her own cheeks, than blackening other people's characters."[88]

Boswell's report does not suggest that Macaulay's interest in her toilet is diminishing her political energy, but Johnson's response assumes that her fondness for dress must be indulged at the expense of or as an alternative to her pen. His remarks are reminiscent of those earlier satires which suggested that fashionable behavior was preferable to learning in women. But Johnson's comments also echo Walpole's, in suggesting that Macaulay's reputations as a fashionable woman and as a republican historian may be interchangeable. Their comments are about the proper contrast between history writing and personal adornment, and imply that Macaulay has never been able to maintain the

86. Lucy Aikin, ed., *The Works of Anna Laetitia Barbauld. With a memoir,* 2 vols. (London: Longman, 1825), 2.19, letter to John Aikin, Palgrave, 19 January 1778.

87. Peter Cunningham, ed., *The Letters of Horace Walpole Earl of Orford,* 9 vols. (London: Bohn, 1861), 5.196, Walpole to Sir Horace Mann, Calais, 8 October 1769.

88. Boswell, *Life of Johnson,* 749, 26 April 1776.

appropriate masculine distance from personal vanity and personal spite in "using her pen."

In retrospect, after her remarriage, the earlier incidents of Macaulay's statue and of the birthday celebrations seemed part and parcel of the more or less explicitly sexualized vanity her later action was seen to demonstrate. In the satirical poem, *The Female Historian to the Patriot Divine; or, A Modest Plea for the Right of Widows* (1779), Macaulay is imagined to explain to Wilson that her second marriage is her patriotic duty, recognition of the "civic debt" of her sex, "which she alone repays, / Who strives the civic fund of living wealth to raise." She claims that the vanity he has encouraged in those earlier incidents has culminated in her grandiose conception of her remarriage, which perpetuates the theatricality of the birthday scenes,

> When on a gorgeous throne you seated high,
> Me the dear idol of your dazzled eye:
> When softest poets hail'd your mimic queen,
> And you the hero of that puppet-scene.
> Where open Vanity mov'd all the wires;
> While motley Muses squeak as she inspires.[89]

The idea of the birthday celebrations as puppetry, theater, a suitable preface to the "abject idolatry of the living Catharine"[90] that was seen to be involved in the business of placing her statue in the church, associates Macaulay with precisely the kind of courtly parade to which her work was most hostile, and to which the virtues of the domestic wife and mother were increasingly seen as inimical—the queen herself being, of course, the exception that proves the rule.

I have already mentioned Carter's comments on the earlier "farcical parade of foolery," which had culminated in the presentation of six odes to the historian, who "was seated in a conspicuous elevated situation" and "very elegantly dressed."[91] In the same letter, Carter reflects that "I think one never heard of any body, above the degree of an ideot, who took pleasure in being so dressed out with the very rags and ribbons of vanity, like a queen in a puppet show."[92] Carter's language here is close to that of contemporary satirists, for she, like

89. Anon., *The Patriot Divine to the Female Historian; an elegaic epistle. To which is added, the lady's reply. The Female Historian to the Patriot Divine; or, a Modest Plea for the Rights of Widows. A Didactic Epistle* (London: Fielding, 1779), 38–39.

90. [?Jodrell], *Female Patriot,* l. 156 n.

91. [?Wilson], "Introduction," in *Six Odes Presented to the Justly-Celebrated Historian, Mrs. Catharine Macaulay, on her Birthday, and publically read to a polite and brilliant audience assembled April 2nd at Alfred House, Bath to congratulate that Lady on the happy occasion* (London: 1777), vii. For a fuller account of the ceremonies and of responses to them, see Hill, *Republican Virago,* 94–99.

92. *Carter to Montagu,* 3.99, letter ccxviii.

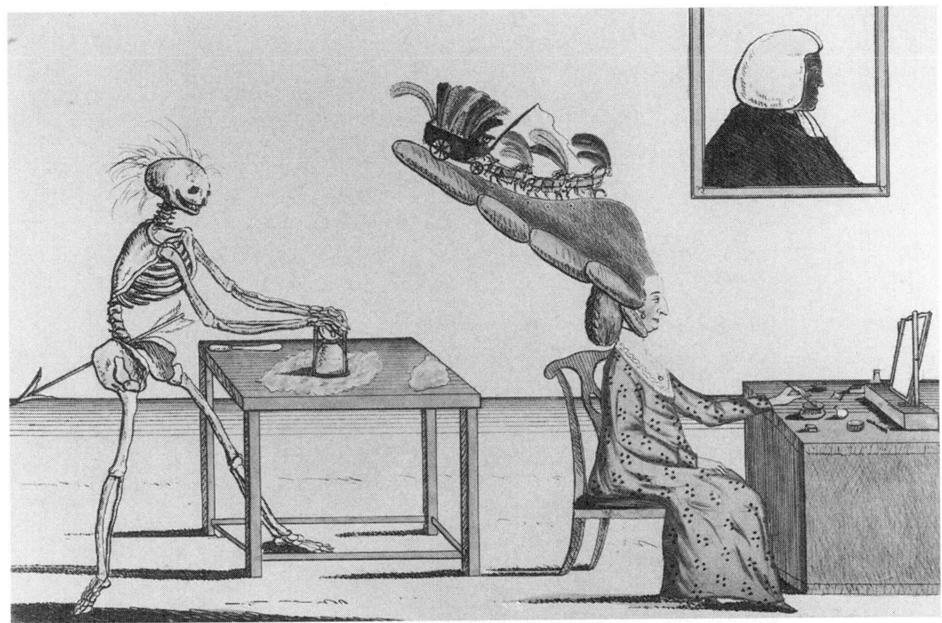

Figure 11 M. Darly, *A Speedy & Effectual Preparation for the Next World*, 1777, engraving, $8\frac{3}{8} \times 12\frac{13}{16}$ in. BM 5441. © The British Museum.

them, condemns the historian for having violated the privacy appropriate to feminine sensibility. She remarks in another letter that "magnificence and show have no connexion with the feelings of the heart, or the real comforts of private life."[93] The representation of Macaulay's second marriage as the acknowledgment of her "country's higher claims" denies its possible "connexion with the feelings of the heart," and identifies it as an unfeminine form of patriotism that resembles a sexually scandalous drama more appropriate to the public theater than to private life. The notion of Macaulay as the "mimic queen" in a puppet show points to the sense in which her involvement in republican politics, the patriotism that was seen to have defeminized or disembodied her, had hollowed out her image for public display, evacuated the "feelings of the heart," to create a doll-like figure who could represent history, or political beliefs incompatible with her own convictions, or indeed less exalted qualities. Matthew Darly's print of 1777, for example, shows Macaulay at her dressing table, wearing one of the high adorned "heads" fashionable in the late 1770s (fig. 11). The print is titled *A Speedy & Effectual Preparation for the*

93. *Carter to Vesey*, 3.313, letter cxvii, Deal, 12 November 1778.

Figure 12 Carington Bowles, *Abelard and Eloisa,* 1778, $4\frac{1}{2} \times 6$ in. The caption reads: "Madam your wondrous Beauty I admire. / Sir your Politeness all my thanks require. / Madam, I love you most sincerely well. / Your Passion Sir I by my own can tell. / Madam, my Gout and Dropsy are no Crimes / O Sir! they're merits in these modish times. / My Person Ma'am eternally is thine—/ Sir, My Charms and Fortune I to thee resign."

Next World, and the plumed horses and hearse, with suitably urgent driver, balanced on Macaulay's head emphasize the connection between her taste for fashionable adornment, her worldliness, and her mortality. A print produced for Carington Bowles in 1778, representing Wilson and Macaulay as *Abelard and Eloisa* (fig. 12), shows her as an aged fashion victim, responding to Wilson's flattery with the assertion of her passion and the assurance that his "Gout and Dropsy," the afflictions of old age, are "merits in these modish times."

High heads of the kind that satirical prints of Macaulay use to adorn and even to identify her image were often perceived to make women into the puppets of fashionable vanity. In, for example, Christopher Anstey's *New Bath Guide,* first published in 1766 but reissued repeatedly throughout the 1770s, a commentator deplores the "MODERN HEAD-DRESS," telling the ladies: "Ye have eyes, lips, and nose, but your heads are no more / Than a doll's that is plac'd at a milliner's door."[94] Anstey was obviously pleased with his joke, choosing to be posed for William Hoare's portrait of c. 1775 with his daughter who brandishes a fashion doll suitably bewigged (fig. 13). The image contrasts his solidly familial and private virtues with the miniature mannequin of the fashionable lady, so frequently satirized for lacking domestic virtue, and spurning the simplicities of private family life. And Anstey returned to the theme in his later satire, *An Election Ball, In Poetical Letters* (1776). There Mr. Inkle, writing from Bath to his wife in Gloucester, describes the attempts of his daughter Madge "to appear like a Lady of very high Fashion," exploiting the well-worn theme of the rustic in town. Madge's most ambitious scheme is to create a fashionable head for herself, ornamenting her father's old red wig with dripping and flour, jewels, fruit and flowers, and, to add the final touch, "Laying hard at the tail of our Dunghill Cock! / She pluck'd it—and pull'd it—and tore from the Stump / All the Feathers that cloath'd his unfortunate Rump." The frontispiece shows Madge, with earnest concentration, sticking the crowning, scatologically loaded glory into her headdress (fig. 14). The effect, Mr. Inkle goes on to relate, of "Head and Feather / And Wig altogether" is to make Madge resemble a picture of "th'adorable Queen" of Tahiti, who, with her "black Maids of Honour," distracted the eyes of the Europeans who intended to witness the transit of Venus "From the Orbs in the Skies, / To gaze at THEIR Heavenly Bodies."[95] The appeal of the wig, for the satirist, lies in the way it brings into one focus so many strains of antifeminine discourse: the doll, shit, racial difference, violence and sexuality, the indelicacy of the most elegant and luxurious excesses of fashion.

The headdresses are signs of superfluity, signs of luxury. In 1775 Frances Boscawen was told that "the sight of a milliner's box would make my hair stand on end! Others tell me that Miss . . . wears chesnuts in her hair, Lady . . . Leeks,

94. [Christopher Anstey], *The New Bath Guide; or, Memoirs of the B—r—d Family. In a Series of Poetical Epistles,* 9th ed. (London: Dodsley, 1773), 108, 112, letter XII. On satires on fashion from the 1770s onward, see James Raven, *Judging New Wealth: Popular Publishing and Responses to Commerce in England, 1750–1800* (Oxford: Clarendon Press, 1992), 177–81.

95. [Christopher Anstey], *An Election Ball, in Poetical Letters from Mr. Inkle, at Bath, to his Wife at Glocester: with a Poetical Address to John Millar, Esq. at Batheaston Villa,* 2d ed. (Bath: S. Hazard, 1776), 32, 35, 38–39. The first edition, also published in 1776, claimed to be written "in the Zomerzetshire dialect."

Figure 13 William Hoare, *Christopher Anstey with his Daughter, Mary,* c. 1775, oil on canvas, $49\frac{5}{8} \times 39\frac{1}{4}$ in. Reproduced by courtesy of the National Portrait Gallery, London.

and Mrs. . . . oranges. The names you may put in as you please, I have forgot them, but the facts are so, and the headdress ridiculous and odious and unbecoming beyond the example of former times" (fig. 15). Her comments seem to gain force from their juxtaposition with the observation that "beef in Boston is fourteen pence a pound, mutton only a shilling. Judge you therefore

Figure 14 Coplestone Warre Bampfylde, engraving of 1776, frontispiece to [Christopher Anstey], *An Election Ball, in Poetical Letters from Mr. Inkle, at Bath, to His Wife at Glocester,* 2nd ed. (Bath: S. Hazard, 1776), engraving, $6\frac{3}{4} \times 8\frac{7}{8}$ in. (pl.).

whether the collection for poor soldiers is not very proper."[96] The high heads of high fashion often, and with some directness, identify themselves as perversions of trade, signs of that rapacious colonial policy that threatens to strip Britain of her profitable dependents, as Boscawen's comments imply. For Hannah More, visiting London in the mid-1770s, the heads are primarily signs

96. Aspinall-Oglander, *Admiral's Widow,* 70, 69, letter to Julia Sayer, Glan Villa, 21 November 1775.

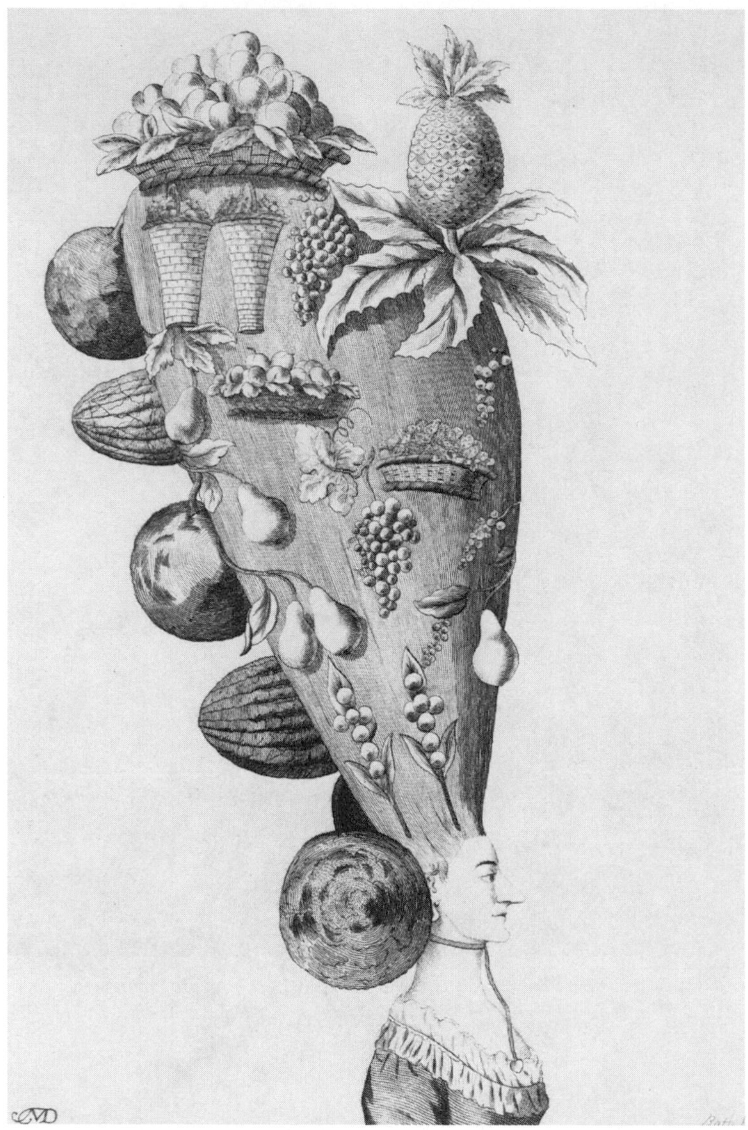

Figure 15 M. Darly, *The Fruit Stall*, 1777, engraving, $12\frac{3}{4} \times 8\frac{1}{2}$ in. BM 5448. © The British Museum.

of the decadence of fashionable life. She writes to one of her sisters in 1775 that "nothing can be conceived so absurd, extravagant, and fantastical, as the present mode of dressing the head. Simplicity and modesty are things so much exploded, that the very names are no longer remembered." But her rather self-righteous disgust is tempered, as condemnation of extravagance turns almost to pity for disease, when she explains that she has just been dressed for dinner by "one of the most fashionable disfigurers." Though she asks for simplicity, she finds when the treatment is finished that "I absolutely blush at myself, and turn to the glass with as much caution as a vain beauty, just risen from the small-pox; which cannot be a more disfiguring disease than the present mode of dressing. Of the one, the calamity may be greater in its consequences, but of the other it is more corrupt in its cause."[97] There is an intriguing omission in More's account here, as though her failure to identify with her own image precluded the possibility of reflecting on what corrupt cause might have prompted her to visit the fashionable disfigurer in the first place. But by the following year she can condemn with confident disdain: "Again I am annoyed by the foolish absurdity of the present mode of dress. Some ladies carry on their heads a large quantity of fruit, and yet they would despise a poor useful member of society, who carried it there for the purpose of selling it for bread."[98] The remark is reminiscent of mid-century comments on vulgar fashion, which fails to homogenize its ornaments, and to conceal beneath a unifying veneer of elegance the possibility that they might be perceived as a "robbery on the shop."[99] But where earlier satires had claimed to unveil and thus deny the aspirations of trading and artisanal women, More's comments suggest that for her the problem of the fashionable woman is that she is not "a poor useful member of society." The point of the headdress, More suggests, is to confirm the distance between fashionable luxury and useful trade (fig. 16).

Fashion is more readily identifiable as a folly where it is associated with the aristocracy. For in "the later periods of commerce and luxury," as Adam Ferguson argues in his *Essay on the History of Civil Society* (1767), aristocrats "become the first victims of that wretched insignificance, into which the members of every corrupted state, by the tendency of their weaknesses, and their vices, are in haste to plunge themselves."[100] Increasingly, in the second half of the eighteenth century, full membership in society is seen to belong only to those who do useful work, who perform one of those divided labors in the uniting of which society itself is seen to consist. Excluded from the division of labor, by the 1770s "people of fashion" are coming to be seen as the victims of their own idleness, and at the same time as the victims of fashion, reduced to competing for status by devoting themselves to trivial occupations which, whether

97. William Roberts, *Memoirs of the Life and Correspondence of Mrs. Hannah More,* 4 vols. (London: R. B. Seeley, 1834), 1.51–52, London.

98. Ibid., 1.65, letter "to one of her sisters," London, 1776.

99. *Connoisseur,* no. 25, 18 July 1754. See pp. 24–29 above.

100. Adam Ferguson, *An Essay on the History of Civil Society,* intro. Louis Schneider (New Bruswick, N.J.: Transaction Publishers, 1980), Part vi, sect. iv, 260.

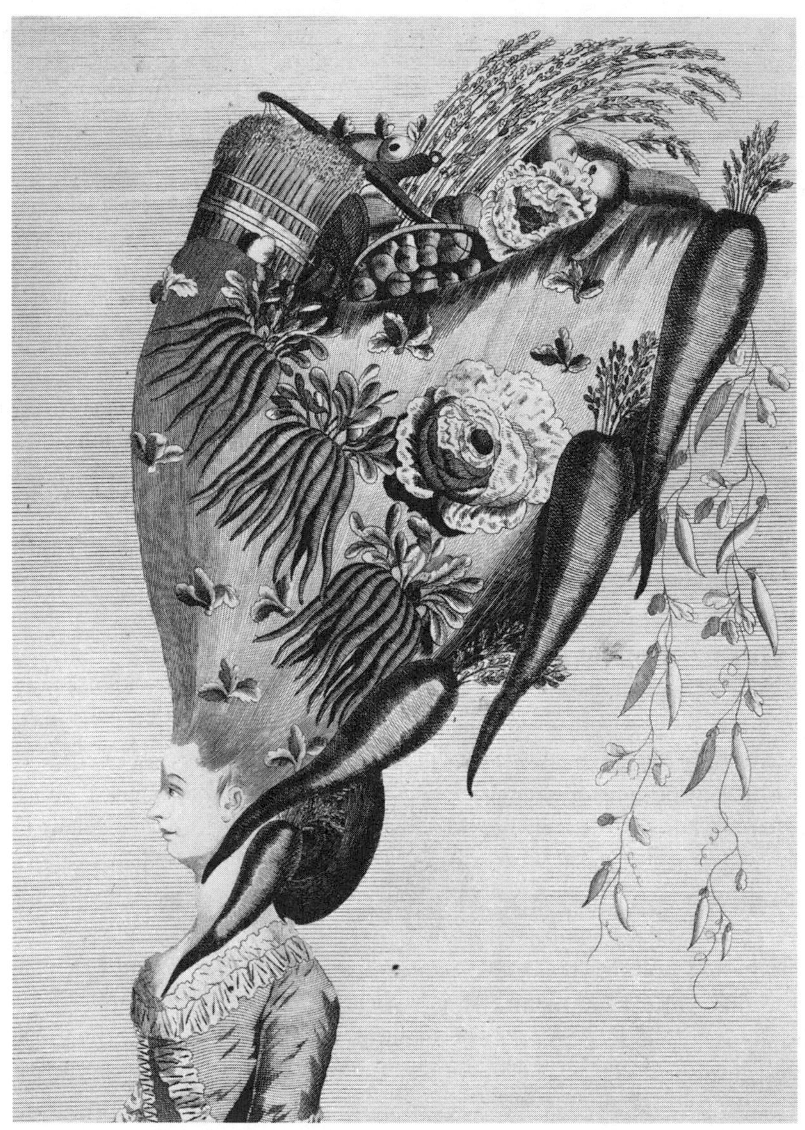

Figure 16 M. Darly, *The Green Stall,* 1777, engraving, $12\frac{3}{4} \times 8\frac{1}{2}$ in. BM 5449. © The British Museum.

they are seen to be innocent or vicious, are the sign at once of their idleness and of "the elegance and refinement of their living."[101] John Millar explains:

> From the improvement of arts and manufactures, the ancient simplicity of manners is in a great measure destroyed; and the proprietor of a landed estate, instead of consuming its produce in hired retainers, is obliged to employ a great part of it in purchasing those comforts and conveniences which have become objects of attention, and which are thought suitable to his condition.[102]

The aristocracy are obliged, by the "logic" of the "wretched insignificance" that distinguishes them, to exchange paternalistic employment policies for elegant and spectacular purchases which indicate only the acquisitive taste and wealth "thought suitable" to their station.

In the spring of 1776, Lady Harriot Pitt, the daughter of Lady Chatham, was spending the season in London with Mrs. Molly Hood and her husband, the future Rear-Admiral. Molly Hood wrote to Lady Chatham, warning that she and her husband had become "alarmd least that dignity should be wanting in Lady Harriot Pitt that markd Lady Mahon to the World as your well educated daughter." Lady Harriot, she fears, is "certainly in danger" of "infection . . . from the mode of the Bon Ton." She explains: "The dress of her Head which makes her sit double in a coach and her stays little at the Bottom and broad at the Top are certainly to be remarked with some other Ladys who like to be distinguished, and who may run some hazard to their healths by such enormous fashions."[103] Molly Hood is unsure of whether these "other Ladys" are "much below [Lady Harriot's] imitation," or whether her disapproval simply indicates that she is "an old woman who sees so little of the great Ladies," but Lady Chatham immediately recalled her daughter to the country. Lady Harriot's sister, who displayed such exemplary dignity in resisting the allure of "enormous fashions," had in 1774 married Lord Mahon, the future Earl "Citizen" Stanhope, who, following his return from the continent in 1773, involved himself in the political circles in which Catharine Macaulay moved and was admired.[104] In 1790, Macaulay addressed her public letter of *Observations* on Burke's *Reflections* on the French revolution to Stanhope, thinking that he would welcome her arguments "as a patriot, a philosopher, and the firm friend

101. Millar, *Origin,* 233.

102. Ibid., 232–33.

103. Molly Hood, *Letters to Hester Pitt* [Harley Street, March 1776], 118.

104. See Caroline Robbins, *The Eighteenth-Century Commonwealthman: Studies in the Transmission, Development and Circumstances of English Liberal Thought from the Restoration of Charles II until the War with the Thirteen Colonies* (Cambridge: Harvard University Press, 1961), 358–62, 368–72.

Figure 17 M. Darly, *The Vis. A. Vis. Bisected. Or the Ladies Coop,* 1776, engraving, 8 $\frac{9}{16}$ × 12 $\frac{15}{16}$ in. BM 5373. © The British Museum.

of the general rights of man."[105] But neither Lady Mahon's rank nor her connection with radical politics had infected her with the desire for "a true polite Figure" which her sister shares with Anstey's Madge Inkle, who, in pursuit of her ambition, must "*shove up* her Bosom, and *shove down* her Stays," and be conveyed like "The Lady you've seen in a Lobster confin'd," with "her Head almost jamm'd to her Knees" (fig. 17).[106]

In representations of Macaulay and of the Duchess of Devonshire, however, female patriotism becomes involved in fashionable dress. The Duchess was, of course, frequently represented as a figure of high fashion. William Combe's *The First of April: or, The Triumphs of Folly* (1777), for example, a satirical poem elaborating the notion that "FOLLY loves the Toilette of a Woman of Fashion!" was dedicated to the "Celebrated Dutchess," and explored in Combe's predictable and venomous manner the predilection of the aristocracy for fashion-

105. Macaulay, *Observations on the Reflections of the Right Hon. Edmund Burke, on the Revolution in France, in a letter to the Right Hon. the Earl of Stanhope* (London: Dilly, 1790), 5.

106. Carter identifies Mahon as one of the "pert republican boys" in *Carter to Montagu,* 2.231, letter clxv, Deal, 30 October 1773. [Anstey], *Election Ball,* 42, 46, 45.

Figure 18 T. Rowlandson, *Liberty and Fame introducing Female Patriotism to Britania*, 1784, engraving, $8\frac{1}{2} \times 6\frac{5}{8}$ in.

able excess.[107] The Duchess appeared again as the "wild . . . laughing" leader of "A giggling throng, by ev'ry folly led," in *Fashion. A Poem. Addressed to the Ladies of Great-Britain* (1778).[108] Images celebrating or satirizing her involvement in Fox's election campaign frequently emphasized the fashionability of her dress, both as the recognizable sign of her identity, and because fashion might signify either the elegance or the dissipation of the party she endorsed. In, for example, the engraving of *Liberty and Fame introducing Female Patriotism to Britania* [*sic*] (fig. 18), which appeared as the frontispiece to the 1785 edition of *The Westminster Election,* the well-dressed figure of the Duchess, smilingly "Infused with a Fortitude from Heaven," is led toward Britannia with eyes modestly downcast. The image celebrated the Duchess's contribution to

107. [William Combe], *The First of April: or, The Triumphs of Folly: A Poem, Dedicated to a Celebrated Duchess. By the author of the Diaboliad* (London: Bew, 1777), Dedication, ii, i.

108. *Fashion. A Poem. Addressed to the Ladies of Great-Britain. In Two Books. Book First* (London: Williams, 1778), 21.

Figure 19 *The Auspicious Marriage!* in *Town and Country Magazine,* vol. 10 (1778), engraving, $4\frac{1}{4} \times 4$ in.

the election campaign, but I think her fashionable appearance tinges the accolade with uncertainty about the implications of the grace she lends to patriotism, for her appearance is the sign of desirable elegance and of excessive refinement, of patriotic virtue and luxury. But fashionable appearance is still more appropriate to Devonshire, as one of "the great Ladies," than it could be to Macaulay, the female representative of republican politics and city wealth.

Representations of Macaulay as a well-dressed lady with a Roman nose include in one gesture reference to her republican politics and to her status as a woman of wealth and fashion (fig. 19). Her sexuality, her dress, and her political activities are interchangeable signs of the imperial corruption against which she had always argued so strenuously. In Macaulay's progress from republican heroine to image of feminine frailty her fashionable dress seems, as it were, to get snagged on the machinery of the cultural shift in the idea of patriotism. Fashion is perceived to be the sign of a lack of sensibility. *The Lounger,* for example, comments in 1786 that "our fashionable ladies have brought up Indifference with their gauzes and feathers; both (in the words of my friend the Milliner of Prince's-Street) 'light easy wear, and fit for all seasons.'" The essayist adds that

> The highest fashions must always properly belong to certain orders of the people. This ease and indifference, in their greatest extent, should only be worn by privileged persons. It might not be amiss, if, like the rouge of the French, they were put on by married women only, who may be supposed to bestow all their feelings at home; or by ladies of very high rank, who (as travellers tell us of the calm that reigns on the summit of the Alps) have got into a superior region, undisturbed by the emotions of ordinary life.[109]

Apart from that jibe at married women, whom the essay implies, with heavy irony, ought to be expending "all their feelings at home," the satire depends on the notion not that there is still a real difference in the livery of station, but that there should be. The woman who wishes to establish that she is a "useful member of society," in Hannah More's terms, or to claim the virtue of a sensibility that is both domestic and patriotic, cannot appear to be "so made up of ornaments, so stuck around with finery, that an ill-natured observer might say, their milliner had sent [her] hither, as she places her doll in her shopwindow, to exhibit her wares to the company."[110] Modern patriotism is based in sensibility and local emotion, but these are feminized qualities which, when removed from a private and familial register, are involved in the discourse of corruption employed in the narrative on the decline of the Roman empire. The negative implications of these qualities are most fully explicit when they are associated with women of fashion, or with women involved in the public life of politics. But representations of those women confirm that the focus of concern in these decades is the coincidence of civilized progress and imperial decline, politeness and corruption.

109. *Lounger,* no. 55, 18 February 1786.
110. *Lounger,* no. 4, 26 February 1785.

9

Anna Laetitia Barbauld and the Mighty Mothers of Immortal Rome

I

In 1775, Josiah Wedgwood produced a portrait medallion of Anna Laetitia Barbauld as a Roman matron (fig. 20). In contrast to the engraving of Macaulay as Roman matron that had appeared as the frontispiece to the third volume of her *History* in 1767 (fig. 21), the image of Barbauld seems softer, made more girlish by the copiousness of Barbauld's ringlets, the youthful curve of her cheek, the absence of jewelry. But the Roman style nevertheless endows both women with an uncompromising seriousness or monumental impassivity that is intriguing in its implications for their femininity. The image of Barbauld builds most obviously on the exceptional success of her volume of *Poems,* first published in 1773 and frequently republished in the following four years. But if it does exploit the associations of the *Poems,*[1] then it emphasizes that they establish Barbauld as a poet of defeminizing seriousness and authority. When the *Poems* were republished in 1792, Mary Wollstonecraft took Barbauld to task for

Portions of this chapter appeared in "Femininity and Anna Laetitia Barbauld: A Supposed Sexual Character" in *Women and Literature in Britain, 1700–1800,* ed. Vivien Jones (Cambridge: Cambridge University Press, 2000).

1. On the importance of "appearance and associations" to the success of Wedgwood's work, see Hilary Young, "Introduction. From the Potteries to St Petersburg: Wedgwood and the Making and Selling of Ceramics," in *The Genius of Wedgwood,* ed. Hilary Young (London: Victoria and Albert Museum, 1995), 14.

Figure 20 Wedgwood Portrait Medallion of Anna Laetitia Barbauld. The image shows a modern white on pale blue Jasper portrait medallion taken from the mould of 1775. No eighteenth-century copies of the medallion have been located. Reproduced by permission of the Trustees of the Wedgwood Museum, Barlaston, Staffordshire, England.

perpetuating in them the notion of women as merely decorative and excessively feminine. In this chapter I will explore the contrast between the implications of Wollstonecraft's criticisms and Wedgwood's image. First I will consider the changing demands on women's writing indicated by the reception of Barbauld's work in the last three decades of the century; and second I will look briefly at representations of the women of classical antiquity. In chapter 8 I mentioned that the public lives of the women of imperial Rome were seen as the signs and causes of decline and fall, but the Roman matrons alluded to as exemplary models in positive images of Macaulay and Barbauld are those of the Roman republic, and in the conclusion to this chapter I consider their currency as models for learned women of the later decades of the century.

In her *Vindication* of 1792, Mary Wollstonecraft wrote of the "false system of female manners" which, she argued, "robs the whole sex of its dignity, and

Figure 21 G. B. Cipriani after J. Basire, engraving of *Catharina Macaulay,* 1767. Originally used as the frontispiece of vol. 3 of the first edition of Macaulay's *History,* this is an apparently reversed image, with the text re-engraved, and was used as the frontispiece to vol. 1 of the third edition (London: Dilly, 1769). $4\frac{1}{2} \times 7\frac{1}{8}$ in. (pl.).

classes the brown and fair with the smiling flowers that only adorn the land." She remarked that the evaluation of women as merely ornamental "has ever been the language of men, and the fear of departing from a supposed sexual character, has made even women of superior sense adopt the same sentiments." In a footnote, she identified the woman of "superior sense" she had in mind as Barbauld, who had explored what Wollstonecraft saw as the "ignoble comparison" between women and flowers in her poem, "To a Lady, with some painted flowers." Wollstonecraft quotes the eighteen lines of the poem in full, emphasizing what she finds most offensive, including almost all of the second half of its short length (here cited with her emphases):

Flowers, the sole luxury which nature knew,
In Eden's pure and guiltless garden grew.
To loftier forms are rougher tasks assign'd;
The sheltering oak resists the stormy wind,

The tougher yew repels invading foes,
And the tall pine for future navies grows;
But this soft family, to cares unknown,
Were born for pleasure and delight ALONE.
Gay without toil, and lovely without art,
They spring to CHEER *the sense, and* GLAD *the heart.*
Nor blush, my fair, to own you copy these;
Your BEST, *your* SWEETEST *empire is*—TO PLEASE.

What adds fuel to Wollstonecraft's indignation is her admiration for Barbauld as an educationalist and a poet. Barbauld spent her childhood at the Dissenting academy at Warrington, where her father, John Aikin, taught. Following her marriage to Rochemont Barbauld in 1774, the couple ran a school for boys, and after their resignation from the school in 1785 she continued to teach small numbers of male and female pupils independently for most of the rest of her life. The educational theory set out and practiced in the various publications she produced for children was widely admired. At the Warrington Academy, she met Joseph and Mary Priestley. In her footnote Wollstonecraft cites an early poem Barbauld had addressed to Mary Priestley, as an example of the high standard the poem on flowers departs from, and the terms in which Wollstonecraft castigates the ignoble comparison between women and flowers—"virtue . . . must be acquired by rough *toils,* and useful struggles with worldly *cares*"—echo Barbauld's claim in the earlier poem that in order to achieve his destined virtue and glory man must accept that "His course with toil concludes, with pain began"; he must learn from his struggles in the world that is "misfortune's school."[2]

Wollstonecraft accuses Barbauld of adopting a masquerade of femininity, a disguise that conforms to the "supposed sexual character" that the language of

2. Mary Wollstonecraft, *A Vindication of the Rights of Woman* (1792), ed. Carol H. Poston (New York: Norton, 1975), 53 and n. 7. "To Mrs. P[riestley], with some Drawings of Birds and Insects," in *The Poems of Anna Letitia Barbauld,* ed. William McCarthy and Elizabeth Kraft (Athens: University of Georgia Press, 1994), ll. 98, 100; Wollstonecraft quotes ll. 101–2. For fuller accounts of Barbauld's life see her niece Lucy Aikin's memoir of her, prefixed to Lucy Aikin, ed., *The Works of Anna Laetitia Barbauld. With a memoir,* 2 vols. (London: Longman, 1825); Betsy Rogers, *Georgian Chronicle: Mrs Barbauld and her Family* (London: Methuen, 1958); and the Introduction to *Poems of Barbauld* (1994). See also Penny Bradshaw, "Gendering the Enlightenment: Conflicting Images of Progress in the Poetry of Anna Laetitia Barbauld," *Women's Writing* 5, no. 3 (1998): 353–71; and William McCarthy, "'We Hoped the Woman Was Going to Appear': Repression, Desire, and Gender in Anna Letitia Barbauld's Early Poems," in *Romantic Women Writers: Voices and Countervoices,* ed. Paula R. Feldman and Theresa M. Kelley (Hanover, N.H.: University Press of New England, 1995), 113–37. I have chosen to refer to Barbauld by her married name throughout this chapter, though she was of course known as Aikin before her marriage in 1774.

men creates. To the political opponents of both women, however, Barbauld's pamphlets of the early 1790s defending the revolution in France and its basis in universal natural right marked precisely her departure from that sexual character, and characterized her as one of the "*Unsex'd Females*" closest to Wollstonecraft. Horace Walpole, for example, depicted the "Amazonian allies" of those who attacked Burke's *Reflections on the Revolution* as "headed by Kate Macaulay and the virago Barbauld, whom Mr. Burke calls our *Poissardes*" [fishwives].[3] He told Hannah More that he would never read Barbauld's poetry because "I cannot forgive the heart of a woman . . . that curses our clergy and feels for negroes," and he warned More "not to let your piety lead you into the weakness of respecting the bad, only because they hoist the flag of religion, while they carry a stiletto in the flag-staff."[4] Walpole alludes to Barbauld's published contributions to the campaigns for the repeal of the Corporation and Test Acts in 1790, and for the bill for abolishing the slave trade in 1791. Her support for these causes Walpole attacks as unfeminine, inappropriate to the "heart of a woman."

Walpole also alludes to the rumor that Barbauld intended to publish a reply to Burke's *Reflections.* Barbauld commented in a letter to her brother probably written early in 1791:

> I do not wonder at your asking whether I am answering Burke, for the question has been asked me even from Paris. The truth is, I have not been without thoughts of it, and I have now some sheets of loose thoughts written out, but whether they will see the light I know not; to answer him regularly I am afraid is an undertaking too big for me, and a little skirmishing which might have done very well at first, comes with an ill grace now.[5]

For Walpole and Burke, the possibility that Barbauld might publish a response to the *Reflections* links her with Catharine Macaulay, and associates both with the "Thracian orgies" of "the vilest of women" in revolutionary France.[6] Barbauld's connection with Burke's political opponents was more sympatheti-

3. Horace Walpole to Charlotte Berry, "Strawberry Hill, Dec. 20, 1790, very late at night," in *Extracts from the Journals and Correspondence of Miss Berry, from the year 1783 to 1852,* 3 vols., ed. Lady Theresa Lewis (London: Longmans, 1865), 1.268.

4. Horace Walpole, letter 2561, to Miss Hannah More, Berkeley Square, 29 September 1791, in *The Letters of Horace Walpole, Earl of Orford,* 9 vols., ed. Peter Cunningham (London: Bohn, 1861), 9.354. Walpole alludes to Barbauld's *Address to the Opposers of the Repeal of the Corporation and Test Acts* (1790), and her poetic *Epistle to William Wilberforce, Esq. On the rejection of the Bill for Abolishing the Slave Trade* (1791).

5. Letter to John Aikin, dated 28 February, in Rogers, *Georgian Chronicle,* 210.

6. Edmund Burke, *Reflections on the Revolution in France,* ed. A. J. Grieve (London: Dent, 1964), 69.

Figure 22 [? Frederick George Byron], *Don Dismallo Running the Literary Gantlet,* 1790, engraving, $10\frac{3}{4} \times 23\frac{1}{4}$ in. BM 7685. © The British Museum.

cally represented in a print published late in 1790 by William Holland and titled *Don Dismallo Running the Literary Gantlet* (fig. 22). The print shows Barbauld preparing to strike Burke as he runs past a line of his opponents, including Helen Maria Williams, Richard Price, Richard Sheridan, Horne Tooke, and Catharine Macaulay, each of whom is armed with a cat-o'-nine-tails. Barbauld's zeal as a chastiser of political wrongs is satirically linked with her fame as an educationalist, as she is shown exclaiming that "the most incorrigible Urchin in my School never felt from my hands what this Assassin of Liberty shall now feel!"

It was not only Barbauld's political activities of the early 1790s that were seen to transgress the "false system" on which feminine identity depended. The *Monthly Review* had praised the *Poems* when they were first published in 1773, but lamented that Barbauld "has, in pursuing the road to fame, trod too much in the footsteps of men." The reviewer thought that she should have "taken her views of human life from among her female companions, & not altogether under the direction of men, either living or dead." In contrast to what Wollstonecraft's later strictures suggest, however, this reviewer implied that it was "the direction of men" that had caused Barbauld to neglect the appropriate sexual character, and to forget that "there is a sex in minds as well as in bodies." He is disappointed with Barbauld's work because "we hoped the *Woman* was going to appear; & that while we admired the genius & learning of her graver compositions, we should be affected by the sensibility & passion of the softer pieces."[7] He was disappointed by the absence of feminine sensibility and passion, by Barbauld's failure to display something very close to the "sexual character" that Wollstonecraft deplored in her poetry. What this range of responses to Barbauld's work has in common is that for all of them it is the gendered character of her writing that is at issue: it is her willingness or failure to appear properly feminine that is the central focus of their criticism.

The character of femininity is central to much of Barbauld's writing, and perhaps most contentiously in the poem on "The Rights of Woman," which she may have written in response to Wollstonecraft's criticisms in the *Vindication* of 1792, though the poem was not published in her lifetime, and first appears in the posthumous collected *Works* of 1825. The poem echoes the lines Wollstonecraft found so ignoble in revisiting the theme of woman's "sweetest empire." It begins in what are, in the context of Walpole's remarks about "Amazonian allies," strikingly aggressive and militaristic terms:

> Yes, injured Woman! rise, assert thy right!
> Woman, too long degraded, scorned opprest;
> O born to rule in partial Law's despite,
> Resume thy native empire o'er the breast!
>
> Go forth arrayed in panoply divine;
> That angel pureness which admits no stain;
> Go, bid proud Man his boasted rule resign,
> And kiss the golden sceptre of thy reign.
>
> Go, gird thyself with grace; collect thy store
> Of bright artillery glancing from afar;
> Soft melting tones thy thundering cannon's roar,
> Blushes and fears thy magazine of war.[8]

The lines employ courtly conventions of gallantry of the kind, for example, that Pope had mocked in his portrayal in *The Rape of the Lock* (1714) of "the fierce Virago" Thalestris, who scatters metaphorical death "from both her Eyes."[9] But those conventions have a more ambivalent resonance coming from the pen of "the virago Barbauld"—an ambivalence that might be traced in these lines to that notion of women "born to rule in partial Law's despite."

7. The *Epistle to Wilberforce* is the only addition to the collection of 1773, which had appeared in five editions by 1777. The review, by William Woodfall, is quoted in Rogers, *Georgian Chronicle,* 58–60.

8. "The Rights of Woman," ll. 1–12, in *Poems of Barbauld* (1994), 121.

9. Alexander Pope, *The Rape of the Lock: An heroi-comical poem in five canto's,* in *The Poems of Alexander Pope: A One-Volume Edition of the Twickenham Text with Selected Annotations,* ed. John Butt (London: Routledge, 1968), ll. 37, 58.

Women might claim "native empire o'er the breast" because both they and the emotions of the breast are ignored by the law, treated by it only with contempt or "despite," or because they act in defiant opposition to the law, in "despite" of it. The second possibility, that what women do is somehow a defiant claim to native rights that should be universal, but which the partiality of the law denies to all but a few, seems to animate the militaristic language of the following stanzas with an energy out of step with conventions of gallantry.

In the earlier poem that Wollstonecraft had so disliked there was a clear contrast between the "sweetest empire" of feminine softness and leisure, and the "rougher tasks" of national defense against "invading foes," and perhaps of imperial expansion by "future navies."[10] In this later poem that division is blurred. Barbauld writes in the fourth stanza: "Thy rights are empire: urge no meaner claim," but the boldness of this imperative is qualified and obscured when the rights of women are compared with the "sacred mysteries" of ancient Greece, which "Shunning discussion, are revered the most." The poem goes on to suggest that women may command men as their "imperial foe," but implies that relations between imperial conqueror and slave, idol and worshipper, must always be mutually contaminating, must always involve the interchangeability of those positions.[11] The language of idolatry, and the reference to the pagan mysteries of Eleusis, work to show that the dominance of women can only be a frail fiction, an illusion. The poem concludes that as a result of their power women will become both "Subduing and subdued," and will abandon their claim to rights:

> Then, then, abandon each ambitious thought,
> Conquest or rule thy heart shall feebly move,
> In Nature's school, by her soft maxims taught,
> That separate rights are lost in mutual love.

Women are rather ambiguously predicted or conjured to abandon the inequality and struggle implicit in the notion of "separate rights" in favor of the promised equality of "mutual love." The final lines suggest that domestic bliss offers a haven from "misfortune's school," and from the condition in which women have been "too long degraded, scorned, opprest."[12]

Barbauld's "Rights of Woman" is a troubling text because its use of the language of rights seems to pull it in a different direction from its conclusion, and to emphasize a violence in the language that is at odds with the praise of

10. "To a Lady, with some painted Flowers," ll. 18, 9, 11, 12, in *Poems of Barbauld* (1994), 77.
11. "Rights," ll. 13, 15, 16, 18, in *Poems of Barbauld* (1994).
12. "Rights," ll. 29–32, 2, "To Mrs P[riestley]," l. 100, in *Poems of Barbauld* (1994).

mutual love. For G. J. Barker-Benfield, the poem is best understood as a "rejection of politics . . . repudiating the case Wollstonecraft made against such cultural segregation" in favor of the claims of feminine sensibility. He argues that "Barbauld directly restates the 'SWEETEST empire' that Wollstonecraft had just challenged."[13] But he does not discuss the relation between this rejection of political involvement for women and Barbauld's own political activities in the 1790s. The editors of the admirable 1994 edition of Barbauld's *Poems* argue that though "revolutionary rhetoric and ideals inform much" of Barbauld's poetry, here the use of that rhetoric is "ironic as she opposes what she sees as Wollstonecraft's declared war with the male sex."[14] Later they note that the poem "need not be read as representing [Barbauld's] considered judgement on women's rights; rather, it is an outburst of anger at Wollstonecraft."[15] These remarks are clouded by the difficulty of assessing the relation between Barbauld's opinions on politics and on domesticity; they imply that if we take her views on mutual love seriously, then we must perceive her political language as ironic, or indeed as a rejected system of value. The source of this critical embarrassment can, I think, be traced to the assumption that the final lines of the poem defend a sentimental feminine identity that abandons ambition for "mutual love," and is incompatible with a politically articulate femininity—or feminism—based in the defiant language of natural right.

The "Rights of Woman" does not, however, represent a departure from Barbauld's earlier views on the value of women's contribution to domesticity. From her earliest publications of poems and essays Barbauld had articulated the public language of politics, for example in the unambiguous classical republicanism of her poem on *Corsica,* written in 1769, alongside poems to women which praised a characteristically "soft" and domestic femininity. In an early essay of 1773, for example, Barbauld alludes to women as "that part of the species who are formed to shine in families and sweeten society."[16] When, in the 1770s, it was suggested that Barbauld should establish a college for young ladies, she refused. She argued that though she had "stepped out of the bounds of female reserve in becoming an author. . . . My situation has been peculiar, and would be no rule to others." She thought that a regular course of instruction could not improve the situation of women while they were "subject to a

13. G. J. Barker-Benfield, *The Culture of Sensibility: Sex and Society in Eighteenth-Century Britain* (Chicago: University of Chicago Press, 1992), 222, 266.

14. Introduction, in *Poems of Barbauld* (1994), xxv.

15. *Poems of Barbauld* (1994), 289.

16. "On Monastic Institutions," in J. and A. L. Aikin, *Miscellaneous Pieces, in prose* (London: J. Johnson, 1773), 115.

regulation like that of the ancient Spartans," under which "thefts of knowledge in our sex are only connived at while carefully concealed, and if displayed, punished with disgrace." She argued, in a manner that might be regretful but cannot be swept aside as merely ironic, that middle-class women would be best occupied in learning to become "good wives or agreeable companions."[17] But this notion of women's domestic duty does not imply the kind of choice between different kinds of femininity, between sensibility and politics, that Barker-Benfield's discussion suggests. James Barry, the history painter and republican, wrote of Barbauld in the early 1780s as a national treasure. He suggested that the fruits of her genius, in the form of "some epic or other great work," were denied to the public because her work as a teacher left her no time to write, but not because domestic duty was incompatible with public or political life:

> Leisure will, I hope, be found; the world of imagination lies still before her, and there is no region of it which Mrs. Barbauld's muse may not appropriate to itself. However interesting it may be to some affectionate parents to have such talents employed in the wise and virtuous culture of a few children, yet the thing is not right; talents, like her's, belong to the country at large and to the age, and cannot, in justice, be monopolized, or converted into private property.[18]

Barry argues that Barbauld's talents should be employed in the service of the public because they are public property.

Mary Hays notes with approval in 1793 that her friend, the radical George Dyer, includes Barbauld among the list of "respectable names" of those women who, as a result of their experience of oppression, feel "a generous indignation; which when turned against the exclusive claims of the other sex, is favourable to female pretensions; when turned against the tyranny of government, . . . is commonly favourable to the rights of both sexes."[19] For Hays and Dyer, and indeed for those hostile to Barbauld's politics, her views on feminine domesticity are not at odds with her role as a political pamphleteer and campaigner.

George Dyer's accounts of women involved in radical politics assert that women are peculiarly capable of disinterested and liberal views. His ode "On Liberty" of 1792 is, he explains in the Preface to his *Poems,* intended to praise patriotic virtue that transcends mere political differences. He writes that "some

17. Letter to Elizabeth Montagu, quoted in Aikin's Memoir in *Works of Barbauld* (1825), 1.xvii–xix.

18. *An Account of a Series of Pictures, In the Great Room of the Society of Arts, Manufactures, and Commerce, at the Adelphi* (1783), in *The Works of James Barry, Esq.,* 2 vols., ed. Dr. Edward Fryer (London: Cadell, 1809), 342, 344.

19. Mary Hays, *Letters and Essays, Moral, and Miscellaneous* (London: T. Knott, 1793), no. II, 11.

may smile to see . . . a duke and an impugner of dukes, a doctor of divinity and a quaker, in the same company. The author has only to say, that his respect is meant to be addressed to public spirit, and not to titles, or mere opposers of titles." In a stanza which initially imagines Liberty inviting Tom Paine to "rouse the languid hearts / Of Albion's sons" so that "Britons kindle into rapture," the poet praises a collection of women whom Liberty has warmed "With more than manly fire." The women he names were all more or less closely—and notoriously—associated with radical politics, but the publications by them that he lists in his footnotes to their names are not always what most obviously earned them that reputation. Dyer's lines praise their feminine capacity for poetic sentiment as much as or rather than their explicitly political publications. Addressing Liberty the "sweet enthusiast" he claims to

> . . . hear thee warble in Laetitia's song;
> Or see thee weep in Charlotte's melting page;
> And from Macaulay learn to scourge a venal age.

The feminine warbling and weeping of Barbauld and Charlotte Smith (in her *Elegiac Sonnets*) convince the poet as unambiguously as had Macaulay's attacks on political corruption in her *History* that "the most sensible females, when they turn their attention to political subjects, are more uniformly on the side of liberty than the other sex."[20] Defending retrospectively his decision to name the women he admired for their commitment to liberty, Dyer later explained that "the perfecting of the female understanding promotes at once the truest morals, and the best interests of society; a sentiment, that I hold with all the coldness of dispassionate inquiry, and with all the firmness of a settled belief."[21] Dyer's comments confirm that Barbauld's political reputation as an advocate of liberty and the rights of man—the reputation that identified her as a virago—was tied to the notion that her work promoted "the best interests of society," and was based in the more feminine qualities of her poetry, and not only in her more polemical publications.

20. George Dyer, "Preface," in *Poems* (London: J. Johnson, 1792), viii; Ode VII, "On Liberty," stanza 7, and see 36–37 nn. Dyer praises Wollstonecraft for her *Vindication* of 1792, Ann Jebb for her political essays of the 1780s, Helen Maria Williams for her *Letters from France* (probably a reference to those of 1790), and Mary Hays as "an admirer and imitator of Mrs Charlotte Smith." The notes also specify Charlotte Smith's *Elegiac Sonnets,* which had first been published in 1784, and appeared in a sixth revised and enlarged edition in 1792. Exceptionally, in this catalogue, no particular publication of Barbauld's is singled out in the notes.

21. George Dyer, "Preface," in *Poems* (London: J. Johnson, 1800), lxvi–lxvii. Dyer noted Russell's translation of Thomas's *Essay on the Character of Women* in support of this belief (lxvi n.). Only the title page and Preface of this edition of Dyer's *Poems* were published.

II

Throughout her career, Barbauld was strongly committed to the belief that men and women should occupy different social stations, and cultivate the gendered characteristics appropriate to them. In an early poem of 1768, "To Dr. Aikin on his Complaining that she neglected him," she reassures her brother of her constant affection for him by addressing to him an account of their personal histories. At first, she writes, gender difference was not a factor in their relationship:

> The first warm impulse which our breasts did move,
> 'Twas sympathy, before we knew to love.
> As hand in hand with innocence we stray'd
> Embosom'd deep in Kibworth's tufted shade;
> Where both encircled in one household band,
> And both obedient to one mild command,
> Life's first fair dawn with transport we beheld, . . .

She and her brother were "like two scions on one stem," and it is a measure of the unity, the at-one-ness that these lines repeatedly emphasize, that the "first . . . impulse" between them should be sympathy (which depends on similarity) rather than love (which implies a greater degree of individual distinction).[22] The poem goes on to argue that in continuation of that shared impulse they are now "By stronger ties endear'd," although gender difference does separate them:

> Our path divides—to thee fair fate assign'd
> The nobler labours of a manly mind:
> While mine, more humble works, and lower cares,
> Less shining toils, and meaner praises shares.

They are separated by a gendered division of labor which allocates professional ambition exclusively to the "manly mind," and briefly the poet chafes against this division of minds:

> Yet sure in different moulds they were not cast
> Nor stampt with separate sentiments and taste.
> But hush my heart! nor strive to soar too high,

22. "To Dr. Aikin on his Complaining that she neglected him, October 20th 1768," ll. 19–25, 27, in *Poems of Barbauld* (1994), no. 7. Cp. Coleridge's "Frost at Midnight" (1798), where the poet's reflections on his "dim sympathies" with the "fluttering stranger" on the grate lead him to recollect how at school he longed to see his sister, "My play-mate when we both were clothed alike." In *Poetical Works,* ed. E. H. Coleridge (London: Oxford University Press, 1967), ll. 18, 26, 43.

Nor for the tree of knowledge vainly sigh;
Check the fond love of science and of fame,
A bright, but ah! a too devouring flame.
Content remain within thy bounded sphere,
For fancy blooms, the virtues flourish there.[23]

Barbauld encourages herself to accept the constraints of the gendered division of labor, and achieve contentment "within thy bounded sphere." But this is not necessarily an act of self-effacement or self-abasement. The assertion that their minds were not cast in "different moulds" or "stampt with separate sentiments" remains unchallenged, and she prophesies that her brother's future success in the medical profession will result from his capacity to display sentiments usually characterized as feminine. She advises that he should "Join to the sage advice, the tender sigh; / And to the healing hand the pitying eye," arguing that "cordial looks" and "words of balm" will work "when drugs would fail."[24] The reference to the "tree of knowledge" suggests that his professional labors involve a kind of fall from the prelapsarian innocence of their undifferentiated childhood, and that the "virtues flourish" in the "bounded sphere" appropriate to feminine works because they are not understood to involve specialized ambitions.

The poem celebrates the fact that though Barbauld and her brother pursue paths divided by gender difference, their common upbringing and similarities of mind have forged "stronger ties" between them. That emphasis on the primacy of what they share is repeated in the concluding discussion of their writing, where Barbauld asserts that "both our breasts at once the Muses fir'd, / With equal love, but not alike inspir'd." Their writings are also differentiated by the gendering of genres, but their love of the liberal arts is equal. This emphasis on a primary and undifferentiated equality may imply that gender difference, or at least the inequality it implies, is largely an effect of the ability of the brother to choose a specialized profession, a choice that is represented as a decree of fate which determines that brother and sister shall no longer pursue the "same studies."[25] Barbauld herself, though she had to "Check the fond love of science and of fame," participated in the culture of middle-rank liberal whiggery and religious dissent. Clearly, she valued professionalism, and was modest about claiming professional status for her own "humble works" as a teacher and a writer of educational books as well as poetry and political pamphlets. In this poem she accepts the divergence between masculine profession-

23. "To Dr. Aikin," ll. 49–52, 53–61.
24. Ibid., ll. 78–79, 81–82.
25. Ibid., l. 49.

alism and the "bounded sphere" of femininity, but represents that as secondary or supplementary to a primary equality of inspiration and capacity.

Barbauld wrote a number of poems to and about women, who are usually named only in her autograph copies. Most of these are short "Characters," which praise the women as exemplary figures for demonstrating the qualities and performing the duties appropriate to their "bounded sphere": she praises them for rearing their children, caring for the elderly or sick, for piety, and of course for "that most useful science, how to please."[26] In what Barbauld's recent editors suggest is probably an early "character" of a woman identified in the poet's annotation as Mrs. Sarah Vaughan, the subject's domestic virtues are described in an extended comparison with those of "The mighty mothers of immortal Rome." Barbauld writes of the Roman matrons:

> Obscure, in sober dignity retir'd
> They more deserved, than sought to be admir'd:
> The houshold virtues o'er their honour'd head
> Their simple grace, and modest lustre shed;
> Chaste their attire, their feet unus'd to roam[,]
> They lov'd the sacred threshold of their home, . . .[27]

Barbauld's account clearly alludes to the women of pre-imperial Rome, who represented for many of the theorists of the Enlightenment an ideal model of familial domesticity. The *Essay on the Character of Women,* for example, praised early Roman women for their "austere manners," to which it was believed they "joined an enthusiastic love of their country."[28] Barbauld turns to this capacity for patriotism in the second half of her "Character." The poem continues:

> . . . Yet, true to glory, fan'd the generous flame,
> Bade lovers, brothers, sons aspire to fame;
> In the young bosom cherish'd virtue's seed,
> The secret springs of many a godlike deed!
> So the fair stream in some sequester'd glade,
> With lowly state glides silent through the shade,

26. "Characters: [Sarah Taylor Rigby]," l. 6, in *Poems of Barbauld* (1994), no. 42.

27. [A Character of Sarah Hallowell Vaughan], ll. 4, 5–10, in *Poems of Barbauld* (1994), no. 14. The editors explain that in 1769–70 the government was attempting to discredit Sarah's husband, Samuel Vaughan, "in the eyes of his fellow radicals" by accusing him of attempting to bribe the Duke of Grafton. Some newspapers argued that Vaughan had "betrayed the oppositionist cause." Barbauld's poem offers the Vaughans encouragement and support in these difficult circumstances. See the note to the poem (240).

28. William Russell, *Essay on the Character, Manners and Genius of Women in Different Ages. Enlarged from the French of M. Thomas,* 2 vols. (London: G. Robinson, 1773), 1.53.

> Yet by the smiling meads her urn is blest;
> With freshest flowers her rising banks are drest;
> And groves of laurel, by her sweetness fed,
> High o'er the forest lift their verdant head[.][29]

That "Yet" of course is teasing—do the "mighty mothers" contribute to the laurels of Rome despite or because of their domestic confinement? The poem sustains a degree of ambiguity about the relation between their "household virtues" and the virtues they nurture in the young bosom.

In Barbauld's later writing, however, the notion that women must limit their ambitions to a more bounded sphere than that available to middle-class men is not understood to preclude the notion that women have public identities and responsibilities. In 1792, Barbauld published a pamphlet of *Remarks on Mr. Gilbert Wakefield's Enquiry into the expediency and propriety of public or social worship.* She argued that

> Public worship is a civic meeting. The temple is the only place where human beings, of every rank and sex and age, meet together for one common purpose, and join together in one common act. Other meetings are either political, or formed for the purposes of splendour and amusement; from both which, in this country, the bulk of inhabitants are of necessity excluded.

The argument of the essay is important, because though it is here conducted in terms of the notion that the public, truly civic business of collective religion can be distinguished from a merely political assembly, the argument is thoroughly and unambiguously politicized. Barbauld writes that this is "the only place where man meets man not only as an equal but a brother; and where, by contemplating his duties, he may become sensible of his rights." She alludes here to the revolutionary principles of liberty, equality, and fraternity, and to the slogan of the movement for the abolition of the slave trade—"Am I not a man and a brother?"—and confirms those references in characterizing this as "the age which has demolished dungeons, rejected torture, and given so fair a prospect of abolishing the iniquity of the slave-trade." She explains rather cautiously that the worshipper "learns philosophy without its pride, and a spirit of liberty without its turbulence." But in the next sentence she expands on the nature of that philosophy and liberty in terms that also explain the need for caution: "Every time Social Worship is celebrated, it includes a virtual declaration of the rights of man."[30]

29. [Vaughan], ll. 11–20.

30. *Remarks on Mr. Gilbert Wakefield's Enquiry into the expedience and propriety of Public or Social Worship,* in *Works of Barbauld* (1825), 2.446, 470, 448.

In the pamphlets she published in the 1790s Barbauld repeatedly emphasizes the inclusiveness of her conceptions of the civic, public, and national, but she very rarely explicitly mentions gender as a factor in these arguments. The pamphlet on public worship is unusually direct in its statement that the congregation assembled for this "virtual declaration of the rights of man" acquires the civic character that lends weight to this declaration because it includes "human beings, of every rank and sex and age." But in other pamphlets of the 1790s she includes women at least implicitly in her conception of the public. So, for example, in the second of her *Civic Sermons to the People* (1792), she represents the relation between family and state in the analogy of the stream that she had sketched in the "Character of Sarah Vaughan." She explains that the "first society is called a Family," and argues, echoing Burke, that "it is the root of every other society. It is the beginning of order, and kind affections, and mutual helpfulness and provident regulations. If this spring be pure, what proceeds from it will be pure: if it be polluted, the broader waters will be discoloured." She describes the relation between family, locality, and country in a Burkean analogy with travel, but she emphasizes that the citizens she addresses must "Love your Country" not only because of its associations with "early pleasures, and tender recollections" but because of their voluntary contributions to it: "because it includes every other object of love, because it unites all separate energies into one energy; all separate wills into one will; and having united and declared them, calls it Law." The idea of the nation, she argues, is bound into everyday life, however private or "obscure": "Love then this Country; unite its idea with your domestic comforts . . . remember that each of you, however inconsiderable, is benefited by your Country; so your Country, however extensive, is benefited by every one of the least of you." The argument emphasizes that what seems most private, domestic, and feminine is bound up with what is most public and perhaps masculine, and that all citizens, however weak and defenseless their situation, have a right to a say in how government is conducted—"for the plain reason, that all have an equal desire to be happy, and an equal right to be so."[31] The theme Barbauld's essays of the 1790s repeatedly return to is that of the constitution of the public as a religious, civic, and national body, and she is always concerned to emphasize the continuity between the rights of private individuals and those of the public defined in capaciously inclusive terms. Barbauld's pamphlets of the 1790s are radical in their insistence that every individual participates in the national political identity, though their lives may be as private as those of the matrons of ancient Rome,

31. *Civic Sermons to the People. Number II. From mutual Wants spring mutual Happiness* (London: J. Johnson, 1792), 6, 21, 22, 25–26.

and in their implication or assumption that the rights claimed for men are also those of women.

III

Barbauld's writing could suggest to her contemporaries that she was, on the one hand, a dangerously radical virago, and on the other, a timid creature, complicit in robbing "the whole sex of its dignity" because of her "fear of departing from a supposed sexual character" acceptable to men. When Barbauld first published her poetry and essays in the 1760s and 1770s, her writing was recognized to be "very different from that of other 'Daughters of the Nine'" in its "justness of thought & vigour of imagination." The *Monthly Review* commented that "a woman is as perfect in her kind as a man: she appears inferior only when she quits her station, & aims at excellence out of her province." Barbauld appeared to be differentiated from the ideal woman writer, imperfect in her femininity, not because "softer pieces" were absent from her collection, or because she could write with masculine justness and vigor on Corsican republicanism, but because both the "graver compositions" and the "softer pieces" were "out of her province," they avoided "the subject of Love" and the "particular distress of some female situations." Barbauld's poem on the character of Sarah Vaughan identified the proper province or bounded sphere of femininity in familial domesticity, but it represented that sphere not as inward-looking, but as the source of civic virtue. It suggested that Barbauld modeled her arguments for the civic role of the private individual on the image of the Roman matron. But the implications of that image were contested and shifting in the second half of the century. I want to look now at some of the range of representations of the women of classical antiquity, focusing in particular on the 1770s and 1780s, and on William Alexander's *History of Women.*

In *The Origins of Modern Feminism* (1985), Jane Rendall draws on Mary Beth Norton and Linda Kerber's accounts of American women's history to argue that for radical and feminist writers in Britain and France as well as America "in the 1780s and 1790s, the ideal of 'republican motherhood' seemed to offer a way of uniting public and private responsibilities for women":

> The domestic sphere was no longer to be merely the backcloth to public and social life, but to have a positive educational and inspirational function. A woman's position was no longer to be merely that of a passive partner, and the practical organiser of the household; her nature would allow her, in the right setting, to uplift and regenerate the spirit of her society.[32]

32. Jane Rendall, *The Origins of Modern Feminism: Women in Britain, France and the United States, 1780–1860* (Basingstoke: Macmillan, 1985), 34, 32, and see chapter 2, "Feminism and Republicanism:

I have suggested that a notion of femininity which is in some respects quite close to this ideal of republican motherhood had a much wider currency in the 1770s and 1780s. The ideal of a feminine role which unites "public and private responsibilities for women," and which distinguishes the feminism of politically radical thinkers, seems to emerge out of the increasing emphasis on the private virtues as the basis of public and social morality, out of a notion of the continuity of private and social life, the nature and implications of which are debated in accounts of femininity, learning, and national feeling. But republican motherhood is also an ideal which involves particular definitions of what Rendall calls the domestic sphere, and extensive debates over the representation of women of classical antiquity as its prime historical exemplars. In this section, I want to look at some of the ways in which the example of women in ancient history might have been perceived as inspirational or problematic for modern women. This is of course a very wide field of study: in plays, poems, histories, and polite essays of these decades there are numerous discussions either of the women of antiquity in general or of particular heroines, and more than a brief foray into that field is not my purpose here. But the limited number of texts and examples I want to discuss will I think provide some indication of the diversity of notions of "republican motherhood" emerging in this period, and of some of the debates which informed allusions to, for example, Roman matrons or Spartan women.

What most obviously seems to reshape notions of domesticity in the second half of the eighteenth century is the increasing persuasiveness of the account of modern commercial society articulated by the discourse on the division of labor—an account which, of course, marginalizes or obscures the productivity of women's work. Kathryn Sutherland argues, for example, that Adam Smith's version of the discourse, in his *Wealth of Nations* (1776), "refuses or conceals the female contribution to the economy. . . . Informalising women's labour as extrinsic to the formal structures of its argument."[33] Above all, women's work that goes on within the home is not recognizable as labor within the terms of the discourse. William Alexander's *History of Women* alludes to the language of the division of labor in its claim that the restriction of women to the domestic sphere is a distinguishing characteristic of polite or advanced

'Republican Motherhood.'" See also Linda Kerber, *Women of the Republic: Intellect and Ideology in Revolutionary America* (Chapel Hill: University of North Carolina Press, 1980); and Mary Beth Norton, *Liberty's Daughters: The Revolutionary Experience of American Women, 1759–1800* (Boston: Scott, Foresman and Co., 1980).

33. Kathryn Sutherland, "Adam Smith's Master Narrative," in *Adam Smith's Wealth of Nations: New Interdisciplinary Essays,* ed. Stephen Copley and Kathryn Sutherland (Manchester: Manchester University Press, 1995), 117.

civilization. He explains that "in England, France and Italy, and those other parts of Europe which have arrived nearly at the same degree of politeness; prompted by a mixture of humanity and love, the men have entirely exempted the women from every species of labour, except where it is absolutely necessary among the poor."[34] Focusing in particular on "women of middling fortune," he comments that their "proper office . . . is the care, inspection, and management of everything belonging to the family, while that of the man is to provide by their labour and industry what the women are to manage with care and frugality."[35] Women manage what men produce through their "labour and industry," and this feminine exemption from productivity seems central to women's civilizing role: their capacity to soften and polish the manners of men.

Alexander explains:

> in this country it is too much the fashion to suppose that books, and the company of men only, are necessary to furnish every qualification requisite for the scholar and the gentleman; but . . . it is only the company and acquaintance of the ladies, which can bestow that easiness of address by which the fine gentleman is distinguished from the mere scholar, and man of business.[36]

His comments here allude to Hume's remark, in his essay "Of the Rise of the Arts and Sciences":

> What better school for manners than the company of virtuous women, where the mutual endeavour to please must insensibly polish the mind, where the example of the female softness and modesty must communicate itself to their admirers, and where the delicacy of that sex puts every one on his guard, lest he give offence by any breach of decency?[37]

This notion of the polish men gain from the company of women is, of course, a commonplace of eighteenth-century theories of civilized progress. But in Alexander's *History* the civilizing influence of women is tied more particularly to their exclusion from productive work. In their company a man cannot speak the jargon of his trade; the "easiness of address" that mixed company demands refines the gentleman from the specialist absorbed in the pursuit of his occupation. Alexander claims that men have exempted women from labor "prompted by a mixture of humanity and love," and he implies that they are reminded of that mixture in themselves whenever they converse with women.

34. Alexander, *History of Women* (1782), 2 vols. (Bristol: Thoemmes Press, 1995), 1.315–16.

35. Ibid., 1.315–16, 134.

36. Ibid., 1.489–90.

37. David Hume, *Selected Essays,* ed. Stephen Copley and Andrew Edgar (Oxford: Oxford University Press, 1993), 74.

Alexander acknowledges that there are classes of women who are obliged to engage in "the labours necessary to procure daily bread." His account of what these women do involves a sort of mimicry of the social graces expected of middle-rank women. They are involved in manufactures which "do not depend so much upon strength as upon delicacy," they produce "works of taste and elegance," or, where they contribute to the production of goods "of a rougher kind," these, according to Alexander, "receive a last polish from their softer touch." Clearly his account feminizes their work, in contrast to, for example, that of women who perform butchery on "the lesser animals used in our kitchens"; this work, Alexander believes, results in "that masculine ferocity, which distinguishes many of the lower classes of women in Britain."[38] Feminizing women's work implicitly "refuses or conceals the female contribution to the economy" because gender difference is fundamental to the division of labor, as Sutherland suggests, but the representation of women's work in Alexander's account also shadows their civilizing role; their capacity to soften and polish the manners of men.

The slippage or overlap between the qualities attributed to women's work, or to women as a result of their exemption from labor, is important to Alexander's argument that softness, polish, and common humanity are not only off-duty or sabbatical pleasures for the scholar or man of business. For in his *History* femininity is not associated with retirement. He claims that

> female society . . . seems not only to be the cause of the rise and progress of polite manners, and of sentimental feeling, but also of the fine arts. When we view the countries where women are confined, we find the inhabitants of them distinguished for want of invention and barbarity of manners; when we view the same countries in periods when the women begin to have their liberty, we immediately perceive invention arising, and manners beginning to improve.

It is because men wish to please women, he argues, that they cultivate "elegance of manners, and perhaps all their acquisitions of mind."[39] Alexander's account of women's paid work, I suggested, shadowed or mimicked his account of the civilizing influence of middle-rank women, and that correspondence implies both that women's work is not acknowledged as a form of labour, and conversely that women's social role may be in some sense productive. The feminizing terms appropriate to women's work suggested that what they produced were luxuries, the production and consumption of which was superfluous and therefore not laborious. Where women's work produced

38. Alexander, *History* (1782), 1.133, 135, 546.
39. Ibid., 1.495–96, 487.

something useful, in the kitchens for example, it was masculinizing. In this account of how the company of women is "the cause of the rise and progress" of fine arts and indeed "perhaps all . . . acquisitions of mind," that suggestion of luxury is the positive sign of civilized progress.

In his accounts of ancient Europe, Alexander is perhaps understandably keen to emphasize that not all mixed company contributes to the progress of civilization. His account of ancient Greece, for example, is consistently hostile, apparently because he believes they achieved progress in "the fine arts" at the expense of "the rise of . . . polite manners." He argues that though the people of ancient Greece "shone so illustrious in arts and arms," not much else can be said for them: "When we consider them as men, and as citizens of the world, they greatly disgust us." He alludes to the "glaring proof" that "public prostitution" was "so fashionable that it is attended with no disgrace" in Athens, and comments that the Greeks were a "rude and barbarous people . . . during the heroic ages," and scarcely improved when "they became famous for their knowledge of the arts and sciences." He concludes that "it is not therefore arts, sciences, and learning, but the company of the other sex, that forms the manners and renders the man agreeable. But the company and conversation of that sex, was among the Greeks shamefully neglected." Consorting with women Alexander labels prostitutes enabled the Greeks to improve in invention, but in the absence of "polite manners, and of sentimental feeling" this does not constitute civilization.[40] The *Essay on the Character of Women* commented on the ancient Greeks that "The laws and the public institutions, indeed, by authorising the privacy of women, set a high value on the sanctity of the marriage vow. But in Athens imagination, sentiment, luxury, the taste in arts and pleasures, was opposite to the laws. The courtezans therefore may be said to have come in support of the manners."[41] Alexander's discussion of modern women's contribution to the civilizing process suggests that his hostility to the Greeks is aimed precisely at the degree of contrast between the excessive publicity of the courtesans and the excessive privacy of the married women—a contrast which allows the Greeks to excel in the arts of luxury while remaining rude and barbarous in their lack of civilized politeness.

Alexander's *History* presents a contrasting case in its treatment of Tacitus' "beautiful picture of ancient German simplicity and chastity."[42] As Jane Rendall has shown, Tacitus' account of the ancient Germans was regarded as the

40. Ibid., 1.360–61, 365, 480.

41. Russell, *Essay,* 1.43.

42. Alexander, *History* (1782), 1.391.

basis for a radically divergent historical narrative of the progress of civilization in relation to gender difference.[43] Gilbert Stuart's *A View of Society in Europe, in its progress from rudeness to refinement* (1778), for example, used Tacitus to argue that "the state of society, which precedes the knowledge of extensive property and the meannesses which flow from refinement and commerce, is in a high degree propitious to women."[44] Ancient German society did not provide evidence that lack of commercial civilization was indexically manifested in the oppression of women, or the grotesque exaggeration of what were seen as the inevitable social consequences of gender difference, for among these people the public role of women commanded respect, and childcare was shared by both partners. The terms of marriage established the wife's "equality with the husband," Stuart thought, because "they admonished her, that she was to be the partner and the companion of his toils and his cares, and that, in peace and in war, she was to sustain the same fatigues, and to bear a part in the same enterprise."[45] Alexander concluded from Tacitus' account that "the ancient Germans appear to have exceeded in some points of morality, the most polished and instructed nations of Europe." Their history showed that there was no necessary connection between "the greatest purity of manners," which they had attained, and "particular states of cultivation and refinement."[46] The Germans had purity, but lacked the polish that is in Alexander's *History* associated with the exemption of women from labor or the feminization of their work—the implicit recognition of its superfluity. His account suggests that where the Greeks had achieved the invention without the manners necessary to civilization, the Germans achieved the manners without the invention.

IV

Alexander's account of Roman women is a good deal more complex, and perhaps more confused. On the one hand he argues that

> it was the Romans who first gave the sex public liberty, who first properly cultivated their minds, and thought it as necessary to do so as to adorn their bodies.

43. See Jane Rendall, "Writing History for British Women: Elizabeth Hamilton and the Memoirs of Agrippina," in *Wollstonecraft's Daughters: Womanhood in England and France 1780–1920,* ed. Clarissa Campbell Orr (Manchester: Manchester University Press, 1996), 79–93; and her important essay, "Tacitus Engendered: 'Gothic Feminism' and British Histories, c. 1750–1800," in *Imagining Nations,* ed. Geoffrey Cubitt (Manchester: Manchester University Press, 1998), 57–74.

44. Gilbert Stuart, *A View of Society in Europe, in its progress from rudeness to refinement,* 2d ed. [1792], reprinted with introduction by William Zachs (Bristol: Thoemmes Press, 1995), 12.

45. Ibid., 18.

46. Alexander, *History* (1782), 1.392.

> Among them were they first fitted for society, and for becoming rational companions; and among them was it first demonstrated to the world, that they were capable of great actions, and deserved a better fate than to be shut up in seraglios, and kept only as the pageants of grandeur, or instruments of satisfying illicit love.

But on the other hand he emphasizes that "the Romans were a people but little acquainted with decency, and entire strangers to that delicacy which takes place between the two sexes, among nations tolerably advanced in civilization and society."[47] I can perhaps best make sense of his account by considering it in the context of some of the accounts of Roman and Spartan women published in the 1770s and 1780s.

In his *Sketches of the History of Man* (1774), Henry Home, Lord Kames, expressed enthusiastic admiration for the exemplary qualities of the women of Sparta and Rome, singling out in particular their capacity for patriotism. He argued that if women received a "virtuous and refined education," men would have to display "every manly talent in public and in private life" in order to please them, and as a result "the two sexes, instead of corrupting each other, would be rivals in the race of virtue." His argument for women's education as a social panacea is based in classical examples of women's patriotism. So, for example, he claims that Coriolanus "made a capital figure in the Roman republic" because, though "others behaved valliantly, in order to acquire glory: he behaved valliantly, in order to give pleasure to his mother." He concludes:

> Let the most profound politician say, what more efficacious incentive there can be to virtue and manhood, than the behaviour of the Spartan matrons, flocking to the temples, and thanking the gods, that their husbands and sons had died gloriously, fighting for their country. In the war between Lacedemon and Thebes, the Lacedemonians having behaved ill, the married men, as Plutarch reports, were so ashamed of themselves, that they durst not look their wives in the face. What a glorious prize is here exhibited to be contended for by the female sex![48]

The *Essay on the Character of Women* also praises the women of Rome for their "enthusiastic love of their country," but its admiration for the domestic virtues in which this patriotism was based is perhaps more ambivalent. The *Essay* suggests that the virtue of the women of Rome may have been the result of ignorance, as they were

> shut up in their houses, where a simple and rustic virtue paid everything to instinct, and nothing to elegance; so nearly allied to barbarism, as only to know what it was to be wives and mothers; chaste, without apprehending that they

47. Ibid., 1.203–4, 202.

48. Henry Home, Lord Kames, *Sketches of the History of Man*, 2 vols. (Edinburgh: Creech, 1774), 1.Bk. 1, sketch 6, 217, 218, 219.

> could be otherwise; tender and affectionate, before they had learned the meaning of the words; occupied in duties, and ignorant that there were other pleasures, they spent their lives in retirement, in nursing their children, and in rearing to the republic a race of labourers and of soldiers.

The claim that the virtues of Roman women indicate that they were "more susceptible of habits than of principles," and the suggestion that those principles might go hand in hand with elegance, may be echoed in Alexander's comments on the lack of civilized decency and delicacy in relations between Roman men and women; both accounts may imply that Roman women were attributed the virtue of patriotism at the expense of the virtues of educated principle or polished elegance which might be the cause or effect of civilization.

The *Essay* suggests, as did Kames, that women, including modern women, display patriotic virtue in enduring bereavement for the sake of their country. A woman (who appears to be modern) is imagined addressing Thucydides in defense of women's "equal right to praise" and "public esteem," apparently with the historian's account of Pericles' oration in mind. She argues that "sometimes also the name of citizen demands from us the tribute of fortitude. When you offer your blood to the state, think that it is ours. In giving it our sons and our husbands, we give more than ourselves. You can only die on the field of battle, but we have the misfortune to survive those whom we love the most."[49] This sacrifice is represented as the basis for female citizenship, as it is in Kames's purer strain of classical republican panegyric. But here there is perhaps some concession to modernity in the acknowledgment that bereavement is a misfortune, and not a cause for celebration. For Alexander, however, and for James Fordyce, the classical patriotism of Roman and Spartan women seems completely incompatible with the feminine sensibility which they manage to imply is both universal or timeless and peculiarly modern and civilized. Alexander argues that the willingness of women to sacrifice those they love to "wars, undertaken to defend or enlarge their country" is undesirable because it may "overcome the natural propensity of women to preserve their own offspring." He equates this "romantic patriotism" with the willingness of Egyptian women to see "their children . . . devoured by their sacred crocodiles." He implies that the classical patriotism of women is analogous to Egyptian piety, and "superstitious almost beyond a possibility of belief." Both violate what he sees as the natural maternal character. He reflects in passing that in modern times maternal feelings "often yield to causes more frivolous and not less

49. Russell, *Essay,* 1.53, 49, 68, 15, 16. On Thomas's failure to discuss the effects of women's sociability, see Dena Goodman, *The Republic of Letters: A Cultural History of the French Enlightenment* (Ithaca, N.Y.: Cornell University Press, 1994), 10–11.

culpable," but his own willingness to value more properly maternal propensities seems clearly to imply that these are merely the aberrations and excesses of modern fashion.[50]

James Fordyce's brief discussion of Roman women in his *Sermons* of 1767 also implied that patriotism should be rejected where it conflicted with feminine sensibility. He writes:

> The virtues of a Roman matron, in the better times of that republic, appear on some accounts to have been greatly respectable. They are such as might be looked for, from her education amongst a people where ideas of prowess, patriotism, and glory, ran high; where, in effect, these things were regarded as the summit of human excellence and felicity. But not to insist on national pride, and ungenerous prepossessions, on which those ideas were founded; it is manifest to me, that whatever force or grandeur the female mind might in other views derive from them, such advantage was over-balanced by the loss or the diminution of that gentleness and softness, which ever were, and ever will be, the sovereign charm of the female character.

The "women of Great Britain," he concludes, "profess a system so much more just, amiable, and happy." For Fordyce, patriotism has come to seem too narrow and ungenerous—a matter of "national pride" rather than of dedication to a more comprehensive ideal of the public good. But it seems inappropriate to women, even in that reduced form, because it is incompatible with the "meek and quiet spirit" he sees as properly feminine; it suggests a "force and grandeur" which (perhaps like the effects of learning elsewhere in his *Sermons*) can only be gained at the expense of "gentleness and softness."[51]

Alexander concludes his discussion of the patriotism of Roman women with the observation that "we have reason to believe that the Romans sacrificed more to merit than to love; and that while their women shared with them almost every honour and every privilege, they were in general treated rather with the cool esteem of friendship, than with the warm indulgence of tenderness and affection." This "cool esteem" rapidly becomes the sign of a "political virtue so rigid and severe, that it never suffered humanity in the least to interfere where the interest of their country was concerned." Esteem turns out to indicate in the Romans a lack of humanity that leads to the "still worse" treatment of conquered women, and in particular to the ravishing and scourging of "the daughters of the British queen Boadicea."[52] Alexander suggests that the capacity to recognize and esteem the patriotism of women indicates a failure

50. Alexander, *History* (1782), 1.341.

51. James Fordyce, *Sermons to Young Women* [1765] (London: Cadell, 1809), Sermon xiii, 2.183–84.

52. Alexander, *History* (1782), 1.216–17.

of "warm indulgence"; it indicates in Roman men the lack of that humanity which the domestic sensibility of less patriotic women would presumably have nurtured. The female defender of "the cause of her sex" who addresses Thucydides, in the *Essay on the Character of Women,* for example, asserts:

> We are wives and mothers. 'Tis we who form the union and the cordiality of families; 'tis we who soften that savage rudeness which considers every thing as due to force, and which would involve man with man in eternal war. We cultivate in you that humanity, which makes you feel for the misfortunes of others; and our tears forewarn you of your own danger.[53]

For Alexander, the patriotism of Roman women, and the ability of Roman men to admire it, indicates that Roman women fail to cultivate the humanity of men, and forgo its benefits. He asserts that the condition of Roman women "was much preferable" to that of other women of classical antiquity, but he suggests that the respect shown for their public virtues, as much as their "subordination to the men," results in their being "coldly and indelicately treated by their husbands and lovers," and confirms that the Romans "had not yet learned, as in modern times, to blend the rigidity of the patriot, and roughness of the warrior, with that soft and indulging behaviour, so conspicious in our modern patriots and heroes."[54]

For Alexander and Fordyce, classical patriotism is an inappropriate model for modern women to emulate because it is incompatible with feminine sensibility and humanity. Alexander extracts some perhaps unexpected support for this view from the example of ancient Sparta. He writes that

> Lycurgus . . . seems to have thought women almost below his notice: nor need we wonder at this, when we consider, that his sole intention . . . was to divest his countrymen of every thing implanted in them by nature; and, upon the principles of art, to form a race of heroes, who should be insensible to every feeling but love of their country. Women . . . were but ill calculated for this purpose. Patriotism is a principle seldom so strong in them as in men, and humanity is generally much stronger. The acuteness of their feelings made them less able to bear all the pains and difficulties of eradicating whatever is natural, and the weakness of their bodies disqualified them for becoming heroines.[55]

The opposition Alexander sets out here between the natural humanity of women and the artificial idealism of men alludes to the familiar dualism of mind and body. Men are capable of becoming "insensible to every feeling,"

53. Russell, *Essay,* 1.15, 16.
54. Alexander, *History* (1782), 1.209–10.
55. Ibid., 1.53.

whereas women are engrossed by the acute feelings of their weak and painful bodies. Women seem here to be debarred from patriotism by something very close to the "gentleness and softness" Fordyce admired, or that capacity to exist "more in themselves, and in the objects of their sensibility" insisted on in the *Essay on the Character of Women.*[56]

I have suggested, however, that in the 1770s and 1780s changing notions of patriotism reconfigure that stark opposition between women's physical absorption and men's ideal heroism, and Alexander's unusual reading of Spartan history marks that shift. Alexander's surprising emphasis on the denial of patriotic virtue to Spartan women—who were of course more usually seen, as they were by Kames, as prime examples of its most severe and self-denying results—is introduced as part of his argument that the women of ancient Greece and Sparta were valued chiefly as "healthful and robust bodies," which could "give strong and healthful children to the state." Alexander suggests that it was because this was the "chief qualification" of women that their minds were left uncultivated, and they were encouraged to pursue only the "masculine amusements" of physical exercise. This emphasis on physical strength, Alexander argues, "must have tended, in the strongest manner, to destroy every seed of delicacy that nature had implanted in their minds; and . . . in all probability, gave birth to that boldness and effrontery, for which the Athenian women at last became so remarkable."[57]

Physical strength was, of course, important to the notion of Spartan women as exemplars of classical republican femininity. Catharine Macaulay noted, for example, in her *Letters on Education* (1790), that "instead of entailing the curse of feebleness on their women for the sake of augmenting their personal beauty," the Spartans "endeavoured to improve their natural strength, in order to render them proper nurses for a race of heroes." Macaulay argued that the combination of moral, mental, and physical robustness is necessary to "a conduct uniformly virtuous."[58] In the 1780s and 1790s almost every advocate of women's rights endorses the view that this combination is indivisible, suggesting that it is almost impossible to achieve a virtuous and healthy mind without regular physical workouts. An interesting example of the argument is provided by Alexander Jardine's *Letters from Barbary, France, Spain, Portugal, &c* (1788), which Mary Hays claimed expressed views on women so "nearly similar" to her own that they made working on her *Appeal to the Men of Great*

56. Russell, *Essay,* 2.50.

57. Alexander, *History* (1782), 1.52.

58. Catharine Macaulay Graham, *Letters on Education. With Observations on Religious and Metaphysical Subjects* (London: Dilly, 1790), 24–25.

Britain (1798) seem (temporarily) superfluous.[59] Jardine argues that the only "remedy to that growing disposition to indulgence, affectation, and perpetual change, which attends on civilization, arts, and taste" lies in raising women "to that equality with men in natural rights, and in the use of their talents, which seems intended by nature." He cites the example of Sparta, which showed what "a wise government might do," and urges that in order to achieve this end "the children of both sexes should be educated together and alike." He observes that in families which permitted this, "the most manly of the sisters, who keep up the nearest to the brothers in their laborious exercises or employments, are generally every way the superior characters," and comments that "those who pretend to be so highly disgusted with learned or masculine women" are not "the most manly or learned of men," but are "fribbles and triflers." His argument admits no distinction between the manly virtues of liberal education and of physical strength, and concludes with the hope that "ladies will have courage enough to go on to be as manly or learned as they please."[60]

Alexander's account of the women of Sparta is opposed to this model perhaps most obviously in its insistence that delicacy is natural, and not false, immoral, or diseased; and that notion of delicacy as a natural and desirable feminine quality is of course common to many of the more conservative accounts of women published in the last few decades of the century. What is perhaps more striking is the way his account distinguishes between physical robustness and the unnatural or unfeminine demands of patriotism, or between strength of body and strength of mind. Physical exercise, he implies, may have made Spartan women fitter to bear children, but not necessarily to nurture or educate them. There may be a discursive link between the way patriotism involves "eradicating whatever is natural" and the apparent ease with which physical training can "destroy every seed of delicacy that nature had implanted," but for Alexander this is not a causal link, and physical health does not result in the moral virtue of patriotism. The importance of that distinction may be that it leaves open the possibility of a more modern idea of patriotism based in humanity, rather than in the artificial heroism of Spartan men, or the coldness and indelicacy of the Roman warrior.

The female examples of classical patriotism most frequently cited in the late

59. [Mary Hays], *Appeal to the Men of Great Britain in behalf of Women* (London: Johnson, 1798), Advertisement, n.p.

60. [Alexander Jardine], *Letters from Barbary, France, Spain, Portugal, &c. By An English Officer*, 2 vols. (London: Cadell, 1788), 1.310, 332–34. On Jardine, see Jane Rendall, "'The Grand Causes which Combine to Carry Mankind Forward': Wollstonecraft, History, and Revolution," *Women's Writing* 4, no. 2 (1997): 159–60.

century, by Alexander among many others, are those of Cornelia, the mother of the Gracchi, and Veturia (or Volumnia), the mother of Coriolanus.[61] I have already mentioned that Kames, following Plutarch, remembered Veturia for having prompted her son to pursue glory, but most commentators in the late century praise her primarily for her intervention to save Rome from the fury of her son. Alexander praises her for having "prevailed upon" her son "to sacrifice his resentment to the love of his country."[62] The *Essay on the Character of Women* described her intervention in terms which emphasized the importance of maternal humanity rather than patriotic severity: "the mother had softened her son."[63] An odd example of the currency of the image of Veturia is provided by the *Morning Herald and Daily Advertiser* in 1784. Defending the Duchess of Devonshire's campaign to purchase shopkeepers' votes in the Westminster election, it commented that her "interference . . . in behalf of Mr Fox is but a counterpart of those Roman Ladies who sued to Coriolanus for the welfare of the City of Rome."[64] The strained analogy between Coriolanus and the Westminster shopkeepers, or Fox and the city of Rome, may indicate that the image is so familiar that it defies scrutiny. It seems here simply to focus attention on the parallel between the Duchess's actions and the exemplary patriotism of Coriolanus' mother and wife.

Representations of Veturia as the acceptable image of female patriotism in the second half of the eighteenth century probably owe as much to James Thomson's *Coriolanus* (1749), or to the spectacular stage adaptations of Sheridan and Kemble, as they do to Shakespeare's play; but these different versions have much in common, particularly in the way they represent the mother's intercession. In Thomson's tragedy, Veturia emphasizes in her approach to Coriolanus that she is not "a deputy from Rome," not the representative of the "dignity of senates." Instead she portrays in her own maternal body the affective ties Rome extends to its sons. When Coriolanus speaks of the "base seditious herd" which has made Rome ungrateful, she replies:

> Thou has not thence a right to lift thy hand
> Against the whole community, which forms
> Thy ever-sacred country—That consists

61. For an illuminating discussion of representations of Cornelia, see Kate Davies, "Gender and Republicanism in Britain and America: The Meanings of Catherine Macaulay," (unpublished Ph.D. dissertation, University of York, 1999). Veturia is known as Volumnia in Shakespeare's *Coriolanus* and in Plutarch's *Lives.*

62. Alexander, *History* (1782), 1.212.

63. Russell, *Essay,* 1.54.

64. *Morning Herald and Daily Advertiser,* 15 April 1784, cited in Amanda Foreman, *Georgiana, Duchess of Devonshire* (London: HarperCollins, 1998), 150.

Not of coeval citizens alone:
It know no bounds: it has a retrospect
To ages past; it looks on those to come;
And grasps of all the general worth and virtue.
Suppose, my son, that I to thee had been
A harsh obdurate parent, even unjust:
How would the monstrous thought with horror strike thee,
Of plunging, from revenge, thy raging steel
Into her breast who nurst thy infant years!—

The decision to conquer and sack Rome, she claims, will make Coriolanus a "double parricide!"[65] Veturia suggests that the physical bond of mothering implies analogous physical ties between Coriolanus and his country, so that the possibility of violating either seems a "monstrous thought," despite the vice or corruption that may accidentally characterize them. She does not attempt to appeal to a Spartan idea of patriotism, which might make her son "insensible to every feeling, but love of . . . country"; instead she reminds him of ties of sentiment and humanity, of a kind of "local emotion" that may make it possible to appropriate her image to a more modern idea of patriotism.

V

In conclusion, I want to reconsider those portraits of Barbauld and Macaulay as Roman matrons with which I began this chapter. For they perhaps begin to look rather different in the contexts I have sketched. The image of Macaulay may now seem to allude more obviously than does the medallion of Barbauld to the severity of the ideal of classical patriotism. Macaulay is framed with a garland of oak leaves, which in contrast to, say, a laurel wreath is distinctively military and heroic in its implications. Beneath the portrait roundel itself, in both the editions I have consulted, appears a small coinlike stamp, showing Brutus, the founder of the Roman republic, followed by lictors bearing fasces. Brutus is of course identified with the most heroic or inhuman sacrifice of private feeling to the public good. Adam Smith uses the example of Brutus' sacrifice of his two sons, who had conspired against the republic, to illustrate the masculine generosity of public spirit, which consists in "thwarting, from a sense of duty and propriety, the strongest of all natural propensities." He explains that

65. *Coriolanus: A Tragedy,* in *The Works of James Thomson, with his last corrections and improvements,* 3 vols. (London: Baldwin, 1802), 3. 293, 295–96, 300.

> Brutus ought naturally to have felt more for the death of his own sons, than for all that probably Rome could have suffered from the want of so great an example. But he viewed them, not with the eyes of a father, but with those of a Roman citizen. He entered so thoroughly into the sentiments of this last character, that he paid no regard to that tie, by which he himself was connected with them; and to a Roman citizen, the sons even of Brutus seemed contemptible, when put into the balance with the smallest interest of Rome.

Smith goes on to explain that the generosity of Brutus' action may also be the sign of its barbarity. He argues that "humanity is the virtue of a woman, generosity of a man," but he later makes it clear that this degree of manliness may be excessive in "ages of humanity and politeness" when "abstinence from pleasure becomes less necessary, and the mind is more at liberty to unbend itself, and to indulge its natural inclinations." He writes:

> Among civilised nations, the virtues which are founded upon humanity, are more cultivated than those which are founded upon self-denial and the command of the passions. Among rude and barbarous nations, it is quite otherwise, the virtues of self-denial are more cultivated than those of humanity. . . . Every savage undergoes a sort of Spartan discipline, and by the necessity of his situation is inured to every sort of hardship.[66]

Macaulay's decision to represent herself as the pseudomilitary scourge of modern corruption, the female Brutus who values liberty more than natural affection, marks the idealism of her patriotism, but it may also characterize it as premodern or uncivilized in its inhuman or antifeminine severity.[67]

Critics have emphasized that Barbauld's politics were more liberal than Macaulay's. But it is worth remembering that the two women did share common ground; both were celebrated and linked in Dyer's lines, and both appeared shoulder to shoulder with male radicals in the lineup depicted in the print of Burke "Running the Literary Gantlet." As I have mentioned, Sarah Vaughan was celebrated for encouraging the patriotic virtues of "lovers, brothers, sons" in Barbauld's "Character" poem, which the editors believe was probably written early in 1770. In 1769 her husband, Samuel Vaughan, attended meetings of the Society of Supporters of the Bill of Rights along with Macaulay's brother John Sawbridge and Thomas Wilson.[68] The patriotism that led both women to be portrayed as Roman matrons involved some shared

66. Adam Smith, *The Theory of Moral Sentiments,* ed. D. D. Raphael and A. L. Macfie (Oxford: Clarendon Press, 1976), IV.2.11, 10; V.2.9, 8.

67. On Macaulay's savagery, see Kate Davies, "Gender and Republicanism."

68. See S. Maccoby, *English Radicalism, 1762–1785: The Origins* (London: George Allen & Unwin, 1955), 105–6, 106 n. 2.

features, some overlap in political definition as well as in hairstyle. But the medallion of Barbauld as a Roman matron was softened in comparison to that of Macaulay. In her writing, Barbauld explicitly distances herself from the model offered by the women of Sparta. She praises the "mighty mothers of immortal Rome" for their domestic virtues, which she suggests are the necessary basis for "the generous flame" of what Smith characterized as masculine patriotic zeal. Her sermons of the 1790s suggest that Barbauld might best be understood in the context of an ideal of "republican motherhood" which represents the "household virtues" as continuous with and necessary to more obviously patriotic virtues because their privacy is the basis for an inclusive conception of the civic. If Macaulay's patriotism echoed that which whiggish writers of the mid-century had admired in the mother of Coriolanus as she sent her son to battle, then that of Barbauld was closer to the maternal solicitude with which Veturia pleaded for Rome, in which the historians of the late century found more to admire.

10

Britain Mourn'd: Anna Seward's Patriotic Elegies

In 1791, a visitor to Lichfield wrote of entering the home of Anna Seward while the poet was away in Bristol: "in I ran, impatient to see where genius and poetry had fixed their abode, and happy even in the opportunity of treading the same ground. Indeed it would be impossible for the most rigid stoic to enter such a spot without emotion." The Bishop's Palace at Lichfield evokes what Samuel Johnson had called "local emotion"—a powerfully doubled language of patriotism and piety rooted in the associations of the place. The account continues:

> From this hallowed spot originated that beautiful bud of British poetry, which, like the morning rose impearled with the dew of heaven, expanded in tears. It was here that the distracted mourner imprecated vengeance upon the base abettors of an ignominious doom, that sent the soldier and the lover to an early grave. It was here that the genius of Britain sung the fall of heroes, and, scattering her inspired lays, would "Light with vestal flame her André's hallow'd pyre," or wander "With wild unequal step, round Cook's morai."[1]

1. Edward D. Clarke, *A Tour through the South of England, Wales, and part of Ireland made in the Summer of 1791* (1793), quoted in E. V. Lucas, *A Swan and her Friends* (London: Methuen, 1907), 80. Seward lived in the Bishop's Palace with her father, who was canon of Lichfield Cathedral. For a fuller account of Seward's life see Margaret Ashmun, *The Singing Swan: An Account of Anna Seward and Her Acquaintance with Dr. Johnson, Boswell, and Others of Their Time* (New Haven, Conn.: Yale University Press, 1931).

It is important to this account that Seward was not in Lichfield at the time, for it is the trace of her, the idea of her, that is so rich in elegiac associations. The Bishop's Palace where Seward lives is hallowed by clustered notions of dead British heroes and of the poet who is "the genius of Britain," as though their status as national heroes accrued to her reputation, and found its focus in her home as the site of local emotion.

Anna Seward's reputation, in the 1780s, depended largely on the two publications the tourist mentions: *An Elegy on Captain Cook* (1780), and the *Monody on Major André* (1781). The nature of the success those enjoyed is indicated by the comment, in *The Lady's Monthly Museum,* on her later *Ode on General Eliott's Return from Gibraltar* (1787). The *Museum* noted that "it is some doubt, whether her strains derived more lustre from the popularity of the hero, or the hero from them."[2] Seward's reputation, her importance as a national poet, looms so large that the achievements of Cook, André, or Eliott, significant as they are recognized to be in their own right, are magnified because they contribute to her almost mythological status. Two poems by H. F. Cary which were printed as prefatory addresses to Seward's *Original Sonnets* (1799) and *Llangollen Vale* (1796) celebrate Seward as the personification of national identity, as "Our British Muse," "th'immortal MUSE of Britain."[3] In an "Impromptu" of 1781, William Hayley represents Seward as uniquely able to comfort the grieving nation. He writes that following the deaths of Cook and André, "Britain mourn'd, with all a Mother's pain, / Two Sons, two gallant Sons, ignobly slain"; the Goddess of Britain is represented as "plung'd in grief too vast to speak." The muse of elegy then offers her comfort:

> "Take, injured Parent, all we can bestow,
> To sooth thy heart, and mitigate thy woe!"
> Speaking, to earth the kind enthusiast came,
> And veil'd her heavenly power with SEWARD's name. . . .

The muse conceals her presence by causing Seward to announce that she has known André since youth, and speaks so affectingly and effectively in the poet's "fair semblance" that "the weeping Goddess owns the blest relief, / And

2. *The Lady's Monthly Museum, or Polite Repository of Amusement and Instruction: Being an assembly of whatever can tend to please the fancy, interest the mind, or exalt the character of the British Fair. By a Society of Ladies,* March 1799, "Miss Seward."

3. "Verses by the Rev. H. F. Carey, on reading the following paraphrases," l. 10, in Seward, *Original Sonnets on Various Subjects; and Odes Paraphrased from Horace,* 2d ed. (London: Sael, 1799); and H. F. Cary, "Sonnet," l. 7, in *Llangollen Vale, with Other Poems* (London: Sael, 1796).

fondly listens, with subsiding grief."[4] Seward is attributed an extraordinary ability to speak for and to the nation.

In this chapter I will consider the nature of that ability—its dependence on the conjunction of the particular historical circumstances of the early 1780s, when Britain's imperial power was at its lowest ebb, with the privacy and depth of feeling which can define virtuous femininity. Seward's reputation clearly owed much to her ability to exploit her provincial position as the leader of polite society in Lichfield, as John Brewer argues in his illuminating essay in *The Pleasures of the Imagination* (1997). She can be seen, Brewer points out, as perhaps the most prominent exponent of an idea of poetry that is "woven into the fabric of genteel social life," and removed in its feminized and "provincial tranquillity" from metropolitan professionalism.[5] I argue, however, that Seward's emphasis on her own privacy, her exclusion or exemption from the professional or public circles of the metropolis, is important in the 1780s also because it enables her poetry to articulate a distinctively female patriotism that is a form of both national celebration and private consolation. Margaret Ashmun, Seward's biographer, notes that the *Monody on Major André* "reaped the reward of timeliness. In the *salons* of London her lines were read and quoted; and in distant country houses her name was repeated beside the hearth."[6] The poem offers an account of responses to the American war in a narrative that represents some of the complexity of liberal whiggish attitudes to the war as though they were the private and impassioned perceptions of the poet for her friend. It is important both as an index to the kinds of patriotic or national feeling that provincial liberal whigs could salvage from the war, and as an indication of why women's poetry should have become central to national culture in the 1780s.

Seward's letters were published posthumously by her direction, and carefully selected and rewritten by her to establish her reputation as the arbiter of polite and sentimental taste. In the letters she is at pains to establish that her ambitions as a poet did not—were never allowed by her to—compete with her feminine duties. She writes to Thomas Christie in 1788, to turn down his invitation to contribute regularly to the *Analytical Review,* explaining that:

4. Hayley's "Impromptu," in Seward, *Monody on Major Andrè. To which are added Letters Addressed to her by Major Andrè, in the year 1769,* 2d ed. (Lichfield: Jackson, 1781), v–vi.

5. See John Brewer, "'Queen Muse of Britain': Anna Seward of Lichfield and the Literary Provinces," in his *The Pleasures of the Imagination: English Culture in the Eighteenth Century* (London: HarperCollins, 1997), quotation from 611.

6. Ashmun, *Singing Swan,* 86.

> To maintain household economy, social intercourse, and the established claims of a very large correspondence, I am obliged but very seldom to admit the visits of the Muses. With great fondness for literature, my life has been too much devoted to feminine employments to do much more than study, in every short and transient opportunity, with eager avidity, and intense attention, that science, the first and fairest, "Which set on fire my youthful heart. . . ."[7]

Her account of herself suggests some chafing against the restrictions imposed by genteel provincialism. This may also be apparent in, for example, a letter to Helen Maria Williams, warning her against corresponding with George Hardinge (the lawyer and M.P.), whose epistolary solicitations to herself Seward had rejected (for the time being). She explains to the younger poet that she has pointed out on her behalf to Hardinge that "an author's time was his or her source of profit and of fame; that where talents exist, capable of engaging the attention of the public, it was deplorable extravagance to turn them almost all into the covert channel of private letters."[8] Seward endorses Williams's professionalism, but her approbation of the younger poet's claim to profit and fame emphasizes her own acceptance of the prior claims of "feminine employments" despite the "deplorable extravagance" with her talents that they might involve. She terminates her own developing correspondence with Hardinge, she explains to him, because she does not believe their lives have enough in common: "You are in high life, I am in obscurity, from which I do not wish to emerge, since peace is dearer to me than distinction."[9]

The *Lady's Monthly Museum* commented in its portrait of Seward in 1799 that

> with all our deference for the powers of Composition she possesses in a very eminent degree, and the sincere admiration in which we hold many of her verses, we still presume to think, that all her productions are very inferior to what she might have yielded in a conjugal state, as a mother of a family. But what so likely to prevent her utility in this humble, but natural sphere, as an attachment to studies rather unfavourable to its duties, and which is seldom either an excitement to marriage, or a source of happiness in a marriage state.[10]

In a letter of 1786, Seward claims to support a similar notion of the "natural sphere" of femininity. Writing of an acquaintance who "married a

7. *The Letters of Anna Seward: Written between the years 1784 and 1807,* 6 vols., ed. A. Constable (Edinburgh: Ramsay, 1811), 2.4, letter 1, to Christie, Esq. of Edinburgh, Lichfield, 15 January 1788.

8. *Letters of Seward,* 1.398, letter lxxxvi, to Miss Helen Williams, Lichfield, 25 December 1787.

9. *Letters of Seward,* 1.233, letter 1, to George Hardinge, Esq., Lichfield, 20 December 1786.

10. *Lady's Monthly Museum,* March 1799, "Miss Seward."

Warwickshire squire . . . and squiresses it with much loquacious importance," she comments:

> but away with everything like sarcastic comment upon a prudent wife, a kind mother, and a cheerful desirable neighbour. Ah! how much a more useful creature than such a *celebaic* cypher as myself! You coin a word now and then, so pray welcome my stranger-epithet. Her sons are fine youths; and her eldest daughter is "the fairest flower of the vicinage."[11]

Seward's self-abjection is of course doubled, tinged with irony. Denial does not purify her praise of sarcasm, and even in her apparently modest claim to be a *"celebaic* cypher" she hints at her sense of her own worth, for she thought coining neologisms was an obligation on the literate, as a result of which "higher will rise the reputation of English literature."[12] The implication of her comments on the proper duties of femininity is to turn criticisms such as those expressed by the *Lady's Museum* to her own advantage. Her letters represent her as a woman primarily concerned to look after her aged parent—"my aged nursling," as she often calls him, whose "entire dependence upon my care and attention, resulting from the decay of his corporeal and intellectual faculties, has doubled our bond of union, and engrafted the maternal upon filial tenderness." By emphasizing the dutiful sensibility she displays in caring for the man who "seems at once my parent and my child,"[13] Seward represents herself as having sacrificed all ambition to properly "feminine employments," and it is this that licenses the production of a huge correspondence, and a very considerable body of poetry, and an active involvement in a fairly intensive social life.

Seward represents her ability to write poetry as continually subject to a peculiarly feminine form of virtuous self-denial. She writes to Humphry Repton, for example, that "I have ever made it a point to omit no duty, to neglect no claim of friendship, or even of civility, for the idle business of the muses." She tells Repton that even if she could spare the time to write, she would be deterred from publishing by the "arrogance and ignorance of the public critics" who "keep dragon-watch around the Hesperian tree of fame."[14] The letter is typical of many of Seward's comments on her own writing in the 1780s in forging a curious but undeniably strong link between her desire to be perceived both as committed to virtuous domesticity and as a figure of public fame: she would write more, she suggests, if that "idle business" were compat-

11. *Letters of Seward,* 1.109, letter xxiii, to Mrs . Knowles, Lichfield, 25 January 1786.
12. Ibid., 2.155, letter xxxv, to Edward Tighe, Esq., Lichfield, 23 September 1788.
13. Ibid., 1.221, letter xlix, to Mr. W. Newton, Lichfield, 17 December 1786.
14. Ibid., 2.311, letter lxxvii, to H. Repton, Esq., Lichfield, 15 July 1789.

ible with private life, and if she could be confident of the reward of fame. Seward's commitment to domesticity, with its familial ties, is important to her sense of herself as a patriot. She tells Helen Maria Williams, about a visit to "my native Derbyshire," that the county is significant to her because it is the site of "the village that gave me birth, and of which my dear father is rector." As a result of these associations, and in particular the strength of her feeling for her father, she writes that the "pleasures I feel from the contemplation of romantic scenery, is [*sic*] there always heightened by the patriot passion." But it is the combination of her industrious domesticity with the "idle business" that should secure her fame that establishes her claim to middle-class merit. She writes of Burke's *Reflections* in 1791 that she dislikes his

> Quixotism about the Queen of France, and his vindication of hereditary honours. They are much more likely to make a man repose, with slumbering virtue upon *them,* for the distinction he is to receive in society, than to inspire the effort of rendering himself worthy of them. They are to men what beauty is to women, a dangerous gift, which has a natural tendency to make them indolent, silly, and worthless.[15]

It is Seward's writing of poetry and letters, in conjunction with her diligence in private duties, that implicitly supports her claim to a peculiarly feminine social distinction that approximates to the professional ambition she praises here.

John Brewer's argument that Seward opposes the claims of her own polite amateurishness to the metropolitan professionalism of Johnson and other critics suggests the extent to which Seward's capacity to speak for and to the nation is based in the meanings and value of her gender in the 1780s. Seward did not abjure fame, or at least some of its material rewards. She is, for example, unambiguously resentful about the lack of public and material reward to accompany praise for her poetry, noting that she never received the "medal in honour of Captain Cook," though "Mr Green of our museum had one, and indeed every person who had interested themselves at all publicly in the memory of that philanthropic hero."[16] She reconciles her claim to a public voice and fame with feminine and retired virtue by opposing both to the notion of the corrupt metropolis, devoid of sentiment, in a maneuver similar to that which reconciles the self-denying virtue and self-gratifying happiness of the

15. Ibid., 3.52, letter xviii, to Mrs. Taylor, 10 January 1791.

16. Ibid., 2.31, letter v, to J. Wedgewood, Esq., Lichfield, 18 February 1788. This perceived slight continued to rankle—see 3.31–32, letter x, to David Samwel[l], Esq., 16 August 1790, and 3.59–60, letter xxi, to David Samwell, Esq., Mansfield Woodhouse, 15 May 1791.

protagonists of *Louisa,* the *Poetical Novel* she published in 1784. There the heroine and her lover, divided by the demands of commerce and filial duty, are reunited through the active and passive agency of the hero's fashionable wife. The wife dies because "'Midst the light Throngs, that croud the garish Mart, / Consuming Fever hurls her fiery dart";[17] because of the pathological effects of metropolitan society, rejection of which brings the hero and heroine together; and the wife, seeing the error of her ways, pleads for them to be united by her death.

In a parallel movement, the virtue of the hero of her *Elegy on Captain Cook* is established by his departure from the charms of London in pursuit of more masculine ambitions. The poet asks:

> Say first, what Pow'r inspir'd his dauntless breast
> With scorn of danger, and inglorious rest,
> To quit imperial London's gorgeous plains,
> Where, rob'd in thousand tints, bright Pleasure reigns. . . .[18]

The nature of Cook's mission is here opposed to the sensual luxuries of London, which are represented by fruits available out of season and the wanton behavior of women. Cook's expeditions are represented as anti-imperial, in the sense in which empire is linked with metropolitan corruption, because they involve a kind of industrious and masculine heroism, and are inspired by humanity, whose personified form led him to "Unite the savage hearts, and hostile hands, / In the firm compact of her gentle bands."[19] As Bernard Smith has argued, the "heroising process" which fashioned Cook's image immediately after his death modeled him, in the wake of the publication of *The Wealth of Nations,* "as [Adam] Smith's global agent," the "first European to *practise* successfully on a global scale the use of tolerance for the purpose of domination."[20] Seward's *Elegy* is in keeping with this process, representing Cook as primarily concerned to distribute European flora and fauna and promote Christian family values of "chasten'd love" and "parental duty." Cook is a hero of sensibility and humanity, who weeps for the suffering of his men; he is a Christian martyr, who has not "bled in vain" because his "angel-goodness" blesses those he visits with progressive arts and virtues. Cook is the figure for an idea of empire

17. Seward, *Louisa, A Poetical Novel, in Four Epistles,* 3d ed. (Lichfield: J. Jackson, 1784), Ep. 4, 85.

18. Seward, *An Elegy on Captain Cook, to which is added, An Ode on the Sun,* 2d ed. (London: Dodsley, 1780), 4.

19. Seward, *Cook,* 5.

20. Bernard Smith, "Cook's Posthumous Reputation," in *Imagining the Pacific in the Wake of the Cook Voyages* (New Haven, Conn.: Yale University Press, 1992), 227, 236, emphasis in original.

that is free from the vices of imperial corruption in its implications for both the imperial center and the colonized.

In the concluding verse paragraph of the poem, Seward addresses Cook's widow, whom she imagines braving storms at night in the forlorn hope of glimpsing her husband's sails. She conjures the widow to take comfort from the assurance that Humanity, personified as Nordic holy mother with "golden hair" and "Blue . . . robe," is bearing the hero to "th'immortal plains" to await her. In this funereal tableau, the nation takes a supporting or subordinate role. Humanity bears Cook to heaven "while Britannia, to his virtues just, / Twines the bright wreath, and rears th'immortal bust."[21] The emphasis on the sorrow and pious consolation of Cook's widow, and on the bereavement and maternal solicitude of humanity, portrays his martyrdom as matter for domestic and universal grief, and Britannia's role in hailing Cook the national hero as merely supplementary. The positioning of the widow "aloft on Albion's rocky steep" recognizes her as a figure for the private grief of the nation, and denies the representativeness of Britannia's public and memorializing response to Cook's death. In the opening lines of the *Elegy,* Seward portrays the muses, made mute by sorrow, but adds that "not in silence sleep their silver lyres; / To the bleak gale they vibrate sad and slow, / In deep accordance with a Nation's woe."[22] In the representation of Cook as the hero of a new and enlightened imperialism which is primarily characterized by the virtues of humanity, piety, and domesticity, the *Elegy* claims to express national but private sentiment, to be itself "In deep accordance with a Nation's woe."

Seward's *Monody on Major André* built on the notions of patriotism expressed in the *Elegy on Cook,* and indeed the two poems are usually mentioned together in the late eighteenth century, as though they were the complementary parts of one project. English (but not American) editions of the monody in the 1780s identified the poet on the title page as the author of the *Elegy on Cook.*[23] The poet comments on the relation between the two poems in the later *Monody,* asking whether the muse can remain silent when imagining the grave of André after she has been animated by "public fame" to "hymn a Stranger." The poet asks if the muse can offer no more than a tear to the irresistible appeal of memories of one whose "virtues stole / Thro' Friendship's softening

21. Seward, *Cook,* 17–18. Seward changed "Humanity" to "Benevolence" in subsequent editions.

22. Seward, *Cook,* 6, 16, 3.

23. ESTC records that the *Monody* was issued in New York in 1781, 1788, and 1792; in Philadelphia probably in 1788; in Hanover, New Hampshire, in 1794; and in Boston in 1798. Only the first New York edition, printed by James Rivington, seems to have identified Seward as the author of the *Elegy on Cook.*

medium on her soul!"[24] The *Elegy on Captain Cook,* I have suggested, represented maternal and marital bereavement as the model for the expression of national loss; it explored some of the possibilities of the notion that "Britain mourn'd, with all a mother's pain."[25] The *Monody* takes that theme a step further in its claim to be based in strong personal feeling and private recollection.

The *Monody on Major André* is a remarkable patriotic poem because of the extraordinary skill with which it moves between public issues and private, impassioned feeling. Most of the first half of the poem is devoted to portraying André as the perfect sentimental hero, and detailing the virtues he displays in his relations to women, as son, brother, friend, and lover. Seward represents him as the victim of "ill-starr'd passion" for her friend, Honora Sneyd, with whom he could have created the ideal matrimonial home:

> Dear lost Companion! ever constant Youth!
> That Fate had smil'd on thy unequal'd truth!
> Nor bound th'ensanguin'd laurel on that brow
> Where Love ordain'd his brightest wreathe to glow!
> Then Peace had led thee to her softest bow'rs,
> And Hymen strew'd thy path with all his flow'rs. . . .

Had they been able to marry, Seward claims, their home would have been the center for the cherished private virtues of "social Joy," "Science, and soft affection"; André, the model sentimental husband, would quickly have learned that "the magic of her face" was "Thy fair Honora's least engaging grace." The couple are, however, represented as separated by her parents, and the poem manages to suggest that national war is a direct consequence of this: if he cannot enjoy domestic bliss, then there must be a war for André to turn to. Seward writes that "Pow'r Parental sternly saw, and strove / To tear the lilly-bands of plighted Love," whereupon André exclaims: "Honora lost! I woo a sterner Bride, / The arm'd Bellona calls me to her side."[26]

Richard Garnett notes severely, in his article on John André in the *Dictionary of National Biography,* that Seward misrepresents the circumstances of his enlistment. André took out his army commission in 1771, two years before Honora Sneyd married Richard Edgeworth, and well before Britain embarked on war with the thirteen colonies. But the point, in the *Monody,* seems to be that by 1781 André's willingness to "win bright Glory" in what many saw as an

24. Seward, *Monody on Major Andrè. By Miss Seward (Author of the Elegy on Capt. Cook.) To which are added Letters addressed to her by Major Andrè, in the year 1769* (Lichfield: Jackson, 1781), 2–3.

25. Hayley, "Impromptu," in Seward, *Monody,* 2d ed., v.

26. *Monody,* 6–7, 7, 9.

unjust and unwinnable civil war can best be represented as appropriate to his identity as sentimental hero if it is the negative effect of star-crossed love. In Seward's *Monody,* André chooses the war in response to the unjust use of "Pow'r Parental"; he is the victim of parental oppression, and in the context of pervasive representations of the American war as a struggle between parental authority and maturing offspring, this role implicitly identifies him as a displaced colonial son. Seward does suggest that André's military zeal finds some justification in patriotic feeling—the hero intends to fight against "dire Sedition"; but this is very much an afterthought, a rather vague coda to the more lengthy and impassioned discussion of André's need for an alternative bride, a manly objective that will allow him to reject the possibility that he might "languish in inglorious ease" amid the "soft'ning Luxuries" of "Voluptuous LONDON!"[27]

When André does embark on battle in America, the poet portrays both sides as heroic victims:

> Firm in their strength opposing Legions stand,
> Prepar'd to drench with blood the thirsty Land.
> Now Carnage hurls her flaming bolts afar,
> And Desolation groans amid the War.
> As bleed the Valiant, and the Mighty yield,
> Death stalks, the only Victor o'er the field.

These lines refer to a battle of 1775, in which André was taken prisoner, but the narrative of his captivity in the *Monody* is dominated by a detailed description of his successful attempts to preserve Honora's miniature by hiding it in his mouth, and he continues to be represented as a romantic hero whose struggles against oppressive fate merely coincide with what Seward later called "the absurd and ruinous attempt to conquer America."[28] At this stage of the war, as Seward explains in the *Monody,* the Americans seemed to her to be animated by principles that appealed to her liberal whig ideals: by

> . . . the generous active rising Flame,
> That boasted Liberty's immortal name!
> Blaz'd for its rights infring'd, its trophies torn,
> And taught the Wise the dire mistake to mourn,
> When haughty Britain, in a luckless hour,

27. Ibid., 8, 10, 13, 9, 8.

28. Ibid., 15. *Letters of Seward,* 3.45, letter xvi, to Miss [Helen Maria] Williams, Colton, 12 December 1790. Seward is arguing here that Burke's *Reflections* seem "the twin-brother of Johnson's 'Taxation no Tyranny.'"

With rage inebriate, and the lust of pow'r,
To fruitless conquest, and to countless graves
Led her gay Legions o'er the western waves!

For much of the poem, the American cause represents ideals and virtues the lack of which in England, and in London in particular, had, the *Monody* implies, led André to enlist. The poet observes that she mourns Britain's fate because years of war "Exhaust my Country's treasure, pour her gore / In fruitless conflict on the distant shore." But she recognizes the virtue of the cause her country opposes, and therefore she "rever'd her Foes."[29]

Seward's patriotic principles are, however, realigned with her feeling for her country by the circumstances of André's death. General Clinton, the commander of the British forces in America, sent André to negotiate with Benedict Arnold over his plan to betray West Point. André became trapped behind the American lines, was captured, and as a spy, was sentenced by a military court to death by hanging. Seward represents this as a "Ruffian's fate," because to be hanged was ungentlemanly, but she suggests that the decision to use the rope was itself less than genteel. André appealed to Washington before his execution:

> Sympathy towards a soldier will surely induce your Excellency and a military tribunal to adopt ["adapt"?] the mode of my death to the feelings of a man of honour.
>
> Let me hope, Sir, that if aught in my character impresses you with esteem towards me, if aught in my misfortunes marks me as the victim of policy, and not of resentment, I shall experience the operation of these feelings in your breast, by being informed that I am not to die on a gibbet.[30]

Seward cites in a footnote André's reported last words: "I die as becomes a British Officer, while the manner of my death must reflect disgrace on your Commander." André's dishonourable death concluded a wretched tale, but not—as sympathetic British publications noted—one that reflected on Washington's honor. Seward herself reported that Washington, who said that "no circumstance of his life had been so mortifying as to be censured in the *Monody*," later sent an officer commissioned to vindicate his innocence to her, and

29. *Monody*, 22, 23.

30. Letter from John André, Tappan, 1 October 1780, in "Public Papers," *The New Annual Register, or General Repository of History, Politics, and Literature, For the Year 1780*, 158. A full account of the affair can be found in these "Public Papers," 146–160. For a briefer account see "Proceeding on the Trial of the unfortunate Major André," *The London Magazine: or, Gentleman's Monthly Intelligencer. For January, 1781*, 46–48.

on examining the evidence she was "filled . . . with contrition for the rash injustice of my censure."[31] In the *Monody* she wrote:

Oh Washington! I thought thee great and good,
Nor knew thy Nero-thirst of guiltless blood!
Severe to use the pow'r that Fortune gave,
Thou cool determin'd Murderer of the Brave!
Lost to each fairer Virtue, that inspires
The genuine fervor of the Patriot fires!

Washington is no longer the hero of whiggish patriotism, and, in the *Monody,* the moral opprobrium attached to the oppressive parental authority exercised by the British is exchanged for condemnation of what Seward saw as the unfeeling tyranny of the Americans.[32]

What makes sense of this exchange, in the impassioned narrative of the poem, is the representation of André's fate as a direct consequence of the treaty of alliance between the Americans and the French in 1778. Seward, like other British whigs, saw this alliance as an "Unnatural compact," because she believed that the American commitment to ideals of freedom was incompatible with the system of government in France, which had of course in British eyes made the French "a Race of Slaves." She did not, like some of the radicals discussed by Linda Colley in her essay on radical patriotism, believe that the alliance pointed to redeeming features in the French national character, and saw André's death as evidence of the corruption of the American cause.[33] She writes:

Infatuate Land!—from that detested day
Distracted Councils, and the thirst of Sway,
Rapacious avarice, Superstition vile,
And all the Frenchman dictates in his guile
Disgrace your Congress!—Justice drops her scale!
And radiant Liberty averts her sail!
They fly indignant the polluted plain,
Where Truth is scorn'd and Mercy pleads in vain.

In the context of what she sees as the outrage of the American alliance with France, the poet forgets that she had earlier condemned the feminizing vices

31. *Monody,* 25 and n. *Letters of Seward,* 5.143, letter xxi, to Miss Ponsonby, Buxton, 9 August 1798.

32. *Monody,* 24, 27.

33. Linda Colley, "Radical Patriotism in Eighteenth-Century England," in *Patriotism: The Making and Unmaking of British National Identity. Vol. 1: History and Politics,* ed. Raphael Samuel (London: Routledge, 1989), 169–87.

of "Voluptuous LONDON," with its "soft'ning Luxuries" and "polish'd Arts." André is no longer represented as having made a herculean choice between the pleasures of London and the hardships of war, but as "polish'd André," a relatively feminized figure whose civilized virtues can be contrasted with the corrupt lack of moral sentiment among the Americans.[34]

The *Monody* concludes with the reappropriation of pastoral sentiment to the British cause, as the poet reflects on the grave of André:

Yet on thy grass-green Bier soft April-Show'rs
Shall earliest wake the sweet spontaneous Flow'rs!
Bid the blue Hare-bell, and the Violet there
Hang their cold cup, and drop the pearly tear!
And oft, at pensive Eve's ambiguous gloom,
Imperial Honour, bending o'er thy tomb,
With solemn strains shall lull thy deep repose,
And with his deathless Laurels shade thy brows!

The lines allude to the elegiac pastoral mode of Collins's "Ode, to a Lady on the Death of Colonel Ross" (written in 1745), and of *Cymbeline.* The personification of Imperial Honor bends over the tomb in the pensive attitude of philosophical melancholy that is appropriate to "Eve's ambiguous gloom." This is a very different notion of empire from that of the opening verse-paragraph of the poem, where the Genius of Britain

Bids steel-clad Valour chace that dove-like Bride,
Enfeebling Mercy, from his awful side;
. . . .
Then, in her place, bids Vengeance mount the car,
And glut with gore th'insatiate Dogs of War!—

Imperial honor as the philosophical mourner of the closing verse-paragraphs of the poem is more obviously reminiscent of the notions of humanity celebrated in the *Elegy on Captain Cook* than of this barbaric Genius.[35]

This transition from national vengeance to pensive imperial mourning might best be understood in the context of the account of herself and her poem that Seward gives in her prefatory address to Clinton: "With the zeal of a religious Enthusiast to his murdered Saint, the Author of this mournful Eulogium consecrates it to the memory of Major Andrè, who fell a Martyr in the

34. *Monody,* 21–22, 23, 8, 9, 21.

35. *Monody,* 27, 2. See William Collins, "Ode, to a Lady on the Death of Colonel Ross in the Action at Fontenoy" (1746), esp. ll. 19–24, in *The Works of William Collins,* ed. Richard Wendorf and Charles Ryskamp (Oxford: Clarendon Press, 1979); and William Shakespeare, *Cymbeline,* Act IV, sc. ii.

Cause of his King and his Country, with the firm intrepidity of a Roman, and the amiable resignation of a Christian Hero." The address insists on the notion of André's history as a religious narrative, a tale of resigned martyrdom that provokes an enthusiasm that is most obviously reminiscent, in the context of the poem, of Gothic chivalry. But André is also credited here with the "firm intrepidity of a Roman," with the character portrayed by William Alexander and other theorists of the Scottish Enlightenment as obviously incompatible with sentimental humanity and indulgence in feminine softness. In the *Monody,* André is shown as a figure of Roman virtue and unsoftened masculinity in his death, in his rejection of the luxurious attractions of London, and in his approximation, as the victim of parental oppression, to the Americans who are initially perceived to fight for patriotic and Roman ideals of liberty. In representing the death of André and the apparently simultaneous corruption of the American ideal of freedom by French slavery the *Monody* implicitly presents itself as a "mournful Eulogium" to the death of liberty, the death of the ideals most cherished by liberal Whigs.

Recent historical debate between, for example, John Sainsbury, Linda Colley, and Kathleen Wilson has tended to focus on the response to the American war of metropolitan radicalism, on one hand, and pro-government loyalism on the other.[36] The polite and provincial liberal whiggery of Seward's *Monody* was a long way, both discursively and geographically, from the radical utopianism of city whigs like Catharine Macaulay in the 1770s and 1780s, or from the radical reformist tradition which flourished in the Corresponding Societies of the 1790s, and to which Sainsbury and Wilson allude. Her *Monody* offers, I have suggested, a lament for the passing of the values of liberal whiggery, which marks the replacement of the ideal of liberty with a sentimental notion of humanity. It signals a patriotism identified with notions of loss and bereavement, and best expressed in elegiac consolation: "that beautiful bud of British poetry, which . . . expanded in tears." Indirectly, perhaps, it has something in common with the universalism Colley represents as the recourse of radical patriotism in the 1780s, and with the "activist model of political subjectivity" which, in Wilson's account, radical patriots derived from the American example, and used to justify the right of private individuals to scrutinize and if necessary intervene in the conduct of public affairs.[37] But that model of activism is appropriate

36. John Sainsbury, "Afterword," in *Disaffected Patriots: London Supporters of Revolutionary America 1769–1782* (Kingston, Ontario: McGill-Queen's University Press, 1987), 163–65; Kathleen Wilson, *The Sense of the People: Politics, Culture and Imperialism in England, 1715–1785* (Cambridge: Cambridge University Press, 1998), chapter 5; Colley, "Radical Patriotism."

37. Wilson, *Sense,* 278.

more directly to Barbauld's pamphlets of the 1790s, which I discussed in chapter 9. The *Monody* is more obviously about forging a delicate relation between personal grief and a national identity which mourns for what Britain has lost, for lost ideals of political liberty and perhaps for diminishing imperial power. By 1783, Ian Christie has argued, "Britain was generally regarded as finished, reduced to the rank of a second- or third-class power by the loss of her American empire."[38] Seward's elegy anticipates mourning for that loss in identifying imperial honor not with conquest or the ideal manliness of the struggle for liberty, but with sentimental humanity, with those more feminized qualities that her *Elegy on Captain Cook* had shown as the key to the extension and maintenance of empire in other parts of the globe.

Those themes were taken up by Helen Maria Williams in her *Ode on the Peace,* first published in 1783, and included in a slightly revised form in her *Poems* of 1786. Williams, like Seward, emphasizes that the domestic affections are the primary victims of the war, which is personified as indiscriminately wreaking violence on family life in both Britain and America. War elicits "Orphan's cries," "parental sighs," and "The wild impassion'd tear of fond Connubial Love." These forms of grief find a focus in the image of "hapless ANDRÈ's tomb," and a voice in Seward's monody. Williams writes:

> While SEWARD sweeps her plaintive strings,
> While pensive round his sable shrine
> A radiant zone she graceful flings,
> Where full emblaz'd his virtues shine,
> The mournful Loves that tremble nigh
> Shall catch her warm melodious sigh,
> And drink the precious thrilling drops that flow
> From Pity's hov'ring soul, that pants dissolv'd in woe.

Seward's poetry both speaks for the grief of less articulate "mournful Loves," and makes available to them the consolations of the pity her *Monody* excites; and Williams's lines suggest that Seward's readers find libidinized pleasures in the sense of their own pathos, their own capacity to feel the pains and pleasures of sensibility. Williams goes on to discuss the case of Charles Asgill, which, like the plight of André, provided an opportunity to discuss the war in terms of familial feeling rather than imperial politics. The *Ode* asserts that it is because the British nation is capable of participating in the grief of individuals, and the pleasure of Seward's poetry, that peace finally comes about: "The private pang

38. Ian Christie, *Wars and Revolutions: Britain, 1760–1815* (Cambridge: Harvard University Press, 1982), 193.

shall ALBION trembling share, / And breathe with fervid zeal, a warm accepted prayer." Peace is the reward of "a warm accepted prayer," of a national sensibility that shares in private grief. In Seward's elegiac poetry the "distracted mourner" intervenes between the silent maternal grief of Britannia and an imagined body of national sympathy to articulate a feeling that is apparently confident of public audibility, confident it speaks for the nation and its imperial honor, just because it is private, sentimental, and impassioned.[39]

39. Williams, *An Ode on the Peace* (London: Cadell, 1783), 5, 7, 9. On Asgill, see Sarah Knott, "A Cultural History of Sensibility in the Era of the American Revolution," chapter 5 (unpublished Ph.D. dissertation, Oxford University, 1999). Clarke, *Tour,* quoted in Lucas, *A Swan,* 80.

PART FOUR

Politics, Sensibility, Domesticity, 1790–1810

11

The Dream of a Common Language: The Strictures on Femininity of Hannah More and Mary Wollstonecraft

I

In part 3 I discussed the feminization of patriotism in the 1770s and 1780s, and considered the implications of that for the way Catharine Macaulay, Anna Laetitia Barbauld, and Anna Seward were perceived, or represented themselves. Each of these women is associated with whiggish politics, but their positions within that broad spectrum of political opinions are diverse, which may help to explain some of the differences between the ways they write or are written about. My next two chapters focus on Mary Wollstonecraft: in this chapter paired with Hannah More, and in the next with Mary Hays. Wollstonecraft's political opinions are of course closest to those of Macaulay, among the three women I have discussed, and certainly Wollstonecraft's severity toward the figure of the middle-class feminine consumer in her *Vindication* of 1792 owes much to the antifeminine cast of Macaulay's classical republican discourse. But the turn to sensibility which I discuss in chapter 12, and which I tie specifically to the political climate of 1796, has strong connections to my discussion of the importance of sensibility in the work of Anna Seward, where, similarly, the language of sensibility reconciles a patriotic and whiggish discourse on liberty and independence with the defeat of those ideals.

An earlier version of this chapter appeared as "The Dream of a Common Language: Hannah More and Mary Wollstonecraft" in *Textual Practice* 9, no. 2 (1995): 303–23, published by Taylor and Francis, Ltd. (P.O. Box 25, Abingdon, Oxfordshire, OX14 3UE).

I do not, however, want to overstate the degree of continuity between these final chapters and the earlier parts of this book. While I do in these final three chapters return to the various themes I have discussed earlier, the arguments of chapters 11 and 12, on the 1790s, are predominantly structured around discussions of implications of the discourse on the division of labor for representations of femininity. Much has been written, in the past few decades, about the place of Wollstonecraft's work in relation to the oppositional politics of the 1790s, and I have not attempted to offer an overview of those critical debates, or indeed to address them directly. Mary Lyndon Shanley writes:

> Given her understanding of the psychological, cultural, and legal reach of patriarchy, it is neither surprising that Wollstonecraft suggested that women needed political representation, nor that she did not give it more than the passing mention she did in *A Vindication of the Rights of Woman.* The workings of patriarchy infused everything from the legal rules governing marital property to the dynamics of sexual attraction.[1]

Shanley suggests that the account of femininity presented in Wollstonecraft's *Vindication* of 1792 reveals the pervasive "reach of patriarchy," and the fundamental importance of gender difference, in structuring the political and personal discourses of the 1790s. I have chosen in these two chapters to focus in particular on the implications of the discourse on the division of labor for languages of femininity in the 1790s because, as part 3 of this book has indicated, those become increasingly important in articulating the relation between gender difference and the public/private divide in the late century.

II

"Have you read that wonderful book, The Rights of Woman," wrote Anna Seward to Mr. Whalley, on February 26, 1792. "It has, by turns, pleased and displeased, startled and half-convinced me that its author is oftener right than wrong."[2] Seward's enthusiasm for Wollstonecraft's work, and sympathy for the trials of her life, seems to have endured despite her passionate antagonism to political radicalism in England in the 1790s. By August 1792, she writes, with what is clearly a deeply felt sense of personal as well as political alarm, of "Paine's pernicious and impossible system of equal rights, [which] is calculated to captivate and dazzle the vulgar; to make them spurn the restraints of legis-

1. Shanley, in *Women Writers and the Early Modern British Political Tradition,* ed. Hilda L. Smith (Cambridge: Cambridge University Press, 1998), 164.

2. *The Letters of Anna Seward: Written between the years 1784 and 1807,* 6 vols., ed. A. Constable (Edinburgh: Ramsay, 1811), 3.117.

lation, and to spread anarchy, murder, and ruin over the earth."[3] But neither Wollstonecraft's use of the discourse of natural rights, nor the scandal of her personal career, seem to have dismayed her. In 1798 she reports that Wollstonecraft's "death shocked and concerned me,"[4] and, in a letter to Humphry Repton, she writes in praise of Godwin's *Memoirs:* "Bearing strong marks of impartial authority as to the character, sentiments, conduct, and destiny of a very extraordinary woman, they appear to be highly valuable. Since, on balancing her virtues and errors, the former greatly preponderate, it is no disgrace to any man to have united his destiny with hers."[5] Seward found in Wollstonecraft's work and life principles she could continue to admire even though she recognized the sympathy between Wollstonecraft's political opinions and the radicalism she hated and feared.

Seward suggests in discussing the *Vindication* of 1792 that "though the ideas of absolute equality in the sexes are carried too far, and though they certainly militate against St Paul's maxims concerning that important compact, yet they do expose a train of mischievous mistakes in the education of females."[6] Seward links her admiration for Wollstonecraft as an educational theorist with her feeling for her as a woman victimized by what she described as her "basely betrayed attachment to that villain Imlay," rather than with arguments for rights to sexual and political equality.[7] I do not want to suggest that it was commonplace for women who rejected Wollstonecraft's political views to see her theories on the education of women as a distinct body of beliefs, uncolored by her radicalism, and capable of being uncoupled from the claim to sexual equality. Writing in July 1792, Sarah Trimmer, for example, remembered the second *Vindication* exclusively as a claim for "a further degree of liberty or consequence for women" within marriage—a claim which, she felt, threatened her own "happiness in having a husband to assist me in forming a proper judgement, and in taking upon him the chief labour of providing for a family." Trimmer regretted that Wollstonecraft had not employed her "extraordinary abilities . . . to more advantage to society."[8] In August of the same year, Horace Walpole wrote congratulating Hannah More on not having read the *Vindication.* Apparently confident of More's agreement, he observes that "I

3. Ibid., 3.160, to Lady Gresley, 29 August 1792.
4. Ibid., 5.47, to Mrs Jackson of Turville-Court, 13 February 1798.
5. Ibid., 5.73, 13 April 1798.
6. Ibid., 3.117, to Mr Whalley, 26 February 1792.
7. Ibid., 5.74, to Humphry Repton, 13 April 1798.
8. *Some Account of the Life and Writings of Mrs Trimmer, with original letters, and meditations and prayers, selected from her journal. In two volumes,* 2d ed. (London: R. & R. Gilbert, 1816), 2.60–61, to Mrs M., 12 July 1792.

would not look at it, though assured it contains neither metaphysics nor politics; but as she entered the lists on the latter, and borrowed her title from the demon [Paine]'s book, which aimed at spreading the *wrongs* of men, she is excommunicated from the pale of my library."[9] More herself claimed to find the notion of the rights of woman both absurd and a regrettable staining of "domestic manners . . . with the prevailing hue of public principles."[10] Whether or not they had actually read the second *Vindication,* these writers clearly perceived it in the context of a polemical genre associated primarily with the discourse of rights—they perceived it as a political text.

For a surprising range of readers, however, the educational theories of Wollstonecraft's work did represent a common currency apparently uninflected by political differences. These readers seem to identify substantial parts of the text, at least, with a subgenre of educational conduct books and satires on social morality which they do not perceive to be appropriate to the articulation of political views. They see gender, perhaps, as a category of concern that cuts across political differences. Mary Berry, the society hostess and correspondent of Walpole and More, acknowledges this possibility most directly. She writes, in a letter of 1799:

> I have been able . . . to go entirely through Hannah More, and Mrs Woolstonecroft [*sic*] immediately after her. It is amazing, or rather it is not amazing, but impossible, they should do otherwise than agree on all the great points of female education. H. More will, I dare say, be very angry when she hears this, though I would lay wager that she never read the book.[11]

In Hannah More's *Strictures on the Modern System of Female Education* (1799) and Wollstonecraft's *Vindication of the Rights of Woman* of 1792, Mary Berry detects an agreement on "all the great points of female education" that would

9. *The Letters of Horace Walpole, Earl of Orford,* 9 vols., ed. Peter Cunningham (London: Bohn, 1861), 9.385, 21 August 1792. Walpole's remark about the absence of politics in the text implies the absence of direct or explicit comment on the political events of the day. In the preceding paragraph of the letter he describes "the second massacre of Paris" in some detail, and suggests that these events have confirmed his "abhorrence of politics" (384).

10. *Strictures on the modern system of female education. With a view of the principles and conduct prevalent among women of rank and fortune* (1799), in *The Works of Hannah More, in Eight Volumes: including several pieces never before published* (London: Cadell, 1801), 7.172–73. This work is hereafter cited by volume and page number in the text.

11. *Extracts of the Journals and Correspondence of Miss Berry, from the year 1783 to 1852,* 3 vols., ed. Lady Theresa Lewis (London: Longmans, 1865), 2.91–92, to Mrs Cholmeley, 2 April 1799. On perceptions of Wollstonecraft as an educational theorist see Regina M. Janes, "On the Reception of Mary Wollstonecraft's *A Vindication of the Rights of Woman,*" *Journal of the History of Ideas* 39 (1978): 293–302; and Virginia Sapiro, *A Vindication of Political Virtue: The Political Theory of Mary Wollstonecraft* (Chicago: University of Chicago Press, 1992), 28.

be amazing if it were not inevitable. Her observation may point to that aspect of the *Vindication* that seemed to Anna Seward to remove the text from political controversy, and to make it praiseworthy despite its arguments for sexual equality.

In a footnote to *The Unsex'd Females,* Polwhele wrote that "Miss Hannah More may justly be esteemed, as a character, in all points, diametrically opposite to Miss Wollstonecraft."[12] The polarization of the public and private characters of the two women is evident in the texts they produced, but nevertheless what is common to them is the language, the discourse in which they characterize the corruptions of femininity. Their texts propose, on the whole, different remedies for that corruption, and identify its causes in markedly divergent terms. But the figure of the corrupt woman presented or produced in these texts seems indistinguishable, and she is characterized in terms that can stand independent of what Walpole or Polwhele saw as the absolute moral and political opposition of their views. That figure is, of course, familiar to any student of eighteenth-century writing on women. But I want now to examine her familiar features again, and to consider how they may illuminate the politics of feminism in the 1790s.[13]

12. Richard Polwhele, *The Unsex'd Females: A Poem* (London: Cadell, 1798), 35 n.

13. The relation between More's *Strictures* and Wollstonecraft's second *Vindication* has been explored most fully by Mitzi Myers, in her important article, "Reform or Ruin: 'A Revolution in Female Manners,'" *Studies in Eighteenth-Century Culture* 11 (1982): 199–216. Myers argues that Wollstonecraft and More are united, despite or across their political differences, in "perceiving a society infected with fashionable corruption, [to which] both preach a militantly moral middle-class reform grounded in women's potentiality" (211). As will I hope become apparent, my chapter is concerned to unpack—to specify and complicate—what is involved in those rather generalized notions of fashionable corruption and middle-class morality. But I also question Myers's reading of the second *Vindication* as primarily concerned with reforming women's domestic role, as well as her assumption that middle-class and affluent women are, in some sense, really corrupted by fashionable amusements. My approach is much more extensively indebted to Cora Kaplan's reading of Wollstonecraft in her brilliant and influential essay, "Wild Nights: Pleasure/Sexuality/Feminism," in *Sea Changes: Essays on Culture and Feminism* (London: Verso, 1986). Kaplan's essay (first published in 1983) argues that Wollstonecraft's text is "interested in developing a class sexuality for a radical, reformed bourgeoisie" (35), through the reform of something resembling Myers's "fashionable corruption." Kaplan persuasively identifies the figure of the fashionable or middle-class woman in the text with the representation of feminine sexuality and pleasure, and argues that the second *Vindication* "expresses a violent antagonism to the sexual; it exaggerates the importance of the sensual in the everyday life of women, and betrays the most profound anxiety about the rupturing force of female sexuality" (41). I am concerned to explore some of the implications of that identification of female sexuality with the forms of desire attributed to middle-class women, which may be implicit in Kaplan's essay, and to some extent in polemical texts on women of the 1790s. My chapter attempts to build on Myers's account of the cultural and political significance of feminine morality in the 1790s, by taking up Kaplan's suggestion that "the negative construction of the sexual in the midst of a positive and progressive construction of the social and political" (36) should be questioned.

III

Both More and Wollstonecraft allude, early in their arguments, to Hamlet's speech to Ophelia—"You jig, you amble, and you lisp, and nickname God's creatures."[14] The allusion seems to trigger, in their very different polemical texts, strikingly similar rehearsals of an apparently misogynistic discourse. Wollstonecraft argues that women—and particularly middle-class women—are encouraged to acquire "a kind of sickly delicacy . . . a deluge of false sentiments and overstretched feelings, stifling the natural emotions of the heart" (10). More similarly believes that "unqualified sensibility" has been cultivated in affluent women, "till a false and excessive display of feeling became so predominant, as to bring into question the actual existence of . . . true tenderness" (7.79–80). It should be enough here to sketch only the outlines of the discursive construction of corrupt femininity that both texts then elaborate. In both, the feminine subject is represented as peculiarly the creature of her material circumstances, which absorb her perceptions and adapt or accommodate them to their own nature. More writes: "Women too little live or converse up to the standard of their understandings. . . . The mind, by always applying itself to objects below its level, contracts its dimensions, and shrinks itself to the size, and lowers itself to the level, of the object about which it is conversant" (8.57). As a result of their preoccupation with trivial and unconnected phenomena, women are unable to generalize their ideas, are peculiarly localized, and cannot maintain a coherent train of thought. They are enthralled by novels; fascinated by manners, superficial appearances, surface ornamentation; distracted by isolated incidents and random, occasional events. These habits of mind produce a debilitating absorption in the sensible body, in the addictive pleasures of luxury, the lowest forms of taste. Women are slaves to the demands of the fashionable body for adornment, for epicurean and sexual sensation, for an endless diet of ever novel and artificial stimuli. More writes: "To attract admiration, is the great principle sedulously inculcated into [a woman's] young

14. See *Strictures,* 7.78–79; and Mary Wollstonecraft, *A Vindication of the Rights of Woman* (1792), ed. Carol H. Poston (New York: Norton, 1975), 10 (cited hereafter by page number in the text). The subtext here may be Burke's notorious use of Hamlet's speech. He writes that in "sensible objects," "so far is perfection . . . from being the cause of beauty; that this quality, where it is highest in the female sex, almost always carries with it an idea of weakness and imperfection. Women are very sensible of this; for which reason, they learn to lisp, to totter in their walk, to counterfeit weakness, and even sickness. In all this, they are guided by nature." *A Philosophical Enquiry into the Origin of our Ideas of the Sublime and Beautiful,* ed. J. T. Boulton (London: Routledge, 1958), 110. For a brilliant analysis of More's account of the woman reader, see Peter De Bolla, *The Discourse of the Sublime: Readings in History, Aesthetics and the Subject* (Oxford: Basil Blackwell, 1989), chapter 10.

heart; and is considered as the fundamental maxim; and, perhaps, if we were required to condense the reigning system of the brilliant education of a lady into an aphorism, it might be comprised in this short sentence, *To allure and to shine*" (7.98). Corrupted femininity is all surface, all display, lacking the detachment, the critical distance necessary to the production of a continuous consciousness or integrity of identity capable of deferring its gratifications.

In Wollstonecraft's *Vindication* the analogy of travel provides a revealing figure for the incoherence of feminine subjectivity. She argues that

> A man, when he undertakes a journey, has, in general, the end in view; a woman thinks more of the incidental occurrences, the strange things that may possibly happen along the road; the impression that she may make on her fellow-travellers; and, above all, she is anxiously intent on the care of the finery that she carries with her, which is more than ever a part of herself, when going to figure on a new scene; when, to use an apt French turn of expression, she is going to produce a sensation.—Can dignity of mind exist with such trivial cares? (60)

Wollstonecraft's writing seems, in this passage, almost to yield to the pleasures of the narrative afforded by the feminine attraction to incidental events and details, and almost to acknowledge that the woman does have an "end in view" in her desire to produce a sensation, though it is an end that could only be appropriate to genres more amenable to sentiment, such as those to which Wollstonecraft turned later in the decade. But the point is that feminine lack of purpose is represented here as producing a kind of dissipation of subjectivity into a succession of accidents, so that feminine identity becomes indistinguishable from the finery, the things which "are more than ever a part" of what it is that constitutes its tenuous and apparent continuity. More argues, in an intriguingly similar image, that

> The female . . . wanting steadiness in her intellectual pursuits, is perpetually turned aside by her characteristic tastes and feelings. Woman in the career of genius, is the Atalanta, who will risk losing the race by running out of her road to pick up the golden apple; while her male competitor, without, perhaps, possessing greater natural strength or swiftness, will more certainly attain his object, by direct pursuit, by being less exposed to the seductions of extraneous beauty, and will win the race, not by excelling in speed, but by despising the bait. (8.31–32)

In the *Strictures,* the analogy of masculine direction and feminine aimlessness provides a much more explicit image of the feminine incapacity to regulate desire for tangible and immediate gratifications. But for both Wollstonecraft and More, corrupt femininity is characterized by its attachment to what is incidental or extraneous, and by the absence of the sense of purpose and direction that seems to them necessary to self-possession and moral control.

The image of corrupt femininity, abandoned beyond all coherence or control, is familiar enough. In her *Appeal to the Men of Great Britain in Behalf of Women,* for example, Mary Hays implies that it is unnecessary to detail the character of immoral femininity again. It seems enough, on the whole, merely to allude to women's "state of PERPETUAL BABYISM," and occasionally to flesh out the fascination with dress, the slavery to fashion, the addiction to what she calls "the idle vagaries of the present moment," that characterize the feminine role in commercial culture.[15] Wollstonecraft writes:

> The conversation of French women . . . is frequently superficial; but, I contend, that it is not half so insipid as that of those English women whose time is spent in making caps, bonnets, and the whole mischief of trimmings, not to mention shopping, bargain-hunting, &c. &c.: and it is the decent, prudent women, who are most degraded by these practices; for their motive is simply vanity. The wanton who exercises her taste to render her passion alluring, has something more in view. (75–76)

The general characteristics here echo those of representations of corrupt femininity from earlier in the century. Wollstonecraft is careful to emphasize, for example, that attention to "the frippery of dress" weakens the mind, and distracts it from social duty. Middle-class women are here condemned for making their own clothes because this is a failure to consume and participate in affective exchange, as it had been at mid-century. But here, more specifically, these women show lack of feeling because they deprive the poor of employment, and themselves of the leisure necessary to self-improvement, for they "work only to dress better than they could otherwise afford" (75). The most remarkable feature of this characterization is the suggestion that absorption in self-adornment, in the almost unmentionable folly of shopping and bargain-hunting, is more contemptible and degrading than the behavior of the sexually voracious woman, who at least has "something more in view."

Wollstonecraft's comments confirm that by the 1790s economic considerations have taken priority in the characterization of corrupted femininity. The problem is not that absorption in self-adornment may encourage an insatiable

15. *Appeal to the Men of Great Britain in Behalf of Women* (London: J. Johnson, 1798), 97, 82. William Thompson attributed the *Appeal* to Mary Hays in the Introductory Letter to Mrs Wheeler, in their *Appeal of one-half of the human race, Women, against the pretensions of the other half, Men* (1825). The attribution may also be indirectly supported by the apology for writing in the first person that is appended to the *Appeal*—see *Appeal,* 295–300. Wollstonecraft wrote to Mary Hays on 12 November 1792, commenting on a draft of her *Letters and Essays, Moral and Miscellaneous,* which was to be published in 1793. She argued that the text was "too full of yourself. . . . [T]rue modesty should keep the author in the back ground." In *Collected Letters of Mary Wollstonecraft,* ed. Ralph M. Wardle (Ithaca, N.Y.: Cornell University Press, 1979), 220.

sexual rapacity disturbing to the social confidence placed in the system of propertied inheritance, though that remains an important ingredient of the discursive construction at issue. In these years, when fortunes may be more likely to be acquired through commercial speculation than through inheritance of landed estates, the dangers of social disruption that cluster and find focus in the familiar figure of feminine excess, at least in the context of the polemical genre of vindications, appeals, and strictures, result from the vices of consumerism, rather than the more colorful sins of bad sexuality. The figure of corrupted femininity, I suggest, needs to be understood primarily as a set of gendered characteristics appropriated to the requirements of the discourse of commerce and its feared inverse, the anticommercial horrors of profiteering, greed, and consumerism run riot. In the later eighteenth century, the discourse of commerce projects out of itself the image of its own amoralism, producing the figure of insatiable feminine desire that shadows the morality of middle-class men and women, and that, in its confirmed and acknowledged immorality, works to consolidate the shaky moral values of commerce itself. The vices of commerce are embodied in the figure of immorally desirous femininity, which serves, as it were, to draw that poison off from the system of commerce itself. But in this context, of course, the poison is also the antidote—commerce needs the image of corrupt femininity to account for the consumption of its commodities, to represent the ceaseless stimulations to desire in the marketplace, and to figure, in its own shining form, the radiance of the commodity. It needs corrupt femininity to moralize and masculinize its own self-image.

Wollstonecraft's shoppers are caught up and implicated in the changing nature of the retail trade—they hunt for bargains in violation of the code of trust that was believed to have existed between tradesmen and their customers. They are implicitly promiscuous in awarding the favors of their custom, responding to the seduction of window displays and cut-price offers, undercutting traditional channels of supply with the industry of their busy fingers, rather than participating in those steady and trusting relationships of reciprocal recognition between consumer and supplier that are imagined to have characterized the more paternalist society of the past.[16] In Hays's *Appeal,* in particular, these shoppers and stitchers are reprimanded for their failure to fulfill the

16. On the changing nature of consumption see Neil McKendrick, "Introduction. The Birth of a Consumer Society: The Commercialization of Eighteenth-Century England," and chapter 1, "The Consumer Revolution in Eighteenth-Century England," in Neil McKendrick, John Brewer, and J. H. Plumb, *The Birth of a Consumer Society: The Commercialization of Eighteenth-Century England* (London: Europa, 1982); and E. P. Thompson's essay of 1971, "The Moral Economy of the English Crowd in the Eighteenth Century," reprinted in his *Customs in Common* (London: Merlin, 1991).

obligations of their class and gender, their failure to provide poor women with steady employment.[17] They are the counterpart of those men Wollstonecraft describes to Imlay in her *Letters written during a short residence in Sweden, Norway and Denmark* (1796). She writes:

> men entirely devoted to commerce never acquire, or [they] lose, all taste and greatness of mind. An ostentatious display of wealth without elegance, and a greedy enjoyment of pleasure without sentiment, embrutes them till they term all virtue, of an heroic cast, romantic attempts at something above our nature; and anxiety about the welfare of others, a search after misery, in which we have no concern. But you will say that I am growing bitter, perhaps, personal. Ah! shall I whisper to you—that you—yourself, are strangely altered, since you have entered deeply into commerce . . . never allowing yourself to reflect, and keeping your mind, or rather passions, in a continual state of agitation.[18]

Imlay here is represented as partaking in those feminized qualities that the second *Vindication* attributes to corrupted femininity. What is personal, what strikes home to his self-image, she suggests, is the moralized and gendered discourse of anticommerce, rather than the reflections produced by the discourses of sentiment on the one hand, or civic humanism on the other. Wollstonecraft's letter implies that Imlay the dealer in alum and soap will recognize and wish to reject the gendered and impassioned image of its own amoralism that commerce has produced.

Hannah More is prepared to locate value and virtue in the feminine image of the good consumer much more straightforwardly and explicitly than are Wollstonecraft and Hays—both of whom might be seen as more concerned to define middle-class women as something other than consumers. More's prose seems to register no flicker of doubt, none of the hesitancy that might point to a sense of incongruity, as she invests the figure of the good housewife with many of the virtues necessary to public spirit. She writes that

> ladies whose natural vanity has been aggravated by a false education, may look down on *oeconomy* as a vulgar attainment, unworthy of the attention of a highly cultivated intellect; but this is the false estimate of a shallow mind. Oeconomy . . . is not merely . . . the shabby curtailments and stinted parsimony of a little mind, operating on little concerns; but it is the exercise of a sound judgement exerted in the comprehensive outline of order, of arrangement, of distribution; of regulations by which alone well-governed societies, great and small, subsist. . . . A sound oeconomy is a sound understanding brought into action; it is calculation

17. See, for example, *Appeal,* 242–43.

18. *Letters written during a short residence in Sweden, Norway and Denmark,* facsimile of first ed. of 1796, with an introduction by Sylva Norman (Fontwell: Centaur Press, 1970), 251–52.

> realized; it is the doctrine of proportion reduced to practice; it is foreseeing consequences, and guarding against them; it is expecting contingencies, and being prepared for them. The difference is, that to a narrow-minded vulgar oeconomist, the details are continually present. . . . Little events and trivial operations engross her whole soul. . . . (8.5–7)

The argument that the practice of the good consumer indicates what More identifies as "real genius and extensive knowledge" (8.8) can clearly only be supported in juxtaposition to the representation of the "vulgar oeconomist," endowed with the narrow-minded absorption and capacity for engrossment in the physical that characterize corrupted femininity.

More writes of properly domesticated women:

> Both in composition and action they excel in details; but they do not so much generalize their ideas as men, nor do their minds seize a great subject with so large a grasp. They are acute observers, and accurate judges of life and manners, as far as their own sphere of observation extends; but they describe a smaller circle. A woman sees the world, as it were, from a little elevation in her own garden, whence she makes an exact survey of home scenes, but takes not in that wider range of distant prospects which he who stands on a loftier eminence commands. (8.29–30)

The good domestic economist seems, on the one hand, to perceive with the kind of commanding and comprehensive grasp that distinguishes the vision of public men, from their loftier eminences. But on the other hand, within her "smaller circle," she excels in her attention to detail. Her "survey of home scenes," in other words, seems ambiguously "exact"—it seems to be true and right, in the sense that the perceptions of great men are imagined to be true, disinterested, and unbiased, and it seems to be exact in the sense that it is precise, and preoccupied with detail. Those qualities, I think, can only be represented as though they were compatible, and the notion that women do not generalize their ideas "so much" as men can only be represented as though it made sense, as a result of the introduction of the contrasting figure of the vulgar economist, who neutralizes the problem by absorbing into herself what are seen as the more degrading implications of engrossment in the physical detail and menial drudgery of housekeeping.

IV

The appropriation of the image of corrupted femininity to an anticommercial discourse is thoroughly problematic, as both More's *Strictures* and Wollstonecraft's *Vindication* demonstrate. The very currency, the power and resonance of the image in so many eighteenth-century texts serves to indicate the extent to which it has hoovered up the available languages of desire. It acts as a magnet for gendered characteristics in excess of those necessary to its function as a guarantee of the moral discourses from which it is projected and excluded, and assumes the power to characterize not only what is excessive, corrupted, and feminized, but those qualities that are necessary to the distinction of gender in the discourses of the period. In the particular, anticommercial form which I have suggested is specific to the 1790s, the image of corrupted femininity can seem to embrace and to represent all femininity, and thus to identify anticommercial discourse as misogynistic. This can be seen in many of the polemical texts of the period, but is perhaps most unmistakably marked in More's *Strictures.* Writing of women's fashionable publicity, she argues:

> If, indeed, women were mere outside, form and face only . . . it would follow that a ball-room was quite as appropriate place for choosing a wife, as an exhibition room for choosing a picture. But, inasmuch as women are not mere portraits, their value not being determinable by a glance of the eye, it follows that a different mode of appreciating their value, and a different place for viewing them antecedent to their being individually selected, is desirable. The two cases differ also in this, that if a man select a picture for himself from among all its exhibited competitors, and bring it to his own house, the picture being passive, he is able to fix it there: while the wife, picked up at a public place, and accustomed to incessant display, will not, it is probable, when brought home, stick so quietly to the spot where he fixes her; but will escape to the exhibition-room again, and continue to be displayed at every subsequent exhibition, just as if she were not become private property, and had never been definitively disposed of. (8.178–79)

More's argument is remarkable because of the twist, the change of direction that registers the problematic instability of discourses of gender. In the first place it seems that women are more valuable than portraits because they are more enigmatic, because they conceal hidden depths that cannot be known at a glance. The association of corrupt femininity with surface display is established by portraiture, which can only paint the superficial appearance suitable for the exhibition room. But as More develops the image, that very addiction to surface, that sense in which femininity is fully manifested in its exhibitable and commodified form, becomes the valued and apparently uncorrupted site. Women who fail to recognize that they have become private property, which has been definitively disposed of, women who continue to desire to be seen, but unlike commodities do not apparently desire to be possessed, become identified as corrupt. They seem corrupt, shop-soiled, because of their suspect motivation and mobility—because, unlike portraits, they are not all surface.

The analogy between women and their portraits, in More's argument, makes it clear that the identification of femininity with surface and display which is central to the discourse on feminized corruption has become ambiguous. The stable but superficial image which respects its status as private property is here a marker of relative purity and value.

Mary Hays's argument, in her *Appeal,* runs into similar difficulties in employing the analogy between women and works of art. She writes of corrupt women as "mere automatans" [*sic*], who "put on the semblance of every virtue," and may appear "as captivating—perhaps even more so, than women of real sensibility." She contrasts their "varnish of surface" with "real, unaffected, unassuming goodness," which is analogous to "marble of the most exquisite quality,—which, without flaw or blemish, admits of an equal polish through all its parts as on its surface; and on which the sculptor may lastingly impress the sublimest efforts of his art" (*Appeal,* 255–56). What is curious about this contrast between automata and sculpture, what seems excessive to the familiar language of surface and depth, is the emphasis on the sculpted image of virtuous femininity as a production, lastingly impressed by the hand of its maker. Both the automaton and the sculpture, that emphasis on production serves to point up, afford pleasure to the spectator because of their visible surfaces and polished finish. The fact that marble statuary has a more enduring polish does not call into question the characterization of both corrupt and virtuous femininity in the desire to excite desire, in qualities common to commodities. What seem to distinguish corrupt from virtuous femininity are the aesthetic criteria which articulate discrimination between different kinds of art, between the value of different kinds of private property. The analogy between women and painting or sculpture makes explicit the commodification of femininity, while veiling that commercial form in the decent and acceptable drapery of aesthetic value; but the analogy also elides the distinction between virtue and corruption that it is apparently called upon to support. In this context, all femininity is identified as spectacle, and caught up in those transactions of desire that characterize both consumers and commodities.

The perceived erosion of what was imagined to have been the clear distinction between virtuous and corrupt femininity is a matter of explicit concern and alarm for conservative writers of the later eighteenth century. John Bowles, for example, in his *Remarks on Modern Female Manners* (1802), laments that women of unblemished character "no longer . . . pride themselves . . . on the distinction which separates them from the abandoned part of their sex." He argues that virtuous women should not tolerate the society of known adulteresses—a point of etiquette that Hannah More also stressed in her *Strictures* of

1799, although in her *Essays for Young Ladies* of 1777 she had argued for the exercise of Christian forgiveness and tolerance. Bowles advances his case with an excessive strength of feeling that borders on panic. He writes: "Honour, especially in women, can admit of no compromise with dishonour; no approaches from one towards the other must be suffered; the boundary between them must be considered as impassable; the line by which they are divided is the RUBICON of female virtue."[19] His insistence can be taken as an indication of the frailty of definition, the discursive instability, of the categories of feminine virtue and corruption—categories which cannot be kept distinct by the mere device of social maneuvering that he advocates. The blurring of these categories, he argues, represents "a much more formidable enemy that Buonaparte himself, with all his power, perfidy, and malice." It indicates a social change which, he writes, "would be more tremendous than even the suspension of those wonderful powers of nature, which confine the planets to their respective orbs, and maintain, from age to age, the harmony of the universe." Bowles believes that apocalyptic chaos will result from virtuous women adopting immodest fashions of dress. Confronting the discursive confusion this represents, he exclaims that "compared with such a woman, the bold and abandoned profligate, who with dauntless effrontery, appears publicly in her true character, is less disgraceful to her sex, and less injurious to society."[20] Like Wollstonecraft contemplating the horrors of shopping, he finds himself welcoming the unambiguously scandalous woman as a more socially acceptable and useful figure than the fashionable woman of indeterminate morality. For, as I suggested earlier, it is the feminine image of corrupt desire, of bad sexuality, that is necessary to inoculate the morality of commercial culture. The danger represented by the confusion of the signs of vice and virtue, or by the possibility that anticommerce might be recognized as a feature of commerce itself, is greater than the danger represented by the bold and abandoned face of bad sexuality or Napoleonic perfidy.

19. *Remarks on Modern Female Manners, as distinguished by indifference to character, and indecency of dress; extracted chiefly from "Reflections political and moral at the conclusion of the war. By John Bowles, Esq."* (London: Woodfall, 1802), 4, 6.

20. Ibid., 16, 20, 15. Bowles's discussion may echo Hannah More's argument that as a result of excessive cultivation the arts have become "agents of voluptuousness" (*Works,* 7.91). She writes: "May we not rank among the present corrupt consequences of this unbounded cultivation, the unchaste costume, the impure style of dress, and that indelicate statue-like exhibition of the female figure, which, by its artfully disposed folds, its seemingly wet and adhesive drapery, so defines the form as to prevent covering itself from becoming a veil? This licentious mode, as the acute Montesquieu observed on the dances of the Spartan virgins, has taught us 'to strip chastity itself of modesty'" (*Works,* 7.92).

V

The problem that I believe these texts of the late century respond to and articulate in their shared and apparently misogynistic discourse is clearly set out in Barbauld's essay of 1773, "Against Inconsistency in our Expectations." She explains that

> We should consider this world as a great mart of commerce, where fortune exposes to our view various commodities, riches, ease, tranquillity, fame, integrity, knowledge. Every thing is marked at a settled price. Our time, our labour, our ingenuity, is so much ready money which we are to lay out to the best advantage. Examine, compare, choose, reject; but stand to your own judgement; and do not, like children, when you have purchased one thing, repine that you do not possess another which you did not purchase.[21]

It is apparent from this initial image of society that Barbauld's essay attempts to wed a moral discourse on the use of talents, on those differences of character that may result in tranquility, fame, or integrity, to a discourse on the division of labor concerned to explain the diverse specializations of commercial society in a way that seems also to justify its inequalities. Barbauld concludes that

> There is a cast of manners peculiar and becoming to each age, sex, and profession. . . . Each is perfect in its kind. A woman as a woman: a tradesman as a tradesman. We are often hurt by the brutality and sluggish conceptions of the vulgar; not considering that some there must be to be hewers of wood and drawers of water, and that cultivated genius, or even any great refinement and delicacy in their moral feelings, would be a real misfortune to them.[22]

The inclusion of women here, as though gender were a category immediately comparable to occupation or class, is thoroughly problematic. What women in their capacity as The Sex bring to the great mart of commerce is, most obviously, their sexuality. They may figure in the great mart as consumers or commodities, but as I have tried to show, those roles are at least morally ambiguous.

What women are more commonly valued for by the late century, I have argued, is their exclusion from the marketplace—the marginal position from which, according to John Bowles,

21. In Lucy Aikin, ed., *The Works of Anna Laetitia Barbauld. With a memoir,* 2 vols. (London: Longman, 1825), 2.185.

22. Ibid., 2.194.

> they soften, they polish, the rougher sex, which, without their mild and genial influence, would never exhibit any thing better than a race of barbarians. . . . They constitute the very ties of those family connections, those domestic societies, which can alone foster in the human heart those tender sympathies, the social affections. . . . In short, they adorn, they harmonize the world.[23]

That image of women as social glue is common to many of the polemical texts of the 1790s, including Wollstonecraft's and More's. But in Barbauld's essay it is clear that even this vague notion of a social function for virtuous femininity is incompatible with the model of society that the division of labor articulates. Barbauld laments that in modern society "every one is expected to have such a tincture of general knowledge as is incompatible with going deep into any science; and such a conformity to fashionable manners as checks the free workings of the ruling passion, and gives an insipid sameness to the face of society, under the idea of polish and regularity."[24] The qualities that Barbauld here regrets, because they militate against specialization and against the division of labor on which the great mart of commerce is perceived to depend, are precisely those of polish and regularity which it is the business of women to instill. Barbauld acknowledges that the idea of society which it is the function of women to harmonize and polish is made redundant by the more powerful and persuasive model of the great mart described by political economy. In the context of that commercial model, there is no moral or professional language available to articulate feminine virtue. It has no place and no value. By the 1790s, I think, that perception has become inadmissible. The problem of feminine virtue, the problem of what women are wanted for, has become an issue capable of producing that anxiety about policing the division between good and bad women that John Bowles articulated—an anxiety that animates the spate of conservative and radical texts on the education of women in the 1790s. The most obvious function of women in the 1790s is to fuel the discourse of anticommerce—a discourse that I have suggested shows an alarming tendency to become fully misogynistic, and to become the only available, or at least the dominant, discourse on femininity.

I have argued that Barbauld herself responds to this erosion of the moral language of gender difference by turning to an inclusive notion of humanity, in her sermons of the 1790s. Barbauld emphasizes the citizenship, the civic rights, available to women and men when differences of race, class, and occupation

23. Bowles, *Remarks,* 18.
24. *Works of Barbauld,* 2.193–94.

are set aside. Wollstonecraft, Hays, and More, in contrast, respond to the impossible demands commercial culture makes on femininity by recourse to the language of professionalization, which they use to reclaim respectability for the notion of virtuous femininity. Hays and Wollstonecraft both argue strongly that the exclusion of women from the division of labor as anything but consumers means that the terms in which they can be represented are restricted almost completely to those of corrupt feminine desire made available by what I have called the discourse of anticommerce. Emphasizing the dominance of the model of society produced by political economy, Wollstonecraft writes:

> Taught from their infancy that beauty is woman's sceptre, the mind shapes itself to the body, and, roaming round its gilt cage, only seeks to adorn its prison. Men have various employments and pursuits which engage their attention, and give a character to the opening mind; but women, confined to one, and having their thoughts constantly directed to the most insignificant part of themselves, seldom extend their views beyond the triumph of the hour. (44)

What women are perceived to be for, the character of femininity, is for Wollstonecraft produced by their allocated place and employment within the division of labor, which dictates that they will consume goods for their personal adornment, goods which the middle-class woman finds become "more than ever a part of herself" (60), and constitute her social identity.[25] Hays's *Appeal* is more explicitly concerned than is the *Vindication* with the issues raised by differences of class. She argues that what she identifies as the "misemployed talents" that middle-class women expend on "ribbons, gauze, fringes, flounces and furbelows . . . might have placed thee on the woolsack, or have put a mitre on thy head, or a long robe on thy back, or a truncheon in thy hand" (*Appeal,* 79). The vanity of corrupt femininity is ambition misemployed, she claims. She argues strongly for the reappropriation to women of trades and professions that had become masculinized in the course of the eighteenth century. Hays emphasizes that the masculinization of women's work has left prostitution as the only available professional course open to poor women obliged to compete in the marketplace.

More, in contrast, employs the language of professionalization to characterize both corrupt and virtuous femininity. The life of fashionable women, she argues, "formerly, too much resembled the life of a confectioner," but "it now too much resembles that of an actress; the morning is all rehearsal, and the evening is all performance" (7.120–21). The passions women bring to

25. On Wollstonecraft's views on employment for women, see Sapiro, *Vindication,* 158–61.

their public performances resemble those that "might be supposed to stimulate professional candidates for fame and profit at public games and theatrical exhibitions" (7.123). More argues that

> Most men are commonly destined to some profession, and their minds are commonly turned each to its respective object. Would it not be strange if they were called out to exercise their profession, or to set up their trade, with only a little general knowledge of the trades and professions of all other men, and without any previous definite application to their own particular calling. The profession of ladies, to which the bent of their instruction should be turned, is that of daughters, wives, mothers, and mistresses of families. They should therefore be trained with a view to these several conditions, and be furnished with a stock of ideas, and principles, and qualifications, and habits, ready to be applied and appropriated, as occasion may demand, to each of these respective situations. (7.111–12)

More's suspicion of those who are equipped "with only a little general knowledge" echoes Barbauld's distrust of the "tincture of general knowledge" that is valued "under the idea of polish and regularity." It is a suspicion of what has come to seem an anachronistic lack of specialization, appropriate to an idea of society innocent of commercial progress. In More's *Strictures,* women can only become properly modern and professional by subjecting themselves to an extraordinary degree of restraint—by accepting the confinement of their different presence within the "smaller circle" of domesticity. More argues that fashionable men are peculiarly subject to the allure of the ambiguously public world of clubs, which "generate and cherish luxurious habits, from their perfect ease, undress, liberty, and inattention to the distinctions of rank" (8.184). Clubs, she argues, "promote . . . every temper and spirit which tends to undomesticate" (8.185). It is the duty of the wife to correct what More represents as the democratical spirit of club life by cultivating in her husband the "love of fireside enjoyments" (8.186). By confining her own circle of understanding and activity to the domestic, More suggests, the wife will be able to produce in herself and her husband the belief that "those attachments, which . . . are the cement which secure the union of the family as well as of the state" (8.187), are those which are nourished in the asocial world of the family, of domesticity. The kind of limited publicity and professionalism to which Wollstonecraft and Hays wish to secure women access is associated in More's argument with "inattention to the distinctions of rank," with the blurring of the boundaries of public and political space—boundaries which are for More secured by the polarization of family and state, and confirmed by the antagonism that she and John Bowles wish to see between virtuous and immoral women. For Wollstonecraft and Hays, however, women seem left with the possibility of entering more fully into the political and economic marketplace. As Wollstonecraft observes: "The world cannot be seen by an unmoved spectator, we must mix in the throng, and feel as men feel" (112).

What is problematic about that statement is of course its apparent denial of the value of gendered difference. And that problem, I hope to have shown, is produced by the specific historical moment in which the *Vindication* participates. The apparently misogynistic discourse that is common to Macaulay, Wollstonecraft, and More, and to a lesser extent to Hays, in their polemical texts if not in their writing in other genres, needs to be understood, I think, as peculiar to the late century. The general terms in which it characterizes corrupt femininity are, of course, common to writing about women throughout the eighteenth century. Mary Astell, for example, has some very similar things to say about fashionable women at the beginning of the century. But in Mary Astell's writing the image is not misogynistic, it is not a representation of all femininity. It is a set of terms appropriated, broadly speaking, to those women who are seen as surplus on the marriage market, marriageable women who may be made redundant by the newly emerging relationship between the city and the landed gentry. By the late century, however, the requirements of anti-commercial discourse appropriate the image of corrupt femininity, and extend it into the nightmare of a language that has the potential to represent all women, and all forms of feminine desire.

12

Modern Love: Feminism and Sensibility in 1796

I

Over the past decade or so, feminist studies of the Romantic period have returned repeatedly to the question of the relation between Wollstonecraft's hostility to the language of sensibility in her *Vindication* of 1792 and her adoption of that language in her later work. It is as though that transition were the touchstone which revealed the character of the critical analysis that contained it. I find it most fruitful to think about that transition in the context of the very different political situation Wollstonecraft's writing addressed by 1796. But in this chapter I also emphasize the continuity of concern with Wollstonecraft's earlier work—the continuing importance of the discourse on the division of labor as a major constituent of the way gender difference is represented and conceived in the late century. It is also, I suggest, important to recognize the extent to which Wollstonecraft's use of the language of sensibility in her later work builds on the way that language had been transformed by its uses in women's writing in the 1770s and 1780s. This is not simply a reappropriation of the language of Burke, but a signal that the language of sentiment and sensibility is bound up with a feminine patriotism based in loss.[1]

An earlier version of this chapter appeared in *New Formations* 28 (spring 1996). Reproduced with permission of Lawrence and Wishart, London.

1. I take issue here with Claudia Johnson's representation of Burke's use of the language of sentiment and sensibility as decisive. Johnson, "Introduction," in her *Equivocal Beings: Politics, Gender, and Sentimentality in the 1790s* (Chicago: University of Chicago Press, 1995).

This chapter is about two texts—Mary Hays's *Memoirs of Emma Courtney,* and Wollstonecraft's *Letters written during a short residence in Sweden, Norway and Denmark.* These texts invoke complex notions of sensibility in ways which are directly concerned with the difficulty of articulating radical political positions in 1796—the year in which both texts were first published—when in Britain the penalties for publishing political writings judged to be libels had been made suddenly much more severe by the Treasonable Practices Act of December 1795, and when the Terror in France had fueled conservative and counterrevolutionary arguments against everything that could be represented as part of a radical agenda. Both of these texts can be understood as engaged in constructing responses to those counterrevolutionary arguments as well as in attempting to salvage an ideal of republicanism that would not result in terror, and would not neglect or betray the interests of women. But they do so at least partly in a language not apparently political at all—a language of personal and commercial desire. I do not want to suggest their invocation of the language of sensibility can be seen directly as representative of its use in other texts by women. But indirectly, I think, these texts do indicate how the extraordinary volatility of notions of sensibility might make such language peculiarly amenable to the articulation of women's complex position in relation to the commercial and political cultures of the period.

The notion of sensibility in these texts can be understood in the context suggested by Habermas's *Structural Transformation of the Public Sphere.* Habermas writes:

> To the degree to which commodity exchange burst out of the confines of the household economy, the sphere of the conjugal family became differentiated from the sphere of social reproduction. The process of the polarization of state and society was repeated once more within society itself. The status of the private man combined the role of owner of commodities with that of head of the family, that of property owner with that of "human being" *per se.* The doubling of the private sphere on the higher plane of the intimate sphere furnished the foundation for an identification of those two roles under the common title of the "private"; ultimately, the political self-understanding of the bourgeois public originated there as well.[2]

The uneasy relation Habermas describes between affective and commercial relations is an effect of the "doubling of the private sphere," the complex of relations that tied "intimate relationships between human beings" to commodity exchange. Habermas's argument suggests that the production of a

2. Jürgen Habermas, *The Structural Transformation of the Public Sphere: An Inquiry into a Category of Bourgeois Society,* trans. Thomas Burger with Frederick Lawrence (London: Polity, 1989), 28–29.

bourgeois public sphere in eighteenth-century Britain required that that knot of relations be cut, or at least denied, so that "'purely human' relations" could transcend the demands of the marketplace, and create a conceptual space in which men could pursue "ideas of freedom, love, and cultivation of the person"—generate, in other words, an oppositional culture. This notion of an intellectual community of liberal and literate men is, of course, difficult, because it either ignores gender difference or excludes women, and because it ignores differences of material circumstance between men.[3] But the difficulty I want to focus on for the purposes of this chapter lies in the extent to which, in the texts I am concerned with, feminine sensibility is articulated as intertwined with or implicated in the division of labor and the business of commodity exchange. In Habermas's terms that might seem to indicate its conservatism, its failure to be engaged in the modern differentiation of the spheres of intimacy and of social reproduction. But it might also be thought of as involved in the articulation of a sense of self—an interiority—that is both feminine and modern[4] in the complexity and the difficulty of the relations it constructs between those "spheres."

II

In his *Memoirs* of Mary Wollstonecraft of 1798, William Godwin wrote of his enthusiastic reception of her *Letters written during a short residence,* explaining that "if ever there was a book calculated to make a man in love with its author, this appears to me to be the book." He locates the power of the book in the distinctive language of sentiment: it "irresistibly seizes on the heart" because "the occasional harshness and ruggedness of character, that diversify her *Vindication of the Rights of Woman,* here totally disappear. . . . Affliction had tempered her heart to a softness almost more than human; and the gentleness of her spirit seems precisely to accord with all the romance of unbounded attachment."[5] If Godwin found the sincerity of the book irresistible, this seems

3. Ibid., 48. For a fuller discussion of some of these problems see Rita Felski, *Beyond Feminist Aesthetics: Feminist Literature and Social Change* (London: Hutchinson, 1989), 164 ff.; and Nancy Fraser, "What's Critical about Critical Theory: The Case of Habermas and Gender," in *Feminist Interpretations and Political Theory,* ed. Mary Lyndon Shanley and Carole Pateman (Cambridge: Polity, 1991).

4. I borrow my terms here from Carolyn Steedman, "Introduction: Lost and Found," in *Strange Dislocations: Childhood and the Idea of Human Interiority 1780–1930* (London: Virago, 1995).

5. In Mary Wollstonecraft, *A Short Residence in Sweden, Norway and Denmark,* and William Godwin, *Memoirs of the Author of the Rights of Woman,* ed. Richard Holmes (Harmondsworth: Penguin, 1987), 249.

to have been because he perceived the sentimental reveries of the text as unmistakably gendered.[6] But perhaps there is a slight hesitation, a slight indication of what is problematic about this thorough feminization and eroticization of the text, in the suggestion that the seduction it effects is "calculated." The juxtaposition of calculation and love in this sentimental context hints at a hesitation about the character of ideal femininity that is carefully erased in the conclusion to Godwin's *Memoir,* where he considers himself and Wollstonecraft as paradigmatic figures of gender difference, a pair who (in the words of the second edition) "perhaps each carried further than to its common extent the characteristic of the sexes to which we belonged." He claims that "her religion, her philosophy . . . were . . . the pure result of feeling and taste. She adopted one opinion, and rejected another, spontaneously, by a sort of tact, and the force of a cultivated imagination . . . perhaps, in the strict sense of the term, she reasoned little."[7] All trace of calculation is here repeatedly denied, so that Wollstonecraft emerges, in his characterization, as a pure creature of feeling, all but bereft of reason.

The problem that Godwin's account of Wollstonecraft's character responds to is indicated in his essay "Of Trades and Professions," published a few months earlier in 1797. There Godwin writes of

> the servile and contemptible arts which we so frequently see played off by the tradesman. He is so much in the habit of exhibiting a bended body, that he scarcely knows how to stand upright. Every word he utters is graced with a simper or a smile. He exhibits all the arts of the male coquette; not that he wishes his fair visitor to fall in love with his person, but that he may induce her to take off his goods. An American savage, who should witness the spectacle of a genteel and well frequented shop, would conceive its master to be the kindest creature in the world, overflowing with affection to all, and eager to contribute to every one's accommodation and happiness.[8]

The tradesman exhibits the arts of manipulative persuasion and seduction which, Godwin suggests, are calculated—the word would be exact here—to make the female consumer in love with his goods. A stranger to commercial culture would imagine that he (or perhaps his shop) was the central figure in a romance of unbounded attachment. But the point of Godwin's vilification of

6. On the perception of Wollstonecraft's reveries as gendered see also G. J. Barker-Benfield, *The Culture of Sensibility: Sex and Society in Eighteenth-Century Britain* (Chicago: University of Chicago Press, 1992), 364–65.

7. Godwin, *Memoirs,* Appendix 2, 276, and 272–73.

8. *The Enquirer. Reflections on education, manners, and literature. In a series of essays* (London: Robinson, 1797), 218.

salesmanship is not only that it is based on the seductive techniques of the "systematic, cold-hearted liar," that it exposes the obvious catch in attributing irresistible power to sincerity of sentiment.[9] What troubles him is that this display of benevolence is stimulated by the business of commodity exchange, and participates in the romantic eroticization of the inequalities produced by the division of labor. He introduces his discussion of the tradesman with the comment: "The ideas of the division of labour, and even of barter and sale [are] . . . the means of enabling one of the parties to impose an unequal share of labour or a disproportionate bargain on the other. . . . Is it to be expected that any man will constantly resist the temptations to injustice, which the exercise of trade hourly suggests?"[10] In the context of the division of labor, the language of feeling is intertwined with the calculated perpetration of "fraud and injustice." For the shop is the theater for a social exchange in which kindness and affection are the means of commercial (and perhaps colonial) exploitation.

The Edgeworths, writing on the cultivation in children of the "social affections" of "Sympathy and Sensibility," express a similar sense of suspicion, a similar sense of the contiguity of these forms of feeling and trade. Children, they argue, should not be encouraged or applauded for showing charity or generosity, for

> even generous children are apt to expect generosity equal to their own from their companions; then come tacit or explicit comparisons of the value or elegance of their respective gifts; the difficult rules of exchange and barter are to be learned; and nice calculations of *Tare and Tret* are entered into by the repentant borrowers and lenders. A sentimental, too often ends in a commercial intercourse; and those who begin with the most munificent dispositions, sometimes end with selfish discontent, low cunning, or disgusting ostentation.[11]

The social affections of children are for them inappropriately bound up in the competitive economy of the gift. Their comments invoke that sense of commerce as the site of excessive passion that Godwin forcefully makes explicit: "Nothing," he writes, "is more striking than the eagerness with which tradesmen endeavour to supplant each other. The hatred of courtiers, the jealousy of artists, the rivalship of lovers attached to a common mistress, scarcely go beyond the fierceness of their passions."[12] Passion is of course an important constituent of the discourse on commerce throughout the eighteenth century,

9. Ibid., 219.

10. Ibid., 217.

11. Maria and R. L. Edgeworth, *Practical Education* [1798], 2d ed. (London: Johnson, 1801), 2.34–35.

12. *Enquirer*, 219.

which tends to represent shopping and acts of charity as peculiarly libidinized transactions.[13] But there is a more particular awareness apparent in these texts by Godwin and the Edgeworths of the commodification of the language of affection, a language that too often and too easily ends in a "commercial intercourse" from which it should be distanced. That awareness distinguishes the modernity of the commercial cultures of this period.

In general terms, I think, these kinds of usages of the language of feeling, where affection is identified with desire, and more or less deeply implicated in the business of commercial exchange on the one hand, and of sexuality on the other, have more in common with the cluster of notions that make up ideas of sensibility in this period than they do with notions of sentimentality.[14] It is possible to make too much of this distinction; but I think it can be useful to mark the difference between sentiment, which might be understood as a moralized language of feeling articulated in certain overdetermined structures of narrative which deal with the victimization of feminine or feminized subjects, and sensibility, which can be perceived as a set of notions much more closely associated with what is instinctive or physical, and which represent desire both as the necessary and even aspirational force or motor of sociability, and as the source of antisocial corruption and disease. The difference between the two is unstable—indeed, sometimes and significantly, impossible to mark—but it seems worth attempting to register the distinction between sensibility as a set of notions which articulate the moral ambivalence of desire, and sentiment as a much more thoroughly moral language which denies desire, or seems to obscure it. In what is perceived as a modern commercial culture, sensibility marks those appetites of the sexual or profiteering subject which are, in a sense that the Edgeworths perhaps come closest to acknowledging, most central to the social contract, and most difficult for it to contain or accept. In this chapter I want to explore some of the implications of notions of sensibility—and, more incidentally, sentiment—as they are used by women writers of the

13. J. G. A. Pocock, *The Machiavellian Moment: Florentine Political Thought and the Atlantic Republican Tradition* (Princeton, N.J.: Princeton University Press, 1975), chapters xiii, xiv.

14. For a persuasive analysis of the unstable meanings of sensibility, see Markman Ellis, *The Politics of Sensibility: Race, Gender and Commerce in the Sentimental Novel* (Cambridge: Cambridge University Press), chapter 1. See also Janet Todd, *Sensibility: An Introduction* (London: Methuen, 1986), 6–9, for further discussion of the relation between sentiment and sensibility. See also Stephen Cox, "Sensibility as Argument," in *Sensibility in Transformation: Creative Resistance to Sentiment from the Augustans to the Romantics,* ed. Syndy McMillen Conger (London: Associated University Presses, 1990), 63–82, esp. 67. But see also John Mullan, *Sentiment and Sociability: The Language of Feeling in the Eighteenth Century* (Oxford: Clarendon Press, 1988), and Barker-Benfield, *Culture of Sensibility,* introduction.

1790s. Because notions of sensibility are involved in representations of gendered sexuality on the one hand, and commodity exchange on the other, they are, I want to suggest, central to the attempt to understand the politics of feminine identity in the commercial culture of modernity.

III

It is perhaps surprising, in the context I have sketched, that Godwin should imply that active sexuality can rescue the language of feeling from the sordid exchanges of commerce. Godwin's revulsion toward salesmanship is so powerful, in that essay from the *Enquirer,* that he concludes that he would rather his child be exposed at birth than that it enter into trade, and his account of the shop implies that it would be morally preferable for the tradesman to "wish his fair visitor to fall in love with his person," and for him to be engaged in a directly sexual seduction, than for him to be involved in "the consideration of how to make the most of every one that enters his shop."[15] If Wollstonecraft's *Letters* are "calculated to make a man in love" with their author, then her act of seduction is rescued from ending in the grime of "a commercial intercourse" by the degree to which, in Godwin's account, the presence of the author of the *Letters* is eroticized. Sexuality seems at once to be deeply involved in commercial intercourse—in the representation of the desires of the consumer and the ambitions of the tradesman—and yet distant from or even hostile to the forms of exchange that structure those identities.

The heroine of Wollstonecraft's unfinished novel, *The Wrongs of Woman* (1798), considers the uneasy conjunction of sensibility with the economic and the sexual in her reflections for her daughter on the morality of her sexual relations with a husband she no longer desires, or when, as she puts it, "compassion, and the fear of insulting his supposed feelings, by a want of sympathy, made me dissemble, and do violence to my delicacy. What a task!"[16] In retrospect, she suggests that her conduct exemplified the extent to which women understand their duties as wives through an internalization of the discourse of the division of labor. Women who dissemble from motives of compassion or prudence transpose the notion of the duties of sexual compliance required of their marital station into the moral register of sentimental victimization. Women who do not effect that transposition, she suggests, have accepted the fact that sexuality is involved in "the secrets of trade"; for them, "indeed it is a mere affair of barter." In either case, they succumb to the arguments of "Men,

15. *Enquirer,* 219.

16. Wollstonecraft, *Mary* and *The Wrongs of Woman,* ed. Gary Kelly (Oxford: Oxford University Press, 1980), 152.

[who] more effectually to enslave us, may inculcate this partial morality, and lose sight of virtue in subdividing it into the duties of particular stations."[17] They show an "indelicate" lack of "*active* sensibility, and *positive* virtue." Sexualized sensibility, for Wollstonecraft's Maria as well as for Godwin in the *Memoirs,* seems valuable and virtuous when it can be represented as opposed to notions of barter, or the duties of particular stations—when it manifests "a softness almost more than human."

The point, however, is not that active sensibility should transcend the division of labor and inhabit the sphere of pure humanity. At the beginning of the novel, when she is confined in the madhouse, "in the heart of misery," the heroine reflects in terms reminiscent of the second *Vindication* on "how difficult it was for women to avoid growing romantic, who have no active duties or pursuits." Later she adds that romance fosters "a sickly sensibility."[18] Imprisonment in the madhouse, or in the "bastille" of marriage, represents in this novel a doubled exclusion from both the full legal rights which are the focus of the existing fragments of the narrative, and the "active duties or pursuits" which participation in the division of labor would entail. Whether women are perceived to be enslaved by the demands of the division of labor as it extends into marriage, or are corrupted by their exclusion from it, their oppression seems to produce in them the prostituted sensibility, appropriate to the "wife being as much a man's property as his horse, or his ass":[19] the feminine sensibility appropriate to the property or commodity. For the specialized duties and forms of exchange that structure commercial modernity mark feminine desires as redundant or excessive, unable to remain stationary, or to keep their station. The heroine of Wollstonecraft's novel seems to be most elusively sentimental when she contemplates escape from the horrors of the madhouse, or from her marriage: contexts which force her to consider "the world a vast prison, and women born slaves," and which, she later reflects, license "sickly sensibility" in its pursuit of "the phantoms of elegance and excellence, which sported in the meteors that exhale in the marshes of misfortune."[20] The purest and most active forms of sensibility seem also to be those which are most obviously diseased and addicted to the production and consumption of fantasy. Like the heroine of Mary Hays's *Memoirs of Emma Courtney,* Maria almost knowingly pursues an illusory ideal which she can only embody in the inadequate figure of her lover, and the domesticity he seems to promise.

In *Emma Courtney* the representation of sensibility as both pathological and

17. Ibid., 153.
18. Ibid., 197, 87, 193.
19. Ibid., 158.
20. Ibid., 79, 193.

salvific is perceived more explicitly as a function of the anomalous position of women in relation to the discourse of the division of labor. Echoing the arguments and language of Wollstonecraft's second *Vindication,* the heroine considers that though she suspects "that all mankind are pursuing phantoms, however dignified by different appellations. . . . Should I, at length, awake from a delusive vision, it would be only to find myself a comfortless, solitary, shivering, wanderer, in the dreary wilderness of human society."[21] In the passage to which the novel seems to allude, Wollstonecraft contemplates the delusive vision and naked, phantasmagoric reality, and arrives at the relatively open-ended conclusion that "we must mix in the throng, and feel as men feel." This entails being "hurried along the common stream" of "ambition, love, hope, and fear," and participating in the characteristic passions and delusions of commercial culture. Wollstonecraft argues specifically that the value of engaging in the common pursuit overrides the difference between love and professional success as objects of desire. She argues that "the habit of reflection, and the knowledge obtained by fostering any passion, might be shewn to be equally useful, though the object be proved equally fallacious." Because the passage employs the ambiguous language of projection, it elides the difference between sympathizing in pursuits from which women are excluded in the present, and the imagined participation of women in those pursuits in the future. The notion of feeling as men feel therefore works to elide the distinction between "the ambitious man consuming himself by running after a phantom," in the second *Vindication,* and the heroine of her later novel whose "sickly sensibility" pursues "phantoms of elegance"—the difference between the desires of professionalism and sensibility.[22]

Emma Courtney explores the relation between sensibility and ambition when she argues that her "ardent sensibilities" (2.54) must be focused on love. She writes:

> The mind must have an object:—should I desist from my present pursuit, after all it has cost me, for what can I change it? I feel, that I am neither a philosopher, nor a heroine—but a *woman, to whom education has given a sexual character.* It is true, I have risen superior to the generality of my *oppressed sex;* yet, I have neither the talents for a legislator, nor for a reformer, of the world. . . . Ambition cannot stimulate me, and to accumulate wealth, I am still less fitted. Should I,

21. Mary Hays, *Memoirs of Emma Courtney* (London: G. G. and J. Robinson, 1796), 2.51. This work is hereafter cited by page number in the text. This first edition is reproduced in facsimile, with an introduction by Jonathan Wordsworth (Oxford: Woodstock Books, 1995).

22. Mary Wollstonecraft, *A Vindication of the Rights of Woman* (1792), ed. Carol H. Poston (New York: Norton, 1975), 112, 111. The passage to which the novel refers begins on 111.

> then, do violence to my heart, and compel it to resign its hopes and expectations, what can preserve me from sinking into, the most abhorred of all states, *langour and inanity?* (2.53)

She determines to offer to become the mistress of Augustus Harley in terms that indicate that for her this is a career choice, to be considered and weighed against other possible occupations and specializations. She seems to believe that a language of professional ambition can be appropriate to the articulation of her desires, and that it will indicate their moral respectability. She does not consider that the professionalization of her sexuality might approximate to prostitution, and the difference seems to depend on the nice distinction between the desires appropriate to women as either commodities or agents in the field of commercial enterprise.

As though she were preparing her résumé for a job application, she writes that "I have laboured to improve myself, that I might be worthy of the situation I have chosen" (2.53–54). The situation she has in mind will, she argues, save her from sins ranked high in the commercial catalogue: "*langour and inanity.*" These are, of course, sins to which middle-class women are represented as particularly inclined, throughout the eighteenth century: the abhorred states of those perceived to lack any positive social function, and for whom the only socially worthy ambition is that chosen by Emma Courtney. The situation she desires, she notes in preparation for her formal application, is that "I would unite myself to a man of worth—I would have our mingled virtues and talents perpetuated in our offspring—I would experience those sweet sensations of which nature has formed my heart so exquisitely susceptible" (2.54). The situation she desires appears to be moral because her desire for it can be articulated in the language of professional specialization and ambition; but, of course, marriage locates middle-class women outside the division of labor, and denies them access to that professional language. The discourse of the division of labor, in which Emma Courtney articulates the morality of her pursuit of her lover, her chosen vocation, is precisely the discourse which marks sexuality as an immoral and excessive form of labor—marks it not as a specialization, but as a product of the way "nature has formed" her heart.

The language of natural inclination, juxtaposed as it is here rather suddenly with a notion of professional morality, indicates the uneasy status of feminine sensibility in the context of commercial culture. For the way nature has formed her heart seems at once to confirm her choice of "situation," and to indicate that it is no choice at all. Her problem, after all, may be her sex (and the natural inclinations that is perceived to imply), and not that she simply lacks "the *talents* for a legislator" (my emphasis). Later in the novel, when she has given up hope of Harley, and is searching for a different "occupation fitted to my talents," she reflects in terms that allude to her earlier thoughts about her career:

> I walked through the crowded city, and observed the anxious and busy faces of all around me. In the midst of my fellow beings, occupied in various pursuits, I seemed, as if in an immense desart, a solitary outcast from society. Active, industrious, willing to employ my faculties in any way, by which I might procure an honest independence, I beheld no path open to me, but that to which my spirit could not submit—the degradation of servitude. Hapless woman!—crushed by the iron hand of barbarous despotism, pampered into weakness, and trained the slave of meretricious folly!—what wonder, that, shrinking from the chill blasts of penury . . . thou listenest to the honied accents of the spoiler; and, to escape the galling chain of servile dependence, rushest into a career of infamy. . . . (2.149)

She sees the world here as though she had awoken "from a delusive vision," and what this reveals to her (as Jemima knew in Wollstonecraft's novel) is that for women the choice is between "the degradation of servitude" and the infamous independence of prostitution. Though the passage does not allude to her earlier fantasy of becoming Harley's mistress, it may indirectly and ambiguously suggest that these desires might be identified with those of the fallen woman. For middle-class men independence is, in the words of the heroine's Godwinian correspondent Mr. Francis, "the first lesson of enlightened reason, the great fountain of heroism and virtue, the principle by which man alone can become what man is capable of being" (2.100). But for women honest independence is the mephitic phantom of sensibility.

Earlier Emma Courtney laments that women are obliged to remain "insulated beings," excluded from the pursuits of men which make up the "drama of life," and she comments:

> Hence the eccentricities of conduct, with which women of superior minds have been accused—the struggles, the despairing though generous struggles, of an ardent spirit, denied a scope for its exertions! The strong feelings, and strong energies, which properly directed, in a field sufficiently wide, might—ah! what might they not have aided? forced back, and pent up, ravage and destroy the mind which gave them birth! (1.169)

Her comments identify feminine sensibility as the product, the luxury of indolence. Women are defined in relation to the division of labor either through "the vilest of all interchanges" (1.169), which gives them a positive but immoral role as commodities, or through their exclusion, which makes them not purely human (in Habermas's terms), but negative sources of corrupting and destructive energy, peculiarly libidinized in their eccentricity. As Mr. Francis points out to Emma Courtney, it is this exclusion which leads her to cultivate "an excessive sensibility, a fastidious delicacy" (1.90)—a capacity to foster in herself and others a combination of desire and discrimination that seems at once to be the limit of what commercial culture can hope to achieve, and excessive to that culture, the inverse of its productive energies. This notion of sensibility seems appropriate to the representation of the desirous consumer as the feminine counterpart to the masculine professional in his pursuit of independence. And yet, in the novels of both Wollstonecraft and Hays, sensibility acquires a radical edge, a political inflection, which that account cannot indicate. For there is a positive sense in which the energy of sensibility parallels as well as inverts the masculine—republican and commercial—drive for virtuous independence.

IV

The value of the language of sensibility is apparent in Hays's account of the education of Emma Courtney. In many novels of this period, as in conduct books and texts on the education of women, the key to feminine character is, in a crude form, the quantity of novels consumed. The novel or romance is perceived as "a commodity catering to 'infantile' female taste":[23] the commodity which provides early training in the self-regulation necessary to the good consumer. Emma is of course an inordinate consumer. With "inconceivable avidity" (1.30), she gets through "from ten to fourteen novels in a week" (1.26). When her father takes her education in hand, she reads Plutarch, and the primary texts of republican political and ethical theory: "Accounts of the early periods of states and empires, of the Grecian and Roman republics, I pursued with pleasure and enthusiasm: but when they became more complicated, grew corrupt, luxurious, licentious, perfidious, mercenary, I turned from them fatigued, and disgusted, and sought to recreate my spirits in the fairer regions of poetry and fiction" (1.40). On reading Descartes, she is "seized with a passion for metaphysical subjects" (1.40), and when she encountered Rousseau's *Julie, ou la Nouvelle Héloïse,* "the pleasure I experienced approached the limits of pain" (1.41). Reading continues to be for her an act of libidinized consumption. She imbibes the values of classical republicanism, but apparently without perceiving their opposition to the commodities purveyed by the circulating library. For she does not accept the stadial theory in

23. Terry Lovell, *Consuming Fiction* (London: Verso, 1987), 54.

which republicanism is involved, and rejects the lessons of decline and fall.[24] Her politics are represented as tinged with romantic idealism, and it is in response to her observations on having been "brought up in retirement—conversing only with books," and her acknowledgment that she is "at a loss to understand the distinction between theory and practice" (1.86), that Francis accuses her of "fostering an excessive sensibility" (1.90).

The narrative of the education of Emma Courtney works to produce the context for the articulation of her political ideals. It offers a doubled commentary on, in particular, the notion of independence that is central to her discussion of sexual inequality. On the one hand, this commentary might seem to confirm the reading of her dream of independence as the product of "excessive sensibility," as a dangerous luxury produced by and yet antagonistic to commercial culture. On the other hand, the vision of an independence for women that is both financial and moral can be understood, in the novel, as both the extension or consolidation and the perversion of classical republicanism. By playing these readings off against one another, the novel is able in a single gesture to endorse what it disavows. So, for example, if we think about this novel as a kind of commentary on or extrapolation from Wollstonecraft's second *Vindication*—a reading to which the novel unambiguously makes itself available—then we might understand it both as a celebration of all that Wollstonecraft set out to vindicate, and as the articulation of the "sexual character" that Wollstonecraft repudiated.[25] In this novel (and to some extent this seems also to be the case with *The Wrongs of Woman*) it is important that this double-edged gesture be staged most explicitly in the domestic theater of sexual politics. The "exquisite sensibility" of the heroine has an unimpeachable aim: "To have been the wife of a man of virtue and talents was my dearest ambition, and would have been my glory: I judged myself worthy of the

24. In volume 1, Emma Courtney is warned both by her aunt and by Mr. Francis about the primacy she gives to theoretical ideals of republicanism, which they suggest results in her failure to understand the imperfect and corrupt practice of modern society. See 1.44, 91–95. The heroine explains that because of the ideals she imbibed from her reading, "Everything I see and hear is a disappointment to me." Experience of the modern world leads her to believe that virtue may "exist only in the regions of romance" (1.86), rather than having been the result of the political institutions of civil societies of the past. The novel changes direction quite markedly with the second volume, where the heroine's difficulties are represented as having more to do with the primacy that she gives to passionate practice over theoretical ideals.

25. Hays herself later expressed concern about this ambivalence, and seemed anxious to confirm in retrospect that the novel should be read simply as a warning about the dangers of excessive sensibility. See the preface to her later novel *The Victim of Prejudice* (1799). Barker-Benfield accepts this retrospective reading, and suggests that the text's ambivalence resulted from Hays's failure in "mastering" her language. *Culture of Sensibility,* 365–68.

confidence and affection of such a man—I felt, that I could have united in his pursuits, and shared his principles—aided the virtuous energies of his mind, and assured his domestic comfort" (2.30–31). The heroine's ambitious desires find their focus in ideal domesticity, their excessive sensibility or sexual aggression neutralized and moralized in the self-abnegating fantasy that she will "contribute to your happiness, and to the worth of your character" (2.31).

Gary Kelly has argued that the sexual politics of the text are revolutionary,[26] and clearly its representation of sexuality is both scandalous and of a piece with the heroine's political beliefs. But the text is ambiguously radical. Its sexual politics may represent the form of excessive desire that, in 1796, commercial culture could afford to contain, or to exclude and dismiss. For the heroine's sexual radicalism may be the ultimate (perhaps quixotic) expression of "republican ardour" (1.33). Her romantic reading of republicanism leads her to believe that love "operated as a powerful, though secret spring" in "ages less degenerate than this, and states of society less corrupt" (2.106–7). But the examples she cites, and celebrates, perversely enough, are examples of civic manliness emasculated by sexual desire: Hercules taking the distaff, Sampson shorn, Jupiter crawling as a reptile.[27] Or her politics may manifest the sense in which the sexualization of feminine ambition is an accomplishment implicit in the cultural dominance of commerce. In passages such as those I have quoted on her romantic ambitions, the heroine offers to sublimate her own desire for independence in that of her husband—to exchange the phantoms of ambition for the phantoms of romantic sensibility. Sensibility as a feminized language of professional ambition comes uncomfortably close, in the heroine's visions of domesticity, to the language of the wife as property, defined (as Walter Benjamin might have it) by the relations of desire between commodities. Conservative and radical constructions of feminine sensibility seem here to be indistinguishable, and the opposition between aspirational and diseased sensibility seems blurred, perhaps even dissolved.

V

Finally, I want to turn to Wollstonecraft's extraordinarily seductive *Letters written during a short residence.* But first I want to look briefly at one of the

26. Gary Kelly, *Women, Writing, and Revolution: 1790–1827* (Oxford: Oxford University Press, 1993), 101.

27. For further discussion of the implications of sexual desire in the context of classical republicanism, see John Barrell, "'The Dangerous Goddess': Masculinity, Prestige and the Aesthetic in Early Eighteenth-Century Britain," in his *The Birth of Pandora and the Division of Labour* (London: Macmillan, 1992).

"Hints. [Chiefly designed to have been incorporated in the Second Part of the Vindication of the Rights of Woman]," which Godwin published in the *Posthumous Works* of Wollstonecraft in 1798. She writes:

> Nothing can be more absurd than the ridicule of the critic, that the heroine of his mock-tragedy was in love with the very man whom she ought least to have loved; he could not have given a better reason. How can passion gain strength any other way? In Otaheite, love cannot be known, where the obstacles to irritate an indiscriminate appetite, and sublimate the simple sensations of desire till they mount to passion, are never known. There a man or woman cannot love the very person they ought not to have loved—nor does jealousy ever fan the flame.[28]

The terms of this discussion allude to the arguments of Millar's *Origin of the Distinction of Ranks* which suggested, in brief, that the inequalities of commercial society create the obstacles necessary to refinement of passion. In her second *Vindication,* Wollstonecraft cited Johann Forster's account of Tahiti, in his *Observations made during a voyage round the World* (1778), in which the islanders were represented as free from all but the most rudimentary divisions of labor.[29] Here she suggests that as a result they have no knowledge of romantic love. Wollstonecraft's use of Millar's argument is striking: it suggests that she, like Hays's Mr. Francis rather than like Emma Courtney, believes that romantic love, or what in the *Letters* she calls "voluptuousness," is peculiarly the product of modern civilization, but she does not suggest here that she therefore thinks of it as immorally excessive, or as what Francis describes as "the unnatural and odious invention of a distempered civilization" (2.98). The "Hint" suggests that inappropriate or disappointed passion—like the desire of Emma Courtney for Augustus Harley, or of the subject of the *Letters from Sweden* for her absent lover—which is the characteristic expression of excessive sensibility, is not diseased. Or else that it is valuable just because it is corrupt, because of its pathological relation to "commercial intercourse."[30] Emma Courtney claims, in her response to Francis's characterization of her passion as the symptom of "distempered civilization," that passion is valuable because it is the motor of social change. She writes: "Is it possible that you can be insensible of all the mighty mischiefs which have been caused by this passion—of the great events and changes of society, to which it has operated as a powerful,

28. No. 5, in *The Works of Mary Wollstonecraft,* ed. Janet Todd and Marilyn Butler with Emma Rees-Mogg (London: Pickering, 1989), 5.271. Compare *Letters from Sweden,* letter 4.

29. See Wollstonecraft, *Vindication,* 70–71. For further discussion of these issues see my "Looking at Women," in Johann Forster, *Observations made during a Voyage around the world,* ed. Nicholas Thomas, Harriet Guest, and Michael Dettelbach (Honolulu: Hawaii University Press, 1996).

30. Maria and R. L. Edgeworth, *Education,* 2.35.

though secret, spring?" (2.106). She seems to ignore or sweep aside her own acknowledgment that in the discourse of classical republicanism immoderate love wreaks mischief, or injures masculinity, in order to insist with apparent perversity on its positive value. Wollstonecraft's *Letters from Sweden* attribute value to the manifestations of excessive sensibility through a more complex process, but for her, as for Mary Hays and John Millar, it is a value bound up with the involvement of sensibility in commercial culture.

Wollstonecraft represents Scandinavia, in her *Letters,* through the doubled lens of disappointed love and disappointed enthusiasm for the revolution in France. In her first letter, she writes: "I forgot the horrors I had witnessed in France, which had cast a gloom over all nature, and suffering the enthusiasm of my character, too often, gracious God! damped by the tears of disappointed affection, to be lighted up afresh, care took wing while simple fellow feeling expanded my heart."[31] At this early stage, she emphasizes the conjunction, the correlation of personal and political feeling that is one of the most striking features of the whole volume. That correlation draws on the centrality of conceptions of the family to political debate in the 1790s, inflecting that debate with notions of sensibility which focus its articulation in the sexual and political desires, the libidinized reveries, of the individual subject. The narrator displays her own subjectivity, her political and personal sensibilities, as the theater for that debate. But this display does not depend on an easy sentimental notion of the continuity of the personal and political, for the text dramatizes the difficulties and discontinuities of their correlation.

The narrator's estranged lover is, of course, the addressee and, as it were, thematic motif for the reveries on or of sensibility that are so essential to the gendered character of this text. If we set aside, for the moment, the identification of this addressee with Gilbert Imlay, then the characteristics of this figure, as the object of feminine sensibility, emerge more clearly. He is the type of the modern lover: he seems to be the most inappropriate object of affection, and the narrator's desire for him seems to be heightened or irritated, refined, by the obstacles of distance that his indifference and their shared involvement in commercial business create.[32] He is repeatedly characterized as representative of modern commerce: a man deeply involved in and colored by what is most

31. *Letters written during a short residence in Sweden, Norway and Denmark,* facsimile of first ed. of 1796, with an introduction by Sylva Norman (Fontwell: Centaur Press, 1970), 11. All further references in the text are to this edition.

32. For an illuminating discussion of this shared involvement, see Mary A. Favret, *Romantic Correspondence: Women, Politics and the Fiction of Letters* (Cambridge: Cambridge University Press, 1993), chapter 4. On the increasing bitterness of Wollstonecraft's comments on commercial culture, see Gary

corrupt and perhaps also most enlightened about commercial culture. The final letters are, of course, quite explicit in attributing the alienation of her lover's affections to the effects of his involvement in commercial enterprise, as a result of the process which, she believes, dictates that "a man ceases to love humanity, and then individuals, as he advances in the chase after wealth" (255). But the earlier letters suggest, perhaps more indirectly, that his commercial nature is a part of his sexual attraction. As she leaves rural Norway, for example, she observes that though she wishes to retreat from the "vices and follies" of "the polished circles of the world" into "simplicity of manners," she recognizes that the "advantages obtained by human industry" which are demonstrated in polished society are necessary to the "wisdom and virtue which exalts my nature." She concludes that these reflections on the follies and advantages of commercial civilization "increase my respect for your judgement, and esteem for your character" (115–17). She writes of Imlay as though he were a figure for commerce itself, caught up in the historical process in which it produces both social progress and corruption.

The narrator's observations on the state of commercial progress or civilization in northern Europe are conducted in the context of a kind of dialectic of sensibilities, of fantasies of desire. In her later letters, Wollstonecraft emphasizes the extent to which France has been in her thoughts as she has assessed her experiences of Scandinavia. She writes:

> The interesting picture frequently drawn of the virtues of a rising people has, I fear, been fallacious, excepting the accounts of the enthusiasm which various public struggles have produced. We talk of the depravity of the french, and lay a stress on the old age of the nation; yet where has more virtuous enthusiasm been displayed than during the two last years, by the common people of France and in their armies? I am obliged sometimes to recollect the numberless instances which I have either witnessed, or heard well authenticated, to balance the account of horrours, alas! but too true. I am, therefore, inclined to believe that the gross vices which I have always seen allied with simplicity of manners, are the concomitants of ignorance. (216)

Experience of the contrast between France and Scandinavia enables her to "guard against the erroneous inferences of sensibility," which in 1794 had made it difficult for her to maintain her sense of the value of the revolution.[33] Earlier she argues that discussion of the revolution will bring enlightenment

Kelly, *Revolutionary Feminism: The Mind and Career of Mary Wollstonecraft,* rev. ed. (London: Macmillan, 1996), 181–82.

33. Preface to *An Historical and Moral View of the Origin and Progress of the French Revolution* (1794), in *Works,* 6.6.

and public spirit to the Norwegians of the coast, whose interests she represents as confined to the accumulation of wealth and the aggrandizement of their families. And she alludes to the exemplary republicanism displayed in the "virtuous enthusiasm" of the French in her account of what attracts her to the idea of the "substantial farmers" of northern Norway:

> The description I received of them carried me back to the fables of the golden age: independence and virtue; affluence without vice; cultivation of mind, without depravity of heart; with "ever smiling liberty;" the nymph of the mountain.—I want faith! My imagination hurries me forward to seek an asylum in such a retreat from all the disappointments I am threatened with; but reason drags me back, whispering that the world is still the world, and man the same compound of weakness and folly, who must occasionally excite love and disgust, admiration and contempt. But this description, though it seems to have been sketched by a fairy pencil, was given me by a man of sound understanding, whose fancy seldom seems to run away with him. (168–69)

Here the combination of independence, virtue, and liberty with agriculture identifies the ideal community with the founding fables of republicanism. But what may be most fanciful about the representation of this ideal here is, as the narrator recognizes, the hope that it might provide an asylum for a woman. The strategy involved in its representation is similar to the one I discussed in the education of Emma Courtney, in that here masculine republican ideals are identified with precisely the kind of fantasy to which they are most hostile—the sketch of a "fairy pencil." As was the case in Hays's novel, this works here to produce a kind of perversely feminized narrative of a masculine ideal—a narrative which suggests that this ideal community might be hospitable to the sentimental heroine in distress, and might not reject her as the source of "mighty mischiefs."[34] And this ideal is represented as the fantasy of a politicized sensibility. Greg Claeys shows how in the later 1790s primitivism became an ideal attributed to radical thinkers by their conservative and counterrevolutionary adversaries—an ideal that made their thinking appear not just contemptibly and ridiculously idealistic but pointlessly regressive.[35] Revolutionary arguments for the redistribution of property, it was argued, had degraded the "once-polished and civilized" French "below the savage tribe" of North America. As a result of revolutionary disrespect for private property, "their distresses increase daily; Commerce lost—Trade ruined—Credit at

34. For further discussion of this issue, see Carole Pateman, "The Patriarchal Welfare State," in *The Disorder of Women: Democracy, Feminism and Political Theory* (Cambridge: Polity, 1989).

35. Gregory Claeys, *Thomas Paine: Social and Political Thought* (Boston: Unwin Hyman, 1989), chapter 6.

an end."[36] In representing this ideal community as a feminized fantasy in which she has little faith, and as located in a place which she does not visit partly for practical reasons, but partly because she does not want to establish that her fantasy has no basis, Wollstonecraft is able both to endorse and to deny the attraction of republican primitivism. Like her lover, it is an object of desire the value of which is increased, or even produced, by the obstacles to its possession.

In her later letters, however, Wollstonecraft suggests that the reveries of sensibility are not about radical politics, but about a much more conservative form of consolation. In these final letters, written from Denmark and Germany, her criticisms of the "whirlpool of gain" (259) that is commercial culture become increasingly harsh, as does her sense of estrangement from her lover. She looks back at northern Scandinavia with affection, as a place

> where I seemed to have retired from man and wretchedness; but the din of trade drags me back to all the care I left behind, when lost in sublime emotions. Rocks aspiring towards the heavens, and, as it were, shutting out sorrow, surrounded me, whilst peace appeared to steal along the lake to calm my bosom, modulating the wind that agitated the neighbouring poplars. Now I hear only an account of the tricks of trade, or listen to the distressful tale of some victim of ambition. (258–59)

What these later letters work to do, I think, is to reposition or recontextualize the reveries of sensibility interspersed among the earlier letters. These on the whole more urban letters identify sublime sensibility as the projection of modern, commercial dis-ease, its voluptuous fantasy of peace the consolation for the wretchedness of the victims of ambition. Peace here is not about a politicized vision of "fellow feeling," but about oneness with material objects, that "empathy with inorganic things"[37] that is the dream of the commercial subject freed from desire through satiety. They position the sorts of visions of a rural golden age that had been the focus of the fantasies of sensibility in the earlier letters as the objects of a nostalgic desire fostered by the oppression of commercial surroundings.

Wollstonecraft might almost be thought to have had that passage in mind

36. *An Address to the Inhabitants of Great Britain, containing an Account of the French Revolution, the Sufferings of the unfortunate King and Royal Family of France* (London, 1793), 41.

37. I quote from Walter Benjamin's discussion of the empathy between the *flaneur* and the "soul of the commodity," in "The Paris of the Second Empire in Baudelaire, II. The *Flaneur*," in *Charles Baudelaire: A Lyric Poet in the Era of High Capitalism,* trans. Harry Zohn (London: Verso, 1983), 55. Benjamin explains that "inorganic matter" is "matter that has been eliminated from the circulation process" (56, n. 41).

when she wrote, in *The Wrongs of Woman,* of the "artificial forms of felicity, sketched by an imagination painfully alive." There she argued that the "heaven of fancy" had "an insipid uniformity which palls. . . . We dose over the unruffled lake, and long to scale the rocks which fence the happy valley of contentment, though . . . danger lurks in the unexplored wilds." In the enclosed and secluded landscape of fantasy, "the heart is often shut by romance against social pleasure; and, fostering a sickly sensibility, grows callous to the soft touches of humanity."[38] The landscape which may be constructed as a retreat from commerce here shares with "the chase after wealth" the capacity to deaden the civilizing love of humanity.

In the first letter from Sweden, the narrator engages in a reverie which is important in establishing the status of this kind of writing, and the complex relation between revolutionary politics and fantasy as the refuge of the commercial agent or victim. In a passage which clearly influenced Coleridge in the composition of "Frost at Midnight" (1798) she reflects:

> I could write at midnight very well without a candle. I contemplated all nature at rest; the rocks, even grown darker in their appearance, looked as if they partook of the general repose. . . .—What, I exclaimed, is this active principle which keeps me still awake?—Why fly my thoughts abroad when every thing around me appears at home? My child was sleeping with equal calmness—innocent and sweet as the closing flowers.—Some recollections, attached to the idea of home, mingled with reflections respecting the state of society I had been contemplating that evening, made a tear drop on the rosy cheek I had just kissed; and emotions that trembled on the brink of extacy [*sic*] and agony gave a poignancy to my sensations, which made me feel more alive than usual. (14–15)

The passage confirms that the privacy of family life cultivates an excessive sensibility which seems sick because it is restless. But in the next paragraph the narrator goes on to suggest that this restlessness may be the mark of humanity:

> What are these imperious sympathies? How frequently has melancholy and even mysanthropy taken possession of me, when the world has disgusted me, and friends have proved unkind. I have then considered myself as a particle broken off from the grand mass of mankind;—I was alone, till some involuntary sympathetic emotion, like the attraction of adhesion, made me feel that I was still a part of a mighty whole, from which I could not sever myself—not, perhaps, for the reflection has been carried very far, by snapping the thread of . . . existence. (15)

38. *Wrongs of Woman,* 193.

Here she suggests that sickness lies in considering herself as "a particle broken off from the grand mass." In the context of meditations on the idea of home and the state of society, thoughts which lead her to weep over her daughter, the disease of sensibility might be understood to be produced by the exclusion of women from the division of labor, and the increasingly compelling construction of domestic space as the atomized and asocial unit of affective relations. Sympathy, which acts imperiously and involuntarily, like a gravitational or magnetic force, overrides that isolation with an energy which she suggests effects a kind of religious redemption. This irritable and irrepressible sympathy is represented, in the concluding phrases of the first paragraph, in strongly libidinized terms. It is contrasted with the sense of repose, of being "at home," that the sleeping child shares with the rocks, and that is strongly reminiscent of the peace that characterized the narrator's fantasy of escape from the "tricks of trade" in the passage I quoted earlier. The restlessness of sympathetic desire is opposed to the properly infantile enjoyment of sublime emotions of satiety which are the consolation of commerce. In the conclusion to the reverie, Wollstonecraft writes: "Futurity, what hast thou not to give to those who know that there is such a thing as happiness! I speak not of philosophical contentment, though pain has afforded them the strongest conviction of it" (15–16). The passage is not, finally, about "philosophical contentment" or religious resignation, but about the capacity of a restless and forceful desire to make demands on the future despite the disappointments of the past.

VI

Coleridge's poem is of course much more suspicious of the "dim sympathies"[39] of retired sensibility. His reflections on it may be closer to those of Rousseau, which Mary Hays used as the epigraph to both volumes of *Emma Courtney:* "the perceptions of people in retirement are very different from those of people in the great world. . . . The same small number of images continually return, mix with every idea, and create those strange and false notions, so remarkable in people who spend their lives in solitude."[40] But the point, I think, is that by 1796, when Hays's novel and Wollstonecraft's letters were first published, the extraordinary ambivalence of sensibility, as a language of fantasy and of sexual and material desire, made it peculiarly amenable and appropriate to the ex-

39. S. T. Coleridge, "Frost at Midnight," l. 18, in *Poetical Works,* ed. E. H. Coleridge (Oxford: Oxford University Press, 1967).

40. From Rousseau's *Eloisa: Or, A Series of Letters,* trans. William Kendrick (London: Becket, 1776); the reference is traced in Mary Hays, *Memoirs of Emma Courtney,* ed. Eleanor Ty (Oxford: Oxford University Press, 1996), 197 n. 1.

pression of radical political aspirations that might be difficult, perhaps even dangerous, to articulate in any other form. Both Wollstonecraft and Mary Hays argue that the radical projects of republican politics are vitiated by their failure to accept the need to reform the social and political condition of women, and particularly middle-class women. The dreams of sensibility are peculiarly appropriate for the articulation of the desire for this reform. The language of sensibility links the feminine pursuit of financial and moral independence with the masculine pursuit of professional ambition. In that sense, it is a language which takes advantage of the blurred public and private character of professional or commercial ambitions, which for men, as well as perhaps for women, are the phantoms of libidinized pursuit, of an idea of self-fulfillment which is as much about the desires of the private and sexual subject as it is about the more thoroughly moralized aim of independence. But manifestations of sensibility also confirm the exclusion of women from commercial culture, in the "idea of home" and peace that is projected as the consolation for its restlessness. This sensibility is modern insofar as it speaks a language of political aspiration, which situates the subject of sensibility in the context of the "sphere of social reproduction" and commodity exchange, and not only in terms of exclusion from that sphere. It is modern because it articulates a conservative and nostalgic ideal of family life and of community, and projects it into a commercial future.

In her critique of the gender blindness of Habermas's model of classical capitalism or modernity, Nancy Fraser argues that "gender norms run like pink and blue threads" through the four elements of his model, "through paid work, state administration, and citizenship as well as through familial and sexual relations." Those "gender norms" are of course the "forms of male dominance"[41] which subordinate, exclude, or oppress women, and to some extent they might therefore be thought of as indications of that rather starker dualism which Carole Pateman perceives as fundamental to modernity. In what has been an influential formulation, Pateman writes:

> The fraternal social contract creates a new, modern patriarchal order that is presented as divided into two spheres: civil society or the universal sphere of freedom, equality, individualism, reason, contract and impartial law—the realm of men or "individuals"; and the private world of particularity, natural subjection, ties of blood, emotion, love and sexual passion—the world of women, in which men also rule.[42]

41. Fraser, "What's Critical," 263.

42. Pateman, "The Fraternal Social Contract," in *Disorder,* 43. See also Chantal Mouffe, "Feminism, Citizenship, and Radical Democratic Politics," in *Feminists Theorize the Political,* ed. Judith Butler and Joan W. Scott (New York: Routledge, 1992).

The network of relations that structure paid employment, state administration, citizenship, and the family seem predicated on the privacy and privation of women, but the forms of consciousness or interiority that those relations distinguish as feminine cannot readily be characterized as purely intimate sources of "human feeling." My concern in this chapter has been to unpick some of Fraser's pink and blue threads in, as it were, a different direction, from the wrong end. For in the texts I have discussed feminine subjects conceive of themselves in terms of discourses of politics, of the division of labor, of civil and commercial culture. The domestic and intimate world of sensibility is folded into that other sphere, those other elements of modern society, not just by the presence in that world too of men who rule. It is also folded in, I suggest, because for women to think of themselves as modern subjects necessarily involves a refusal of the exclusion, the division, fundamental to modernity; it involves thinking of themselves as modern because their desires are structured and articulated as those of commercial agents and political citizens.

Godwin continued his reflections on Wollstonecraft as a paradigmatic example of femininity, from which I quoted at the beginning of this chapter, with the observation that her "intuition" was "of use to her in topics that seem the proper province of reasoning," and "much more so in matters directly appealing to the intellectual taste."[43] Her capacity for intuition—which, it is worth noting, had for most of the eighteenth century been considered an exclusively masculine quality—is for Godwin what marks her as feminine, yet it seems to allow her access to what was seen as the "proper province" of masculinity. It is clearly important to Godwin's estimation of Wollstonecraft's exceptional qualities that she should possess a semilegitimate capacity for reasoning and intellectual taste, but that this capacity should be differentiated from his own, and so should secure her no more than an oblique access to the province of modern citizenship. For the notion of citizenship is defined by its opposition to what her gender represents, and as an inclusive category. Wollstonecraft is characterized here, as middle-class and educated women were with increasing frequency in the first half of the nineteenth century, in terms not just of exclusion, but of an access that is valuable because it is mediated and in most senses denied by gender difference.

43. Godwin, *Memoirs,* 273.

13

The Neutral Situation of Domesticity

I

In her *Letters on the Elementary Principles of Education* (first published in 1801–2), Elizabeth Hamilton writes that the "path of duty" for women does not lead to "the theatre of public strife." Women, she argues, should be educated to fulfill a distinctive private role:

> Did the cultivation of judgement once become an object in female education, the zeal of fair politicians might, perhaps, suffer some abatement; an evil that would not probably be productive of any very fatal consequences to society. . . . To heal the wounds of contention; to cool the raging fury of party animosity; to soften the rugged spirit of resentment; to allay the fervour of ambition; and to check the cruelty of revenge; would, to enlightened judgement, appear as the peculiar duty of those, who, not being called on to take an active part, are, by this neutral situation, marked out as the mediators and peace-makers of society![1]

She believes, in retrospect, that the "spirit of party" in politics which had characterized the 1790s was "radically vicious,"[2] and incompatible with the

Portions of this chapter appeared in "Femininity and Anna Laetitia Barbauld: A Supposed Sexual Character" in *Women and Literature in Britain 1700–1800,* ed. Vivien Jones (Cambridge: Cambridge University Press, 2000).

1. Elizabeth Hamilton, *Letters on the Elementary Principles of Education,* 2 vols., 4th ed. (London: J. Johnson, 1808), 2.221–23. The *Letters on Education* were first published in one volume in 1801, and the revised and enlarged edition, with expanded title, first appeared in two volumes in 1801–2.

2. Miss [Elizabeth] Benger, *Memoirs of the late Mrs. Elizabeth Hamilton, with a selection from her correspondence, and other unpublished writings* [1818], 2d ed., 2 vols. (London: Longman, 1819), 2.86, letter to Dr. S—, Ambleside, Kendal, 12 June 1808.

demands on femininity of religion, humanity, and domesticity. Like most cultural commentators of the early years of the nineteenth century, she perceives middle-class women to be led by their path of duty—fortunately both for themselves and for men—away from political dispute, and toward the "neutral situation" of familial and domestic life.

Hamilton's emphasis on the neutrality of middle-class women's domestic situation seems to identify her unambiguously with what Catherine Hall and Leonora Davidoff describe as the central cultural values of the early nineteenth century. They comment on accounts of domesticity in this period that

> What is important about such writing . . . is the scale on which it existed, the market which it commanded, and the evidence it provides as to the centrality of domestic values in middle-class culture. This was the voice of the middle class uniting Anglican and Dissenting audiences. Uniting, furthermore, Radicals, Liberals and Tories from all strata of the occupational spectrum and uniting men and women in a celebration of their different and separate spheres.

Davidoff and Hall argue that these central notions of domesticity commanded consensus, and united those who wrote about them (and particularly poets) to such an extent that their ideas and images are "predictable, their values familiar."[3] It can sometimes seem, when we consider narratives of femininity in the eighteenth century, as though the rich and varied panoply of discourses, trajectories, and stories the century affords takes a kind of nose dive into the comfortable retreat of domesticity at the close of the century, when the doctrine of separate spheres rules supreme and untroubled, while everyone sinks back exhausted from the turbulence of the revolutionary decade. That narrative direction has, of course, been persuasively challenged, most notably in the work of Amanda Vickery, and by the contributors to Hannah Barker and Elaine Chalus's *Gender in Eighteenth-Century England.* What interests me is the discursive persistence of the image of middle-class domesticity, and the way so many writers, and in particular middle-class women writers whose own lives might have seemed to question its pertinence, defer or enthusiastically sign up to an apparently uniform set of ideas about the domestic role of women. I am intrigued by the extent to which, in the work of Hamilton and other writers, this apparently uniform consensus conceals, and thus perhaps make it possible to articulate, significantly divergent definitions or notions of domesticity, and

3. Leonore Davidoff and Catherine Hall, *Family Fortunes: Men and Women of the English Middle Class, 1780–1850* (London: Hutchinson, 1987), 179, and see 162–79. See also Catherine Hall, "The Sweet Delights of Home," in *The History of Private Life. IV. From the Fires of Revolution to the Great War,* ed. Michelle Perrot, trans. Arthur Goldhammer (Cambridge: Harvard University Press, 1990), 47–93.

the femininity appropriate to them. In the postrevolutionary decade, what looks like "a celebration of . . . different and separate spheres" turns out, on closer inspection, to be the polite form of debate and dissension about them.

The differences I am concerned with focus on the terms in which the "neutral situation" of domesticity can be valued. This issue is succinctly debated in Maria Edgeworth's *Letters for Literary Ladies* (1795, 1798). In Edgeworth's text, the two gentlemen who initially exchange letters on women's education agree that "women of literature are much more numerous of late than they were a few years ago. They make a class in society, they fill the public eye, and have acquired a degree of consequence and an appropriate character." Their disagreement turns on the extent to which these women can be thought of as exemplary. The first correspondent, who is opposed to the education of women, argues that this literary character is inappropriate or unfeminine, and describes "female prodigies" of learning as monsters. He writes: "One power of the mind undoubtedly may be cultivated at the expense of the rest; as we see that one muscle or limb may acquire excessive strength, and an unnatural size, at the expense of the health of the whole body: I cannot think this desirable, either for the individual or for society."[4] Learning, according to this correspondent, causes in women something analogous to those forms of "physical difference" which, as John Barrell has shown, "can best be understood as an image of occupational difference"; and because the excess it produces makes women appear deformed rather than sublime, Barrell's argument suggests, it indicates that their labors are not considered socially useful, or appropriate to their social function.[5] The correspondent goes on to explain that women have neither the time nor the opportunity to compete with men in learning:

> we mix with the world without restraint, we converse freely with all classes of people, with men of wit, of science, of learning, with the artist, the mechanic, the labourer; every scene of life is open to our view; every assistance that foreign or domestic ingenuity can invent, to encourage literary studies, is ours almost exclusively. From academies, colleges, private libraries, private associations of literary men, women are excluded, if not by law, at least by custom, which cannot easily be conquered.

The world that opens to the view of men of liberal education here is a kind of Habermasian bourgeois public sphere of unimpeded exchange of ideas, from

4. Maria Edgeworth, *Letters for Literary Ladies, to which is added, An Essay on the noble science of self-justification* (1795), ed. Claire Connolly (London: Everyman, 1993), 7, 2. This text uses the second revised edition of the *Letters,* published in 1798.

5. John Barrell, "The Birth of Pandora and the Origin of Painting," in *The Birth of Pandora and the Division of Labour* (London: Macmillan, 1992), 156, and see 150–59.

which women are excluded. The gentleman concludes that "we see things as they are; but women must always see things through a veil, or cease to be women." If women attempt to enter this social exchange, they do so at the expense of their gender, which is constituted and defined by domestic exclusion from the world where private associations facilitate converse between classes and occupational specialisms. What women enjoy as the solace for this domestic confinement is their freedom from distortion by occupational difference, and a quality the correspondent calls "moral instinct."[6]

The gentleman who responds to this letter takes the opposing view, claiming that women are able to become learned precisely because they are not subjected to the distorting effects of occupational specialism. He argues that for men, "business, the necessity of pursuing a profession, the ambition to shine in parliament, or to rise in public life, occupy a large portion of their lives.— In many professions the understanding is but partially cultivated; and general literature must be neglected by those who are occupied in earning bread or amassing riches for their family." He points out that in the modern world of divided labors and specialisms "men of genius" complain that their professions "contract their inquiries," statesmen are servants to accidental expediency, and men of letters, however unwillingly, become " 'literary artisans.' " He adds:

> "Literary artisans," is the comprehensive term under which a celebrated philosopher classes all those who cultivate only particular talents or powers of the mind, and who suffer their other faculties to lose all strength and vigour for want of exercise. The other sex have no such constraint upon their understandings; neither the necessity of earning their bread, nor the ambition to shine in public affairs, hurry or prejudice their minds: in domestic life they have leisure to be wise.[7]

In this second letter, it is men whose understandings are distorted and whose scope of vision is contracted by specialization. The exclusion of women from "such constraint" affords them the opportunity to develop something closer to

6. Edgeworth, *Letters,* 2, 3, 7.

7. Ibid., 27. The philosopher alluded to here is Dugald Stewart, who argued in his *Elements of the Philosophy of the Human Mind* (1792) that in many professions a man would be "more likely to excel, the more he has concentrated the whole force of his mind to one particular object." This man, Stewart claimed, "is educated to be merely a literary artisan." He compared the effects of this employment with the kinds of physical distortion discussed by Edgeworth's first correspondent: "It is not in the awkward and professional form of a mechanic, who has strengthened particular muscles of his body by the habits of his trade, that we are to look for the perfection of our animal nature: neither is it among men of confined pursuits, whether speculative or active, that we are to expect to find the human mind in its highest state of cultivation." Dugald Stewart, *Elements of the Philosophy of the Human Mind,* 6th ed., 2 vols. (London: T. Cadell, 1818), 1.21–22, Introduction, Part II, sect. i. See Edgeworth, *Letters,* 85 n. 37. Stewart's work was also an important influence for Hamilton's *Letters on Education.*

that liberal comprehensiveness of view which the first correspondent attributed to educated men.

The different positions Edgeworth articulates in these *Letters* provide, I think, a useful key to the debate about the nature of domesticity in the late 1790s and 1800s. Women's learning and literary achievements are, as Edgeworth notes, clearly in the public eye; feminine capacities for learning are too well established to be ignored or wished away. But despite (or because of) this, there also seems to be a consensus that gender difference depends on the exclusion of women from the public sphere of masculine activity. What is then at issue is the discourse appropriate to the description of that domestic exclusion; or the cultural values, in Hall and Davidoff's terms, that domesticity is credited with securing. On the one hand, the public sphere might be thought of in terms of the discourse on the division of knowledge, as Edgeworth's first correspondent suggests. In terms of this discourse, men in pursuit of their different occupational and professional specialisms are capable of gaining a specialized knowledge not available to the generalist. The man of liberal education, however, will gain through sociable interaction in the masculine world of debate and exchange a hoard of cultural capital, a degree of knowledge and understanding of the cultural riches produced by these different pursuits, that will make "every scene of life . . . open to our view." Their knowledge, the first correspondent claims, becomes the received opinion on which further advances can then be built, and without the accumulation of which "the mutual intercourse of individuals and of nations must be only for the traffic or amusement of the day."[8] Women, excluded from this intercourse, only have access to what it produces in the form of the prejudices that guide their "moral instinct." They are, as it were, the trust funds, the repositories, for the cultural capital men produce and put to work. They are also, in the first letter, the only example of the potentially distorting effects of the division of labor if they choose to forgo or violate the exclusion necessary to the definition of their gender.

According to Edgeworth's second correspondent, however, the world men inhabit is too divided by the different occupational specialisms to which its agents are devoted to produce any possibility of sociable exchange or knowledge for those agents beyond that appropriate within any particular profession. This is a world structured according to a division of labor that allows only those excluded from labor to view "every scene of life" or survey what is produced by different professional pursuits. Here it is only women who have the leisure to be wise or to understand that the divergent paths of different

8. Edgeworth, *Letters,* 6.

occupational specialisms may be involved in contributing to a social unity its agents cannot see. The correspondent is—perhaps judiciously—vague about what the acquisition of this wisdom involves. He writes:

> The more men of literature and polished manners desire to spend their time in their own families, the more they must wish that their wives and daughters may have tastes and habits similar to their own. If they can meet with conversation suited to their taste at home, they will not be driven to clubs for companions; they will invite the men of wit and science of their acquaintance to their own houses, instead of appointing some place of meeting from which ladies are to be excluded.

This account exploits the capaciousness of the notion of conversation in the late eighteenth century, which did not of course imply that women had to speak or participate actively, but could suggest, more minimally, that women create the kind of environment in which men like to talk, and to which the husband is happy to invite his male acquaintances. The correspondent continues:

> This mixture of the talents and knowledge of both sexes must be advantageous to the interests of society, by increasing domestic happiness.—Private *virtues* are public benefits: if each bee were content in his cell, there could be no grumbling hive; and if each cell were complete, the whole fabric must be perfect.[9]

The correspondent may be celebrating the mixture of the equally distributed talents of both sexes: the combination of the specialized knowledge of men and the general wisdom of women in a private space from which "the political self-understanding of the bourgeois public" could trace its origin.[10] But if the role of women here is more passively to create the domestic comfort to which the man will be happy to invite his friends—if their leisured wisdom has become no more than the ability to facilitate men's off-duty chat—then this may represent the denial of public or political exchange, in an atomized world where "there could be no grumbling hive." In this second letter, the domesticity of women understood to be excluded from the division of labor may be valuable because it affords women the opportunity actively to cultivate the wisdom necessary to guarantee the wholeness of a society only apparently ruptured and divided by occupational specialisms, or it may be valuable because it offers asylum from and consolation for a social division or atomization recognized as inevitable and irreparable.

9. Ibid., 36–37.

10. Jürgen Habermas, *The Structural Transformation of the Public Sphere: An Inquiry into a Category of Bourgeois Society*, trans. Thomas Burger with Frederick Lawrence (London: Polity, 1989), 29.

II

The arguments of Edgeworth's correspondents, I think, provide a means of grasping the intriguing possibility of a kind of discursive overlap or alliance between writers apparently as diverse as Priscilla Wakefield and Mary Ann Radcliffe on the one hand, and Jane West and the young Felicia Hemans on the other. In her *Reflections on the Present Condition of the Female Sex; with Suggestions for its Improvement* (1798), Priscilla Wakefield is concerned with the employment prospects of women in the modern age. She considers the position of women within the context of her endorsement of Adam Smith's argument "that every individual is a burthen upon the society to which he belongs, who does not contribute his share of productive labour for the good of the whole." She argues that since "women possess the same qualities as men, though perhaps in a different degree, their sex cannot free them from the claim of the public for the proportion of usefulness"; and she urges women to make "the virtuous attempt" to participate in the division of labor. Some women, she suggests, are able to fulfill the "peculiar office" appropriate to their gender within the home, were they should "smooth the inconveniences of domestic life," and educate their daughters. Her account clearly implies that the appropriate education of daughters is a form of "productive labour." When she considers the folly of those who educate their daughters to have aspirations inappropriate to their rank she asks, "Of what use would it be to a seaman to learn the theory of agriculture?" The skills and knowledge appropriate to women of different ranks seem to her conclusively analogous to those appropriate to diverse employments. Wakefield also considers the plight of "genteelly educated" middle-class women who lack the financial support of a male relation. She asks, "Is it not time to find a remedy" for this situation,

> when the contention of nations has produced the most affecting transitions in private life, and transferred the affluent and the noble to the humiliating extremes of want and obscurity? When our streets teem with multitudes of unhappy women, many of whom might have been rescued from their present degradation, or who would perhaps never have fallen into it, had they been instructed in the exercise of some art or profession, which would have enabled them to procure for themselves a respectable support by their own industry.[11]

The plight of these women is similar to that of the perhaps not so "genteelly educated" women discussed by Mary Ann Radcliffe in *The Female Advocate;*

11. Priscilla Wakefield, *Reflections on the Present Condition of the Female Sex; with Suggestions for its Improvement* (London: Johnson, 1798), 66–67.

or, an Attempt to Recover the Rights of Women from Male Usurpation (1799). Radcliffe argues that poor women are "left destitute in the world, without the common necessaries of life . . . even without any lawful or reputable means of acquiring them," as a result of "the vile practice of men filling such situations as seem calculated, not only to give bread to poor females, but thereby to enable them to tread the paths of virtue, and render them useful members, in some lawful employment, as well as ornaments to their professions and sex."[12] Both Wakefield and Radcliffe suggest that employment and the financial independence it could afford would preserve the moral and sexual independence of women. Wakefield takes the argument a step further, and suggests that some form of employment is necessary to moral virtue even where there is no obvious danger of the hardship that might lead to vice. She believes that "interesting employment" in occupations "such as deserve the name of business" should "be pursued as a talisman, to preserve those women who are virtuous" from adultery and divorce.[13] Like so many other texts on women of this period, Wakefield's *Reflections* repeatedly return to the threat of prostitution as the only profession which seems already available to define the position of women in the language of the division of labor. Women seem either to become prostitutes and adulterers, or, if her suggestions for the improvement of their condition are adopted, to be able to pursue interesting employment which is the talisman that guarantees their virtue. The occupations of women which cannot be represented in the discourse on the division of labor in Wakefield's *Reflections* can only be represented in negative terms.

Jane West's long poem *The Mother* (1809) and Felicia Hemans's *The Domestic Affections* (1812), in contrast, represent domesticity as the fullest expression of feminine duty. But like Wakefield and Radcliffe, West and Hemans seem to find this station difficult to represent positively. Their poetry represents labor in terms of division and isolation, but it nevertheless seems to absorb the available terms of value, and to leave the idea of domesticity peculiarly evacuated and empty. When, for example, Jane West writes of the family in *The Mother* she describes with a nostalgic regret reminiscent of Wordsworth's *Michael* the days before the coherence of the family unit was broken up by the division of labor. She writes that in modern Britain "the manners of her swains. . . . Preserve their old simplicity no more" because they are "Loos'd from the ties which to one house, one task, / One interest, the laborious

12. Mary Anne Radcliffe, *The Female Advocate; or an attempt to recover the Rights of Woman from Male Usurpation* (London: Vernor and Hood, 1799). Reprinted with introduction by Jonathan Wordsworth (Oxford: Woodstock, 1994), "To the Reader," vii and 26–27.

13. Wakefield, *Reflections,* 34, 61, 1, 2, 68, 46.

brethren bound." Now, she suggests, family unity is only available in childhood, before the anxious mother must watch her son depart for "labour's prison-house" and the rigors of imperial service. These are common enough images of the opposition between the divided world of masculine industry and ambition, and the peace and coherence of domesticity. But the idea of the family that this involves in West's poem is given a peculiar definition by the conflation of the good old days with infancy; by the familiar recapitulation of phylogeny in ontogeny. For the ideal family of infancy seems here to continue into the present the image of a feudal domesticity in which "affection knits / The strong, fraternal cord." In feudal times, West writes,

> every house
> Became a little monarchy, compos'd
> Of children-citizens, and kindred slaves,
> Distinguish'd from the world beside, which seem'd
> A horde unknown of aliens or of foes.

This distinction from the alien or hostile world beyond the domestic family seems still to characterize the mother's vision of labor as a prison house. As the image of the domestic is extended to embrace the nation, the outer darkness of the "world beside" becomes the field for the heroic struggles of the imperial servant:

> Whether beneath
> Thy naval or thy martial banner plac'd,
> Britannia, he with honest zeal contends
> For thy insulted rights, thy slander'd fame,
> And menac'd empire in far distant climes. . . .[14]

West uses the commonplace language of the family as a little monarchy to produce an idea of domesticity distinguished by its fear of and hostility to the world beyond its own limited confines.

The mother who occupies West's fortress state of domesticity is, like the family itself, defined largely in negative terms. She is obliged to send her sons, but not of course her daughters, to be educated by teachers of their own sex in public schools, because her own knowledge cannot extend to the alien world beyond the home. Male schoolteachers must instruct boys because they "know life's subtle maze, untried / By the safe ignorance which bounds thy walk / To the domestic pale." From within the pale of this protective ignorance, West

14. Mrs. [Jane] West, *The Mother, A Poem, In Five Books* [1809], 2d ed. (London: Longman, 1810), Book 4, "Separation from Children," 133, 149, 128, 147.

believes that the mother cannot even imagine what her son should become beyond it:

On a bolder scale
Than female softness can project, with nerves
Brac'd tighter than maternal tenderness
Can strain, must man be form'd, intrepid man,
Lord of this lower world, pilot of state,
Rough mariner, pilgrim of every soil. . . .

The mother is unable to plan or project her son's future because she cannot conceive of the mobility his life will demand, or apparently, the size and hardness of the masculinity he will need to display. But this inability is of course fortunate, because the fulfillment of her maternal duty seems to depend on her passive pliability and ignorance: duty demands that the mother give up her sons, her "dear delights to strangers," even though, West points out, it has first enjoined her to identify herself in their proximity. Duty, she writes, has first fixed

The careful mother in the narrow walk
Of her own family, and bid her eye
Direct the little commonwealth, till use
Render'd confinement pleasure, and the prate
Of gay simplicity and wonder bland,
Than deep discussion or colloquial wit
More grateful. . . .[15]

West's conservatism begins to indicate the extent to which the language of domesticity is hospitable to markedly divergent views. Even in the short passage from Elizabeth Hamilton's *Letters on Education* at the beginning of this chapter, it was clear that her notion of feminine neutrality, despite the contrast it represents to the masculine and "active part" of society, involved an understanding of the value and nature of the domestic very different from that West describes. For Hamilton's domestic neutrality is the result of the "cultivation of judgment" rather than of the confinement to passive ignorance that West celebrates. But West's unattractively conservative and repressive image of domesticity as something that needs to be made pleasant by habit, I think, speaks to the sense in which domesticity is valued in negative terms, as a space evacuated of almost any possible subjectivity, any positive content.

Felicia Hemans's poem of 1812 on *The Domestic Affections* builds with considerably more skill on the negative characteristics of the space. The poem

15. West, *Mother,* Book 3, "Education," 87–88, 85.

circles continually around the idea of the space dedicated to domestic affection as a site that is always lost, always longed for:

> Hail, sacred home! where soft Affection's hand,
> With flow'rs of Eden twines her magic band!
> Where pure and bright, the social ardors rise,
> Concentring all their holiest energies!
> When wasting toil has dimm'd the vital flame,
> And ev'ry power deserts the sinking frame;
> Exhausted nature still from sleep implores
> The charm that lulls, the manna that restores!
> Thus, when oppress'd with rude tumultuous cares,
> To thee, sweet home! the fainting mind repairs;
> Still to thy breast, a wearied pilgrim, flies,
> Her ark of refuge from uncertain skies!

In Hemans's poem home is the place not just of feminized ignorance but of a sort of denial of consciousness analogous to sleep. The activities that go on outside the home are all represented more or less explicitly as solitary, isolated. Whether men heroically engage in imperial, military, or maritime adventures, or embark on the intellectual excursions of genius, their forays seem here to be typified in the fates of the solitary Siberian exile and the "shipwreck'd wanderer" alone on his island: they all dream of a lost domesticity sacred to familial affections and "social ardors," a home associated with both the exercise of social sympathies and, perhaps at the same time, sleep.[16] Domesticity seems to be a kind of respite from individual labor in a dream of sympathetic community.

Domesticity describes a space which, for much of Hemans's poem, seems to be uninhabited; the space itself, with its sheltering breast, is redolent of maternity, but ideas of wives and children are a part of its fabric, associations of its form. When the poem does finally turn to the representation of the domestic woman, she too, as she is individuated and distinguished from the space that defines her, turns out not to possess or inhabit the full ideal of the domestic dream, for she is a mother grieving for her ailing and then dead child. For her, the ideal of domesticity is as remote, as much the object of nostalgic yearning, as it is for the wandering men, and she is exhorted to have faith that she will find her sympathetic communion of domestic bliss in the afterlife. In both Hemans's poem and West's, the idea of the feminized space of domesticity seems both attractive and elusive because it is the source of social affections

16. Felicia Dorothea Browne [Hemans], *The Domestic Affections, and other Poems* (London: Cadell, 1812). Reprinted with an introduction by J. Wordsworth (Poole: Woodstock, 1995), 151–52, 159.

and sympathies, and yet is constituted by the exclusion of what is social, and in West's poem at least, of what is sympathetic. But Hemans's poem is, I think, clearly more sophisticated than West's. West's poem attempts to resolve these problems by emphasizing the necessary and desirable ignorance of the domestic woman, while demanding from her a kind of moral and pious authority which it is hard to imagine that she could, in her stupefied state, exercise. Hemans seems to accept that the idea of the "Bower of repose" woven by the domestic affections can only be transcendent or interior, and as much the object of women's nostalgia, as "Thro' toil *we* struggle, or thro' distance rove" (my emphasis), as it is that of heroic imperial masculinity.[17]

III

Polemical writers such as Wakefield and Radcliffe, I have suggested, see the sexualized corruptions of prostitution and adultery as the only alternative to the redemption of women through participation in the division of labor. Neither Hemans nor West seems to consider that participation a possibility—though both were professional women attempting to support their families through their writing. If women do participate in the atomized world of modernity in Hemans's poem, then what they share is not the labor or its rewards but perhaps the psychological condition it is understood with increasing persistence to produce. Mary Hays noted, in her *Female Biography* (1803), that Madame de Maintenon had protested that "there is a want, a frightful void, in every state,—a pain and listlessness—a wish for something more: nothing, in short, in this world can ever give us entire satisfaction." Hays commented acerbically: "Is this common complaint really founded in nature; or is it, as there is cause to suspect, a disorder of the imagination, produced by false systems of refinements, by the indulgence of illusions, and the errors of an imperfect civilisation?"[18] Domesticity, in Hemans's poem, seems to represent that "something more," to promise that "entire satisfaction," in a nostalgic ideal of sympathetic community. But for all four of these writers, I think, domesticity is understood as a space beyond knowledge or labor, antecedent to the productive but painful divisions and specializations of cultural modernity; and what Wakefield and Radcliffe represent as its lack, in this respect, becomes in the poems of Hemans and West a value that might best be understood in terms of that transmission of "moral instinct" which Edgeworth's first correspondent saw as the role of ignorant domestic femininity.

17. Ibid., 152.

18. Mary Hays, *Female Biography; or, Memoirs of Illustrious and Celebrated Women, of all ages and countries. Alphabetically arranged. In six volumes* (London: Phillips, 1803), 5.382.

The arguments of Hannah More's didactic novel *Coelebs in Search of a Wife* (1809), in contrast, mock and apparently set out to counter the prejudices of the "eulogist of female ignorance."[19] Her arguments are closer to those of Edgeworth's second correspondent, and there is, I suggest, a sense in which her novel and Elizabeth Hamilton's *Letters on Education* can be seen to elaborate and develop what I represented as the divergent strains of his defense of women's education. For both More and Hamilton the value of women's education is based in their perception of the modest and virtuous privacy of domestic life as the sphere appropriate to women of the landed and middle classes, but whereas in More's novel education seems valuable primarily because it cultivates the pious resignation necessary to domestic contentment, in Hamilton's *Letters* what Jane Rendall identifies as "the rhetoric of republican motherhood," which attributes to the domestic woman the ability "to uplift and regenerate the spirit of her society," is much more clearly in evidence.[20] Hamilton in these *Letters* attributes a degree of public and patriotic significance to women in their domestic role which depends on and yet exceeds the cherished modesty and privacy of domesticity.

The arguments of More's novel and Hamilton's *Letters* share a number of key terms. They both emphasize that the skill of the well-educated domestic woman is shown in her ability to adopt a sort of managerial role, supervising and overseeing the complex organization of the household. Hamilton explains that the "mistress of a family" requires qualities similar to those of "a minister of state," because

> A large family is a complex machine, composed of a great number of individual and subordinate parts. In order to conduct it properly, there must, in the first place, be a comprehensive, *i.e.* a general view of the effect desired to be produced; in the next place, there must be an accurate conception of the powers of each separate wheel, or individual agent, and a just notion of how it can be employed to the best advantage; and lastly, a distinct view of how the whole is to be set in motion, so as most easily to produce the desired effect. It should ever be so constituted, that, like the silk-wheels at Derby, when any one part goes wrong, that part may be stopped and repaired, without arresting the motion of the rest.[21]

More, similarly, understands the domestic organization as a machine. Initially the hero of *Coelebs* argues that the "domestic arrangements" of the superior housewife "resemble . . . those of Providence, whose under-agent she is. Her

19. Hannah More, *Coelebs in Search of a Wife* (1809), in *The Miscellaneous Works of Hannah More*, 2 vols. (London: Thomas Tegg, 1840), 2.399.

20. Jane Rendall, *The Origins of Modern Feminism: Women in Britain, France and the United States, 1780–1860* (Basingstoke: Macmillan, 1985), 32.

21. Hamilton, *Letters*, 2.369–70.

wisdom is seen in its effects. Indeed, it is rather felt than seen. It is sensibly acknowledged in the peace, the happiness, the virtue of the component parts; in the order, regularity, and beauty of the whole system, of which she is the moving spring." Later in the novel her characters return to the analogy of the household as machine, and elaborate on the unseen qualities of its prime mover. They praise superior domestic economists, who

> execute their well-ordered plan as an indispensable duty, but not as a superlative merit. They have too much sense to omit it, but they have too much taste to talk of it. It is their business, not their boast. The effect is produced, but the hand which accomplishes it is not seen. The mechanism is set at work, but it is behind the scenes. The beauty is visible—but the labour is kept out of sight.[22]

The unseen hand that sets More's household machine to work is reminiscent of Adam Smith's notion of the "invisible hand" which in the larger world of the national domestic economy leads the individual unintentionally to use his capital in the interests of society; but for Smith the hand symbolizes an agency no mortal should or could exercise.[23] In More's novel, the role of the superior domestic economist is almost magical or superhuman, and analogous to the agency of providence, but the providential housewife operates by a sleight of hand that denies any connection between the effects achieved and her intentions, and prevents her acknowledgment of her own work, her own moral agency.

More's domestic economist derives a degree of independence from her religion and "mental cultivation":

> the woman who derives her principles from the Bible, and her amusements from intellectual sources, from the beauties of nature, and from active employment and exercise, will not pant for beholders. She is no clamorous beggar for the extorted alms of admiration. She lives on her own stock. Her resources are within herself. She possesses the truest independence.[24]

But this hard-earned intellectual capital does not measure up to the specialized knowledge of professional men. Discussing the "innumerable acquirements" expected of modern young ladies, the men agree that women's learning is like gold "beaten out so wide" that "the lamina must needs be very thin," whereas "among men, learned men, talents are commonly directed into some one channel, and fortunate is he who in that one attains to excellence." Mr. Stanley,

22. More, *Coelebs,* 386, 554.

23. See Adam Smith, *An Inquiry into the Nature and Causes of the Wealth of Nations,* 2 vols., ed. R. H. Campbell and A. S. Skinner, with W. B. Todd (Oxford: Clarendon Press, 1976), 1. IV. II. 9–10.

24. More, *Coelebs,* 624.

the authoritative paterfamilias, embarks on a celebratory catalogue of the subdivisions of men's professional knowledge:

> The linguist is rarely a painter, nor is the mathematician often a poet. Even in one profession there are divisions and subdivisions. The same lawyer never thinks of presiding both in the King's Bench and the Court of Chancery. The science of healing is not only divided into its three distinct branches, but in the profession of surgery only, how many are the subdivisions! One professor undertakes the eye, another the ear, and a third the teeth.

He concludes by contrasting this catalogue with an ironic account of the attempts of "woman, ambitious, aspiring, universal, triumphant, glorious woman," who "even at the age of a school boy, encounters the whole range of the arts, attacks the whole circle of the sciences!" As if to emphasize that this is not about the capacity of women, as generalists, to preserve some sense of the connections between what are increasingly perceived as the divergent branches of masculine knowledge, another character laughingly comments that women's learning is "a mighty maze, and *quite* without a plan."[25] If the role of women is indirectly analogous to that of the invisible hand which conjures social benefit out of self-interested and asocial labors, this is not because women are attributed a more comprehensive sense of the plan of the social maze than could be available to men preoccupied with their specialized pursuits.

These strictures on the superficiality and incoherence of women's learning, in *Coelebs,* are specifically directed at Miss Rattle, a satirical figure whose follies are implicitly contrasted with the wisdom of the ideal wife, Lucilla. But the difference between the two women turns on Lucilla's modest acceptance of her own deficiencies, rather than on her capacity to repair them. Domestic women are represented in More's novel as the willing and therefore virtuous victims of their exclusion from the specialisms of male learning and the divisions of male labor. In concluding their discussion of feminine domestic skills, More's characters celebrate "those meek and passive virtues which we all agreed were peculiarly Christian, and peculiarly feminine," and these virtues turn out to have a distinctly pathological cast: "To sustain a fit of sickness, may exhibit as true heroism as to lead an army. To bear a deep affliction well, calls for as high exertion of soul as to storm a town; and to meet death with Christian resolution is an act of courage, in which many a woman has triumphed, and many a philosopher, and even some generals, have failed."[26] More's hero is "a retired country gentleman" who does not intend to "live in the busy haunts of men," or "to be engaged in public life" or any profession; but this does not make him

25. Ibid., 482.
26. Ibid., 556.

into the kind of disinterested gentlemanly observer who might, early in the eighteenth century, have been credited with the ability to oversee and guarantee the beneficial plan of the mighty social maze. Here it indicates rather that this occupation is more specialized, more asocial and isolating than that of most professional men. Had his occupation obliged him "to live in the busy haunts of men," his "happiness would not so immediately, so exclusively, depend on the individual society of a woman," but as it is he is a kind of avatar of the social atomization of modernity, and the only consolation offered for his isolation is that his wife, in her passive self-sufficiency and her ability to be sick in admirable ways, has even less sense than he does that there might be a plan or social coherence to the mighty maze of divergent masculine pursuits.[27]

IV

The account of the "complex machine" of the household in Hamilton's *Letters,* in contrast, involves the appropriation to the domestic woman of a capacity to grasp the social organization—a capacity articulated in discursive terms that are poised ambivalently between the languages of the public and political on the one hand and of private piety on the other. So, for example, Hamilton like More praises the independence that education will afford women, but in her argument independence is opposed to luxury, and more specifically to dependence on imperial trade in "the blood-stained treasures of the East or West," which she believes sapped "that noble independence of mind, which rests on conscious integrity, and which is the father of all the patriotic and manly virtues." This is an argument which leads Hamilton, as she acknowledges, to "expose myself, by standing forth the champion of that unfashionable virtue, which . . . has been brought into disgrace, as savouring of republicanism."[28] The language of Christian morality, in these *Letters,* continually overlaps with that of republican or at least whiggish virtue; they are concerned to advance the education of women both on the grounds that it is necessary to exemplary housekeeping and parenting, and that it is a patriotic duty, and that doubled direction means that while the political resonances of her ar-

27. Ibid., 390.

28. Hamilton, *Letters,* 1.335, 329, 333. The notion that extensive empire reduces the colonial center to a kind of addictive dependence is of course a key note of the discourses of classical republicanism, but Hamilton's argument here may be indebted more specifically to Henry Home, Lord Kames's work, which she admired. For further discussion of Hamilton's concern with the morality of empire, see Jane Rendall, "Writing History for British Women: Elizabeth Hamilton and the Memoirs of Agrippina," in *Wollstonecraft's Daughters: Womanhood in England and France 1780–1920,* ed. Clarissa Campbell Orr (Manchester: Manchester University Press, 1996), 79–93, esp. 88–91.

guments are contained and defused by their confinement to the organization of the domestic sphere, that domestic confinement works to license the use of a language which is always imminently exposing the housewife as the champion of republican virtue, her household as the site of the values which should govern public life.

Hamilton's earlier satirical novel, *The Memoirs of Modern Philosophers* (1800), had clearly signaled her distance from the radical politics of, in particular, William Godwin's *Political Justice* and Mary Hays's *Emma Courtney,* but the novel's mockery of those did not extend into the blanket condemnation of whiggish radical and liberal politics that Gary Kelly seems to detect.[29] Wollstonecraft's "very ingenious publication" on "the Rights of Women" is praised for its attack on Rousseauvian sensibility, and the representation of eroticized sensibility in Hays's *Emma Courtney* is the focus for the novel's satirization of the feminism of the 1790s.[30] Hays (and occasionally Godwin) is satirically portrayed in the novel's central character, Bridgetina Botherim, who is represented as having become a ludicrous figure precisely because she reads modern philosophy through the lens of romantic fiction. Mrs. Fielding, the moral exemplar of the novel, comments authoritatively on the heroine's errors: "To an imagination enflamed by an incessant perusal of the improbable fictions of romance, a flight into the regions of metaphysics must . . . be a dangerous excursion."[31] Bridgetina is represented as cultivating the excessive sensibility that characterizes the novel reader, because "I never at any time debased myself by houshold [*sic*] cares, never attended to any sort of work, I always enjoyed the inestimable pleasure of leisure. Always idle, always unemployed, the fermentation of my ideas received no interruption. They expanded, generated, increased."[32] Philosophy and novel-reading confirm Bridgetina's distaste for "houshold cares," and encourage her in the libertinism that is represented, in tandem with Godwin's arguments, as destructive of family life. The novel also takes a passing swipe at Charlotte Smith, whose novel *Desmond* (1792) had, like *Emma Courtney,* associated enlightened radicalism

29. Gary Kelly, *Women, Writing, and Revolution: 1790–1827* (Oxford: Oxford University Press, 1993), chapter 4, and esp. 150–55. See also Carol Anderson and Aileen M. Riddell, "The Other Great Unknowns: Women Fiction Writers of the Early Nineteenth Century," in *A History of Scottish Women's Writing,* ed. Douglas Gifford and Dorothy McMillan (Edinburgh: Edinburgh University Press, 1997), 180–83. Jane Rendall, in contrast, associates Hamilton with "other Scottish Whig historians," in "Writing History," 84.

30. Elizabeth Hamilton, *Memoirs of Modern Philosophers,* 2d ed., 3 vols. (Bath: Cruttwell, 1800), 1.196.

31. Ibid., 3.164.

32. Ibid., 2.93.

with feminine sensibility and sexuality;[33] and it seems in particular to be this aspect of the politicization of femininity in the 1790s, this perhaps utopian form of feminism, which Hamilton disowns.

In Hamilton's *Translation of the Letters of a Hindoo Rajah* (1796) the learned Miss Ardent, with her "masculine understanding," to some extent prefigures the caricatural female philosopher of *Modern Philosophers.* It is explained that though Miss Ardent has been able to gain a substantial education in "ancient authors" and "dead languages" from her brother's tutor, the cultivation of her judgment has been neglected, which has led her to "despise not only the weaknesses, but even the domestic virtues of her own sex."[34] Miss Ardent demonstrates the dangers of what Hamilton represents as a partial and therefore flawed education, but frequently the Rajah sees her with some degree of sympathy and even respect. Until the final pages of the novel, she shows no sign of the libertinism castigated in *Modern Philosophers,* and the follies for which she is—quite gently—mocked serve to point up and to inoculate the endorsement of writing and publication by women. Mr. Denbeigh, the ideal father figure of the concluding letters, urges that the woman who does not have "the management of a family" or the riches to "build alms-houses" should occupy herself in writing "not only for your own entertainment, but for the instruction, or innocent amusement of others." The example of Miss Ardent allows him to suggest that authorship does not damage feminine propriety so long as "the virtues of your heart receive no alloy from the vanity of authorship," for vanity has been represented as the cause of Miss Ardent's errors. He is able to suggest that it is more dangerous to allow "the powers of the mind to lie dormant" than to confront the fact that "female writers are looked down upon."[35]

In *Modern Philosophers,* Mrs. Fielding, like Mr. Denbeigh, repeatedly affirms that industry is the key to virtue. She encourages the young hero in "the choice of a profession," concealing her intention to make him financially independent, because his profession "afforded an immediate object to your mind, and

33. The French Goddess of Reason, who is the mistress first of Myope and then of Vallaton, the modern philosophers, is at one point identified as Emmeline, perhaps in reference to Smith's novel of 1788. See Hamilton, *Modern Philosophers,* 3.266.

34. Elizabeth Hamilton, *Translation of the Letters of a Hindoo Rajah; written previous to, and during the period of his residence in England. To which is prefixed a Preliminary Dissertation on the History, Religion, and Manners, of the Hindoos* [1796], 2d ed., 2 vols. (London: Robinson, 1801), 2.102–3. See also Elizabeth Hamilton, *Translations of the Letters of a Hindoo Rajah,* ed. Pamela Perkins and Shannon Russell (Peterborough, Ontario: Broadview, 1999). For a brief but suggestive reflection on the imperial politics of Hamilton's work, see Katie Trumpener, *Bardic Nationalism: The Romantic Novel and the British Empire* (Princeton, N.J.: Princeton University Press, 1997), 166.

35. Hamilton, *Hindoo Rajah,* 2.334–36.

prevented the rust of idleness from corroding your faculties," and because it "put it in your power to be useful to your fellow-creatures." She pronounces that "a man without employment is a cypher in society; dependent upon others for an adventitious value, he is in himself contemptible."[36] Hamilton's *Letters* suggest that education offers the choice of a career of increasing virtue to "those who are born to the privilege or the *curse* of leisure." Of her own decision to become a published author, she writes:

> Placed by Providence in a situation undisturbed by the pressure of life's cares, tho' by an experience of its sufferings called to serious reflection; blest with leisure, and early inspired with such a taste for enquiry as gives that leisure full employment; I should have deemed myself highly culpable, if I had declined the task to which I was called by friendship, and urged by the hope which is dear to every generous mind—the hope of being in some degree useful.[37]

The terms in which she represents her own work as leisure moralized by "full employment" and usefulness contrast with her account of Bridgetina's life of idle and excessively fertile pleasure, and closely parallel those in which Mr. Denbeigh advocates female authorship, and Mrs. Fielding praises her protégé's choice of the medical profession.

Hamilton claims that she writes because she is convinced of "how necessary it is to the happiness of an active mind, to have some object worthy of its powers." Writing for publication, she explained, "was the only way by which it appeared to me possible to get rid of that mortifying sensation, that arises from feeling one's self a piece of useless lumber in creation." She seems to reconcile this need to write for publication with her sense of the propriety of domestic life by denying herself the social pleasures it might have made available. She explains that she prefers to correspond with literary people who are "personally unknown to me" because

> The character of an author I have always confined to my own closet; and no sooner step beyond its bounds, than the insuperable dread of being thought to move out of my proper sphere (a dread acquired, perhaps, from early association,) restrains me, not only from seeking opportunities of literary conversation, but frequently withholds me from taking all the advantage I might reap from those who offer.

It is clear from Elizabeth Benger's *Memoirs of Hamilton* that Hamilton enjoyed "a very high place in the society of Edinburgh." Benger writes that her "private

36. Hamilton, *Modern Philosophers,* 3.245.
37. Hamilton, *Letters,* 2.321, 29–30.

levee was attended by the most brilliant persons in Edinburgh," and endorses the view that her sociability and "liberal-minded" views were largely responsible for "correcting the vulgar prejudices" which had meant that a "female literary character was even at that time a sort of phenomenon in Scotland." She used her position, for example, to effect social rehabilitation for Eliza Fletcher, who had, it seems, been shunned by polite society in Edinburgh because of her support for the views of her husband, Archibald Fletcher, the liberal Whig, burgh reformer, and celebrator of the French revolution. Eliza Fletcher wrote that Hamilton

> did much to clear my reputation from the political prejudice which had, during the first ten years of my life in Edinburgh, attached to all who were not of the Pitt and Dundas faction there. She had good success in persuading her friends that Mrs Fletcher was not the ferocious Democrat she had been represented, and that she neither had the model of a guillotine in her possession nor carried a dagger under her cloak.[38]

Hamilton scrupulously rationed her sociability, however, and admitted visitors on only one morning a week, apparently because she found "the dangerous distinction of authorship" more compatible with the demands of feminine privacy than the more intermediary forms of polite sociability, and because her attention to the proper boundaries of the closet allowed her to define her activities in the moral language of the division of labor without representing herself as engaged in unfeminine professional employment.[39]

The way Hamilton recommends education to women in her *Letters* implies a similar sense that somehow the elision of the intermediary forms of social life, and in particular the eschewing of employment outside the home for women, makes the forms of detailed knowledge appropriate to domestic life compatible with the comprehensive views and capacity for abstract theory that Dugald Stewart had argued were necessary to politicians and ministers of state.[40] She condemns desultory reading of the kind that Hannah More satirized in the figure of Miss Rattle, explaining that it "does not make sufficient impression to produce those trains of thought which are favourable to arrangement; and without arrangement we shall only, by augmenting the number of ideas, augment confusion." Using a characteristic domestic analogy to em-

38. *Autobiography of Mrs Fletcher with letters and other family memorials. Edited by the survivor of her family,* 3d ed. (Edinburgh: Edmonston, 1876), 86.

39. *Memoirs of Hamilton,* 2.52–53, letter to Mrs. S. Coniston, North Hanover-Street, Edinburgh, July 1803; 2.20, letter to Dr. S., Grassmere, Near Ambleside, 29 May 1802; 1.194, 191, 195, 193.

40. Hamilton, *Letters,* 2.369. She alludes to Dugald Stewart's discussion of the importance of general principles to politicians, in his *Elements,* 1.IV, sects. vi–viii.

phasize the practical difficulties disorganized knowledge produces, she adds: "Those who possess but a scanty wardrobe, may cast the few things they have into an open drawer, where they will readily be found when occasion calls for them; but if all sorts of things are stuffed without order into the same place, in vain will you search for the smaller and more delicate articles amid the cumbrous heap." In order to avoid the horrors of this domestic disorder, she suggests, women should acquire "general and comprehensive views on every part of the subject" of study. She does not recommend the sort of specialized knowledge that More's characters had praised as a prerogative of masculine professionalism, because, she argues, "whoever enters the field of knowledge with his eyes fixed upon one object, and thinks to arrive at it, by resolutely remaining blind to every other, will find he has mistaken his path." This figure is reminiscent of Wollstonecraft's man who "when he enters any profession has his eye steadily fixed on some future advantage," and "when he undertakes a journey, has . . . the end in view." But Hamilton argues that he fails to appreciate that "so curiously interwoven" are the "various branches" of human knowledge, and "so dependent on each other all its parts, that none can be thoroughly understood without a comprehensive view of the whole."[41]

Like Edgeworth's second correspondent, Hamilton suggests that the absorption of middle-class men in particular professional pursuits prevents them from acquiring the kinds of knowledge available to women. She explains that "men who boast a knowledge of the world, know mankind only as they appear in one or two particular habits, and these assumed ones." She argues that they can only acquire "a very narrow and superficial knowledge of human character" from the "common intercourse of human society," whereas women see that character "in the nakedness in which it sometimes appears in the domestic scene."[42] This is clearly a version of that discursive construction which confines women and the vulgar to the knowledge of particular details, as the *Letters on Education* acknowledge. There Hamilton writes that "the duties . . . of our sex in particular, are oftener active than speculative: and an ever wakeful attention to the minutiae of which they are composed, is absolutely essential to their performance." What women gain from this is the indispensable requisite of common sense, which "is sterling in every region; the current coin that is equally useful to the high and to the low, to the learned and to the unlearned." Dugald Stewart argued, in his *Elements of the Philosophy of the*

41. Ibid., 2.396–97, 400, 396. Mary Wollstonecraft, *A Vindication of the Rights of Woman* (1792), ed. Carol H. Poston (New York: Norton, 1975), 60.

42. *Memoirs of Hamilton,* 1.270–71.

Human Mind (1792), that "the minds of the lower orders, like those of savages, are . . . habitually occupied about particular objects and particular events," and blurred the distinction between these men and those who had received a "liberal education," but had become "common drudges in business." These "men of business, or, more properly, men of detail," he suggested, require "good sense, or common sense" in order to succeed in their "inferior walks of life." But this good sense was for him the symptom of an "incurable" condition: "an understanding, minute and circumscribed in its views, timid in its exertions, and formed for servile imitation."[43]

To Hamilton, however, the sterling currency of common sense seems the best basis for comprehensive understanding. She argues that "those who would . . . deny the utility of cultivating" in women "the higher powers of the mind, ought, by a parity of reasoning, to consider gold as useless, because small coin is more frequently requisite in transacting the common business of the day."[44] Maria Edgeworth concluded that the treatment of metaphysics in what she refers to as Hamilton's *Letters on Female Education* gave to "a sort of knowledge which had been considered rather as a matter of curiosity than of use . . . real value and actual currency":[45] Hamilton's *Letters,* Edgeworth suggested, confirmed the relation between the refined gold of abstract reasoning and the small change of common sense. In Hamilton's argument, the ability to know "human character" in its domestic nakedness is the basis for the statesmanlike capacity to oversee the whole of society. Exclusion from specialization gives women the "leisure to be wise" in terms that are implicitly political.

V

If, as Davidoff and Hall have argued, domesticity is the focus that unites otherwise disparate social factions and groups in celebration, then perhaps this is because the idea of this separate space seems strangely without content and lacking in definition. Commentators may agree that the domestic site, and the femininity that is associated with it, have some enormous significance in relation to the world beyond its confines, the idea of the nation and of the empire, but that relation seems hospitable to a diverse range of constructions. Hamilton's *Letters,* I suggest, explore and perhaps exploit the ambivalence or strategic vagueness with which domesticity is defined in these decades. The passage in which she compares the housewife to the minister of state provides, I think, a characteristic example of her strategy. She writes:

43. Stewart, *Elements,* 1.IV, sect. vii, 224, 232–33.
44. Hamilton, *Letters,* 2.353, 281, 353.
45. In *Memoirs of Hamilton,* 1.225.

> I know not, indeed, whether the generalization of ideas be more requisite to a minister of state than to the mistress of a family. How necessary it is to the former, has been displayed by the elegant and judicious author of the "Elements of the Philosophy of the Human Mind"; its use to the latter is a more becoming theme to the Author of this humble performance.[46]

The emphasis on her own proper humility in choosing to discuss the mistress of a family rather than the minister works to veil the lack of humility in the suggestion that the two roles require the same qualities, or in the implication that small change has political currency.

A similar strategy, but with a perhaps more overtly political trajectory, can be seen in Lucy Aikin's *Epistles on Women, exemplifying their character and condition in various ages and nations* (1810). Aikin, it is worth noting, visited Hamilton "often by her own fire-side" during her stay in Edinburgh in 1812. She wrote of Hamilton that "I had great pleasure in her conversation; her good sense, her cheerfulness, her knowledge of the world, and her great kindness of heart, make her a delightful companion. Her prejudices indeed are strong, but that did not signify to me, who never sought to conquer them."[47] Aikin also maintained what appears to have been quite a close friendship and correspondence with Eliza Fletcher, whose daughter had been educated in the Stoke Newington home of Anna Laetitia Barbauld, Aikin's aunt.[48] Aikin's *Epistles on Women* may indicate the nature of her sympathy with Hamilton's prejudices in their strategy of taking what seems most restrictive about the definition of domesticity and as it were turning that inside out, making the very self-effacement that women's domestic role seemed to demand into the basis for a claim to equality. Aikin writes, in the Introduction to the *Epistles:*

> Let me in the first place disclaim entirely the absurd idea that the two sexes ever can be, or ever ought to be, placed in all respects on a footing of equality. . . . As long as the bodily constitution of the sexes shall remain the same, man must in general assume those public and active offices of life which confer authority, whilst to women will usually be allotted such domestic and private ones as imply a certain degree of subordination.

46. Hamilton, *Letters,* 2.369.

47. Letter of 1812, quoted in Philip H. Le Breton's Memoir of Aikin, in his edition of *Memoirs, Miscellanies and Letters of the late Lucy Aikin* (London: Longman, 1864), xxiii. For a different reading of women's writing, and Aikin's in particular, in relation to public life and politics, see Anne K. Mellor, "The Female Poet and the Poetess: Two Traditions of British Women's Poetry, 1780–1830," *Studies in Romanticism* 36 (summer 1997): 261–76.

48. See, for example, *Autobiography of Mrs Fletcher,* 113–16. In 1811, Barbauld corresponded with Fletcher about "the uncalled for severity of the *Edinburgh Review* against my niece"—*Autobiography of Mrs Fletcher,* 105.

This concession to masculine physical strength then allows Aikin to claim intellectual equality. She writes:

> Let the impartial voice of History testify for us that, when permitted, we have been the worthy associates of the best efforts of the best of men; let the daily observation of mankind bear witness, that no talent, no virtue, is masculine alone; no fault or folly exclusively feminine; . . . . that there is not an endowment, or propensity, or mental quality of any kind, which may not be derived from her father to the daughter, to the son from his mother. These positions once established, and carried into their consequences, will do every thing for woman. [ellipsis in original][49]

Aikin's argument, like Hamilton's, attempts to represent domesticity as the basis for a kind of liberal comprehensiveness of knowledge and understanding because it affords independence of mind rather than confinement to ignorance. Building on the familiar argument that the status of women is the index to the degree of national civilization, Aikin concludes:

> For you, bright daughters of a land renowned,
> By Genius blest, by glorious Freedom crowned;
> Safe in polisht privacy, content
> To grace, not shun, the lot that Nature lent,
> Be yours the joys of home, affection's charms,
> And infants clinging with caressing arms: . . .

She claims that this "polisht privacy" extends unproblematically into "Taste's whole garden," and into the desire to "Ply the pale lamp, explore the breathing page." These domestic and learned women then "drink in" the lessons of history's "loftiest tone," which encourage them to emulate the patriotic virtues of the Roman matrons. Finally she conjures women, "Thus self-endowed, thus armed for every state, / Improve, excel, surmount, subdue, your fate!" She suggests that women who are content with the "joys of home" will, because of that apparently passive contentment, be able to surmount and subdue their fate with a paradoxical degree of aggression. As a result she imagines that men will invite them to "Rouse thy keen energies, expand thy soul, / And see, and feel, and comprehend the whole."[50] Men will apparently recognize the superior learning and wisdom that their domestic exclusion has enabled women to acquire.

Aikin's views are more recognizably liberal and whiggish than those of Hamilton, as is suggested by her praise in the *Epistles* for the republican virtues of

49. Lucy Aikin, Introduction, in *Epistles on Women, exemplifying their character and condition in various ages and nations. With Miscellaneous Poems* (London: J. Johnson, 1810), v, vi.

50. Aikin, *Epistles on Women,* Epistle IV, ll. 460–65, 466, 472, 476, 478–79, 489–90.

roman matrons such as Veturia and Cornelia. Writing to William Channing in 1832, she recalled that her *Epistles on Women* had attempted to "inspire in my sex" the spirit of patriotism she saw as exemplified in her aunt Barbauld's "Character" of Sarah Vaughan. She argued that because "women are seldom taught to think. . . . Exceedingly few have any patriotism, any sympathy with public virtue." Explaining the scandalous "want of zeal for the reform bill amongst the ladies," she claimed that the effects of luxury and the lack of education led women "to love nothing beyond our own firesides; and when public good and private interest interfere, to feel no generous impulse to sacrifice the less to the greater." In Aikin's comments to Channing, learning "to think" is necessarily a process of political education. Without that education she thought that even the philanthropic endeavors of the "higher and middle classes," which might have seemed valuable because they extended women's interests "beyond our own firesides," could only exemplify "how the precepts of Christianity have been pressed into the service of a base submission to all established power."[51]

Aikin acknowledges, however, that the form of patriotism she wishes to inspire in her contemporaries is not the ideal virtue of the classical past. She writes of the women of Sparta, who "scorned the Woman's for the Patriot's name," that "Souls of gigantic mould, they fill our gaze / With pigmy wonder and despairing praise." She compares knowledge of them to the discovery of the skeletal remains of "the huge mammoth," when

> Columbia's swains in mute amazement eyed
> And heaved the monstrous frame from side to side;
> Saw bones on bones in mouldering ruins lie,
> And owned the relics of a world gone by: . . . .
> Yet self-same clay our limbs of frailty formed,
> And hearts like ours these dreadless bosoms warmed;
> But war, and blood, and Danger's gorgon face,
> Froze into stone the unconquerable race.[52]

The elegiac mode here articulates a deep ambivalence. The public-spirited patriotism of the Spartan women commands admiration; it makes modern women feel small, and inadequate in their patriotism. Yet in those final lines it is not clear that modern women should regard the Spartans as exemplary. The lines might suggest that the transhistorical similarities of hearts and clay have been erased by historical difference. The Spartan women are fossilized in

51. Letter no. 18 to the Rev. Dr. Channing, "Hampstead: April 7, 1832," in *Memoirs of Lucy Aikin*, ed. Le Breton, 258–59.

52. Aikin, *Epistles on Women*, Epistle III, ll. 67, 70–72, 73, 74–81, elipses in original.

their historical moment, and modern women, condemned to timorousness by knowledge of the wars, blood, and danger that have intervened, can regard them only as frozen monuments of a grandeur that cannot now be reanimated or imagined. Or the lines might imply that these Spartan women were just like modern women, but because of their horrible uncivilized lives they were obliged to look into "Danger's gorgon face," which froze them into stone and eradicated that common humanity. Modern women might then be left to congratulate themselves on living in an age which permits warmth of heart, and fosters the domestic affections as the basis for a more enlightened patriotism. The ambivalence here makes it possible for Aikin to argue either (or both) that women will deny their desire for domestic comfort in order to become political citizens, or that it is precisely the capacity to be content with domestic life that enables women to "comprehend the whole."

Hamilton argued, with a more determined neutrality, that education would teach "a just and comprehensive definition of the word patriotism" by abstracting the idea from individual examples of classical civic virtue, of "some turbulent demagogue" who encourages "sedition, conspiracy, and rebellion," or of "narrow, selfish, and unenlightened partiality" for native country. For Hamilton and for Aikin, domestic confinement is the necessary condition for the learning on which the capacity for this abstracted ideal of patriotism depends. It is domesticity that affords the modern woman the leisure to be wise. Hamilton argues that "hitherto . . . champions for sexual equality" have mistakenly argued for "an equality of employments and avocations." She believes that those who "desire for their sex an admission into the theatre of public life" have been swayed by custom to follow the example of men who accept "the false notions of importance which they have themselves affixed to their own peculiar avocations." Misled by these "false notions," she writes, "it is not an equality of moral worth for which they contend, and which is the only true object of regard; not for an equality of rights with respect to Divine favour, which alone elevates the human character into dignity and importance." It is here because domesticity is not an employment or avocation that it can afford women "an equality of moral worth."

As I have indicated, however, Hamilton distinguishes between industriously productive leisure on the one hand, and indiscriminately fecund indolence on the other, precisely in terms of the moral values of the discourse on the division of labor, which define the "man without employment" as "a cypher in society," and the domestic woman as redundant to the needs of society, "a piece of useless lumber." In this context, what can be claimed for domestic exclusion from the division of labor is not independence of mind, but at best a subordinate and auxiliary role. Hamilton writes of the position of women that "the obedience which they are taught to pay to authority, the submission with which they are made to bow to arrogance and injustice, produce habits of self-denial favourable to disinterestedness, meekness, humility, and generosity; dispositions which are allied to every species of moral excellence." She concludes that "seldom do these amiable dispositions fail to be produced by the subjugation of self-will."[53] Here the qualities of disinterestedness and generosity which had once been necessary to the civic virtues of public men, and which had therefore seemed the basis for "every species of moral excellence," begin to look like virtues which can only be cultivated by those unable to participate in the division of labor and production of wealth; they begin to look as though they might be available to women because they can be regarded as no more than the consolations for submission and obedience. The way Hamilton's *Letters* are poised between the public language of politics and the private language of piety make it possible to see in her arguments both the celebration of the separation of spheres that Davidoff and Hall see as characteristic of early nineteenth-century culture, and the emergence of an oppositional discourse.

This book has explored the changing value of the "small coin" of femininity in the second half of the eighteenth century. In some respects it tells a story about progress, about the increasing persuasiveness with which women imagine themselves as public citizens. By the early nineteenth century, it is possible for some women to conceive of their position as peculiarly suited to the cultivation of a stance and a language of liberal opposition, precisely because of the ways women have been excluded from involvement in the political life of the nation, and from professional ambitions. But at the same time, I think, the way this narrative has depended on the interconnections of different discourses, different narratives with quite divergent trajectories, makes it difficult to think of this as a story of the victorious agency of determined women, subduing all opposition. For it is more obviously about the sometimes incidental or accidental effects of the intersection or overlap between the different discourses that constitute gender difference, the voices and aspirations of women, and political or cultural shifts. It is about the importance of small change.

53. Hamilton, *Letters,* 2.345, 1.252–53. Hamilton, *Modern Philosophers,* 3.245. *Memoirs of Hamilton,* 2.53. Letters, 1.251.

INDEX

Numbers in italics refer to illustrations.